THE CHINESE
EXPERIENCE

PHOENIX
PRESS

HISTORY OF CIVILIZATION

For more than thirty years this distinguished series has provided the general reader with a comprehensive picture of the world's greatest civilizations. The series is free from commitment to any single interpretation of history, and seeks to go beyond the standard works of reference. It presents individual and original evocations, by leading scholars in many countries, of the culture and development of a nation, groups of nations or period of history.

The following books in the series
are all available in Phoenix Press editions:

The Japanese Experience, *W.G. Beasley*
The English Experience, *John Bowle*
The Greek Experience, *C.M. Bowra*
The Chinese Experience, *Raymond Dawson*
The Celtic Realms, *Myles Dillon and Nora Chadwick*
The Golden Age of Persia, *Richard Frye*
The World of Rome, *Michael Grant*
The Climax of Rome, *Michael Grant*
The Medieval World, *Friedrich Heer*
The Age of Revolution 1789–1848, *Eric Hobsbawm*
The Age of Capital 1848–1875, *Eric Hobsbawm*
The Age of Empire 1875–1914, *Eric Hobsbawm*
Ancient American Civilisations, *Freidrich Katz*
The Middle East, *Bernard Lewis*
Byzantium, *Cyril Mango*
·Eternal Egypt, *Pierre Montet*
The World of the Phoenicians, *Sabatino Moscati*
The Byzantine Commonwealth, *Dimitri Obolensky*
The African Experience, *Roland Oliver*
The Decline of Rome, *Joseph Vogt*

Raymond Dawson was a University Lecturer in Chinese and Fellow of Wadham College, Oxford.

ALSO BY RAYMOND DAWSON

The Analects, Confucius (*Translator and Editor*)

The Chinese Chameleon, an Analysis of
European Conceptions of Chinese Civilization

Confucius

The Historical Records, Sima Qian
(*Translator and Editor*)

Imperial China

The Invasion of China by the Western World

The Legacy of China

A New Introduction to Classical Chinese

THE CHINESE
EXPERIENCE

Raymond Dawson

PHOENIX
PRESS

5 UPPER SAINT MARTIN'S LANE
LONDON
WC2H 9EA

A PHOENIX PRESS PAPERBACK

First published in Great Britain
by Weidenfeld & Nicolson in 1978
Paperback edition first published in 2000
by Phoenix Press,
a division of The Orion Publishing Group Ltd,
Orion House, 5 Upper St Martin's Lane,
London WC2H 9EA

This paperback edition published in 2005

A CIP catalogue record for this book
is available from the British Library.

Printed and bound in the EC

ISBN 1-89880-049-9

CONTENTS

ILLUSTRATIONS

CHINA
in the last days of Empire

400 miles   0   600 kilometres

RUSSIA

OUTER

SINKIANG

INNER

K A N S U

■ Tunhuang

Yellow River

Wei River

SHE

TIBET

SZECHWAN

Chungking ■

INDIA

Yangtze River

KWEICHOW

YUNNAN

KW

BURMA

VIETNAM

BAY OF BENGAL

ACKNOWLEDGEMENTS

I am grateful to Allen & Unwin for permission to reproduce passages from A. Waley's *Chinese Poems* and *The Poetry and Career of Li Po*; to Clarendon Press for J.D.Frodsham's *An Anthology of Chinese Verse*; to Harvard University Press for S. Bush's *The Chinese Literati on Painting*; to Grove Press for C.Birch's *Anthology of Chinese Literature*; and to Princeton University Press for K.Chen's *The Chinese Transformation of Buddhism*.

Most of the quotations from works in Chinese have been freshly translated by myself, but I am most grateful to my colleagues Anne Lonsdale and Tao Tao Sanders for providing me with some previously unpublished translations. Their contributions are indicated in the notes at the end of the book. My thanks to Glen Dudbridge and Ian McMorran for all their help. I am also grateful to Mary Tregear for reading the art section and giving help with illustrations, and to my wife for giving much help and encouragement of all kinds.

Oxford

Raymond Dawson
February 1978

INTRODUCTION

My most recent book, *Imperial China*, is a narrative account designed to be the middle volume of a trilogy on Chinese history. In it I had little space for philosophy, literature, and art, and restricted opportunity to dwell on the distinctive features of Chinese civilization. The invitation to write the present volume has provided a welcome chance to approach China from a very different angle by describing the essence of the Chinese experience in all the major branches of human activity. In generalizing about thirty centuries of Chinese civilization there is a grave risk of not doing justice to the sweeping changes caused by technological development, submission to foreign conquerors, population growth, the spread of religious and philosophical ideas, and other potentially revolutionary phenomena. But this book is chiefly concerned with elucidating the more constant features of Chinese civilization (which often derived from a conservative acceptance of traditional ways of thought) and with explaining those facets of the Chinese experience which have been most notably different from our own.

The book is in four parts, dealing in turn with the political, philosophical, socio-economic, and aesthetic experience of the Chinese. Certain quite important topics have had to be omitted, for I believe that in order to make the maximum contribution to the reader's understanding it is necessary to be selective rather than exhaustive, and to write as far as possible in terms of individual experience rather than impersonal generalization. Thus in the first part of the book I do not attempt a detailed account of the complexities of Chinese administration. Instead I have tried to give some impression of the roles of individuals caught up in this machine. I have chosen to concentrate first on the role of emperors, who were at the apex of the system. Then, by way of contrast, after some general information about the bureaucracy, I describe the life of the district magistrate at the grass-roots level of administration.

I round off that section of the book by giving a general impression of the great capital cities which were at the heart of the Chinese political system. But before I embark on this topic I must give the reader a brief survey of Chinese history to help him chart his way through the rest of the book.

HISTORICAL SURVEY

At the dawn of Chinese history, according to the traditional view, the throne was occupied by sovereigns remarkable for their longevity who conferred upon the Chinese people the basic tools of civilization, such as writing and agriculture. Later came the famous three dynasties of antiquity – the Hsia, Shang, and Chou. This was afterwards regarded as a Golden Age upon which decadent mankind should look back in awe, seeking models of moral action and wise government. Of the Hsia we still know nothing, since none of the recent accumulation of archaeological evidence can be positively linked with it; but in the present century the Shang has become much more real to us since excavations (started fifty years ago at Anyang, the dynasty's last capital, and recently exploring numerous other sites) have provided a wealth of evidence about the period. Occupying the stage of history for the last half of the second millennium BC, the Shang people are most famous for making bronze sacrificial vessels of unsurpassed quality. Already their culture had distinctively Chinese features: the writing used in inscriptions on bronzes and in oracular questions inscribed on bone and turtle-shell is a recognizable ancestor of the script used in today's *People's Daily*; ancestors were worshipped and the dead kings were given rich provision for their afterlife; jade was imported many hundreds of miles and laboriously carved into objects of great beauty; and the silkworm had been enlisted in the service of mankind.

The Shang people were conquered in the eleventh century by the Chou, who had previously been their satellites. They came from the strong bastion of the mountain-flanked Wei valley, whence conquering armies could pour forth over the North China Plain. The traditional view accepted in later Chou writings was that the revered founders of the dynasty had rightfully banished the Shang because their last ruler had forfeited the Mandate of Heaven by his tyrannical behaviour. At first the Chou sovereign headed a confederation of petty lords linked by ties of kinship or of association in the campaign to supplant the Shang. By the eighth century the power of the Chou royal house had declined and, although the other lords owed nominal allegiance to the Chou sovereign and held him in some respect because of the sanctity of his position, in fact his strength was less than that of the major feudal states which were nominally under his suzerainty. For practical political purposes these states formed a confederation which acknowledged the hegemony of the most powerful among them. This was a time of constant warfare, especially against the civilized state of Ch'u in the Yangtze Valley, which had its own distinctive culture but would before long become part of the Chinese empire. The members of the confederation were also harassed by the barbarian peoples who lived not only outside the frontiers of Chinese settlement but also in the more mountainous and inaccessible regions of their own states (just as aboriginal non-Chinese peoples have continued to occupy areas of China until modern times).

The members of the Chinese confederation also fought among themselves, and gradually the more powerful states swallowed the smaller ones, so that by the middle of the fifth century (the start of the so-called Warring States period) only seven contenders remained, and the scene was set for the contests which would eventually lead to the unification of China by the Ch'in Dynasty and the dawn of the imperial age. These next two centuries were a period of unprecedented social and economic change. Increasingly the powerful states contending for supremacy were administered less by hereditary officials who owed their positions to family ties than by a new class of men who obtained promotion through merit. Feudalistic patterns of political organization gave way to bureaucratic ones. Social change was much accelerated by the rapid development of iron technology, which took the peasants rapidly from the Stone Age to the use of cast iron (which was not developed in Europe until the fourteenth century). This meant a much more efficient agriculture, a much higher level of industrial activity, and a much greater surplus to put into warfare. This became deadlier now that aristocratic chariot-fighting was replaced by mass encounters between peasant armies using iron weapons. At the same time mounted archery was adopted from the northern nomadic peoples. This was still the world's most powerful weapon fifteen centuries later when the Mongols swept across Asia and much of Europe. Trade and communications also developed rapidly, and cities grew enormously. Copper coinages had been in use since the sixth century BC, and the late Chou period saw a great expansion of mercantile activity. The social turmoil of this age caused men to question traditional values and address themselves to fundamental problems about the nature of man and society. These late Chou thinkers laid the foundation of the moral and political philosophy which was to remain the chief intellectual concern of the Chinese people.

Of the philosophical schools founded during this period Confucianism and Taoism had the greatest staying power. Together with Buddhism, which was imported during the Han Dynasty, they formed the 'Three Doctrines', the main branches of religious and philosophical thought; but another one of the so-called Hundred Schools of antiquity had its brief moment of power. This was Legalism, a ruthless totalitarian doctrine which held that all should be stimulated by rewards and punishments to do the state's will. This philosophy was adopted by the north-western state of Ch'in, which eventually came out on top in the struggles of the Warring States period. This state (from which the name China is taken) completed the conquest of the whole of China in 221 BC, and established the first imperial dynasty, with territory already extending from Manchuria to Canton. The achievements of this short dynasty were most influential: the establishment of a professional imperial administration in marked contrast with the old feudal order; the standardization of writing, which greatly facilitated the long-term unification of China; the standardization of weights and measures; the establishment of a network of roads to secure easy communication between the capital and all parts of the empire; and the completion of the Great Wall, which was intended to prevent invasion by the nomadic 'barbarians' who dwelt to the north of China. The Ch'in Dynasty was later reviled for the huge loss of life suffered during this immense undertaking, which failed to save the Chinese from being overrun from the north on several occasions. With their veneration for literature, the Chinese people have also abominated the Ch'in for the notorious 'burning of the books' in 213 BC, the purpose of which was to wipe out the writings of rival philosophies, and indeed to destroy all literature except the historical records of Ch'in and books on certain practical subjects. Although copies of the banned works were kept in the palace, these also perished in a great conflagration when, after a mere fifteen years, the Ch'in's harsh and unpopular regime was overthrown by a man of plebeian origin who founded the Han.

The Han founder could not immediately impose a fully centralized administration, for he had to keep his relatives and supporters happy by rewarding them with hereditary fiefs; and it was several decades before local government throughout the empire came firmly under the control of the central administration. The bounds of empire were further extended in all directions: to the south the Han completed the conquest of what is now south-east China and moved into Vietnam; to the north they occupied much territory beyond the Great Wall and penetrated into Korea; and to the west they conquered the Tarim basin. By the second century AD, the date of the first census, this enormous and prosperous empire had a population of nearly sixty million. By this time Confucianism had become the dominant philosophy of the state. It was a Confucianism which had absorbed some Taoist concepts and been stiffened by Legalism, a philosophy which the Master himself would not have recognized; but its prestige ensured that the Confucian Classics of pre-Ch'in times, copies of which had by now been rediscovered and restored, became the main content of education in China then and thereafter, and so constituted the training and formed the philosophy of many generations of bureaucrats. The dynasty established the kind of bureaucratic administration which was broadly typical of China right through until modern times. It also suffered from the inevitable stresses of unwieldy bureaucracies; and emperors tried to circumvent red tape by relying on eunuchs, favourites, secretaries, and other close personal supporters, another recurrent phenomenon in Chinese history. A perennial economic weakness also made its appearance under the Han: impoverished peasants in increasing numbers had to sell their land, so that vast estates came into the hands of rich landlords, whose power and affluence it was beyond the state's ability to limit. Finally imperial authority was weakened by a series of feeble emperors, and a massive rebellion brought the dynasty to its knees.

The Han came to an end in AD 220 and, except for a brief period under the Western Chin Dynasty (265–316), China was divided for nearly four centuries. From the early fourth century AD the north was overrun by nomad horsemen, whose petty and ephemeral regimes occupied the scene until 439, when the whole of north China was reunited under the Toba people, who established the Northern Wei Dynasty. The south remained free of barbarian invasion, and, although no strong and enduring regime was established, it prospered owing to the influx of refugees from the north, who settled the fertile Yangtze Valley, which was now no longer a sparsely colonized frontier area, but the custodian of traditional Chinese culture. During this period the Buddhist religion, which had first appeared during the Han, swept through the whole of China. The period of division is called the Six Dynasties period after the six successive dynasties that had their capitals at Nanking between 222 and 589.

The country was eventually united by a northern dynasty known as the Sui. The second Sui emperor, at great cost in lives, pursued two ambitious projects: the rebuilding of the Great Wall and the construction of canals linking the capital at Changan both with the north-east and with the Yangtze Valley. These waterways contributed greatly to the unity and strength of the country by facilitating the shipment of government supplies and tax grain, and were a great boon to the T'ang Dynasty which followed; but, like the Ch'in, the Sui had succeeded in unifying China but had tried to do too much too quickly. Costly and unsuccessful military campaigns in north Korea caused further unrest, and the dynasty collapsed in 618.

The first half of the T'ang Dynasty is one of the most splendid periods in Chinese history. Large areas of Central Asia which had been lost since Han times were reconquered. A flourishing overland trade developed, and many Central Asian merchants were to be seen in Changan, which was the greatest city in the world, with a population of over a million. Persian and Arab vessels made their way to Canton, and a very large foreign community resided there also. Art and music were much affected by Central Asian influences, and the foreign religion of Buddhism continued to flourish. It was a most cosmopolitan period. It was also an era of great poets and painters. Civil service examinations, restarted under the Sui, were developed until men recruited through them counterbalanced the aristocrats. Eventually this became the most prestigious way to enter government service and the one which guaranteed the most rapid promotion. At the beginning of the dynasty armed service was provided by a militia, but gradually the strain of defending the long northern frontier and controlling the occupied territories in Central Asia necessitated the recruitment of large garrisons of long-serving soldiers. In 755 An Lu-shan, one of the northern frontier commanders who had acquired too much power as a result of this development, started a rebellion which severely weakened the dynasty. After its suppression central control was no longer effective, and some areas of the country were virtually independent. The expansiveness of the pre-An period gave way to xenophobia, and the Buddhist religion began to decline after a severe persecution in 845. The T'ang was overthrown in 906 and China was again divided. Five short-lived dynasties reigned in the north, and the south broke up into several separate kingdoms.

In 960 the next great dynasty, the Sung, seized power in the north, and by 978 it had brought all the independent southern kingdoms under its sway. The early Sung government, with its capital at Kaifeng, developed highly sophisticated procedures for recruitment and promotion in the civil service, and the bureaucracy was now dominated by examination graduates. The development of printing, which had started in the late T'ang, now made education more widely available, and the great new cities which were growing up began to provide a mass market for popular literature. Territorially the Sung were never able to restore the position of strength enjoyed by the early T'ang. The Peking area and parts of the north-west were controlled by barbarian regimes, which had to be paid large annual sums to keep the peace. In 1126 the Jürched from Manchuria conquered northern China and established the Chin empire. The Sung fled to the south, where they set up a new capital at Hangchow. The loss of the north at this time further accelerated the shift of the economic and cultural centre of gravity southward. The rich area of the Yangtze Valley, further exploited by a burst of technological progress, supported a most flourishing commercial life; and for the first time a great overseas trade was developed, using Chinese instead of foreign vessels.

Mongol invaders wiped out the Chin in 1234 as part of the astonishing series of conquests initiated by Genghis Khan. The effect on northern China was disastrous, but by 1279, when the conquest of the south was completed, the Mongols were prepared to listen to Chinese advice, and Khubilai ruled as a Chinese Son of Heaven rather than as a Mongol khan, so the area suffered less. This was the first time that the whole of China had come under foreign domination. The civil service examinations were temporarily suspended and many foreigners were employed in the administration. Because of the vast extent of the Mongol dominions travel from Europe to China became possible, and Marco Polo and many others were amazed at the enormous size and prosperity of China and the populousness and splendour of its cities even at this time of foreign occupation. At the same time many inventions from this advanced civilization flowed across to the backward countries of Europe.

The Mongols, who retained their own culture and did not blend in with the Chinese, were toppled by popular uprisings and succeeded in 1368 by the Ming, headed by an emperor of peasant stock. The capital was at first at Nanking, but in 1421 it was moved to Peking, where a fine new city was built, the direct ancestor of the capital of the People's Republic. The Mongols continued to be troublesome, and large armies had to be maintained along the line of the Great Wall. In the early years of the dynasty China still had a powerful navy, and great fleets under the eunuch admiral Cheng Ho voyaged as far afield as India, the Persian Gulf, and East Africa. The Ming founder had ruled by terror, and many officials were executed. Later administration settled into a despotic rut, which meant that in times of weak emperors power was wielded by eunuchs or others close to the throne rather than by the now demoralized bureaucracy. Intellectual life became more stereotyped, and the orthodox interpretation of the Confucian Classics established in the Southern Sung period became mandatory. Urban prosperity continued to grow as the great cities became more commercialized and industrialized, but a greatly increased population, unmatched by improvements in agriculture, began to cause pressure on land in some parts of China. During the sixteenth century Europeans began to arrive in the Far East by sea. Portuguese traders reached the Chinese coast soon after the capture of Malacca in 1511. Missionaries followed, but it was not until 1601 that Matteo Ricci was able to establish a Jesuit mission in Peking.

Popular unrest marked the last decades of the Ming, but it was the Manchus, descendants of the Jürched people, who captured Peking in 1644 and inaugurated the last imperial dynasty, the Ch'ing. They had modelled their own state on Chinese patterns, so they interfered little with the Chinese political system. Although they resisted assimilation with the Chinese, forbidding intermarriage and keeping their own homeland as a separate region closed to Chinese settlers, they rapidly adopted Chinese culture and tried to win the support of the intellectuals. Under three great rulers – the K'ang-hsi, Yung-cheng, and Ch'ien-lung emperors, who reigned from 1661 to 1795 – China flourished. Internal stability was matched by successful campaigns to restore Chinese sovereignty over territories in Central Asia and elsewhere which had traditionally been controlled by the most glorious Chinese dynasties. But the success of the first century and a half of Manchu rule could only delay the deterioration in living standards which was bound to be suffered by a population which had increased beyond the capacity of a pre-modern agriculture to sustain. The bureaucracy, recruited through an examination system which stressed ideological conformity and had no place for the techniques required to administer a huge and complex state, was now riddled with corruption and quite powerless to arrest the decline, which was accelerated by the impact of the Western nations during the nineteenth century and the devastation wrought by the

Taiping Rebellion. Finally, in the early twentieth century, the Chinese rejected not only the Manchus but also the old imperial system of government. They began to embrace what the West had to offer, not merely in technology but also in ideology, until after a period of confusion and division such as had often followed the demise of earlier dynasties, the People's Republic was established in 1949.

CHRONOLOGICAL NOTE

The following outline omits the names of minor dynasties, but will be found adequate for the purposes of this book. The dates of emperors will be found in the index.

SHANG	?1523–?1027
CHOU	?1027–256
CH'IN	221–206 (having annihilated Chou in 256 and other rival states afterwards)
FORMER HAN	206 BC–AD 9
HSIN	AD 9–23
LATER HAN	25–220
SIX DYNASTIES	222–589 (north mostly under various non-Chinese dynasties)
SUI	581–618 (ruling in north only before unification in 589)
T'ANG	618–907
FIVE DYNASTIES	907–960 (ruling in north, while south divided into separate kingdoms)
NORTHERN SUNG	960–1126 (LIAO ruled extreme north 947–1125)
SOUTHERN SUNG	1127–1279 (CHIN ruled north China 1126–1234)
YÜAN	1279–1368 (having succeeded CHIN in north in 1234)
MING	1368–1644
CH'ING	1644–1912
REPUBLIC	1912–1949
PEOPLE'S REPUBLIC	1949–

PART ONE
THE POLITICAL EXPERIENCE

CHAPTER 1

SONS OF HEAVEN

I

After his travels in China during the period of Mongol domination, Marco Polo described the Great Khan, Khubilai, as 'the mightiest man, whether in respect of subjects or of territory or of treasure, who is in the world today or who ever has been'.[1] Of the K'ang-hsi emperor a Jesuit description said that 'his bearing, his figure, the features of his countenance, a certain air of majesty tempered with mildness and kindness, inspire at first sight love and respect for his person and announce from the very first the master of one of the greatest empires of the universe'.[2] But Chinese sovereigns were not merely concerned with worldly affairs. It was their awesome responsibility not only to rule over boundless territories and over populations unrivalled in magnitude, but also to ensure by their own conduct the smooth working of the natural order. For disasters would surely follow if they strayed from the ideal path. The role of the Son of Heaven developed through more than three thousand years, from the days of the Shang kings whose funeral rites were accompanied by the sacrifice of men and horses to serve them in the afterlife through to the sad twilight of P'u-yi, the last Manchu emperor, enthroned at three and forced to abdicate at six, doomed to spend the remainder of his youth imprisoned in the gilded cage of the imperial palace, within which the old ceremony lingered on, while outside in the bustling city, whose pedlars' cries he listened to wistfully in the early morning stillness, the infant republic was striving to reach maturity.

Throughout these ages all manner of men – and even one woman – had occupied the imperial throne. Yet in antiquity certain basic concepts of sovereignty emerged to remain as constant themes right through until the twentieth century. Most important was the dogma attributed

3

to Confucius, that just as there are not two suns in the sky, so there are not two Sons of Heaven on earth. This provided a grand cosmic justification of the doctrine that the emperor was not just the ruler of China, but the sovereign of all-under-Heaven. All other peoples near and far were simply awaiting the time when they too would receive the beneficence of the Son of Heaven's rule, so that even embassies from the far ends of the earth, like the Macartney Embassy sent from Britain in 1793, were greeted as tribute missions. Despite all that had happened in the nineteenth century to teach China that there were other sovereign states, and powerful ones too, this saying was still recalled by little P'u-yi five years after his abdication, indignant at Yüan Shih-k'ai's attempt to destroy the republic and set himself on the dragon throne, thus making a second parody of empire to set beside P'u-yi's own.

Also of very ancient origin was the doctrine that the ruler owed his position to the Mandate of Heaven, which could be withdrawn from him if he did not live up to the high expectations of his office. The withdrawal of Heaven's favour would be portended by natural disasters or popular rebellions. Those sovereigns who forfeited the Mandate of Heaven and were superseded by new dynasties were castigated by the historians as bad rulers, while the acts of founder emperors were regarded as highly auspicious because they manifestly possessed the Mandate.

Thirdly this sole sovereign of all-under-Heaven was thought to have an important role to play in securing cosmic order as well as tranquillity among men. His daily conduct and his ritual observances must all be designed to achieve this end. Hence, although some emperors worked long hours and involved themselves in the minutiae of administration, there was also a strong tradition that the emperor's cosmomagical role meant that practical matters should be left to his officials. The emperor would merely be seen as a personification of the virtues which would ensure tranquillity among the people, but for practical administration he only needed to appoint ministers who were men of wisdom and ability. According to the most influential wing of Confucian thought, men were by nature good so, given education in the literature which dealt with the problems of government and men in society, they were all amply suited to the necessary administrative roles. Hence the bureaucracy eventually came to be recruited through examination in the Confucian Classics.

This then is the basic philosophy of kingship which survived great shifts in the practical role of the emperor. Since the theoretical framework did not greatly change, it is possible to examine in turn each of

4

the key features of the Chinese concept of monarchy, to see how they were established in antiquity and how they survived until modern times. Indeed no Chinese emperors were more concerned to cultivate the correct imperial image than the great Manchu sovereigns, especially K'ang-hsi and Ch'ien-lung, who sought to commend themselves to the Chinese by cultivating the ethical concerns, the patronage of literature, scholarship, and the arts, and the general regard for humane and civilized virtues which a Chinese monarch was ideally expected to show.

II

The study of antiquity enables us to discover the sources of this civilian ideal. To Confucius and Mencius, the late Chou Dynasty thinkers whose ideas were to have deep influence on later political thought, the most important event in the previous history of China had been the conquest of the Shang and the establishment of the Chou Dynasty in the eleventh century BC; and the greatest heroes in history were the founders of that dynasty, notably the Kings Wen and Wu and the latter's brother the Duke of Chou, who held the regency during the minority of Wu's son. Wen means 'civilized' and Wu 'martial', the names being clearly posthumous, since these are qualities attributed to them by history. Although his military ardour was approved since it was employed in the just cause of bringing tranquillity to the people, King Wu was a much more shadowy figure than King Wen, who already portrayed many of the qualities later looked for in a ruler: he was filial and had due regard for his religious obligations, he cared for and protected the people, particularly the most hapless of them, he was sparing in punishments, and his government and institutions were exemplary. He was given credit for paving the way for the conquest of the Shang by attracting the people to him with these virtues, thus simplifying the task of military conquest performed by King Wu. Such qualities in a ruler were also seen as an essential solution to contemporary problems by Mencius, writing at a time when the Chou power had waned and China was divided into petty warring states. In these circumstances military force was not the answer. Instead, in Mencius's view, the ruler had to institute ideal economic measures so that the people of neighbouring states would be attracted by them and would flock to his territory. The word *wen* originally meant 'striped', and hence 'ornamented' or 'embellished', and so it came to mean 'civilization' in the sense of the adornments and

5

refinements of life which distinguished the Chinese from the barbarian peoples by which they were surrounded. Thus very early in their history the Chinese thought that it was the duty of their ruler to cultivate the civilized arts which distinguished them from the barbarians and to win the allegiance of a willing and harmonious population by benevolent government.

Apart from magnifying the chieftains who founded the Chou Dynasty into sage kings possessing a wide range of virtues which they could contrast with the vices of rulers in their own decadent age, the philosophers of late Chou times gave substance to shadowy myths about even earlier events by retailing stories about a succession of legendary monarchs who were mainly notable for laying the foundations of civilization. Of these culture-heroes the latest in time was Yü the Great, who saved the country from a vast flood by cutting channels to let the water run away to the sea, which kept him so busy that he passed his own door only three times in eight years and then did not go inside. He was slotted into the chronology as founder of the shadowy Hsia Dynasty which was said to have preceded the Shang. Before him came Yao and Shun, model emperors of great longevity, whose main significance in later Chinese history was that they provided a pattern for abdication; since Shun, a humble farmer and potter renowned for his filial piety in trying circumstances, had been selected as his successor by Yao. Other important mythical culture-heroes were Fu-hsi who was said to have invented writing by studying the marks on a turtle-shell, Shen-nung who was credited with the invention of agriculture, the basic occupation of the Chinese, and the Yellow Emperor, believed responsible for the compass, boats, carts, bows and arrows, coinage, and the calendar. These three sovereigns were latecomers to the mythological scene and so had to be found space as far back as the twenty-seventh century BC, being, as Arthur Waley described it, 'put into this remote period by the chronologists in just the same way as someone arriving late at a crowded concert is put at the back of the room'.[3] All these mythical heroes from the distant past, along with the historical Wen and Wu, were incorporated into the traditional list of rulers accepted throughout imperial Chinese history, thus providing a portrait gallery of examples for the admiration and emulation of later sovereigns.

In addition to descriptions of the sage rulers of antiquity, the Chou philosophers, and particularly those of the Confucian school, provided many other elements in the composite picture of the ideal ruler set before later monarchs. These elements were not all consistent with each other.

In some ancient writings the sovereign's task was described as ruling by non-action, but others went to the opposite extreme and took it to be the diligent and paternalistic regard for the people's everyday concerns. Rule by non-action springs from the belief that the sovereign derives a kind of spiritual power from Heaven, and that it is through the efficacy of this spiritual power and his contacts with spiritual beings that he is able to secure order in all-under-Heaven and freedom from natural disaster, not by any mundane political achievement. The same concept of non-action was one of the paradoxes at the centre of the Taoist philosophy which believed in a kind of state of nature in which everyone unconsciously and without purposive action behaved in conformity with the Tao or Way of nature; but in the hands of the Confucians this attitude developed into a belief that the ideal ruler was not a practical administrator but a perfect moral leader who set an example to the people. A corollary of this was that he must select men of wisdom and virtue to carry out the actual administration of the country. The most extreme statements of this philosophy come in the writings of the Han Dynasty Confucians:

He who is the ruler of men takes non-action as his Way and makes impartiality his treasure. He sits upon the throne of non-action and rides upon the perfection of his officials. His feet do not move but his ministers lead him forward; his mouth utters no word but his chamberlains give him words of support; his mind does not concern itself with problems but his ministers put into effect the appropriate action. Thus nobody sees him act and yet he achieves success. This is how the ruler imitates the ways of Heaven.[4]

If the wisest and most virtuous men in the world have been appointed ministers, then it follows that rulers should leave them to get on with the task of government and show proper respect for them. Thus Mencius compared the task of the minister with that of the jade-carver. Like the minister, the jade-carver was entrusted with extremely valuable material, but the king did not insist on trying to tell him how to cut and polish jade. Nor must wise and virtuous advisers be at the sovereign's beck and call. 'A prince who is destined to achieve great things must have ministers he does not summon,' wrote Mencius. 'If he wishes to be advised by them, he goes to visit them. If his esteem for virtue and delight in the Way is not of this kind, he is not worth associating with in his activities.'[5] These classical references strengthened bureaucratic resistance to autocracy in later times. Given the supreme importance attached to social conventions in China, a salutary message was conveyed by the depiction in literature and art of Emperor Wu, the greatest emperor of the great Han Dynasty, paying a call on one of his ministers. Administration by wise and virtuous ministers also means that aristocrats no longer have a monopoly of government, as they had in the early Chou period. But the shift of power was only gradual. The Confucian tradition strongly emphasized the importance of family ties and the hereditary principle, and it was not until the Sung Dynasty that the intellectuals completely overtook the aristocrats in government.

Thus one conception of the emperor firmly based in the Confucian tradition was of a man aloof atop the misty pinnacles of power, leaving mundane matters to his ministers. Equally Confucian is the ideal of the ruler deeply concerned for his people at the grass-roots level, an attitude which easily derives from an extension of the ruler's patriarchal concern for his own family. The importance of the people is a recurrent theme in ancient literature. Mencius's version is: 'The people are of most importance; the spirits of the land and grain are next; and the sovereign is insignificant.'[6] Hsün Tzu quoted what was evidently a common saying: 'The prince is the boat, the common people are the water. The water can support the boat or the water can capsize the boat.'[7] He also pointed out that 'Heaven does not create people for the sake of the sovereign. Heaven made the sovereign for the sake of the people.'[8] Again Confucius had maintained that to be trusted by the people was more important to government than the supply of arms and food, a sentiment which is echoed by Mencius when he talks of harmony among the people being the predominant consideration in military defence.[9] In these circumstances the main responsibility of the ruler is to treat the people benevolently in order to win their support. He should look after them as a shepherd cares for his flock, for it was said that 'Heaven, when it gave birth to the people, established rulers for them, and made them supervise and shepherd the people.'[10] Another cliché in imperial China was that the ruler should act as father-and-mother of the people; and the popular name of 'father-mother official' was conferred on the district magistrates who represented the emperor at grass-roots level.

Mencius and the Han Confucians strongly argued that economic welfare was the basis of popular morality. 'Only the scholar seems capable of retaining a constant heart although he lacks a constant means of support',[11] said Mencius. The ruler had to provide for the needs of the ordinary people to ensure that law and order prevailed among them. Contemporary rulers were criticized by Mencius for not sharing their pleasures with the people, as compared with the benevolent King Wen who gave them access to his own modest private park. Mencius also devoted much attention to economic measures which would ensure that the people flourished in plenteous years and avoided starvation in calamitous ones. If benevolent government of this kind were carried out, he maintained, nothing could prevent the ruler of the state from attaining true sovereignty and restoring unity to China. The benevolent ruler did not need a large territory from which to set off and unify the empire under just government because, witnessing his goodness, the people would flock to him as surely as water flows downwards.

These are some of the more general ideas in which those who have attempted to rule China since antiquity have been steeped. Some strove mightily to fulfil the requirements of the imperial image. The Sung founder had an especially strong reputation for conforming his conduct to the Confucian pattern, and his successors were carefully trained in the Confucian way. The great Manchu emperors, concerned to commend themselves as true Confucian monarchs, received a thorough education in the Confucian tradition and tried to project themselves as exemplary Confucian scholar-gentlemen with deep concern for the welfare of the people. Even little P'u-yi sat in the Forbidden City mugging up how to be a good emperor long after the empire had ceased to be. Though the great majority failed to live up to the ideal, all emperors knew that, if they did not pay regard to the humane and civil virtues of the sage rulers portrayed in the Confucian Classics that formed the backbone of their education, their vices could be depicted by the Confucian-minded historians who would have the task of compiling the history of their reigns; or, worse still, they might even lose the Mandate of Heaven.

III

After this general introduction to the concept of sovereignty in China we may turn to more specific matters, starting with the emperor's religious role. It is necessary to begin with a more detailed account of the doctrine of the Mandate of Heaven. This doctrine was the invention of the Chou founders, who claimed that Heaven, displeased with Shang misrule, had withdrawn that dynasty's Mandate to govern and conferred it upon themselves. But this was more than a mere piece of Chou self-justification. The theory, as attributed to the Duke of Chou, maintained that the Mandate had been held in turn by the Hsia and Shang

Dynasties and that each had forfeited it by abandoning the virtuous ways of its founders which had caused Heaven to confer upon them the Mandate to rule over mankind, and thus it had come into the hands of the latest exponents of supreme virtue, the Chou conquerors. The theory not only explained the past, but carried implications for the future; for it constituted a pledge that the Chou rulers would continue to govern with piety and wisdom or else run the risk of losing the Mandate in their turn. When they were in course of time overthrown, this confirmed in the minds of the Chinese a way of looking at history which persisted right through to the twentieth century. The doctrine established by the Chou founders was not only developed and stressed by the Confucian philosophers late in the dynasty, who saw themselves as living at a time of dynastic decline, but also confirmed by the Han Dynasty philosophers as part of their elaboration of an ideology of imperial government. The very success of the Han founder, Liu Pang, in conquering Ch'in and uniting the empire, although his peasant qualities did not mark him out as an obvious recipient of Heaven's trust, was firm proof that he had the Mandate, and sound justification for approaching him with the awe and veneration which became the standard treatment for emperors.

The early Chou sources also give reasons why the Mandate of Heaven was withdrawn from the Shang. Drunkenness had led them into evil ways and their last ruler was accused of impiety and failure to carry out the proper sacrifices; but the main reasons for losing the Mandate were naturally given as neglect of the people and failure to attend to the tasks of government. The loss of the Mandate might be portended by floods or other natural disasters, and the K'ang-hsi emperor was particularly noted for taking reports of such calamities as vital means of detecting the Will of Heaven; but a popular uprising would also be regarded as a portent of the loss of Heaven's confidence in the ruler rather than as a sign in itself that the emperor's claim to benevolent and just government was invalid.

The theory of the Mandate of Heaven is only a measure for removing tyrants and contains no positive recommendation on how to choose the most suitable person to rule. But once a new sovereign had emerged, the aura of the supernatural which surrounded him and the sense of divine endorsement of the office confirmed the emperor's position. In a sense the Mandate was vested in the office of the throne rather than in the person of the ruler, and thus the word *sheng* (sacred) used as a conventional epithet for 'imperial' (e.g. Sacred Edict, sacred countenance) obviously describes the institution, not the man. Little P'u-yi was one among many who did not have divine qualities. Emperors indeed were not themselves considered to be divine, despite the title Son of Heaven. This was merely a manner of speaking, natural enough to the family-conscious Chinese, to convey how the ruler acted as intermediary between Heaven and the people, serving as son to the former and parent to the latter, neither relationship being meant literally.

Nevertheless such an awesome responsibility was not lightly taken on by ordinary human beings, and stories of the founding of dynasties recount the reluctance of the new incumbent to be considered worthy of such an honour. Liu Pang, the Han founder, as a man of humble origin who was a minor police official at the start of the rebellion which overthrew the Ch'in, was in an especially difficult position to aspire to an office which had previously demanded noble birth and ideally supreme virtue and wisdom. Like Caesar, he refused three times, and he only accepted on the ingenious plea of his supporters that their own high honours would be invalidated if he did not himself accept the supreme accolade. Soon stories of portents associated with his birth and rise to power were current: his mother was said to have conceived him by a god and a dragon was seen hovering over her at his birth. Later, to bring him into line with other rulers, he was equipped with a genealogy going right back to the legendary Yao. Reluctance to accept the throne became a commonplace of popular fiction: for example, the Sung founder was forced to accede by being dressed in the imperial robes while in a drunken sleep. And the same sort of portentous stories which had accompanied Liu Pang's rise to power were also circulating in 1915 when Yüan Shih-k'ai was planning a restoration of the empire; only this time the stories indicated merely that Yüan planned to become emperor and was pleased to hear of portents, not that he would actually succeed in winning the throne.

The kudos of obtaining the Mandate of Heaven firmly adhered to the founder ruler of a dynasty and gave his words and deeds an especial importance, so that later emperors would be bound to take them as guidelines for their conduct. For example, Ming foreign policy was much influenced by the oft-repeated dicta of the founder emperor, such as his remark that, 'As to the control of the barbarians who surround us, we have only to be militarily prepared and to attend to our frontier defences. Resist them when they invade us but do not pursue them relentlessly when they withdraw.'[12] Such sayings, together with passages culled from ancient literature, helped to provide the framework within which policy was conducted. At the same time it was naturally the custom for founder emperors to introduce new legal codes, and educational and fiscal policies essential to recovery from the mess left behind by the previous dynasty; and great prestige attached to these measures as the work of one who was the conspicuous choice of Heaven. Moreover, dynastic founders were normally vigorous and energetic men of affairs as compared with later rulers, who were often brought up in the seclusion of the palace and cosseted by women and eunuchs rather than hardened by conflict. In popular literature dynastic founders were heroic and charismatic figures who fought their way from humble beginnings to the imperial throne; and even in antiquity the historian, Ssu-ma Ch'ien, reflecting on the Shang, saw a regular pattern in the contrast between the founders and the later mediocrities: 'The rulers at the beginning of each new dynasty never failed to conduct themselves with awe and reverence, but their descendants little by little sank into indolence and vain pride.'[13]

The influence on Chinese history of the doctrine of the Mandate of Heaven cannot be exaggerated. In contrast with Europe, where order depended on the balance of power between separate nation states, China was in theory unified and centralized by the universal pre-eminence of the Son of Heaven. Such a doctrine could even withstand the shock of foreign invasion and conquest, for there was no reason why the Mandate of Heaven should always be conferred on a Chinese: a Manchu too could learn the role and serve as a fitting intermediary between Heaven and Man.

IV

The role of the Son of Heaven, as I have said before, did not imply that the emperor himself was regarded as a divine being. To go back to the beginning of Chinese history, the Shang king was a member of a lineage thought of as existing both in Heaven and on Earth. His ancestors had supernatural powers and their desires could be studied by means of divination. In the early Chou period there was a similar situation, for the *Book of Songs* says:

> The Chou march on in succession,
> And generation after generation there are wise kings.
> Three rulers are in Heaven,
> And the king is their counterpart in the capital.[14]

The king participated in divine tasks, and was regarded as the assessor of Heaven. Later the father of the empire Ch'in Shih Huang Ti was given an aura of divinity. He sought the elixir of immortality and suffered from megalomaniac obsessions. He adopted the new title of *huang-ti*, conventionally translated as 'emperor', although *ti* was used of mythical sages such as Yao and Shun, and often needs to be translated as 'god'. Henceforward the emperor had need of a kind of divine aura to enable him to fulfil his cosmic role. Although in medieval times emperors dealt more informally with their ministers, in the later imperial age they remained more aloof. Seated on the dragon throne, the Son of Heaven was too sacred an object to be gazed on by mortal eyes, so a screen must intervene. Westerners who came to China were struck by the awe in which the emperor was held by his people. Macartney, for example, noted how a sight of the emperor's portrait was sufficient to make people prostrate themselves; and, attending the emperor's birth-day ceremony, he found that the worship and adoration he received on that occasion as he sat behind his screen surpassed any religious cere-mony. When conditions permitted, emperors were kept as separate as possible from ordinary mortals. Thus, as Macartney noted, the common road from Peking to the summer palace was paralleled by a separate one entirely for the use of the sovereign. Receipt of an imperial honour by a high-ranking official miles from the capital would immediately cause him to turn in the direction of the capital and perform the kotow.

But in spite of all this there was no development of a systematic emperor worship. The emperor's ancestors were, of course, powerful gods and guardians of the dynasty's fortunes, but this was only a grander version of the ancestor worship of the ordinary people of China. Among the common people Chinese emperors were often popularly referred to as the Buddha, and indeed the famous nineteenth-century Dowager Empress Tz'u-hsi liked to dress up as Kuanyin, the Buddhist goddess of mercy; but none of this has any serious religious significance. Another common belief was that the emperor was the incarnation of the dragon, the mythical creature associated with the bringing of rain. This idea is reflected in the design of imperial robes, which depict a dragon among clouds, hovering over land and sea. In traditional Chinese society the line of demarcation between the human and the divine was not very clear, but it is plain that there was no systematic worship of the emperor as a divine being.

The nature of the emperor's religious role was already made clear in the ancient *Record of Rites*: 'When the former emperors presented their offerings to God in the outskirts of the capital, wind and rain were duly regulated, and cold and warmth came each in its appointed season, so that the Sage Emperor had only to stand with his face to the south for order to prevail throughout the world.'[15] Needing to maintain harmony between his world and the supernatural, man had to take part in cosmic events by accompanying them with appropriate rituals. The pattern of the emperor's religious duties was already cut out in the Han. Extremely important were the rarely held *feng-shan* sacrifices, which took place at a decent interval after accession to claim that he was fulfilling the Mandate with which he had been entrusted. There were also periodic sacrifices at the famous mountains and great rivers of the empire, which were still being conducted in the nineteenth century, for example in thanksgiving for victory over the Taiping rebels. Important also was the cult of the imperial ancestors, regarded as powerful protectors of the dynasty. But the major responsibility was the worship of Heaven, which he alone, as Son of Heaven, was qualified to perform.

In the ancient ritual it was stated: 'At the winter solstice a sacrifice shall be made to Heaven in the southern suburbs in order to greet the arrival of lengthening days.'[16] The grand imperial sacrifice to Heaven was still being conducted at the Altar of Heaven in the southern outskirts of Peking right through to the end of the Ch'ing Dynasty (1912), when it impressed European missionaries as a ceremony with deep religious significance. The altar itself consists of three circular concentric balustraded terraces of white marble mounted by steps at each of the cardinal points. It is in a walled enclosure approached by a long raised causeway through a grove of pine-trees, symbol of longevity, leading from the magnificent circular Temple of Heaven mounted on its own three-tiered marble base and covered with a triple azure-tiled roof. Here the emperor reverently prepared himself for the sacrifice, and after three days of solemn fasting the ceremony took place before dawn to the light of flaming torches. Escorted by high officials in their magnificent robes, the greatest sovereign on earth prostrated himself before the might of Heaven, something 'not represented by any image, something which was above him and his people as the blue sky was above the white marble altar, something without whose providence in the ordering of the seasons the people could not live, and by whose commission he held his throne'.[17] An unblemished bullock was sacrificed, and the emperor prayed in such words as these: 'All the numerous tribes of animated beings are indebted to Thy favour for their beginning. Men and creatures are emparadised, O Lord, in Thy Love. All living things are indebted to Thy goodness, but who knows whence his blessings come to him? It is Thou alone, O Lord, who art the true parent of all things.'[18] The last time such an act was performed was at the winter solstice at the end of 1915, when President Yüan Shih-k'ai drove to the Temple of Heaven by armoured car, but it was a ceremony which meant nothing if conducted by the mere ruler of China. It had to be done by the sovereign of all-under-Heaven.

V

The emperors' religious activities were their most important function, but now we must turn to the part they played in the business of government. Ideologically the matter was ultimately determined by the conflict between the Confucian and Legalist philosophies, which was mainly played out in the Han period. The two philosophies were diametrically opposed in several respects. Notably the Legalists believed that the people existed for the sake of the state and its ruler while the Confucians believed that the state and its ruler existed for the sake of the people. The Legalists believed that officials must be obedient instruments of the ruler's will, while Confucians claimed that they should be morally superior men accountable in the last resort to Heaven. What emerged as the ideology of imperial administration was a compromise between the Confucian and Legalist extremes, given the label of Confucianism. No emperor ever denied the validity of Confucianism and each sought to rule according to its lights, and it was generally recognized that the success of a dynasty must depend on a kind of harmony or balance of power between the emperor and the various agencies in the government. Although rulers isolated within their palaces tended towards autocracy, total despotism was an impracticable concept, for the emperor was entirely dependent on the kind of advice which came to him from those who acted as his ears and eyes outside the palace, and he must in his own interest sustain their morale by reasonably just conduct of affairs. Even the most autocratic emperor was inevitably restricted by traditions, conventions, and precedents, and by the pressures of relatives as well as by the need to rely on well-informed ministers. Although on occasion emperors could behave with sudden harshness, their right to act in an arbitrary manner served as a threat which was rarely put into practice.

The centre of power shifted as the imperial institution developed and as emperors of different personalities ascended the throne. At the beginning of recorded history, in the Shang period, the king was responsible for all government policies and all decisions were attributed to him. The affairs of state were officially referred to as the king's affairs. Again in the largely self-sufficient manorial type of economy of the Western Chou there was little to distinguish official state business from the private affairs of the lord. Later in the Chou Dynasty rulers delegated more and more military and diplomatic business to their ministers, and interstate conferences were attended by ministers instead of rulers. In the Former Han Dynasty, although it was necessary to develop an administrative machine capable of running a large empire, the emperor still retained considerable power, especially in appointments (since all but junior offices were filled by him), and in matters of law (for he was the sole legislator and chief judge). At the same time his imperial cabinet was a direct descendant of the court of the Chou kings, and the titles of its members were still those appropriate to the running of a large household rather than an empire. Later the rise of Confucian ministers helped to keep the emperor's power in check, but this in turn resulted in the energetic Emperor Wu striving to reassert imperial authority by transferring more power away from the bureaucracy to the inner court. This tension between court and bureaucracy was a familiar feature of later Chinese history, with emperors tending to try to monopolize power by getting the control of affairs into the hands of a small council consisting of their own appointees.

One means whereby emperors involved officialdom in serious discussion on important topics was the court conference. Han emperors, although they were formally the sole policy-makers and legislators, often had recourse to the advice of a court conference when initiating a new policy in foreign, financial, and legal affairs and in matters concerning the imperial house and the state religion. These conferences were often large-scale occasions attended by all officials above a certain rank, ensuring that the views of all departments and interests were considered. Decisions were based on the opinion of the majority and were normally accepted by the emperor. Even under the Ming sovereigns, who have the reputation for being more autocratic than most, such court conferences were held to debate major issues of military and civil policy. Since it is the dominant Chinese view that politics is primarily a matter of human relations rather than of impersonal institutions, such wide consultation is only to be expected. Court conferences in the Ming tried to reach unanimous decisions, which would then, according to custom, be binding on the emperor. If no unanimous decision were reached, the emperor would have to make up his mind in accordance with the minutes of the debates and the advice of leading ministers. Thus decisions on matters of policy were generally the result of consensus rather than the whim of one individual.

The special ruler-minister relationship, one of the five relationships at the heart of the Confucian philosophy, also implied that decisions should be based on consultation. Mencius had insisted on the minister not being at the ruler's beck and call, and the importance of the ruler being a good listener was also a very ancient idea – indeed the word *t'ing* (to hear) was used in the sense of 'to govern' since the essential task of the ruler was to listen to the advice of ministers, who acted as his eyes and ears. 'The great Shun', as Mencius had said, 'delighted to learn from others to practise what was good';[19] and this kind of humility was an essential part of the imperial image, as was acknowledged, for example, by the Ch'ien-lung emperor, who called his study 'The Hall of Delight in Doing Good' in allusion to this passage. Another aspect of the ruler-minister relationship stressed by Mencius is the duty of ministers to remonstrate with their sovereigns if they have faults and to abandon their service if their remonstrance goes unheeded.

The latter tradition developed into an institution commonly known as the Censorate, which combined the function of surveillance over the bureaucracy with that of criticizing the emperor, forming yet another check on tyranny. The ancient belief that the ruler's duty was to be ready to receive advice from all his ministers also developed into the institution of the memorial. At times the right to send in memorials was restricted, but according to the system which was supposed to operate in the Ming, anyone could submit memorials to criticize the ruler and government and make suggestions for improvement. It was said that memorials from the humblest citizens in the capital could reach the emperor's eyes by the same day. These indications of opinion could supplement official reports to form the raw material on which policy decisions could be based. Emperors would normally consult the department concerned before giving their replies. Often, too, memorials which came in from the provinces would contain clear-cut proposals which merely required rubber-stamping. Nevertheless the work involved was arduous. Conscientious emperors handled all memorials themselves, and, as the Shun-chih emperor said: 'The nation is vast and affairs of state are extremely complex. I have to endorse all memorials and make decisions by myself without a minute of rest.'[20] The system got out of control, so that in the Ch'ing Dynasty memorials were strictly limited in length and thus could not go into sufficient detail. They were also subjected to a most elaborate bureaucratic procedure, and in being passed from department to department, they went through so many hands that no vestige of confidentiality remained.

Side by side with this system there developed a new kind of secret palace memorial meant for the eyes of the emperor alone. This new system arose quite casually out of the Manchu practice of sending greetings memorials to the emperor. One such memorial from an imperial bondservant serving as textile commissioner at Soochow added information on weather conditions and rice prices. The K'ang-hsi emperor welcomed this novel source of intelligence and encouraged the imperial bondservants and later an increasingly wide range of officials to send him secret memorials, giving information about conditions in the provinces, which tended not to be given so honestly via the open memorial system. His informants now no longer feared reprisals if they told the truth, but risked being detected by cross-checking if they told lies; so the emperor was able to get a much more accurate impression of economic conditions, the state of law and order, and the accomplishments of officials in remote parts of the country. Memorials had to be submitted in boxes which had locks and keys especially imported from Europe. These were to be kept in the hands of the emperor and the individual memorialist, and death was the penalty for the unauthorized reproduction of keys. The effect of this innovation was not only to be seen in improved intelligence; but more importantly it transformed the role of the emperor, since information came to him directly and he could withhold it from the bureaucracy. Now he was the nerve centre of the whole political system and much more of an autocrat than hitherto. Thus the palace memorial system was one of several devices which emerged in the course of imperial Chinese history whereby the bureaucracy's ability to thwart the emperor was itself thwarted and undermined.

Another means of gathering information was the traditional practice of summoning officials to audience. In the Ch'ing period morning audience was held almost every day for central government officials. They assembled at the palace at dawn and, on their knees, presented their memorials to the emperor in prescribed order. Special audiences were also held for high-ranking provincial officials, and these enabled the emperor to have wide-ranging discussions on local conditions. The K'ang-hsi emperor was one who took these occasions very seriously. He would ask in great detail about the harvest, declare his interest in the welfare of the common people and enquire whether there were any bandits in the locality, and ask about the performance of other officials in the area. He would also question the official about his career and studies and even test him on his knowledge of the Confucian Classics, for this was a matter which had primacy over technical concerns, just as in contemporary China it has often been held more important to be 'red' than 'expert'. Finally he might present him with some Classical books or a farewell poem. Such audiences not only served to provide information but also helped to strengthen the morale and loyalty of officials, just as did the privilege of submitting secret palace memorials; and this was important at a time when Manchu rule meant fewer opportunities for the Chinese scholar-bureaucrats.

VI

Among the more specific aspects of the emperor's role in government, his most important task was the appointment of meritorious officials. This view had been stressed in antiquity as a means to government by non-action, and two thousand years later the Ch'ien-lung emperor thought this the most important of the ideal ruler's attributes. 'Man's individual capacity is limited,' he wrote, 'and even the sage kings Yao and Shun accomplished their great works only with the assistance of talented counsellors. How much the more should those who are not equal to Yao and Shun employ talent!'[21] In the Former Han, as we have seen, the emperor was personally responsible for appointing all high officials, and so was the source of all power and privilege. Later, although appointments theoretically remained in the sovereign's hands, in practice they came forward as nominations from the Board of Civil Office, which because of the emphasis placed on this activity by Confucian doctrine was naturally treated as the senior of the six ministries between which government business was normally divided. But since one explanation of the harmony of the Golden Age of antiquity was that all offices were filled by the right men for the job, conscientious emperors always took a close interest in this aspect of government.

Also of fundamental importance was the emperor's role in education. Confucian texts have much to say about the duty of government to transform and perfect the nature of the people. The first step in this process of civilizing the populace is to provide peace and prosperity.

The next step is to provide moral training and education. This is done by inculcating music, literature and the rites (including everything from the most solemn religious ceremonies to the simplest daily courtesies). Rites and music can be appreciated to some extent by all men, but literature can be pursued thoroughly only by the intelligent and leisured. The final product is the sage who ideally should become emperor, but in practice the hereditary principle is accepted and the sage should become adviser to the emperor. Hence the important role played by the emperors in the patronage of education and the conduct of examinations. In the earliest written tests the Former Han emperors Wen and Wu set the questions for the candidates, and in the fully developed civil service examination system of the late empire it was again the emperor who conducted the highest examination of all, held in the palace. Throughout imperial Chinese history emperors were regarded as the grand patrons of education, frequently paying formal visits to the national university, issuing edicts for the establishment of schools, and paying honour to Confucius as the 'first teacher'.

In these circumstances it was natural that much attention should be paid to the education of emperors themselves. In antiquity the role of tutor to a crown prince in preparing his charge for the throne was an important one – and hazardous too if the tide of political events turned against his protégé. In imperial times there are many accounts of the rigorous Confucian training inflicted upon heirs to the throne and continued even after their accession. Emperors were lectured on Confucianism by venerable Neo-Confucian philosophers. Even the Ming founder, although of rude peasant and bandit origin, had his eldest son and heir exposed to the full rigour of Confucian pedagogy, and many leading officials were assigned the task of preparing him for his imperial role. The K'ang-hsi emperor began his self-imposed Confucian education early in life and throughout his reign had scholars in attendance in his library to expound the Confucian Classics to him whenever necessary. The Ch'ien-lung emperor had a rigorous training, first at home and then in a palace school for princes established by his father, the Yung-cheng emperor. Classes went on almost throughout the year, from 5 a.m. to 4 p.m. His main subjects were the Classics and Histories, which gave him the facility for apt Classical quotation and reference to historical precedent necessary for a ruler. Apart from these subjects, he studied examination questions, verse composition, the Manchu and Mongol languages, horsemanship, archery, and other military subjects. He also had training in painting and calligraphy, and later on in life he learnt much about Western science from the instruction of Jesuit missionaries.

A similar routine was undergone by the boy P'u-yi, long after his abdication. He had various extremely distinguished Chinese and Manchu tutors, and also received English lessons from the diplomat Sir Reginald Johnston. An extract from his diary at the age of fourteen gives an idea of his routine:

> 27th. Fine. Rose at four, wrote out eighteen sheets of the character Prosperity in a large hand. Classes at eight. Read *Analects, Chou Ritual, Record of Ritual*, and T'ang poetry. . . . Listened to tutor Chen lecturing on the *General Chronological History with Comments by Emperor Ch'ien-lung*. Finished eating at 9:30, read *Tso Commentary, Ku-liang Commentary*, heard tutor Chu on the *Explanation of the Great Learning*, wrote couplets. Lessons finished at eleven, went to pay respects to four High Consorts. Johnston did not come today as he had mild flu, so returned to Heart Nurture Palace* and wrote out thirty more sheets of characters Prosperity and Longevity. Read papers, ate at four, bed at six. Read *Anthology of Ancient Literature* in bed: very interesting.[22]

Imperial tutors were meant to be treated with proper deference, and there was a long tradition of debate on the appropriate ritual for greeting them. In the T'ang it had been standard practice for princes to face north and bow to their tutors when they entered (instead of south, the proper direction for rulers to face), and the same recognition of the superior claims of ideological authority was made by the Ch'ien-lung emperor. In the case of P'u-yi, when he had his lessons he sat facing south, and his tutor sat facing west in conformity with the ancient injunction in the *Record of Rites* that 'when the teacher was addressing the Son of Heaven he should not face the north'.[24]

VII

Thus the supreme task of ensuring that the country had the best possible administrators and that they were best educated to fulfil their duties was ultimately the emperor's responsibility. In internal affairs the two main tasks of government were the collection of taxes and the maintenance of law and order, and the emperor had ultimate responsibility for these activities too. As for law and order, many references in bronze inscriptions and early Chou literature refer to the administration of punish-

*The Heart Nurture Palace was the emperor's own residence, named after a quotation from Mencius: 'In the nurture of the heart there is nothing better than to have few desires.'[23]

ments as a kingly task, and King Wu is quoted as saying that if there is any fault in administering justice Heaven will kill him for it.[25] Although ministers of justice were later appointed to take charge of such matters, the ruler remained the person ultimately responsible and the final court of appeal. The primacy of the ruler's legal role can be seen when the Han founder overthrew the Ch'in: his first pronouncement was to abolish the harsh laws of Ch'in and promise instead that the only articles of law would be the death penalty for murder, and that 'he who wounds another or steals shall be punished according to the gravity of the offence'.[26] Later of course a more elaborate code had to be worked out.

In the Han Dynasty all laws had to be approved and promulgated by the emperor and, although the administration of the law was generally left to the commandant of justice, the emperor could overrule him and override the law. The same overriding role remained to the emperor throughout Chinese history, so that in the provincial administration of the later empire all death penalties had to be approved by the sovereign. He could also issue pardons and amnesties, which were especially important because they were seen as a means of restoring harmony to nature when harshness had caused natural catastrophes. It would not, however, be true to describe the emperor as above the law. Emperors felt that their decisions should accord with the law, there being a strong regard for precedent and an especial reverence for the institutions introduced by the dynastic founder.

The collection of taxes depended very much on the peasants being capable of paying them, and to this end it was necessary for the government to concern itself with the prosperity of the people. Since the emperor was described as father and mother of the people, this was very much his affair. In antiquity the Chou rulers worshipped as their founding ancestor an agricultural deity called Hou Chi (Lord Millet). In this predominantly agricultural society it was natural that the government should concern itself deeply with matters of the soil, like the distribution of seed in times of shortage, the dissemination of farming techniques, and the organization of irrigation works and flood control. The emperor was at the apex of all this, his role being symbolized by the ceremonial spring ploughing by which he inaugurated the year's work on the land. This ceremony is described in ancient texts,[27] and was still being carried out by the Ch'ing emperors. It was reported back to Europe by Jesuits at the Chinese court, and in the spirit of admiration for Chinese practices which then obtained in Europe, it was copied by the sovereigns of France and Austria. Apart from this ceremony the emperor had religious duties associated with the promotion of agriculture. As the Emperor Wu of Han once announced to his ministers, 'Recently the Yellow River overflowed its banks and for several years the harvests were poor. Therefore I journeyed about the empire and performed sacrifices to the Earth Lord, praying for the sake of the common people that the grain might grow well.'[28]

Imperial tours were indeed an important branch of the emperor's activities. Mencius stated that the purpose of the Son of Heaven's twice-yearly visitation of the feudal lords was to inspect the ploughing and make good shortages of seed in the springtime and to examine the harvest and supply extra grain where it was needed in the autumn.[29] It was recorded in the *Book of History* that the mythical emperor Shun made quinquennial tours to each of four sacred mountains at the cardinal points on the borders of his terrain, but on these occasions he corrected the calendar and standardized weights.[30] These journeys had more to do with the emperor's cosmomagical role, but later in Chinese history imperial tours were more Mencian in character.

The K'ang-hsi emperor made six famous tours of the southern provinces, the intention being, in his own words, 'to make personal observations and enquiries about the people's hardships . . . and to investigate local customs',[31] as well as to inspect river conservancy projects. These tours would enable him to see for himself what conditions were like, and would also impress the south with the full might of the Manchu regime. His range of activities while on tour provide a useful insight into his concept of the imperial role: he received officials and discussed the local situation with them, inspected conservancy work, talked to local worthies, pardoned criminals, remitted taxes, visited temples, held archery and poetry contests, admired the scenery, and attended banquets and theatrical performances. He once reminded people of his martial heritage by giving a display of his skill in mounted archery. These tours were enormously expensive, for the imperial entourage had to be provided with worthy accommodation in temporary palaces en route; so when the Ch'ien-lung emperor followed his grandfather's example, he gave out that his main motive was to fulfil the requirements of filial piety by giving pleasure to his mother. The venerable tradition of imperial tours of inspection was also utilized as an euphemism for the extremely embarrassing occasions when the court had to flee the capital under pressure from the European barbarians. For example, in 1900, when the Boxer Rebellion had provoked foreign intervention to relieve the diplomats besieged in the Legation Quarter so that the Dowager Empress Tz'u-hsi had to flee the capital disguised as a peasant woman, the emperor's penitential decree referred to 'escorting the Dowager Empress on a progress of inspection throughout the western provinces'.

VIII

Military skill has seemed to be a less essential part of the Chinese emperor's make-up than civil virtues, although in their earlier history the Chinese were not less warlike than other peoples. In the early Chou period the king naturally acted as his own minister of war or commander-in-chief. Later dynasties were generally founded by men who had won military success, but as the Han founder was told by an adviser: 'You might have won the war on horseback, but you cannot govern it on horseback.' However brilliant a general a founder emperor might be, he would have to acquire a reputation for the arts of peace. With the growth of the bureaucracy during the T'ang and Sung, the old military aristocracy of former times finally lost its power, and despite the conquering warriors of the Mongol and Manchu invasions, the civilian ethos triumphed. In contrast with the predominantly military character of European royalty, the Chinese court was remarkably free of military trappings. The soldier's profession was proverbially despised: 'Good men do not become soldiers, and good iron is not made into nails.' Nevertheless war was sometimes a regrettable necessity and, if there had to be a war to restore order and tranquillity to all-under-Heaven, it was obviously the emperor's role to take the main responsibility, just as King Wen tranquillized the barbarians on all four sides, the last he reached complaining that they had not been pacified first. So even as late as the Ch'ing Dynasty the most vigorous emperors took the field in person. The K'ang-hsi emperor led important expeditions in the north-west, and although it is not certain how much direct military experience he had, the Ch'ien-lung emperor was very proud of the martial achievements of his reign. He adopted as one of his names 'The Old Man of Ten Great Campaigns' and composed a self-congratulatory essay entitled *Record of Ten Great Campaigns*, which was preserved for all time in a stone inscription in the Chinese, Manchu, Mongolian, and Tibetan languages.

In conquering neighbouring barbarians the Son of Heaven was merely taking control of what legitimately belonged to him as the ruler of all-under-Heaven. The possession of territory was another attribute of kingship. The main classical authority for this was to be found in the *Book of Songs*:

> Under the vast heaven
> There is nothing which is not the king's land.
> To the very borders of the earth
> There are none who are not the king's servants.[32]

Mencius quoted this passage, and the idea was not only a commonplace in the ancient Chinese world, but also survived throughout imperial Chinese history. In his autobiography P'u-yi referred to the fact that the very height of the buildings in the Forbidden City was an imperial prerogative 'that served to teach me from an early age that everything under Heaven was the emperor's land'.[33] This doctrine strongly influenced the history of land ownership, since the state resisted the concept of private possession of land long after it made any sense to do so. Even in the early Chou period parcels of land had been transferred from one individual to another, with the royal consent; and, as economic life became more complex and trade and a money economy developed, so there was a strong impetus towards the buying and selling of landed property. Yet even the T'ang Dynasty refused to recognize economic realities and insisted on trying to maintain a rigid system of state-controlled land tenure, whereby people received a fixed grant of land from the state for the duration of their working lives. There were strong contemporary political motives for trying to implement this scheme in that it was hoped that it would prevent the accumulation of vast estates by great aristocratic families and so keep power and revenue in the hands of the state, but as always Classical authority was important. Apart from the *Book of Songs*, this policy also had the blessing of the *Record of Rites* which said: 'The lands are not to be sold',[34] and this passage was quoted in the T'ang legal code relating to land tenure.

IX

If one leaves the official conduct of Chinese emperors and tries to find out about their private lives, it is not easy to do so since it was the public image that was of overwhelming importance. In any case biographical writing in China was generally concerned with a person's official career, and the well-rounded biography was a genre not developed in traditional Chinese literature. There are accounts of Ch'ing emperors from the pens of Jesuit missionaries and other Western writers, who were not concerned to present flattering portraits, and some revealing material in Chinese about the later sovereigns has survived into an age when it is no longer necessary to paint out the warts; and there is even an account of one emperor written by himself after he had been transformed into a private citizen. But in general descriptions of life within the palace were fictional, ranging from pious eulogies to the salacious gossip of the popular literature.

But although it may be difficult to see beneath the mask, it is possible to understand the general factors which conditioned an emperor's private life. The most important consideration was his uniqueness among men. In ancient times a ruler would refer to himself as 'the solitary man', and later the emperor enjoyed a unique style of life, wearing special kinds of hats and garments, and having special carriages designed exclusively for himself. Dress regulations were always important in imperial Chinese history, and men wore different coloured robes appropriate to their different ranks. Reserved for the emperor in the Ch'ing Dynasty were the magnificent yellow robes embroidered with the five-clawed dragon. P'u-yi also records the dominance of the imperial yellow colour:

The glazed tiles were yellow, my sedan-chair was yellow, my chair cushions were yellow, the linings of my hats and clothes were yellow, the girdle round my waist was yellow, the dishes and bowls from which I ate and drank, the padded cover of the rice-gruel saucepan, the material in which my books were wrapped, the window curtains, the bridle of my horse . . . everything was yellow. This colour, the so-called 'brilliant yellow', was used exclusively by the imperial household and made me feel from my earliest years that I was unique and had a 'heavenly' nature different from that of everybody else.[35]

The uniqueness of the emperor was also reflected in the special language used to refer to him. He himself had a first person pronoun reserved exclusively for his own use. There was also a taboo against both speaking and writing his personal name, and this meant that the relevant characters were also unusable for other purposes. The names given to emperors in historical sources are their posthumous ones. For example the emperor who reigned from 140 to 87 BC was given the title Wu Ti, the Martial Emperor, after his death, and that is how he has been referred to ever since. Another way of referring to emperors was by reign-period. Starting in the Han Dynasty, auspicious names were used to designate short periods during an emperor's reign (with the purpose of renewing the calendar as a ritually auspicious act). The name was changed every few years, and the Martial Emperor had as many as eleven reign-titles; but in the Ming and Ch'ing periods the practice was altered so that there was only one reign-title for each emperor. Consequently sovereigns of those eras are generally referred to by their reign-titles: the Hung-wu and Yung-lo emperors are the emperors of the reign-periods called Boundless Valour and Eternal Contentment respectively. To address the emperor the term *pi-hsia*, meaning 'under the steps to the throne' was used: it originally referred to the emperor's attendants, but was then used when speaking to the emperor himself, as if pretending that his august person was not really being addressed. Later a common way of addressing the emperor was *wan-sui*, meaning 'ten thousand years', after the convention that he was expected to live that long. Similarly 'after ten thousand years have passed' became an euphemism for 'after your majesty's death'. As mentioned before, the word *sheng*, meaning 'sacred' was also used as a conventional epithet applied to anything concerned with the emperor. The emperor's likeness had also to be regarded with awe, and it is said that the Dowager Empress Tz'u-hsi had a miniature railway constructed for the conveyance of her portrait when it was sent off to an exhibition in the United States, so that the 'sacred countenance' could be borne upright under its canopy of yellow silk and not suffer the indignity of being carried on the shoulders of coolies.

Not only must the emperor be given very special treatment to show his uniqueness. He must also be kept as secluded as possible. In the Han period when an emperor left the palace, guards cleared the route and no one was allowed to pass except his attendants. Execution was the penalty for unauthorized persons who intruded into the palace. Although officials were allowed in to attend court and have audiences, in general males could not stay overnight within the palace walls, except for the eunuchs who staffed the buildings.

X

Within the palace the emperors enjoyed a luxurious style of life which was anathema to Confucian moralists, who believed that economic problems should be solved by frugality, and looked to the Classics for condemnation of pleasure-seeking. To Mencius it was permissible for the king to have his pleasure palaces, his hunting-parks, and his entertainments, provided that he shared them with the people and that he did not distract the peasants from their agricultural tasks so that they could minister to his pleasures. But the splendid palaces and pavilions and gardens which emperors enjoyed were not shared with the people, nor did emperors provide such facilities for their subjects, their concern for the populace being traditionally shown by such measures as amnesties and tax remissions. The luxury and voluptuousness of the court appealed to the imagination of the masses, and popular literature delighted in the most intimate detail of imperial pleasure and credited the occupants of the dragon throne with the most extraordinary sexual prowess. Especially lurid are the accounts of bad last emperors, charged with the ruin of their dynasty and the loss of the Mandate, of whom the emperor Yang of the Sui Dynasty became the most notorious example. Self-gratification is seen as the goal of all his enterprises: his great canal construction projects were all designed to satisfy his desire to travel in the most pleasurable way to his favourite Yangchow. Trees were planted along them to keep the sun off the beautiful girls recruited to pull the imperial barges. A million conscripted workers toiled to build his pleasure palace, while the emperor stayed a month at a time to enjoy the delights of his Maze Pavilion, stocked with several thousand girls of good family provided for his carnal pleasures.

Exaggerated though they are, such stories do reflect the ludicrous scale on which emperors' needs were provided for, which had to eclipse the style of life enjoyed by ordinary mortals. P'u-yi recounts how he was followed by a large retinue of eunuchs whenever he went for a stroll in the garden, ready to minister to every conceivable need – eunuchs of the imperial presence with changes of clothing, eunuchs of the imperial tea bureau with refreshments, eunuchs of the imperial dispensary with medicines and first-aid equipment, and eunuchs to support him as he walked and to bring the sedan-chair in case he wanted to ride, the whole being preceded by a eunuch from the Administrative Bureau, who functioned like a motor-horn, making noises to ensure that anyone in the vicinity would go away.[36]

The luxurious life of the emperors was not to be interrupted by death, for in the vast imperial mausolea lavish quantities of goods were buried for use in the afterlife. Spread over a large plain within easy reach of Peking are the tombs of the thirteen Ming emperors who ruled there. Each has an enormous mound in which the body rested and the treasures were concealed, fronted by a walled compound containing sacrificial halls and other buildings whose splendour accentuated the poverty of the neighbouring villages and pointed an appalling contrast between the conditions of the living and the luxury squandered on the father and mother of the people after his death. Such vast concentrations of treasure invited the attention of the grave robber, and the megalomaniac Ch'in Shih Huang Ti had crossbows arranged so that looters would be automatically shot on attempting to break into his tomb. In the present century the tombs of the Ch'ien-lung emperor and the Dowager Empress Tz'u-hsi were systematically plundered by Chiang Kai-shek's troops. Tz'u-hsi is said to have paid frequent visits to the site of her mausoleum and to have taken great interest in its construction and adornment. This was a common practice among Chinese rulers, just as the ordinary Chinese expected to have his coffin ready in advance of his death.

XI

When the emperor died, there was the problem of finding a replacement. Ideally the job should have gone to someone picked out for his supreme wisdom and morality, but in practice the hereditary principle was adopted. In the Shang Dynasty the succession generally seems to have gone to sons, but sometimes to brothers. In the Chou period the principle of heredity was firmly adhered to, although it inevitably produced some weak sovereigns. In the Han period more regard was paid to the character of the candidates, and emperors were chosen either by the previous emperor or, failing this, by the chief ministers. All of the previous emperor's descendants were regarded as eligible, and scholarship, benevolence, and filial piety were specifically mentioned as qualifications for the job. Generally in Chinese history the principle of hereditary succession prevailed, but this did not mean the simple operation of primogeniture, for the emperor had many wives in addition to the empress, and their offspring might win support. A further complication was that the emperor was normally considered to have the right to choose his heir and so could go for a younger son if he thought him most capable. This resulted in several bitter crises, since factions would gather round one or other contender for the position of crown prince.

The matter was complicated by the influence of the foreign dynasties, the Yüan and Ch'ing. The custom among the nomadic Mongols was for the youngest son to inherit, since he was the last one left at home, his elder brothers having taken their portion of the cattle and gone elsewhere; but this practice was abandoned because of the demands of imperial responsibility. Supreme powers of leadership were now necessary, so the ruler began to be selected by a council of chieftains. This method was also used by the Manchus, but as the power of the throne grew and the influence of the council of chieftains weakened, so the choice fell into the hands of the emperor. The civil service generally hoped that the eldest son would be confirmed as crown prince at an early age and trained for the sovereign's role, and the K'ang-hsi emperor's long refusal to name an heir led to an acute crisis. The problem was solved by his successor, the Yung-cheng emperor, who initiated the practice of putting the next emperor's name in a sealed casket which was not to be opened until after his death.

The other way in which the succession was determined was by abdication, for which there was a hallowed precedent in Yao's yielding the throne to Shun. In the Chinese context abdication had a special flavour since, if a man abdicates in favour of his son, that son, although emperor, still owes the obligations of filial piety towards his father, the retired emperor. As Mencius said, 'To be the father of the Son of Heaven is the highest possible honour.'[37] In these circumstances some special brand of piety is needed, and the Han founder and his father were reported to have been in some difficulty about who should make obeisance to whom. Most abdications in Chinese history, however, were forced, and events in the T'ang Dynasty in particular meant that the title of Retired Emperor ceased to be an honourable one, extravagant displays of filial piety on the part of the new monarch being a facade to cover the fact of usurpation, a very awkward act to reconcile with Confucian morality.

Greater respectability was given to abdication by two successive emperors in the Sung Dynasty, Kao-tsung and Hsiao-tsung, both of whom appear to have retired quite voluntarily. Throughout the quarter century of his reign Hsiao-tsung paid his adoptive father, the retired emperor, the frequent elaborate visitations which their relationship demanded, thus diverting himself from affairs of state. And when the old man finally died, he ascended the very pinnacle of filial piety by abdicating in his turn so that he could complete the full three-year mourning rites for his predecessor, undistracted by the business of government.

A unique abdication was that of the Ch'ien-lung emperor, who declared that on his succession he had confided to Heaven his desire not to exceed the sixty-year reign of his illustrious grandfather, the

K'ang-hsi emperor, and his intention to abdicate rather than do so. Since he did not ascend the throne until the age of twenty-five, it seemed highly unlikely that he would have to fulfil his promise. In the end he did have to, but he was able to make the most of his retirement by displaying it as a grand gesture befitting his moral leadership and an occasion unrivalled since the abdication of the legendary Yao, while he still used his enormous prestige to retain the real power in his own hands. He was not so much to be Retired Emperor as Super Emperor. In memorials and despatches his title was raised three places as compared with the emperor's two, and his birthday was referred to as 'ten thousand times ten thousand years', not a mere 'ten thousand years' like the sovereign's. As for more practical affairs, Ch'ien-lung made it clear in an edict that 'after the change of government we shall continue to instruct personally in matters of high policy, in the choice of talent, and in the administration of the state. Twice daily the succeeding emperor shall respectfully hear our counsel so that in the future he will not be led into error.' [38] The new emperor Chia-ch'ing was to be entrusted only with commonplace and ceremonial matters. For the next three years until the Ch'ien-lung emperor died, two courts were maintained and two calendars kept, so that the period was considered either as the end of the Ch'ien-lung or beginning of the Chia-ch'ing era, and official historiography kept two parallel accounts. At formal banquets the new emperor sat at the old one's side and served him with food as a filial son was expected to do, and when both left for the Summer Palace, it was the Ch'ien-lung emperor who was seen off by foreign dignitaries.

The final abdication, that of P'u-yi, left much of the trappings of power still within the palace. He was allowed to stay on there and he retained his title of Great Ch'ing Emperor and it was agreed that the republic should treat him with the courtesy due to a foreign sovereign. This only made sense because the emperors were not entitled 'Emperor of China' but had dynastic titles, which they could obviously continue to use without impropriety. The abdication edict included the words: 'The minds of the majority of the people are in favour of the establishment of a republican form of government. ... The universal desire clearly expresses the Will of Heaven, and it is not for us to oppose the desires and incur the disapproval of the millions of the people merely for the sake of the privileges and powers of a single House.'[39] What a contrast this makes with the Ch'ien-lung emperor's self-confident review of achievement in his own abdication proclamation:

We have carried on our great heritage, pacified the entire realm, sought conscientiously to rule, and been unsparingly diligent from day to day. We have relied on Heaven's protection and our imperial ancestors' example. The universe enjoys peace, the people enjoy happiness and abundance. The imperial name is known throughout; both near and far, we constitute one family.

Since ascending the throne we have pacified Ili, the Moslem tribes, the great and small Chin-ch'uan rebels. We have added vast tracts to the empire. Burma, Annam, the Gurkhas, and the tributary border kingdoms all tremble before us in awe and respectfully submit tribute to us. Those who have taken it upon themselves to be refractory have all been exterminated.

Meritorious accomplishments have exceeded expectations and our grace and favour have extended to all points of the realm. Thrice have we remitted the grain tribute in all provinces, four times the land-poll tax. . . . Countless sums have gone to debt cancellation and distribution of relief funds. The scholar class has been made prosperous, the officials have been rectified, and the common people . . . have shared in this great age of peace.[40]

This was how the great institution of imperial sovereignty wanted itself to be seen, and none of these aims would have failed to evoke a sympathetic response in the hearts of men at the time, precisely two thousand years earlier, when the Han Dynasty was being founded.

CHAPTER 2

THE MANDARINS

I

The essential corollary of the sage Son of Heaven ruling through the power of his virtue rather than by involving himself in the practical details of administration was the existence of wise and virtuous ministers who would put into practice the principles of kingly government. Hsün Tzu had strongly advocated that education be based on the study of certain classic books,[1] and in the Former Han period the Five Classics (the *Book of Changes*, the *Book of Songs*, the *Book of History*, the *Spring and Autumn Annals*, and the *Record of Rites*) were firmly established as the curriculum for training the promising scholars who would eventually staff the growing bureaucracy needed to administer this great new empire. An imperial academy was formed in 124 BC, when fifty students were selected to study under the wise men and learned doctors used as advisers by the emperor, and before the end of the Former Han their number had increased to three thousand, a figure chosen because Confucius was thought to have had that number of disciples. Students could obtain advancement by passing a test taken at the academy. Another method of recruitment was for officials to be asked to recommend promising scholars, who then merely had to submit essays for the emperor's approval, an early example of the sovereign taking part in the examination system. Scholars could also present memorials to the emperor to recommend themselves.

Although written examinations were used in China in the Han period, many centuries before they were introduced in Europe, office was generally the privilege of powerful families and recruitment depended mainly on heredity and on recommendation right through until the eighth century AD. Then aristocracy was at last outstripped by meritocracy, largely because Empress Wu, having usurped the throne,

33

could not rely on the aristocrats from the metropolitan area who had previously had the monopoly of political strength, but instead had to secure for herself a new political base by drawing on the largely untapped resources of south-east China. After this the examination system remained the predominant channel of entry into the civil service until its abolition in 1905, except for a brief period under the Mongols. By the eleventh century it had already reached an impressive level of sophistication. The authorities strove for high standards of fairness and objectivity: scripts were copied out by members of the Bureau of Examination Copyists, and all papers were marked by three independent readers. Abuses of course occurred: candidates were impersonated by others whose talents seemed more likely to bring success, and there were notorious cases of corruption; but it is remarkable that such sophisticated methods of recruitment should have been introduced at a time so soon after the long decline of the T'ang and the period of division which succeeded it.

During the last five centuries of its life the system failed to preserve the freshness and ingenuity of earlier days. Throughout the Ming and Ch'ing periods the commentaries of Chu Hsi remained the standard interpretation of the Classics and candidates were expected to make their answers conform to this orthodoxy. They also had to write their papers in the form of the notorious eight-legged essay. This type of essay, subject to rigorous rules, required technical expertise rather than intellectual distinction for its composition, so it has been a byword in modern times for the sterility and formalism of the classical tradition. Collections of successful essays were edited by men who had themselves failed to make progress in the examinations, and these were eagerly bought up by men who would find success in imitation rather than in originality.

The examination system of the Ming and Ch'ing periods represented a formidable ordeal, success in which brought great prestige and privilege. There were three main hurdles. The first test, conducted by the provincial education officer in the local city, led to the degree of *hsiu-ts'ai* (Flowering Talent). This entitled the holder to wear distinctive costume, and brought him much local prestige and tax exemption for his family, but it did not secure entry into the bureaucracy. The next examination was held every third year at the provincial capital in a special examination compound honeycombed with tiny cells, in which candidates sat immured for three whole days as they wrote their scripts. As they travelled to the provincial city candidates hoisted banners which read 'Candidate for the Imperially Decreed Provincial Examination' and passed customs stations without having their baggage checked, but on entering the examination compound they were searched to ensure that they were not smuggling cribs into their cells. They had to take in with them a great load of supplies, including ink and brushes, food and water, bedding, and curtains to hang across the entrance to their tiny cells. These were furnished only with three long boards to provide shelf, desk, and seat, and were too narrow to enable the candidate to stretch out and get a proper rest. The famous short story writer P'u Sung-ling vividly described the ordeal in his account of the seven transformations of an examination candidate:

When he first enters the examination compound and walks along, panting under his heavy load of luggage, he is just like a beggar. Next, while undergoing the personal body search and being scolded by the clerks and shouted at by the soldiers, he is just like a prisoner. When he finally enters his cell and, along with the other candidates, stretches his neck to peer out, he is just like the larva of a bee. When the examination is finished at last and he leaves, his mind in a haze and his legs tottering, he is just like a sick bird that has been released from a cage. While he is wondering when the results will be announced and waiting to learn whether he passed or failed, so nervous that he is startled even by the rustling of the trees and the grass and is unable to sit or stand still, his restlessness is like that of a monkey on a leash. When at last the results are announced and he has definitely failed, he loses his vitality like one dead, rolls over on his side, and lies there without moving, like a poisoned fly. Then, when he pulls himself together and stands up, he is provoked by every sight and sound, gradually flings away everything within his reach, and complains of the illiteracy of the examiners. When he calms down at last, he finds everything in the room broken. At this time he is like a pigeon smashing its own precious eggs. These are the seven transformations of a candidate.[2]

After the ordeal the examiners invited the successful candidates to a banquet, at which the guests first turned in the direction of Peking to give thanks for the imperial grace and then pledged themselves to a lifelong disciple-master relationship with the examiners, the whole company being regaled with music to words from the *Book of Songs* describing a memorable imperial entertainment. But the test itself was conducted under harsh discipline and in very trying circumstances, and only a tiny proportion (sometimes only one in a hundred) would be successful in gaining the degree of *chü-jen* (Recommended Man). No wonder it was said that to pass the provincial examination one needed the spiritual strength of a dragon-horse, the physique of a donkey, the insensitivity of a woodlouse, and the endurance of a camel.[3]

Although the prestige of passing this examination meant further social and economic advancement, it led only to minor official appointments. To make one eligible for a career which might lead eventually to high office it was necessary to proceed to the metropolitan examination which took place at the capital a few months later. Here perhaps one in twenty or thirty would pass out as *chin-shih* (Presented Scholars), a term which was of ancient origin, having been used in the *Record of Rites*. Even then their ordeal was not over, nor was their honour complete; for next came the final test, the palace examination presided over by the emperor himself, which did not fail anyone but finally graded candidates in order of merit.

The emperor's role was in practice performed by individuals of high literary ability, but to reflect the sovereign's official responsibility the questions were cast in the style of an imperial rescript, including the words: 'I am the Son of Heaven, responsible for governing the Empire. Night and day I rack my brains so that the people will be able to live in tranquillity. Fortunately I have this opportunity to pose questions to you graduates and I wish to hear your well-considered opinions on the following.' There was also a standard formula for the answers: 'I, Your humble servant, a superficial scholar newly advanced, not realizing where I was, have ventured to state my own views and am so ashamed of offending the Majesty of the Emperor that I do not know where to hide. I respectfully submit my answer.'[4]

The new *chin-shih* were rewarded with an official banquet and later attended a ceremony in which they made obeisances towards the imperial residence to convey their gratitude, followed a few days afterwards by a ceremony at the temple of Confucius. They could also erect triumphal arches in front of their homes. Success in this rigorous competition did not, however, bring automatic appointment. It merely made one a member of a social and intellectual elite from among whom appointments were made. The top palace graduates would go straight into the Hanlin Academy and would expect high office after a period in the imperial secretariat; but there were not enough jobs to go round for those who were qualified, and there was serious concern at the high average age at which men entered upon their civil service careers, particularly during the Ch'ing Dynasty, when many important jobs went to the Manchus.

It would be difficult to over-emphasize the importance of the part played by the examinations in traditional Chinese life. The *hsiu-ts'ai* had to sit a fresh examination every three years in order to retain his status, and there was no limit to the number of times unsuccessful candidates could retake the examinations, so many spent a large part of their lives in quest of success. Fan Chin in the eighteenth-century novel, *The Scholars*, is the classic example of the downtrodden peasant whose success, after years of failure, is followed by a meteoric rise in the social scale, those who previously despised him now currying favour with him and seeking his patronage. None is more put out of countenance than his bullying father-in-law, a butcher by trade, who, when Fan Chin goes berserk at the news of his success, brings him to his senses with a slap on the cheek, only to realize that he has struck a veritable immortal and that the pain in his hand is a sign that the spirits are taking their revenge.[5] The common people regarded those who passed the higher examinations as incarnations of the star gods. An aura of the supernatural also pervaded the examination halls in the minds of the candidates. So intense was their desire for success that many of them were extremely superstitious, and there were many stories illustrating the common belief that success or failure depended on the intervention of the spirits.

The importance of examination success is also reflected in the very special bonds which linked a candidate not only to his teacher but also to the examiner who officiated when he passed the examination. Fellow-examinees of the same examiner, even if they passed at different times, also felt that they had something in common. Such relationships oiled the wheels of social intercourse and of official business outside the formal bureaucratic channels. The poet Yüan Mei, writing thirty years after passing as Recommended Man, expressed his eternal gratitude to his examiner in the following words:

> Parents, however much they love a child,
> Have not the power to place him among the chosen few.
> Only the examiner can bring the young to notice,
> And out of the darkness carry them to Heaven![6]

The chief requirement for success in the examinations, apart from the technical mastery of the 'eight-legged essay' format, was a thorough knowledge of the Confucian Classics and the historical literature, and a mastery of several poetic styles. The more practical content of the examinations varied, but was much less important in the Ch'ing than it had been in the T'ang and Sung, when the study of law had been also required. Obviously those who succeeded were highly literate men, steeped in the political ideology of their time, capable of working under

37

intense pressure to analyse questions and formulate answers to them in accordance with a given format, many of these qualities being highly relevant to the careers of political administration to which they were destined. But would it not have been better if they had had more knowledge of the detailed matters of practical administration which they would face? Should their education not have been more vocational? This was an old controversy. Confucius had made the classic statement that 'the gentleman is not a utensil'[7] and the conflict between the rule of men of high moral quality trained in the Classics and the rule of law was at the heart of the Confucianist-Legalist confrontation. The discrepancy between a training in literature and the career in administration to which it led was often criticized, and the Sung reformer Wang An-Shih wrote: 'What a student should learn is practical matters concerning the world and the nation.'[8] Some concessions to the need for specialization are seen in Ch'ing bureaucratic practice: officials were kept for a long time working for the same government department and there were training schemes to prepare people for departmental work. But on the whole the Confucian ideal prevailed, that good government stemmed from the self-cultivation of the superior man, which could only bear full fruit if he went out and set the world to rights. One may agree that to deal with the numerous different types of problem which confront him, anyone who holds high office in a great empire must have general knowledge and ability (fortified with moral and political consciousness), rather than one-sided specialist knowledge. And the Confucian Classics seemed full of precisely the kind of sentiment appropriate to the administrators of a great empire, since they dealt with the question of how to bring order and prosperity to the people so as to secure peace and harmony for the world. Hsün Tzu put the case for the generalist against the specialist very plainly:

The farmer is skilled in agriculture, but he cannot do the job of a supervisor of agriculture. The merchant is skilled in marketing, but he cannot do the job of a supervisor of markets. The artisan is skilled in craftsmanship, but he cannot do the job of a supervisor of crafts. But there are men who, although they are incapable of these three skills, may be employed to fill these three supervisory posts. This is because they are skilled in the Way.[9]

We are familiar with the amateur ideal in our own civil service tradition, which may owe its style to imitation of the Chinese model,[10] but it did not matter if those who entered on the basis of a Classical education never again read a word of Latin or Greek. By contrast the

Chinese scholar-bureaucrat was expected to keep up his reading of the Classics in order to keep fresh the qualities they had instilled into him. In audience the emperor might even question him on his studies and test him on his knowledge of the Classics. Education was for the Chinese the occupation of a lifetime, or, as Hsün Tzu put it, 'Learning continues until death and only then does it cease.'[11]

The examination system did not go unchallenged in Confucian China; for, if moral qualities were what was needed in government, why should not men of worth be recommended to the ruler by men who were morally well equipped to pick them out? Such a procedure was in tune with the ideals of the ancient sages, and later it took shape as a system of sponsorship in which the sponsor bore some legal responsibility for the acts of his protégé. After the Han, however, the use of sponsorship for recruitment to the service became rare. Instead it developed into the regular method of promotion within the service. The sponsor was rewarded if his protégé did well and penalized if he committed an offence. By the Sung Dynasty a sophisticated method of grading these rewards and penalties had been worked out so as to ensure the effectiveness of the policy.

When the examination system became the regular method of recruitment, did it mean equal opportunity for all? Early Confucianism believed that men were by nature equal and that human beings had infinite potential, for, in Mencius' view, 'Everyone may become a Yao or Shun.'[12] On the other hand there was firm acceptance of the distinction between the gentleman and the small man. As Mencius put it, 'Some labour with their minds, and some labour with their strength. Those who labour with their minds govern others, and those who labour with their strength are governed by others. Those who are governed by others support them, and those who govern others are supported by them. This is a principle generally recognized everywhere in the world.'[13] The only way this could appear just was through the doctrine of equal education for all. Confucius set an example by accepting pupils however poor, and although far from reaching this egalitarian goal, China did go further in this direction than any other pre-modern state. The civil service examinations were open to all males except actors, slaves, children of prostitutes, runners, policemen, and some other menial employees of officialdom. At the same time the school system gradually developed, until in the early Ming there were repeated imperial exhortations that educational establishments should be set up in every county and prefecture, and that village schools should be established by communal effort. Thus a rudimentary nation-wide educational system came into being. This did lay before all the romantic possibility of the humblest obtaining the highest offices in the land. Indeed this did sometimes happen, and – even more surprising – peasants became Sons of Heaven (though not, of course, through academic achievement).

There was indeed much fluctuation in family fortunes in late imperial China. A poor man might rise into the ranks of the bureaucracy by diligent pursuit of his studies, supported either by his family's willingness to make sacrifices in the knowledge of the great rewards his success would win or by the enlightened patronage of a more well-to-do neighbour. He might support himself while he studied by teaching at a village school, or by 'ploughing with the writing brush' as the pursuit of learning while still engaged on farming was called. Other men might easily fall from great heights to poverty and obscurity, either because they suffered from bandits, pirates, or natural disaster, or because they spent too freely on the art collections, libraries, or charitable activities appropriate to their high station in life. Others left their families in reduced circumstances through the mere fact of having too many sons in a society which held that all should inherit equally.

Hsü Kuo, a sixteenth-century prime minister, might be cited as one who rose from extreme poverty. Both his parents were literate, and his mother even had some understanding of Confucian texts, having attended local school lectures before her marriage; but they were very poor. His father earned his living as a small tradesman, which kept him away from home for years at a time, while his mother supported the family by doing embroidery. Being an intelligent and studious child, Hsü Kuo was educated by a cousin of his father, who could afford a family tutor. He obtained his first degree at the age of seventeen, and was then able to support the still impoverished family on the small income he earned as tutor in a local official's household. At thirty-five he passed his provincial examination at the fifth attempt, and three years later he obtained seventh place in the palace examination, which brought him appointment in the Hanlin Academy. Later he became tutor to the heir apparent, which brought him further rapid advancement, leading eventually to the premiership. But none of his descendants was distinguished.[14]

Another who won his way to prominence after early struggles was T'ao Mo, who eventually attained the position of Governor General of Shensi and Kansu in the late nineteenth century. His father died when he was five, so he went every morning to the market-place to sell silks woven by his mother. Afterwards he studied while his mother wove, and he passed his first degree at the age of twenty-one. Later he was captured by the Taiping rebels and forced to do coolie work. When he escaped and returned home his mother and wife had both died. Eventually he remarried, but until he obtained his provincial degree at the age of thirty-two he still had to combine his studies with selling silks in the market and teaching in the village school. A year later he became a Presented Scholar (*chin-shih*), and only after that did he have sufficient resources to bury his ancestors properly.[15] Many such men who achieved very high rank had to combine various kinds of menial work with their studies in order to survive; and their stories illustrate how the prestige of learning permeated the humbler classes of society.

II

The study of recruitment for the civil service tells much about the quality of Chinese society. The nature of the administration which enabled the civil service to control China under the aegis of the emperor is too complex a subject for detailed examination, but certain general features may be described. As far as the central administration was concerned, there was a natural progression away from government by officials whose names betray their origin in the imperial household, such as the Grand Coachman, the Grand Herald, and the Grand Ceremonialist, towards a system more specifically geared to the needs of the state.

The structure of the central administration changed from dynasty to dynasty, but a recurrent feature was the division of the executive tasks of government between six ministries, which remained the same from the T'ang period to the twentieth century. Their various concerns give a clear impression of Confucian conceptions of the tasks of government. Since the most important of these tasks was to find men of the right calibre to run the state, it is not surprising that the senior ministry should have been the Board of Civil Office, charged with all matters concerned with the staffing of the civil service. It was natural too that there should be a Board of Rites, with a general concern for religious and ceremonial matters and with the reception of foreign visitors. The collection of taxes and the administration of state resources was managed by the Board of Revenue, and that other important sphere of governmental activity, the administration of justice, came under the Board of

Punishments. The preservation of external order was the role of the Board of War, while the Board of Works had control of public buildings and state projects of various kinds, including irrigation and river-control schemes and the manufacture of equipment for the government.

The top level of administration which dealt with matters of high policy and supervised the work of the ministries varied from dynasty to dynasty, but in the Ming consisted simply of a Grand Secretariat of between three and six members who assisted the emperor in this work. There were also times when the emperor's private secretariat, engaged by him to draft letters and documents, was able to usurp some of the authority of the major offices of state; and the increasing autocracy of the Ch'ing monarchs was strengthened both by the establishment of a Grand Council, consisting entirely of men appointed by the emperor for indeterminate periods, and by the use of the secret palace memorial system to enable the emperor to have access to knowledge which was not available to the bureaucracy.

A quite separate and remarkable feature of the political system was the Censorate, which was the means used by the government to exercise surveillance over all its affairs. Two separate functions were involved in the Censors' activities: they had to remonstrate when necessary with the formulators of policy in the government, even the emperor himself, and they had to exercise surveillance over the lower echelons of the bureaucracy and impeach anyone guilty of inefficiency or malpractice. These two functions developed quite separately and were not amalgamated until the Yüan Dynasty. The surveillance function had earlier been discharged by men called *yü-shih*, a term which was in continuous use from the Shang Dynasty right through until 1912, a period of more than three thousand years. Earlier used to describe court chroniclers, in the Ch'in and Han Dynasties it signified men who exercised surveillance over bureaucrats. The remonstrance function was also already exercised in the Ch'in and Han Dynasties, by venerable persons considered to be suitable companions and mentors of emperors. Close surveillance of government personnel was a typically Legalist device, while remonstrance obviously had Confucian antecedents. To some extent it was expected of all officials that they should take part in impeachment of other officials or remonstrate with their superiors where necessary, but the Censorate provided an increasingly powerful machine to take the main burden of these activities. By the Ming period there were hundreds of officials in the Censorate, and each province had its own separate office.

The classical insistence on remonstrance had been very strong, with the sayings of Confucius and Mencius providing outstanding examples of how rulers should be spoken to. But when the centralized state developed, compromise was necessary since there was no other state for the unsuccessful remonstrator to escape to as there had been in pre-Ch'in times. The good Confucian would often have to sink his pride, console himself with the thought that loyalty was a good Confucian virtue, and reflect that to enable him to be filial and care for his parents it was necessary for him to keep his head on his shoulders. Nevertheless when the emperor committed what seemed to be a major outrage, many were found to remonstrate at risk of losing their lives or being flogged in open court. For example, it was considered a great scandal that the Chia-ching emperor, on succeeding his cousin in 1521, should have wished to sacrifice to his own parent as 'imperial father' although he had never held the throne. On one occasion during this controversy over two hundred officials wept and wailed their remonstrances at the palace gates, only to receive dismissals, floggings, imprisonments, and exile. The Ming period was notorious for the sufferings of Censors trying to do their duty at any cost.

The whole system of administration was monolithic in the sense that all agencies were created by the central government and all appointments to office were made by it. All local officials were agents of the central government, and local initiative could only operate in an informal way at the grass-roots level. Outside the capital city and the central government, China was for the most part administered through a system of provinces with smaller sub-units. In early times delegation of responsibility for control of regions had been carried out by means of a 'feudal' system of granting fiefs to members of the royal family or faithful allies of aristocratic blood. Following the growing bureaucratization of the late Chou period, the Ch'in Dynasty had introduced a structure of centrally organized provinces, but the Han initially had to fall back on a mixture of the two systems, when that dynasty's founder conferred fiefs on his sons and supporters. Vestiges of the Han practice remained in later dynasties, but in general the provincial system operated throughout imperial Chinese history. In the earlier periods the country was divided into a great number of small units, and it was not until the Yüan that the large provinces which we know today came into being. During the Ming and Ch'ing there was a four-tier system – provinces, of which there were eighteen in the Ch'ing period, prefectures, sub-prefectures, and counties or districts, of which there were over 1600 under the Ch'ing. Naturally, the lower the unit, the less scope there was for specialization in the bureaucracy, and at the lowest level of all, the district or county, there was normally only one official, the district magistrate, who was responsible for all aspects of government in his locality. An account of the part he played in the local community will balance the earlier description of the role of the Son of Heaven.

III

The district magistrate in the Ch'ing Dynasty administered an area about the size of an English county. His was one of the lowest official posts and the first appointment for many people entering the civil service, but he was responsible for being the 'father-mother official' to tens of thousands of people. To minimize the dangers of corruption, favouritism, and local patriotism at the expense of the state, he – together with all other officials working in the provinces – was not allowed to hold office either in his native province or in one which was within five hundred *li* (about 170 miles) of his home town. To try to prevent family concerns from overriding official duties he was also not allowed to occupy a post in the same province as his father, son, brother, grandfather, grandson, or father's brother, or certain maternal relatives. These rules conflicted with the good Confucian's moral obligation not to be far away from aged parents who needed his support: an official career often meant long separation from dearly loved family and native place, but such hardships were tolerated because of the prestige and privileges involved.

The district magistrate had general responsibility for administering the area under his jurisdiction, much as the emperor was at the apex of many different aspects of national life. His primary tasks were the maintenance of law and order, the administration of justice, and the collection of taxes; but he was also responsible for education, welfare, and defence against both internal uprising and foreign invasion, and he also had important religious and ceremonial duties. As the *Draft History of the Ch'ing Dynasty* puts it:

He settles legal cases, metes out punishment, encourages agriculture, extends charity to the poor, wipes out the wicked and the unlawful, promotes livelihood, and fosters education. All such matters as recommending scholars to the court, reading and elucidating the law and imperial edicts to the people, caring for the aged, and offering sacrifices to the gods are his concern.[16]

The official residence (or yamen) of the district magistrate generally occupied a central position in the chief city of the district. Within the yamen compound the court hall was at the front and the magistrate's private residence at the back. The yamen opened its doors before dawn, and the magistrate held court in the morning and afternoon, and occasionally in the evening. He sometimes also worked in his private office behind the courtroom. With the assistance of his secretaries, clerks, runners, and other underlings he dealt with the multifarious business of the yamen, generally reserving the afternoon session for litigation, which was the most time-consuming of his activities. On certain days the people could come to court and submit their complaints. When he left the yamen on official business, his sedan-chair was escorted by lictors clearing the way and by runners carrying placards (or lanterns, if it were after dark) indicating his official position. Twice a month he made offerings at the temples of Confucius and of the God of Walls and Moats (the city god), and on other occasions when prayers were especially needed, he was the proper bureaucratic channel through which the city god could be approached. He might also leave his office to welcome another official or escort him on his way, or to take part in a criminal investigation, or to preside over an execution at the execution ground outside the city.

The magistrate heard all cases within his area, both civil and criminal. There were no juries to give their verdict or advocates to present the cases for and against the accused. The magistrate conducted the hearing alone and alone made his decision. Prior to the hearing he would have investigated the case himself, and so he combined the roles of detective, police chief, prosecutor, judge, and jury. He only had the authority to pronounce sentences in minor cases where beating or the wearing of the cangue were the appropriate penalty. In other cases his recommended punishments were subject to the approval of his superiors. Final approval of sentences more severe than beating had to come from the Board of Punishments, and death sentences usually required ratification from the throne.

The magistrate generally had the advice of a private secretary versed in legal matters, but the latter was not allowed in court during the trial. When he held court, the magistrate put on his formal attire and sat on a raised dais at the top of the hall, behind a bench covered with red cloth. On this bench stood his official seal, his writing brushes and inkstone, his documents, and some bamboo spills in a cylindrical holder, which he threw on the floor to indicate the number of strokes when he wished the accused to be beaten. He was attended by a clerk and a number of runners who were there to guard the prisoners and to administer punishment and torture as required. To this end these minions were equipped with whips, ankle-screws, bamboo rods, and the like. The persons involved in the case, whether plaintiffs, defendants, or witnesses, had to kneel on the bare flagstones before the magistrate throughout the proceedings, flanked by the rows of runners facing inwards. Members of the public were generally allowed in to watch the trials, the purpose of which was to act as a deterrent and secure social order rather than to see justice done to individuals.

So although the law was supposed to perform an educative and corrective function, what the populace saw was suspects being tortured to extract confessions and those found guilty being subjected to floggings. Although the conscientious magistrate did his best to make sure that he had found the proper culprit before bringing him to trial, the method used to obtain the truth does not inspire confidence in its efficacy. Such practices do not seem to accord with the image of the 'father-mother official' whose job was to soothe and tranquillize the people, but on the other hand it may be remembered that fathers did treat their children extremely harshly in traditional China. Moreover, the cruel treatment meted out to the hapless victims of justice was not more sadistic than its European counterparts of that era, and China's judicial system was generally compared favourably to their own by European travellers, even those who had suffered from it.[17]

In harsh times whole clans could be exterminated for the crime of one prominent member, and death penalties could be inflicted by such brutal methods as cutting in half at the waist; but there is little reason to single out the Chinese as the supreme exponents of torture as some European writers have done, since the world in general has a poor record in this respect. Nevertheless the law and its manifestations were deeply repugnant to the Chinese people, who lacked the concept of Justice which has given prestige to the law in Europe.

Their great distrust of the law went back to the saying of Confucius that in litigations he was just like anyone else, but what was necessary was to cause there to be no litigations.[18] 'Litigation' came to have a pejorative sense, so differences were often settled within the clan or guild or local community to avoid submitting grievances to the processes of the state, which could be harsh and expensive. The authorities, too, wanted to minimize the amount of litigation, which took up much of the magistrate's time; and this was one reason put forward for the law's harshness. As the K'ang-hsi emperor put it,

Lawsuits would tend to increase to a frightful amount, if people were not afraid of the tribunals, and if they felt confident of always finding in them ready and perfect justice. . . . I desire therefore that those who have recourse to the tribunals should be treated without pity, and in such a manner that they shall be disgusted with the law, and tremble to appear before a magistrate.[19]

The law was not only too harsh, it was also too rigid and inflexible. It is reported in the *Tso Tradition* that as long ago as 536 BC, when one of the states into which China was divided at that time promulgated a law code, it was said that 'the early kings deliberated on all the circumstances of each crime to make their ruling on it, and did not make general laws, fearing lest this should give rise to a contentious spirit among the people'.[20] This belief in the fallibility of the law persisted. Ideally the problem of crime should be solved by the strengthening of the social and moral order, which leads to a better state of society in which wrongdoing would be minimal. Since the law was such a crude instrument, incapable of taking into account all the special circumstances, magistrates had to be wise enough to use it flexibly. Where possible the law did take into account the relative circumstances: a father might kill his son for disobedience without penalty, but even the unintentional killing of a father by his son was treated as a terrible crime. But it was impossible to codify the infinite variety of special circumstances, so moral criteria were generally regarded as more important in traditional Chinese society. The law was subordinate and ancillary to these, and people only had recourse to it if the moral imperatives failed. Moral questions were understood both by the intellectuals and by the mass of the population, but the legal aspects of a dispute might appeal only to the scholars and seem alien to the people.

The reputation of the law also suffered because magistrates were overworked, having far too large an area under their jurisdiction. They came under increasing pressure in the Ch'ing period because the bureaucracy was reduced in numbers in spite of the huge growth of the population, so that in the nineteenth century there were only about 40,000 official posts altogether. Magistrates also lacked specialist training in the law, and had to rely on private aides, who were not themselves members of the civil service, but were recruited and paid for by the magistrate entirely on his own authority.

These private secretaries lived within the yamen on terms of social equality with the magistrate. They were recruited largely from among holders of the Flowering Talent degree, but some were holders of the Recommended Man degree, some were former clerks who had acquired knowledge of administration, and some were former officials who had failed in their careers. They trained under the private tutorship of someone who already had such a secretarial post, and specialized generally in either law or taxation. Although good secretaries were much in demand and well treated by the magistrates, such an occupation was not thought worthwhile as a career in itself since it lacked the prestige of officialdom. A well-known private secretary of over thirty years' standing wrote a handbook on the subject in which he said: 'If a scholar, because he cannot get himself into administration, therefore assists others to administer, it is because he has no other option.'[21] The system of private secretaries developed during the Ch'ing because the declining status of the clerical workers and the growing responsibilities of the magistrates imposed the need for an intermediate stratum. In addition to their specialist work, the private secretaries drafted letters and documents for the magistrates and took off their shoulders the burden of supervising the clerks, runners, and other yamen underlings. In spite of their obvious value in the administration, they suffered somewhat from the stigma of being specialists in a society which admired the amateur ideal. The government did not introduce a scheme whereby the private secretaries could be recommended for official appointment, so there were no channels of promotion open to them and they remained a body quite separate from the official bureaucracy. Nevertheless this was a useful formula whereby officials could avail themselves of expert help, not merely in the specializations traditionally needed for local administration, but also in the new techniques which were becoming necessary in the nineteenth century in order to deal with the foreign barbarians. It was therefore as the private secretaries of officials that experts in Western subjects sometimes began to play a valuable part in the country's modernization.

Thus the magistrates obtained reasonably expert service from their private secretaries, but the personnel who occupied humbler positions in the magistrate's employment were of very poor quality, and this had been a recurring difficulty in Chinese history. The clerks posed a serious problem, for they were in a very strong position to make life difficult for their superiors. They had the advantage over them in that they were locally recruited and could use their influence in the interest of friends and relations. By contrast the magistrate himself might not even understand the local dialect, and so was very vulnerable to their abuses. They were only supposed to hold their posts for five years, but they either stayed on longer, often changing their names in order to bring about an appearance of legality, or retained their influence by getting relatives to occupy the positions they had vacated. Magistrates were heavily dependent on them because of their greater knowledge of the locality, their familiarity with the complex government regulations, and the heavy pressure of business which had to be got through. They were organized in six sections corresponding to the six government departments. Because they were employed in such tasks as drafting reports, preparing tax records, issuing warrants, and filing documents, they had many opportunities for manipulating business to their personal advantage, the temptation being strong because they received no remuneration apart from fees and the proceeds of the corruption they indulged in. If the gentlemen were the specialists in virtue, it was not surprising that the 'small men' who held such clerical posts behaved improperly. Had there been greater rewards for loyalty and better opportunities for moving up into the bureaucracy proper, the whole system might have worked better; but, as it was, the clerks and other minor employees in the yamen were automatically regarded by the people as corrupt and predatory, and this attitude is reflected in popular literature.

Apart from the clerks the other main group of official underlings was the runners. They were also recruited from among the local people, and so exploited their position in the same way as the clerks. Broadly speaking they were needed as a means of communication with the villages under the magistrate's jurisdiction, to enforce law and order, to collect taxes, to exact labour services, to serve summonses and make arrests, to administer punishment, and to look after the gaol and the official granary. Colloquially they were known as the claws and teeth of the magistrate. There were lictors (whose job was to clear the way for the magistrate in public and to torture and inflict corporal punishment in court), messengers, policemen, and guards, who protected the granary, treasury, and gaol, and escorted criminals. Other more specialized categories included coroners, doormen, sedan-chair bearers, parasol and fan bearers, gong beaters, pipers and drummers, lantern carriers, nightwatchmen, stove attendants, and grooms. Employment as a government runner was looked down on by the people, and some clans went so far as to expel members who embarked on such a career.

In the Ming Dynasty people had been liable to be conscripted into service as government runners. They had been allowed to buy themselves off, and the fees thus obtained had been used to hire men to do the work, so their pay was fixed at a very low level. They were thus largely dependent on fees and what they could squeeze out of people in the course of their duties. Runners sometimes imprisoned people in their own homes to extract money from them. The police were especially notorious and thought to be hand in glove with thieves. Before they would investigate a theft they would first demand from the victim money for travel and subsistence and for the services of informers, as well as a tip for themselves. To some extent the clerks and runners could be controlled by the magistrate's personal servants as well as by his private secretaries, but it is not surprising that people were very reluctant to get involved with the magistrate's yamen.

Such resources were hardly adequate for dealing with the maintenance of law and order, the administration of justice, the collection of taxes, and the other main tasks of government in the provinces of China during the Ch'ing period. But in addition the Chinese concept of government was much broader, including concern for the welfare, education, and morality of the community, so the formal political institutions were quite incapable of discharging these responsibilities unaided. Help fortunately came from the local gentry, who acted as informal leaders of the community. Local gentry in the Chinese context did not mean well-to-do landowners, but people who had graduated in the civil service examinations and were thus either potential or retired officials. A district magistrate on leave in his home district because he was mourning a parent would automatically be a member of the local gentry. The prestige and privileges of the gentry also attached itself to their family members; and the whole social group was given cohesion by the network of ties based on being fellow-examinees of the same examiner or having passed the examination in the same year. So these people formed a powerful and close-knit local group, sharing the same education and ideals as the district magistrate. They were the only people influential enough to represent the local community in discussions with the magistrate, and at the same time the only people with the authority and resources to back the local official and participate informally in the processes of government. Thus as leaders of their community they could settle disputes, advise the magistrate on such matters as public works and defence, command local defence forces, raise funds for charitable purposes, and contribute to the financing of public works, for which government funds were very limited. They were well able to afford their services to the local community. They were much less heavily taxed than the commoners, they had a privileged position in law since they could not be legally tried or given a sentence without the emperor's permission, and they were permitted to pay a fine instead of suffering corporal punishment, while an ordinary person who harmed an official was punished more severely than he would have been if the victim had been his equal. A member of the gentry showed his distinction from the common people by wearing official robes and by displaying before his house a flagpole and a tablet bearing the name of his degree. If members of the gentry chose to exploit their situation, the local officials were in a weak position to keep them under control or punish them, and the system could not work well unless the local gentry did have some sense of responsibility derived from their shared training in Confucian attitudes.

In an attempt to control the population at the grass-roots level and detect law-breakers, magistrates were required to organize households in groups of ten, a hundred, and a thousand, in what was known as the *pao-chia* system, heads being appointed for each unit. Under this system every household had a door placard listing the name, age, and occupation of the family head and the names of other residents, including servants. The *pao-chia* heads had to record the name of anybody who moved, and they were required to report fortnightly whether there had been any unlawful activities in the various families, on pain of being held responsible if they failed to do so. They were also required to organize anti-bandit patrols. There is much evidence that the system did not work very well. It carried the taint of Legalism and was alien to Confucian ideals, so although many decrees were issued by emperors and provincial officials to try to get the system to work, to enforce it would have required much greater manpower than the state was willing to employ.

But in spite of the help the magistrate received from his private secretaries and the support of the local gentry and the attempt to get the people to police themselves through the *pao-chia* system, the main responsibility for many other matters apart from the administration of the law rested on his own shoulders and made demands also on his financial resources. It was his duty to maintain the government buildings and city walls, the main roads and bridges, and to repair dams and keep rivers dredged so that the local irrigation system worked well. In general there was no government money available for these purposes, so the magistrate had to contribute from his own resources, induce the gentry and wealthy people to do so, and recruit local people to provide the labour. He also administered the 'ever-normal granary', a very ancient method of trying to defeat the natural tendency of grain prices to soar in the spring by having state grain available for sale at less than the market price or even on interest-free loan when times were very hard. When flood or drought reduced the people to famine, he had to investigate and report the calamity to higher authority, and administer the tax reduction and famine relief, which was complicated because he had to base it on the actual sufferings of each individual family. Since government relief was often inadequate, it was again necessary for the magistrate to supplement this by raising funds from private individuals. Again, although the government regulations required that schools be organized, no funds were supplied, so their establishment and maintenance was left entirely to the magistrate, who had to rely on gentry contributions for this purpose. The magistrate was also responsible for indoctrinating the masses by convening them to fortnightly lectures on the Sacred Edicts, which were imperial homilies on the Confucian virtues, and it was his general duty to try to improve the moral standards of the people in his care. More specifically he was supposed to give banquets in honour of the aged and worthy people of the community, and to ensure that due honour was given to filial sons and chaste widows. But only the most conscientious of magistrates were able to make an effort to fulfil all these functions.

Finally, a branch of his duties which had to be meticulously observed was the religious role. In the eyes of the people he was not only the local representative of the imperial government but also chief priest of the region. In the popular imagination in late imperial China, the gods had become organized into a kind of bureaucracy which was an extension of the earthly bureaucracy, and there was an especially close link between the county magistrate and the God of Walls and Moats (or city god) of the city in which the magistrate had his official residence. The city god was the magistrate's opposite number in the pantheon, so on arrival to take up office a magistrate would make sacrifice to the god and swear an oath invoking his holy wrath if he were corrupt or unjust in his administration. He also burnt incense at his temple once a fortnight and visited it on occasions of crisis and calamity. The magistrate also made periodic visits to the temples of Confucius, of the Gods of War and Literature, and to a great many other local shrines. In times of drought he was expected by the people to pray to the gods for rain.

Not only would he go to the local temples to pray, but the people would bring images of the gods to his yamen for him to pray to them. Although Confucianism's basic concern with matters of this world rather than the next has often led both Europeans and modern Chinese eager to rescue their culture from the charge of superstition to look upon the Confucian scholar as an agnostic philosopher, in fact the district magistrate spent much of his time engaged in religious ceremonies. This closeness to the supernatural powers together with the people's consciousness that he was also in his official role the representative of the Son of Heaven gave him a kind of superhuman authority which was very necessary if he were to fulfil even a part of the heavy responsibilities which befell him.

Not only was his work demanding, but also his conditions of service had many drawbacks. In the first place appointment to a post did not follow automatically as soon as he obtained the Presented Scholar degree. There would often be many years of waiting, especially since the Manchus retained many important metropolitan posts in their own hands. Once launched on his career, he had to face annual and triennial assessments of his conduct of office. The triennial examination was said to have had its origin in the time of the ancient sages, for the *Book of History* describes Shun's method of disciplining officials by saying, 'Every three years there was an examination of merits, and after three examinations the undeserving were demoted or dismissed and the deserving promoted'.[22] The practice can also be traced back in the historical sources to the Ch'in and Han Dynasties. Although the T'ang had tried to lay stress on moral qualities, in general an assessment was made of administrative achievement. In the Yüan period, for example, growth of population, increases in area of cultivated land, reductions in legal cases, absence of bandits and thieves, and fair administration of taxation and labour services were regarded as indices of administrative efficiency, and all were clearly more quantifiable matters than the possession of the requisite Confucian virtues. In the Ch'ing Dynasty the ability to get the taxes in was the most important qualification for high merit rating. Those who emerged creditably from the assessment were qualified to have an imperial audience and could expect early promotion. Those who fared less well could be degraded, dismissed, and punished. Failure to reach an adequate standard of performance in their various functions carried severe penalties which hampered initiatives and caused local officials to play safe and concern themselves mainly with those tasks which would bring promotion and reward. There were relatively few opportunities of promotion and, after his three- or five-year appointment, the magistrate might be merely transferred to a similar post elsewhere or he might even find himself returning to the same post for further stints.

In the Han period, in particular, officials had been paid handsome salaries for the work they did and at other times they received lands in respect of the offices they held, but at the beginning of the Ch'ing their remuneration was quite inadequate. The Yung-cheng emperor granted a substantial supplementation significantly entitled 'money to nourish honesty', but even then the magistrate's salary was not nearly enough to support his family, pay his private secretaries and servants, and make his expected contribution to financing all the various local activities. The money was made up by exacting fees from the people in connection with his official business, such as tax collecting, land surveying, census taking, and keeping records of the population; so that side by side with the official taxation there were further informal exactions from the populace towards the financing of the civil service, which the government could not have done away with without imposing a much heavier official tax burden on the people. When the magistrate was away from his post to mourn for one of his parents, he was not paid a salary. It was also unusual for permanently retired officials to receive a pension, although they might get a full salary during retirement if their age, rank, and achievement merited it.

In spite of the prestige which the state gave to officialdom, the imperial audiences, the presents of imperial calligraphy, and all the other honours distributed to try to keep up the officials' morale, doubtless many welcomed the days of their retirement as Po Chü-i had done:

Lined coat, warm cap and easy felt slippers,
In the little tower, at the low window, sitting over the sunken brazier.
Body at rest, heart at peace; no need to rise early.
I wonder if the courtiers at the Western Capital know of these things or
   not?[23]

But if they had no nobler reason for seeking a civil service career, at least it brought benefit to their family and clan, who all shared the kudos. As the popular saying went: 'If a man rises to officialdom, then all his dogs and chickens will be promoted.'

CHAPTER 3

THE CAPITAL CITY

I

The city in which the district magistrate was stationed was ideally square and surrounded by walls running due north-south and east-west, following the canonical pattern laid down for capital cities. The ideal plan was described in a text which was incorporated in the *Chou Ritual*: 'The artisans marked out the capital as a square with sides of nine *li*, each side having three gateways. Within the capital there were nine meridional and nine latitudinal avenues, each of the former being nine chariot-tracks in width.'[1] The *Chou Ritual* also describes the method of finding the north-south axis by bisecting the angle between the rising and setting sun. Changan and Peking were the capitals which approximated most closely to the classical ideal.

The squareness of capital cities had nothing to do with practical considerations, but arose entirely from the religious beliefs of the ancient Chinese. As the *Book of Songs* describes it, 'The Shang capital was laid out in orderly fashion, the pivot of the four quarters.'[2] Conscious of the close interaction between the celestial and terrestrial order as the ancients were, they tried to pattern the heart of their political system on the cosmic order by laying their capital city out *in space* to conform with the cardinal directions indicated by the heavenly bodies, just as *in time* they accompanied with appropriate rituals and festivals the important cosmic events marking the passage of the seasons. At the same time an important feature of the capital was the processional way which bisected the city on the north-south axis, thus forming the terrestrial counterpart of the meridian. In more secular times the square city orientated according to the cardinal directions constituted a powerful symbol of the idea that the capital was the centre of the inhabited world, presiding over the peoples on all four sides.

55

In antiquity this delimited space of the capital city was believed to have a sacred quality by contrast with the territory around it. The idea arose from early man's powerful need to maintain contact with the supernatural and his feeling that, since this cannot be done everywhere, there should be certain focal points where prayer and ritual are concentrated on preserving this liaison. In Chinese civilization, as we have seen, it was the role of the emperor to serve as supreme link with the supernatural. He was at the axis of the universe, and the capital was where his role could be made manifest. In the *Book of History* the Duke of Chou is reported to have said at the founding of Loyang: 'May the king come and assume responsibility for the work of God on High and himself serve in that capacity at the centre of the land. I say that, having constructed this great city and ruling from here, he shall be a counterpart to August Heaven. He shall scrupulously sacrifice to the upper and lower spirits, and from there govern as the central pivot.'[3] (The concept of the Son of Heaven being the earthly counterpart of Heaven is a common one in ancient texts.) In the *Chou Ritual* it is explained how the centre of the earth is calculated, and there it is described as the place where 'earth and sky meet, where the four seasons merge, where wind and rain are gathered in, and where Yin and Yang are in harmony'.[4] Mencius also speaks of the gentleman delighting in 'standing at the centre of all-under-Heaven and stabilizing the people within the seas on all four sides'.[5]

The capital was not only conceived as the place where man tried to keep open a channel of communication with the supernatural and demonstrate by appropriate rituals his participation in cosmic events. It was also thought of as the place where supernatural power was channelled down to earth and whence it radiated to the four quarters. Hence the ancient texts commonly referred to the supernatural power or virtue (*te*) of the Son of Heaven radiating from him so as to protect all within the seas on all four sides. This was the reason why the sage emperor Shun was said to have inaugurated his reign by opening gates in his capital city facing towards each of the cardinal points. The monumental proportions of Chinese city gates reflect this symbolical significance.

The square walled city was, however, a Chou Dynasty development, and in the Shang and earlier, the centres of human habitation were very different. Before cities developed at all in China, settlements consisted of small compact self-contained villages, probably consisting of kinship units. Society seems to have been egalitarian, with a marked absence of political and economic exploitation. In the main urban centres of Shang China, however – the famous Anyang, which was the focal point of archaeological activity in pre-Communist times, and the more recently excavated earlier capital at Chengchow – the lay-out is different again. At these two sites there are central areas devoted to administration and ceremonial, surrounded by dependent villages and hamlets. The cities themselves were inhabited merely by the ruling families, the priests, a few craftsmen, and perhaps some soldiers; while not only the peasants but also most of the artisans who catered for the needs of the administrative and ceremonial centre were located in the surrounding countryside. Also out in the countryside was the imposing royal cemetery; and the abundance of treasures buried with the dead, not to speak of the human sacrifices associated with these burials, combine with the large storage-pits found at the ceremonial centre to show that these capitals exercised a very firm control over the labour and resources of the surrounding territory.

In this urban development and accumulation of power it was clearly religion that played the major part rather than technological or commercial progress, or military or political upheavals. The evidence for this is the key role played by the ceremonial centre, as in the case of many other early civilizations, and the close concern of the earliest surviving written records, with religious matters. These were the 'oracle bones', the inscriptions on the scapulae of oxen or carapaces of turtles used to record the results of divination. It is not the citadel or the market-place that dominates these ancient settlements, but the ceremonial complex and the priesthood. The reason for this is not far to seek: it is the inevitable consequence of a trend towards specialization. Once men developed special skills, so that some engaged in crafts to supply the needs of others, it would not be long before those deemed to be most successful in dealing with the supernatural would achieve supremacy; and those who submitted to the authority of the deity would soon find themselves subject to the economic power of the ritual experts who needed to accumulate resources for sacrifice to that deity. At the same time political power would be needed to protect these all-important resources and the shrine at which they were offered. In this way the ordinary people would have lost all political and economic power. The gods would be transformed into formidable figures who needed to be approached through specialists in worship and sacrifice. The priesthood would then develop a philosophy of society which supported the retention of the status quo, a philosophy with hierarchical values and a message about the ceremonial centre and its occupant the Son of Heaven dominating and tranquillizing all-under-Heaven.

When we move on to the Chou Dynasty we find that the square or rectangular walled city becomes the norm. That the wall is an essential feature is indicated by the fact that the word *ch'eng* was used to mean both wall and city. Apart from the wall other essential features of the city were an altar to the god of the soil and a temple to the ruler's ancestors. If a city were conquered, the victors had to keep up the sacrifices if they were not to suffer harm from vengeful spirits, so the city was still important as a focus of religious activity and a receptacle of supernatural power for the benefit of its own locality. These walled cities may have originated from the need of the Chou conquerors settling in the hostile territory of the Shang people to have fortresses within which to withdraw and protect their grain and other resources during the winter season. As the Chou Dynasty progressed, industry and trade developed, but still the majority of the inhabitants of the city went outside to work in the fields every day, and this situation continued in the Han and later periods. Noblemen were sometimes allowed to wall places in return for services rendered to their rulers, but sometimes the walls were built first and the city afterwards, and not all the space within city walls was filled. On the other hand, in places where the population grew rapidly, unplanned settlements sprang up outside the walls, and sometimes an outer city wall was built to enclose these new settlements. Although the tightly packed city with which we are familiar was slow to come to China, already in antiquity fire was a severe hazard, and there is a record of fire-fighting precautions being introduced in the capital of the state of Sung in 564 BC, including the provision of a fire watch, the distribution of baskets, barrows, well ropes, buckets, and water jars, with close attention being paid to the palace area and the repositories in which the state archives were kept.[6]

II

Gradually the primarily religious function of the city yielded precedence to its secular role, and the main concern of the capital became the ordering of society in this world rather than intercession with the supernatural. The Ch'in capital at Changan seems to have been laid out to reflect the disposition of the stars in the Plough or Big Dipper constellation; but later in imperial Chinese history the capital is dominated by the palace, built not only to serve as an appropriate setting for the Son of Heaven who enjoyed a special relationship with the supernatural, but also to provide on a lavish scale for the physical comforts of the sole master of the world. Changan continued to serve as capital during the Former Han Dynasty and the brief Hsin Dynasty which intruded before the Later Han established itself at Loyang in AD 25; and in the period of division which followed several minor dynasties had their capitals in this area. The Sui rulers, who reunified China at the end of the sixth century, also chose this region for the site of their metropolis, but they had too little time to fulfil their plans, and it was the T'ang Dynasty which built a great and glorious city on the basic design laid down by the Sui.

Pan Ku, author of the *History of the Former Han Dynasty*, had long before written of the advantages of the area as a site for the capital:

> In abundance of flowering plants and fruits
> It is the most fertile of the Nine Provinces.
>
> In natural barriers for protection and defence
> It is the most impregnable refuge in heaven and earth.[7]

Apart from the fortress-like nature of the terrain, which had enabled the Chou safely to launch its successful conquest of the Shang and given Ch'in a strong base from which to conquer its rivals and unite China in 221 BC, Changan was also of increasing importance because of its position at the end of the great 'silk route' across Central Asia. So in the T'ang period it became a thriving cosmopolitan city with a large foreign community of merchants. Its population reached more than a million and it was by far the greatest city in the world at that time.

But despite its cosmopolitan nature and mercantile importance and the many foreign influences which entered along the trade routes, its lay-out followed the classic patterns necessary to make it a proper match for the ordered universe. It was almost square in shape, being about six miles broad, and about five miles from north to south. The area enclosed by the walls was laid out as a rectangular grid of streets, described by the poet Po Chü-i as like a great chessboard. These streets were wide tree-lined avenues, flanked by drainage ditches, and the blocks divided off by these avenues constituted separate wards, each surrounded by its own walls, the gates of which were locked at night. According to the classical prescription, each of the city walls should have three gates; and this requirement was observed at Changan, except on the north side, where there was an important departure from the canonical rules in that the imperial palace was situated here instead of occupying the dominant central position in the city. With its garden to the north, outside the city wall, the palace may be seen as an infinitely grand version of the humble Chinese farmhouse fronted by a courtyard and with a plot of garden behind. Immediately south of the imperial palace was the administrative city containing all the government departments, while symmetrically placed in the centres of the eastern and western halves of the city were two great market-places. In 661 the palace city was abandoned as the regular abode of the Son of Heaven in favour of the Great Luminous Palace which had been built in the imperial hunting-park on the north-east edge of the city, because the Emperor T'ai-tsung thought it would be a healthier place for his father, the retired emperor, to pass his old age in. This residence was built on an eminence from which the chessboard lay-out of the city could be seen below, and its elegant painted wooden buildings, rich flower gardens, and weeping willows made it the kind of fairy-tale palace which can still be seen in paintings although the reality has long ceased to exist.

The separate walled quarters within the city were a useful means of keeping the populace under control: they served as units for census purposes and also for the recruitment of the people for military and labour service. Merchants were also kept under control: they were restricted as far as possible to the two great enclosed markets, where all kinds of exotic wares could be bought, and story-tellers, acrobats, and actors entertained the crowds. Another feature which gave colour and variety to Changan and relieved the monotony of the skyline were the temples and pagodas of the Buddhist faith, which on festive occasions provided mass entertainment for the populace, and in general served as centres of philanthropic activities, providing cheap lodgings, public baths, hospitals, dispensaries, and other facilities, which were not at this time provided by the state. Some of these Buddhist establishments rivalled in magnificence the imperial palaces themselves, and their beautiful gardens and rich art treasures were a precious amenity enjoyed by the populace.

Another favourite resort was the Serpentine in the south-eastern corner of the metropolis, where a lake-garden in surroundings of great natural beauty had been embellished with lotus-ponds, gay pavilions, and beautiful plants to make a favourite rendezvous, much loved by poets such as Po Chü-i, who lived nearby and used to go there often.

Many private houses also had beautiful gardens celebrated by the poets; but it was the Serpentine which men regarded as an earthly paradise, especially when decorated for a great festival. Multicoloured silk tents would line the shores of the lake, and there the emperor would entertain his court, and the palace orchestras would play, while some sat in the tents and others in painted boats upon the lake. Early in the year there were gatherings to view the spring flowers, and the poet Tu Fu describes such an occasion at the Spring Festival only two years before the An Lu-shan rebellion temporarily swept all this luxury away. He describes the beauty of the court ladies; the palace eunuchs galloping up with delicacies from the imperial kitchens, including roasted camel hump, a special dish of the time; and the sound of flute and drum at the arrival of the chief minister, who wields a power 'so great you could warm your hands against it'.[8] Four years later the same poet walks sadly in the deserted park where all the waterside pavilions are now locked up, remembering the gay scenes of yesteryear; and there are none for whom the willows and rushes put forth their fresh greenery.

This was not the end of Changan, for it was restored to glory after the rebellion was crushed. But the great Chinese cities did not have the solid lasting qualities of our stone-built antiquities. They were made of more ephemeral materials – wood and tiles, and mudbrick walls. Other great cities had come and gone where the T'ang capital stood, and indeed the ruins of the Han capital were within the walls of the imperial park as a sign of the transience of mortal power. The Chinese sought their memorials in the good reputation that lived after them in the dynastic histories and in the memories of their descendants rather than in more tangible form. In the ninth century many disasters, both natural and man-made, struck Changan, notably the Buddhist persecution of 845 and the occupation by the rebel Huang Ch'ao in 881. When the dynasty finally collapsed, what remained of the palace buildings, public offices, and private dwellings was made into rafts and floated down to Loyang; and gradually the peasants returned to take over the land. Even before this the desolate city had been described in *The Lament of the Lady of Ch'in*, by Wei Chuang, the last of the great T'ang poets:

> Desolate city of Changan, what do you now contain?
> Ruined bazaars, deserted streets where tender wheat-ears grow.
> Collecting fuel, they cut down every flower in Almond Park;
> For barricades they rooted out the willows of the Grand Canal.
> Gay-painted coaches, patterned wheels, have scattered long ago;
> Of splendid mansions, grand vermilion gates, not half remain![9]

On this site there later grew a much smaller city, which is now known as Sian.

In the late T'ang the old rigid hierarchical and aristocratic society had broken down, the system of segregated wards had declined, and shopkeepers spread themselves much more freely about the city. The great urban centres of the Sung and Yüan periods grew up in a more unplanned manner, and as the influence of trade became much greater, the populace spread outside the city walls in a more random fashion. The Northern Sung capital of Kaifeng had grown important during the turbulent Five Dynasties period because of its strategic position on the network of waterway communications. Successive enlargements made it into a city comparable in size with Changan, and the orthodox attention was paid to lay-out, especially within the palace, which enabled the Sung founder to declare to his aides: 'My heart is as straightforward as all this, and as little twisted. Be ye likewise.'[10] But paintings reveal Kaifeng as a bustling city with a thriving commercial life spilling into the streets, which are thronged with people of all classes. And when the Chinese were driven south and the north of their country was occupied first by the Jürched people's Chin Dynasty and then by the Mongols, the Southern Sung capital at Hangchow can be seen from the descriptions of Marco Polo and of contemporary Chinese writers to have been completely different from Changan as it was at the beginning of the T'ang Dynasty.

III

In contrast with the dry plains of the north this was a land of lakes and canals and rice paddies, which in the early T'ang had been on the remote fringes of the area of Chinese culture but had now developed into a centre of flourishing maritime and river-borne trade. In the much warmer climate there was a more outdoor style of life, and houses opened onto the streets instead of being shut off behind walls as they had been in Changan.

Unlike Changan, Hangchow became the capital in a casual, unplanned, and reluctant manner. When Kaifeng fell to the Jürched in 1126 and the emperor was captured, a royal prince proclaimed himself emperor in Nanking and later established his headquarters at Hangchow, which was protected from the enemy by an area of lakes and muddy rice fields which was difficult for cavalry to traverse. But this comparatively small, though scenically attractive, provincial city was thought of as a mere makeshift; and, while dreams of a reconquest of the north were still cherished, it was simply called the 'temporary residence' (which is the meaning of Quinsai, the name given to the city in Marco Polo's account).

The narrow site between the beautiful West Lake and the river Che did not measure up to canonical requirements, for the walled city was about four miles long and half a mile wide, and the walls, which were about thirty feet high, followed a very irregular course. Nevertheless, a thirteenth-century map pretends that it has the conventional rectangular shape with the walls properly aligned on the cardinal directions. A broad thoroughfare, which became the Imperial Way, ran from north to south through the centre of the city. The imperial palace was in the south and the wealthy people lived in the hills beyond, while much of the old walled city became extremely crowded, as the population rose from 200,000 to over a million, a figure which had been absorbed much more easily in the spacious city of Changan. The built-up area spread outside the walls, and within them were erected many multistorey buildings, which had previously been an uncommon feature of Chinese cities. This density of development meant that in the narrow alleyways in the poorer parts of the city there was a seething mass of people jostling each other, and in the maze of wooden tenements fire was a serious danger which could lead to catastrophic destruction of property despite the activities of a large fire-fighting service.

The needs of this densely populated built-up area were mainly supplied by boats on the many canals which traversed it. On land goods were transported by porters or on pack-animals. Carts were used only on the Imperial Way, and then only for transport of passengers. The wealthier people also travelled about on horseback or in chairs. The variety of goods available was amazing. Marco Polo described Hangchow as 'without doubt the finest and most splendid city in the world'.[11] Luxuries came from all over China, South-east Asia, India, and the Middle East, and there was a great variety of specialist shops and trades. There was also a multitude of specialist restaurants, taverns, and teahouses, and in the market-places people could enjoy the story-tellers, jugglers, acrobats, puppet shows, and other entertainments. All this was very different from Confucian solemnity. Indeed there were even humourists 'who gave absurd commentaries on the solemn Classics and demonstrated, by means of erudite word play, that the Buddha, Lao Tzu, and Confucius were women'.[12]

In the southern suburbs of the city there were beautiful parks and gardens, and one could walk along the shores of the West Lake or make an excursion upon it to admire the scenery. The beauty of the lake was very carefully preserved, for every new building had to blend harmoniously with the surroundings. The waters were thronged with boats of all kinds, some, as Marco Polo recounted,

> . . . kept continually furnished with fine seats and tables and all the other requisites for a party. They are roofed over with decks on which stand men with poles which they thrust into the bottom of the lake (for it is not more than two paces in depth) and thus propel the barges where they are bidden. The deck is painted inside with various colours and designs and so is the whole barge, and all round it are windows that can be shut or opened so that the banqueters ranged along the sides can look this way and that and feast their eyes on the diversity and beauty of the scenes through which they are passing. And indeed a voyage on this lake offers more refreshment and delectation than any other experience on earth. On one side it skirts the city, so that the barge commands a distant view of all its grandeur and loveliness, its temples, palaces, monasteries, and gardens with their towering trees, running down to the water's edge.[13]

IV

When Polo was there, Hangchow and the whole of the Southern Sung realm had already been conquered by the Mongols, who built a great new capital at Peking, nearer to their homelands. Peking had begun its career as a dynastic seat by being the southern capital of the Liao Dynasty, the barbarian regime which had ruled part of the far north of China during the tenth and eleventh centuries. Later, after the fall of the north to the Jürched and the retreat of the Chinese to establish their capital at Hangchow, Peking became capital of the Chin Dynasty set up by the invaders and filled this role from 1153 to 1215. Then, after the Mongols had established themselves, it continued as the chief city of China for the remainder of the imperial period, except for several decades in the early Ming when Nanking was made capital.

Although the Mongols had built a new city at Peking, this was replaced by the Yung-lo emperor (who was the third Ming emperor but the first to reign from Peking) with the city which has now developed into the capital of the People's Republic of China. The city he built stood like a flat box on the flat North China Plain. Unlike many of the other great capitals of the world, it was not sited on an important river so as to serve as a key communications centre. The area also seems to be inconvenient because it is remote from China's main economic strength in the Yangtze Valley; but the capital needed to be in the north, both under the Yüan and Ch'ing, so that it was conveniently near to the homelands of the ruling Mongol and Manchu peoples, and under the Ming because the main threat to security came from the Mongols on the northern frontier. Peking also happened to be the principality of the Yung-lo emperor before he usurped the throne, and it could also claim great antiquity since the ancient capital of the feudal state of Yen during the Chou period two thousand years earlier had been on the same site.

Yung-lo's city was almost square and was surrounded by walls forty feet high and more than fourteen miles long, which have been recently demolished, except for forlorn gate towers and an isolated stretch on which the observatory equipped by the Jesuit Verbiert still stands. To the south of the city a large suburb developed, and this was walled round and incorporated into the city in the sixteenth century. Early in the Ch'ing Dynasty the Manchus displaced the Chinese population from the old city and made them reside only in the southern suburb, so that the two separate areas came to be known by Europeans as the Tartar and Chinese Cities.

This Outer or Chinese City contains the Altar of Heaven with its associated temples and also the Temple of Agriculture, but no other buildings of significance to the government and, since it grew up in an unplanned way, its lay-out does not observe canonical rules. However, the planned city of Yung-lo does approximately conform with classical principles. Ideally the seat of power should be at the centre. This requirement had been ignored at Changan, where the palace had been built against the northern wall. In Peking it occupied a position rather south of centre, and it is only the later addition of the Outer City which places the palace in a satisfying central position. The thoroughfares mainly run due north-south and east-west, but they are not spaced out with the chessboard regularity of the Changan street plan. Instead, the overall pattern is of rectangles of varying shapes and sizes, with the centre occupied by the Forbidden City, the heart of the world and the residence of the Son of Heaven, which forms a rectangle surrounded by high vermilion walls and a moat about two miles long. This lay within the Imperial City, which was also walled until the present century. The latter area was of more irregular shape since it had to enclose a string of artificial lakes to the west, where the need for cosmic symmetry gives way totally to the delights of garden scenery; but within the Forbidden City itself all is balance and harmony.

At the very heart of the Forbidden City, and on its north-south axis (which is also the north-south axis of Peking itself) is an imposing group of three buildings, the principle audience halls of the palace. The southernmost, and so the one first reached as one approaches from the main entrance, is the Hall of Supreme Harmony, where the emperor held his grand audiences (and where, for example, the results of the palace examination were announced and degrees conferred by the emperor). The next is the much smaller and square-shaped Hall of Middle Harmony, which was mainly used as a waiting place, and finally one comes to the Hall of Protecting Harmony, which was used for state banquets and for the palace examination, the final test of scholarship for which the emperor himself was officially responsible. This group of three buildings embodies the ancient Chou Dynasty principle that the Son of Heaven must rule from 'three courts'. It was also a very ancient practice in China to raise important buildings on a platform, as can be seen from archaeological remains of the Shang period; and in keeping with this practice the great halls are raised high above ground level on a three-tiered terrace, each tier being surrounded by balustrades of white marble. The whole terrace seen from above is of a squared-off dumb-bell shape to parallel the outlines of the buildings, the waist of the dumb-bell accommodating the square Hall of Middle Harmony, which is much smaller than the other two huge rectangular halls.

The architecture itself has none of the exciting and fairy-like quality of the T'ang palaces, for the halls are simple oblong buildings consisting of rows of huge wooden columns supporting tent-shaped roofs, such walls as exist being mere infilling between the columns. The mass and solidity of form is, however, relieved by the grace of the curving roofs and the delicacy of the white balustraded terraces on which the buildings stand. Their colour is also very important. To us one of the greatest attractions of architecture is when mellowed stone blends with the natural browns, greens, and greys of the environment, so that the build-ing seems to have grown rather than been built; but from ancient times the Chinese had always felt that colour and ornament were primary ingredients of what was meant by civilization. Of the five colours which were equated in antiquity with the five elements all except black are to be found on the walls and palaces of the Forbidden City. The walls and pillars are vermilion red, the marbled terraces are white, the roofs of glazed tiles are yellow, and blue-green is the predominant colour of the painted brackets under the eaves. Just as the colourful silk robes of the court are in glorious contrast with the blue cotton of the ordinary people, so the vermilion walls and bright yellow roofs of the Forbidden City glow in comparison with the grey walls and roofs of the houses huddled below them.

Unlike the Europeans, who built their great houses and castles for lasting strength, the Chinese used more ephemeral materials. These palaces are predominantly made of wood, and frequent fires have made replacements necessary, always rendered in the same style as the original, for imperial Chinese architecture was extremely conservative in its last centuries. Nor do the great audience halls dominate the scene as a European palace or castle often does. They fit into a subtle and harmonious pattern of courtyards, which become much smaller and more intimate at the rear, where the domestic quarters are situated, but are grander to the front, where the great audience courtyard which lies below the Hall of Supreme Harmony is some two hundred yards across. Nor, despite the concentration of the major buildings on the north–south axis, is it possible to enjoy the splendid vistas great European architecture often affords. The cellular arrangement means that one cannot take in the whole complex, except from an aeroplane, for Coal Hill to the north is at the wrong end and not quite high enough. The approach is through a series of gates, each giving entry to a new space more awe-inspiring than the last. In days gone by the foreign tributary arriving from the south, already awed by the distant views of massive walls, would enter via the gate in the centre of the southern wall of the Outer City and then, after traversing an area itself large enough for one great city, would reach the Front Gate, which leads to what is now the vast Square of Heavenly Peace and beyond it to the Gate of Heavenly Peace, which is the ceremonial centre of the present regime, where the country's leaders take the salute of parading masses. Beyond this huge gateway to the old imperial city he would come to the most massive gate of all, the Meridian Gate, which gives entry to the Forbidden City itself, before the Gate of Supreme Harmony finally gives access to the great audience courtyard in front of the Hall of Supreme Harmony.

It was in this great palace that the Son of Heaven presided over all-under-Heaven, filling the role of sage, high priest, judge, and patron of arts and letters, as well as head of government and military leader. Now the people throng in their thousands to wander through the forbidden halls and courtyards; and across on the southern side of the Square of

Heavenly Peace stands the Memorial Hall to their great leader Chairman Mao who wrought more dramatic changes in the lives of his fellow-countrymen than any of the innumerable occupants of the dragon throne.

PART TWO
THE PHILOSOPHICAL EXPERIENCE

CHAPTER 4

CONFUCIANISM AND THE ANCIENT
CHINESE WORLD-VIEW

I

The first part of this book showed how the political practices of the
Chinese in imperial times rested on the authority of remote precedent
and ancient literature, and particularly on the Confucian philosophy;
and it is now time to look more deeply into the intellectual tradition
which underlay this political experience. The close relationship between
the philosophical and political experience of the Chinese follows from
the fact that Chinese philosophy is primarily concerned with the problems of man in society rather than with such matters as logic and
epistemology.

From the outset we must be careful not to be diverted by our own
intellectual tradition into searching Chinese philosophy for truths comparable with those we seek in Western philosophy, for our concern is to
show how the Chinese intellectual tradition developed out of certain
historical circumstances and how it helped to mould the minds of men
in later generations. Nor should we get involved in the business of trying
to discover the real Confucius. Much effort has gone into trying to remove the layers of myth from that intriguing personage, but the lack of
historical evidence makes the task impossible. The earliest extant biography of the sage – in Ssu-ma Ch'ien's *Historical Records* – did not appear
until four hundred years after his death. The *Analects* is considered the
most authentic version of his teachings, but there can be no certainty
that he uttered any of the sayings ascribed to him; and they are so de-
void of context that it is often not easy to follow their meaning. In the
Mencius he is already revered as a sage, in the *Book of Filial Piety* he lauds
filial piety as the supreme virtue, in the ritual texts he is first and fore-
most a ritualist, in the Taoist texts he is depicted either as a fool or a
good Taoist, and in the *Analects* itself he suffers an apparent personality

change since the book includes some material which is much later than the more authentic chapters. Thus the references to him in ancient texts supply a rich assortment of personalities from which to choose according to taste.

Our ignorance of Confucius does not matter for the purposes of this book, for which the myth is much more important than the truth, since it has been much more influential. We may not know whether Confucius ever held office, but what we do know for certain is that we have a corpus of literature dating from antiquity in which Confucius is revered as a sage; and that this literature, however obscure its origin, forms a body of tradition which derives from the ancient Chinese milieu and therefore shares certain common attitudes to the world. We know also that this corpus of literature was studied by the great majority of literate people throughout imperial Chinese history; and that, for the last six centuries of the empire, a part of that corpus known as the Four Books was chosen as the curriculum for the civil service examinations and was committed to memory by all who aspired to succeed in them. What we need to do, therefore, is not to deal piecemeal with the various philosophers and the works which have been associated with their names, but try to isolate and interrelate the major themes in ancient Chinese intellectual history and show how they influenced intellectual life in China right through to the twentieth century.

The Four Books consist of the *Analects*, the *Mencius*, and two short works known as the *Great Learning* and the *Mean*, both of uncertain authorship. Apart from Mencius the other leading early Confucian thinker was Hsün Tzu, who had a profound influence on Han Dynasty Confucianism, although later his work did not have the prestige of Classical status enjoyed by the *Analects* and the *Mencius*. Before talking in general about the early Confucian tradition it will be best to say a few preliminary words about these three giants of early Confucianism.

Although later tradition gave Confucius high offices of state, the Confucius of the *Analects* is a figure disappointed in the failure of his political ambitions, who spends a lifetime teaching and trying to persuade rulers to adopt his doctrines. He appears to have been a member of the small but growing middle class of *shih* (sometimes translated 'knights'), and seems to have been regarded as a specialist on ritual. His teaching was much concerned with moral action and the preparation of young men for careers in government. The style of the *Analects* is brief and aphoristic, and there is no systematic presentation of subject matter. The appearance of this most influential figure at a time when prose literature in essay form was not developed has inclined the Chinese to admire aphorism, to prefer profound lapidary sayings to the long chain of logical argument, and to take naturally to proverb or political slogan. Despite the composite nature of the *Analects*, the book is alive with the personality of a great human being, who is selfless, frugal, and fond of learning, who feels that he has a commission from Heaven and gives inspired utterance to a recognition of the moral nature of man. Most importantly he is seen as a teacher, and has been revered by the Chinese as their first great educator, a very high distinction in a civilization which has placed an enormous emphasis on learning. In this capacity he appears also as the first explainer of Classical texts, the first in that long line of commentators and textual critics who are at the very heart of the Chinese intellectual tradition. Indeed it was as the creator, editor, or transmitter of the heritage of Classical texts that he inspired much adulation among the Chinese people.

'Ever since man came into this world there has never been another Confucius',[1] exclaimed Mencius, who two centuries after his death established him firmly as the founder of the tradition which was to dominate Chinese thought. Mencius had to try to prove his points in the face of criticism from the many rival schools which existed in his day, so his teaching was much more systematic than that of the master. Whereas Confucius stated ethical principles in the context of brief anecdotes, Mencius was forced to look more deeply into the nature of the human being who is responsible for ethical action, and he is particularly famous for his doctrine of the goodness of human nature. Hsün Tzu, who is best known for taking the opposite view of human nature, was an even more systematic writer. From his pessimism he derived a firm belief in the importance of education in certain chosen texts at the feet of a good teacher, and this concept became the basis of training for the civil service when that had to be greatly expanded to cope with the growing Han empire. Hsün Tzu also felt that human conduct had to be restrained by ritual, which he raised to an extremely important place in his system of thought.

II

But, even in the case of the more polished and systematic Hsün Tzu, this early philosophical literature is not so much a collection of arguments leading to conclusions about the nature of man and society; but rather a series of variations on certain themes which are forced on these ancient thinkers, whatever their persuasion, by the world-view which they all shared and by the crisis which they saw affecting their world in the late Chou period. The works of this time naturally reflect a sense of great social and economic change and of the breakdown of the old order. For Mencius 'sage kings do not appear and feudal lords give rein to their desires',[2] and what the world needs is to return to order and tranquillity. Here Mencius is not just talking, as we do nowadays, of a moral decline which may be arrested by the fostering of certain much neglected social virtues. What these ancient Chinese thinkers were concerned with was the collapse of order in a world which embraced nature as well as man, so that human decline went hand in hand with cosmic disaster. Other peoples confronted with similar disorders might have given way to despair or to concern with a life to come since there seemed to be no hope of peace in this world. Or if, like the ancient Greeks, the Chinese had experienced a variety of political systems, they might have turned to other ideologies or invented ideal states. Instead, having no neighbouring great civilizations from which to learn, and living in a society in which cyclical ideas were already deeply entrenched, they naturally sought their solutions by looking back to a Golden Age.

The society of the ancient Greek philosophers was set in an urban context and was open to many outside influences. China was isolated and agricultural. Hence it was natural that the cycle of the seasons had a powerful impact on the way men visualized the course of human history. Early man made constant cross-references between the human and the natural worlds: on the one hand he peopled the heavens with gods having human characteristics, and on the other hand he shaped his view of man in society in accordance with the impact of nature on his imagination. In Egypt, for example, the miraculous annual rebirth of the Nile gave assurance that renewed life would always be victorious over death, while the country's uniform and symmetrical landscape, with eastern mountain range balancing western mountain range and one great river flowing midway between them, helped to give the Egyptians the strong sense of balance and symmetry which is characteristic of their art and literature. Ancient Chinese literature also reflects such a correlation between the world of nature and the world of man, as in the already mentioned remark attributed to Confucius: 'Heaven does not have two suns, and the people do not have two kings.'[3]

The Chinese imagination was not shaped by a conspicuous geographical symmetry, as was the Egyptian. Instead they were deeply conscious of the rhythm of the four seasons and of the basic dualisms which mark man's existence, such as the contrast between night and day and between the vast heavens above and the earth below. The world of man was seen to match this antithesis between heaven and earth with its contrasts between superior and inferior, ruler and subject, gentleman and 'small man'. The earth was referred to as the below-Heaven (or all-under-Heaven, as it is often translated) and as a political entity it was as limitless as the vast skies above. As Hsün Tzu put it, 'Because of the existence of Heaven and Earth distinctions are made between higher and lower.'[4] The contrast between night and day found expression in the well-known belief in Yang and Yin, two complementary principles of nature exemplified by such pairs of opposites as light and dark, sun and moon, and male and female. Finally, set down as they were in this vast land, surrounded as they thought by barbarians and vaguely believing that they were encompassed on all four sides by seas, they naturally thought of the world in terms of a dualism between inner and outer, between private life and public life, and between family and state. And as the world and individuals' relationships with it became more complicated, so a more appropriate image is that of concentric circles, widening from self to family to state to all-under-Heaven — an image of the world which would be quite alien to men brought up in an environment in which they were aware of many different peoples and societies. Ancient geographical speculation envisaged the world in the form of concentric squares, with 'royal domains' in the centre, surrounded by firstly the princes' domains, and then the pacification zone, the zone of allied barbarians, and finally the zone of savagery.

This schematic progression from inner to outer, from self to all-under-Heaven harmonizes well with the hierarchical nature of the social system. A good illustration of this is provided by the *Book of Filial Piety*, which deals in turn with the filial piety appropriate to the Son of Heaven, the feudal lords, the high officials, the knights, and the common people. Man must ensure that harmony prevails in this series of relationships, so that he plays his part in securing cosmic order. Thus the central core of the *Great Learning* reads:

> The ancients who wished to make their luminous virtue shine throughout all-under-Heaven first brought order to their own states. Those who wished to bring order to their own states first regulated their families. Those who wished to regulate their families first cultivated their persons. Those who wished to cultivate their persons first rectified their hearts. Those who wished to rectify their hearts first made their thoughts sincere. Those who wished to make their thoughts sincere first extended to the utmost their knowledge.[5]

III

Thus one of the major principles of Confucian doctrine is that in order to secure harmony and happiness in the world man must bring himself and his activities into a harmonious relationship with the universe: he must adjust the social order to the cosmic order. This has two important implications with immense consequences. Firstly, to complete the cosmic pattern, Man must somehow be envisaged as big enough to stand in this close relationship with the universal order. Consequently many passages in ancient literature link Man with Heaven and Earth. The *Tso Tradition*, for example, has: 'The norms of Heaven and Earth are what men take as their pattern, striving to imitate the brilliance of Heaven and according with the natural diversities of Earth.'[6] The ancient books even show Man forming a trinity with Heaven and Earth, each performing its appropriate function in the cosmic order. Hsün Tzu, for example, says: 'Heaven has its seasons; Earth has its resources; Man has his government. This means that Man is capable of forming a trinity with the other two.'[7] If Man is conceived as forming a trinity with Heaven and Earth, then the qualities which Man needs to make him a fit companion for them must obviously be of heroic, even cosmic proportions. Hence it takes a sage to achieve this proper harmony between the human and the natural order; or, on the other hand, the virtues necessary to enable human beings to match Heaven and Earth grow to the stature of cosmic principles. Thus in the *Book of Filial Piety* the writer's imagination soars and makes this virtue into a cosmic principle, while in the *Mean* it is the turn of sincerity, for it is only he who has complete sincerity who is 'able to assist the transforming and nourishing powers of Heaven and Earth'[8] and form a trinity with them.

So the Chinese really did believe, not as a metaphor or as a piece of poetry, that human moral behaviour interacted with the processes of Heaven and Earth. At the apex of humanity the Son of Heaven was, as we saw in the first chapter, most closely involved in this interaction with the cosmos. And so there survived into modern times the belief that, if the weather was bad, this was due to the emperor's shortcomings; and that, if he ordered executions in the spring, this would have a disastrous effect on the crops.

The second implication of this principle that the social order must be adjusted to the cosmic order is that man comes to believe that the social system is unchangeable because it has a basis in nature as firm and constant as the stars. Hence man is inclined to believe that there is only one solution to political problems and to deplore diversity of opinions. In his memorial proposing the establishment of a university based on Confucian studies and the suppression of other schools of thought Tung Chung-shu of the Han Dynasty wrote: 'The teachers of today have diverse Ways (Tao), men have diverse doctrines, the Hundred Schools have different positions, and the ideas they teach are not the same. Hence the rulers have no means of securing unity.'[9] 'Great unity' (*ta-t'ung*) has been a persistent Chinese ideal. The name was originally given to the classic formulation in the *Record of Rites* of an ideal society in which the Way prevailed, and was included in the title of the nineteenth-century Utopia written by K'ang Yu-wei, the *Book of Great Unity*. Reform in Chinese society was often seen as a fresh search for the true harmony and unity, for, as the *Mean* had said, 'If equilibrium and harmony are secured, Heaven and Earth will dwell in it and all things will be nourished by it.'[10] Even the seventeenth-century reformer Huang Tsung-hsi, who was bitterly critical of the rulers and institutions of his times, pursued the traditional Confucian goal of harmony, based on 'the Truth, one and indivisible, handed down through generations of wise men from those who first revealed it, the sage kings and Confucius'.[11] This is a world in which there is no place for heterodoxy and in which deviationism does not flourish.

IV

The word which was commonly used in the Confucian school to sum up this state of harmony in which good government prevails in the world is Tao, which means 'way' or 'road', both in the literal and in the metaphorical sense. Ideally it meant the Way of the ancient sage kings, but sometimes it was used to mean not ideal government, but simply good government, as when Confucius said: 'When the Way prevails under Heaven, then show yourself; when it does not prevail, then hide. When the Way prevails in your own land, then to be poor and obscure is shameful; and when the Way does not prevail in your own land, then to enjoy riches and honours is shameful.'[12] This saying incidentally illustrates the seminal importance of the *Analects*: it contains the germ of two important elements in the Confucian tradition, firstly the belief that there is no taint on worldly goods and honours as such, and secondly, the teaching that in times of bad government one should withdraw from political life.

77

In his schematic manner Mencius saw the Way and its absence as dependent on whether virtue or force was at the helm: 'When the Way prevails under Heaven men of small virtue serve men of great virtue, and men of small worth serve men of great worth. But when the Way does not prevail under Heaven, the small serve the great and the weak serve the strong.'[13] Mencius considered that his main task was to urge the rulers of his own day to adopt the Way of a true king: this involved the exercise of the ruler's natural benevolence to promote agricultural production and the welfare of the people, so that everyone was well cared for and had the leisure to cultivate the virtues necessary to the harmonious ordering of society. Such kingly qualities had their reward, for 'the one who gets the Way will have many supporters, but the one who loses the Way will have few supporters'.[14]

One who is capable of ensuring that the Way prevails in the world is by definition a sage (*sheng*). Again in his usual schematic way Mencius said that the sage pertains to the Way of Heaven just as benevolence pertains to the relationship between father and son, duty to the relationship between prince and subject, the rites to the relationship between guest and host, and wisdom to the man of worth and ability.[15] It is the sage's task, as Mo Tzu put it, to treat the government of the world as his business, because he is the one capable of integrating the human order with the Way of Heaven.[16] A more pragmatic argument which was often advanced was that government was like a craft, which must be assigned to its own specialist, just as jade, however precious, was assigned to a jade-carver for it to be cut, shaped, and polished; and in the case of government the appropriate specialist was the sage, rather than the ruler, who generally had no real qualifications for the task.[17] Although the analogy with craftsmanship is faulty if only because the ruler himself is part of the polity he rules, Socrates produced similar arguments for treating government as a craft which should be pursued by specialists.

Only in the Golden Age of antiquity had sagehood and kingship gone together, in the person of such revered figures as Yao and Shun. Hsün Tzu put Confucius into the same league by saying: 'He was learned in the arts of government and capable of filling the role of one of the ancient kings. . . . His virtue was equal to that of the Duke of Chou and his reputation was on a par with that of the three dynastic founders.'[18] According to the *Analects*, Confucius explicitly disclaimed the title of sage, but later generations found it difficult to understand why he and others like the Duke of Chou had not attained the position of Son of Heaven in spite of their sagehood. The answer was, as Mencius put it, 'that he who inherits the empire is only rejected by Heaven if he is like the tyrants Chieh and Chou' (the bad last rulers of the Hsia and Shang Dynasties).[19]

The sage was envisaged not only as bringer of harmony and tranquillity to the world through benevolent government, but also as a supreme teacher. As Mencius said, 'A sage is the teacher of a hundred generations.'[20] Teaching in this context was not a matter of presenting intellectual insights into the nature of the world, but rather of providing models for conduct so that people may conform with the pattern of the world. The sages were depicted as embodiments of moral qualities, such as the self-sacrifice of Yü, who saved the world from the flood and wore his limbs smooth and hairless in the process, and the benevolence of King Wen, whom the people rejoiced to aid because he shared his pleasures with them. Ideally the ruler secured harmony and tranquillity by showing himself worthy of the people's imitation. As the *Great Learning* says: 'When the sovereign treats the old as they should be treated, the people become filial; when the sovereign treats his seniors as they should be treated, the people learn younger-brotherly virtue; when the sovereign treats orphans with compassion, the people will not act in a contrary manner.'[21] The ruler in his turn should look higher for a model to emulate, like King Wen who, according to the *Book of Songs*, 'without consciousness and without knowledge accords with the pattern of God'.[22]

This explains Confucius's famous claim to be a 'transmitter, not a creator'.[23] In regarding themselves as guardians and transmitters of the old tradition the Confucians were not merely conserving a literary and cultural heritage for its aesthetic or antiquarian appeal; they were handing on a tradition about the model behaviour of the exemplars of antiquity. Indeed in the Confucian literature men were often judged and evaluated in the light of quotations from the *Book of Songs*, which was thought to be a repository of wisdom on exemplary behaviour. So the Confucian view of politics stressed the importance of officials being models for the people, and the Confucian view of education stressed the pupils' emulation of their models, the teachers.

The importance of this concern with the emulation of models, already a prominent feature of early Chinese writing, has had a profound influence on Chinese literature and thought down to the present day. For example, an important aim of traditional Chinese historians was to hold up a mirror to society so that the acts of the famous and of the notorious might provide examples for later men to follow or avoid. This tradition derived from the conventional interpretation of the *Spring and Autumn*

Annals, a classical work which Confucius was believed to have compiled on the basis of the annals of his own state of Lu, indicating by subtle changes in the use of language his praise or blame for the participants in historical events. It is a tradition which is especially evident in biographical writing. The standard dynastic histories have biographical sections giving accounts of the public careers of distinguished men of the period. The writer does not explore in depth the motives and personalities of the individuals, as we expect biographers to do. Rather the subject is portrayed fulfilling the powerful obligations which in the Chinese view bind the individual to society, the duties to clan and state; and since these are state-sponsored writings, special attention is given to the man's official career, so as to present him as an example for future generations of Confucian officialdom.

The importance attached to social roles rather than individual achievements is also illustrated by the fact that the official histories contain collective biographies of groups such as 'harsh officials', 'virtuous women', and 'filial sons'. Similarly at a local level widows who did not remarry after their husbands' death could be singled out as models of chastity and given honourable mention in the local gazetteers. The same attitude is reflected in popular fiction, in which both good and bad characters are stereotyped. For example, only two types of courtesan seem to appear: the cruel one who squanders a man's money and leaves him penniless, and the tender-hearted one who helps her indigent lover through his studies. The ancient Classics as well as later popular literature frequently use the device of taking a man's name as symbolical of the stereotyped quality he is famous for.

The same strong tradition of moral reform which pervaded historical writing may also be seen at work in the efforts of Neo-Confucian scholars to bring about a rebirth of society and a revival of ancient mores by going back to the ancient texts and achieving a deeper understanding of them. So the idea that the purpose of literature is the reform of society is a strong element in the Confucian tradition which survived in the thought of Chairman Mao.

In the more particular matter of model emulation, one of the most familiar features of present-day China is the setting up of model workers and model organizations for the people to emulate. Much study goes into the question of how to choose and set up models with the right attitudes towards officially approved qualities, such as the spirit of collectivism, or progressive thinking. Model workers are honoured with certificates and banners and paraded round factories as examples to their fellow-workers. When the Ming Tombs reservoir was being built near Peking, a popular play celebrated the model achievements of some of the workers, and Chairman Mao and Chou En-lai were photographed on the site, setting an example by taking part in the manual labour. In recent years Tachai and Taching have been set up as the model places which agriculture and industry respectively should study.

V

The ruler needed to understand the Way and operate in accordance with it and he had to set a good example which the people would emulate, so the ancient philosophers devoted much attention to the virtues of the ideal king. In the book which bears his name Mencius constantly torments the imperfect rulers of his day with his opinion on how the truly moral and benevolent king would treat his subjects. The difference between the ideal ruler and the normal self-seeking ruler is described in terms of a schematic contrast between the legitimate *wang* (king), who really deserved this title (which had been usurped by many of the rulers of the petty states of the day), and *pa*, the paramount princes, who some centuries earlier had in turn held the hegemony among the states because the Chou Dynasty had become too weak to exercise control. Both Mencius and Hsün Tzu schematized the contrast between these two types of ruler, rather as Aristotle compared the tyrant who desires riches with the king who desires honour. The *wang* was said to rule by moral power and the *pa* was said to rule by force. One who rules by force gains men's submission because they have not sufficient strength to deny him allegiance, but one who rules by moral power and practises benevolence gains men's genuine submission; and it is only such a ruler who is capable of uniting 'all within the four seas' and putting an end to the period of warring states. This debate, stated in the simplest terms by Mencius, was crucial for the viability of the Chinese state, since the imprinting on the minds of the people of the notion that government has some moral power behind it and is not just a matter of naked force is a vital element in the survival of political systems, and lay at the heart of the ability of the Chinese empire to survive for such a great length of time. Armed conquest could only succeed if backed up by this kind of moral power, which would ensure that the vanquished would flock to the new ruler and the barbarian peoples would clamour to be liberated by him. Hence it became the accepted view in China that a period of cultural preparation in which a store of moral power was built up was a necessary preliminary to successful conquest, just as Wen Wang (the cultured King) preceded Wu Wang (the Martial King), who defeated the Shang and inaugurated the Chou Dynasty.

The main characteristic of the true king was held by Mencius to be *jen* (benevolence), a quality which he thought was naturally inherent in man and merely needed careful nurturing. Its external manifestation would consist of care for the people. For to Mencius the purpose of political institutions was to benefit the people: he thought that rulers should only retain their stewardship as long as they secured the people's welfare. As we have already seen, this was often described as being 'father and mother of the people'. This expression is sometimes explained in the schematic manner which we have seen to be typical of the ancient texts. According to the *Great Learning*, 'When a prince loves what the people love and hates what the people hate, then that is what is called being the father and mother of the people.'[24] Hsün Tzu rationalizes the expression by saying, 'A father can beget a child but he cannot suckle it. A mother can feed it but she cannot educate it. The ruler can feed his people, and he is also good at educating them.'[25] The concept of the ruler being father and mother of the people had first appeared in both the *Book of Songs* and the *Book of History* before it was taken up by the late Chou philosophers. It was applied to local magistrates from Sung times onwards, and in the Ch'ing period writers on administration still discussed the practical significance of being father and mother of the people.

Care for the people meant concern for their mental as well as their physical well-being, and so required educational as well as economic measures. This was only natural since self-cultivation and character-reform were seen as the essential link in the chain which secured the harmony the world needed; but stress on education gained added strength from the Mencian belief in the goodness of human nature, which was thought only to need satisfactory economic conditions and education for its development. Men must be given a steady livelihood, and to this end must not be taken from the land unduly for purposes of warfare or to cater for the ruler's pleasures. Natural resources must be conserved so that they are not exhausted, and the people must be educated in filial and younger-brotherly duties so that the elderly do not suffer privations. It is wrong for the king to have well-fed horses in his stables while the people starve to death outside. The king must share the pleasures of music and hunting with his people and he must not keep them out of his private park. He must delight in their joys and grieve at their sorrows. The frugality which Confucius and Mencius preached became an important part of the Confucian tradition, which often in later times came into direct conflict with the ostentation of imperial courts.

It was believed that the benevolent ruler could attain to the government of all-under-Heaven without a large territory to start from because the people would all be attracted by his goodness and flock to him. Mencius drew on the examples of the founders of the Shang and Chou Dynasties to support this theory. Hsün Tzu set out the argument in the parallelism which is characteristic of the ancient language:

> The true king's benevolence embraces the whole world, his righteousness embraces the whole world, and his authority embraces the whole world. Since his benevolence embraces the whole world, there is no one in the world who does not draw close to him. Since his righteousness embraces the whole world, there is no one in the world who does not honour him. Since his authority embraces the whole world, there is no one who dares to oppose him. With his unopposed authority and supported by ways which win men's allegiance, he conquers without fighting and wins territory without attacking. Without his weapons or armour being exhausted, the whole world yields to him.[26]

This is an attitude which had a powerful appeal at a time when there was a strong sense of the cultural unity of the Chinese world by comparison with the nomadic barbarians who surrounded and encroached upon it, and when the states into which China was then divided needed to attract large populations to develop the virgin lands within their territories and build up their strength.

The traditional belief has even had confirmation in the twentieth century, which has provided an outstanding example of a 'virtuous ruler', starting off from a small territory, proving that the confidence of the people was more important than superiority in weapons, and finally achieving the conquest of all-under-Heaven. The assumption of the traditional Confucian theory, that the people will be naturally attracted to virtuous rulers, however militarily weak they are, was borne out by Mao's successful emergence from his Yenan retreat to conquer the whole of China and subject it to thorough economic and cultural reform. In the light of these achievements there is nothing surprising in the Maoist doctrine of the primacy of man and his ability to overcome natural obstacles and difficulties. Nature may be tamed, Everest conquered, all manner of great deeds may be done under the inspiration of the thought of Chairman Mao by Man, whose potential is as great as it was when the ancients thought him fit to form a trinity with Heaven and Earth.

The nine rules for sovereigns listed in the *Mean* show how their benevolence should be reflected in their relationships with all classes: they should 'cultivate their characters, honour men of worth, show affection to relatives, respect the chief ministers, deal courteously with the whole body of officials, treat the mass of people as children, attract all kinds o craftsmen, deal kindly with men who come from afar, and be gentle with feudal lords'. Here the whole task of government is seen in terms of the benevolent conduct of personal relationships. If government were thus closely related to ordinary morality and therefore seemed to be deeply rooted in the moral and natural order, then the people could be more easily induced to accept it. The great weakness of this view was that at times of crisis it was felt that moral reform would be enough to solve all problems. Confucian scholars tended to think that the reform of society could be achieved through a better understanding of the moral messages of the early Confucian texts; and even in the nineteenth century, when China was threatened with collapse because of the impact of the West, it was mistakenly thought possible to introduce Western innovations to deal with the practical problems the country faced, while retaining Confucianism for its basic moral and cultural value.

Underlying the concern which the benevolent ruler must show for the welfare of his people is the concept of two basic classes in society, the *chün-tzu* (gentleman, literally 'ruler's son') and *hsiao-jen*, (literally 'small man'). They form a contrast of upper and lower, parallel with Heaven and Earth, father and son, ruler and subject. The *chün-tzu* on the one hand, through their education and culture, have moral sense and provide leadership, while the *hsiao-jen* are intellectually and morally immature like infants and need to be educated into a state of social harmony. The *chün-tzu* preserves his moral sense even in adversity and values righteousness more than his life, while the *hsiao-jen* needs economic security otherwise he will have recourse to crime. But although the two classes played contrasting roles in society, the *chün-tzu* working with their brains and governing others and *hsiao-jen* working with their brawn and being governed by others, it was very strongly appreciated that it was necessary for rulers to win the consent and co-operation of the people.

As Mencius put it, 'There is a way to win all-under-Heaven; if you win the people, then you will win all-under-Heaven. There is a way to win the people; if you win their hearts, then you will win the people.'[27]

Hence the need to examine human nature and the human heart. This was a lively issue in Mencius's time when men's thoughts were turning inwards to try to understand moral feelings as well as moral conduct. It helped to make the world more intelligible if it could be shown that harmonious social order was a product of man's innate moral capacities.

VI

Mencius mentioned that the distinction between men and animals was slight, and indeed he even went so far as to say that the difference between the 'gentleman' and the 'small man' was that the latter loses this distinction but the former retains it.[28] Men differed from animals because they possessed *hsin*, which may be translated as either 'heart' or 'mind', since although it is physically the heart, it was regarded as the seat of thought in ancient China. This is not quite what Aristotle meant when he said that it was the power of reasoning which distinguished man from animals, for Mencius was concerned with moral thinking, i.e. thinking about moral duties. Hsün Tzu also thought it was a moral quality which distinguished men from animals: they were able to form groups or organize themselves in society because of their sense of justice.[29] Hence the main purpose of education in China became not the development of intellectual skills but the development of these innate moral tendencies.

Mencius believed that four principle human virtues – benevolence, righteousness, observance of the rites, and wisdom – sprang naturally from four innate qualities of the heart, which he refers to metaphorically as 'shoots'.[30] Benevolence derives from the compassionate element in the heart, the existence of which can be proved by man's instinctive reaction to the sight of a child about to fall into a well. Righteousness derives from the sense of shame, the observance of the rites derives from that part of the heart which is the seat of courtesy and modesty, and wisdom derives from that part of the heart which distinguishes right from wrong. Wisdom, it will be noted once more, is closely identified with morality. All men alike have these innate moral tendencies, these moral shoots which spring up as naturally as young plants, so Mencius believed that human nature was basically good. This is the humanistic and optimistic doctrine for which he has been most famous, although it did not always endear him to Christian missionaries in China, who preferred to think of man as fallen.

Hsün Tzu has been best known for the contrary view, that human nature is evil, but this is an oversimplified contrast, based largely on one chapter. The book as a whole shows that Hsün Tzu believed that human nature was in need of development through education, ritual, and social organization; but he did not always seem to regard it as inherently evil. Certainly if man's nature is inherently evil, it is difficult to account for the emergence of any goodness, as Hsün Tzu himself implied when he said: 'If man's nature is evil, where do rites and justice spring from? They all derive from the fabrication of the sages.'[31] Moreover Hsün Tzu, like Mencius, believed that men are infinitely perfectible by their own efforts. 'Now suppose the man in the street were to apply himself to training and devote himself to study, concentrate his mind and unite his will, consider things thoughtfully and examine them thoroughly, continuing his efforts over a long period of time and not ceasing to accumulate good acts, then he could commune with spiritual intelligences and form a trinity with Heaven and Earth. Sagehood is what one attains to by such accumulation of good acts.'[32]

This is comparable with Mencius's belief that 'Every man may become a Yao or Shun.'[33] The belief that all men are born equal and are infinitely perfectible is a basic and profoundly humanistic Confucian doctrine, which was not paralleled in the main Christian tradition, which holds that all men are of equal *value*, rather than that they are born with similar characteristics. The belief goes back to the *Analects*, which includes the saying, 'By nature men are close to each other; through experience they become remote from each other',[34] which was accepted as an essential truth in the UNESCO 'Statement on Race' published in 1950. The belief in human equality has not been a characteristic of the Western world until modern times, but the special situation in which the ancient Chinese found themselves was perhaps more conducive to such a doctrine. Geographical circumstances presented them, not with a world of rival peoples and civilizations, but with one in which it was possible to believe in a single civilization to which even the outer barbarians would eventually be assimilated so that 'Within the four seas all men are brothers'.[35] There was also a strong tradition that Heaven and the spirits were impartially receptive to sacrifices and later to virtuous behaviour, so that all men were equal in their ability to influence Heaven. Again it is much easier to believe in the equality of man if moral rather than intellectual standards are seen as the criterion. Moral goals seem to be more universally achievable because they are a matter of will rather than intellectual capacity, so it was possible for the Chinese to say that any man in the street may become a sage, whereas to us it would be nonsense to say that anybody may become an Einstein.

Mencius's interest in human nature was a giant step forward in human self-awareness. His real achievement was to break down the barrier between Heaven and Man and between Heaven's Decree and human nature, because he taught men that acting in accordance with Heaven's Decree is something they can do, not by yielding to an external command, but by willingly looking inwards and finding the roots of morality in their own make-up.

The cultivation of the moral character and the development of virtues was the main task of education, which was naturally an important concern of the ancient Confucian writers. Confucius was revered by the Chinese people as their first teacher, and the *Analects* contains the germ of several important features of the Chinese attitude to education. Firstly his own unwearying diligence as a teacher made him a model for all later members of the profession to emulate. Secondly his saying which has been interpreted to mean 'in education there are no class distinctions'[36] (which has often been displayed in Chinese schools in modern times) and his willingness to receive pupils, however poor, provided they showed enthusiasm for learning, foreshadowed the imperial examination system, which was open to almost all males of whatever social position. Thirdly, like Confucian scholars of later ages, he regarded himself as a custodian of culture in general, as opposed to such philosophers as the Mohists or Legalists who taught only their own doctrines. Fourthly he believed in the attraction of culture and its appeal to barbarians whose own culture was inferior; and throughout history the Chinese would go on trying to inspire awe in tributary peoples through their imperial splendour and superior cultural attainments. So the one who claimed to be 'a transmitter, not a creator', handing on the ancient culture, foreshadowed later Chinese attitudes to education in many respects.

Mencius, whose views of human nature were much coloured by the agricultural society in which he lived, saw a parallel between the cultivation of tender young plants and helping the development of human beings along moral lines. He made casual reference to the existence of schools in his own time and referred to the establishment of schools in the legendary Hsia and the Shang Dynasties as well as the early Chou, saying that their purpose was to cast light on human relationships. Hsün Tzu maintained the same general attitude to education, for he wrote: 'He who does not comprehend moral relationships and categories and who does not wholly devote himself to benevolence and righteousness is not fit to be called a good scholar.'[37] It was he who most firmly established the pattern of later Chinese education, with its bookishness and its concern with particular Classical texts. This curriculum was much less practical than the content of ancient education, which, in addition to ethical teaching, had consisted of the 'six arts' – ritual, music, archery, chariot-driving, writing, and reckoning. For Hsün Tzu, 'Learning begins with the recitation of the Classics and ends with the reading of the ritual texts.'[38] He also stressed the importance of having a good teacher both as a model and as an expounder of the Classical texts.

> In learning, [he said] nothing is more beneficial than to keep close to those who are learned, and of the roads to learning none is quicker than to love such men. Second only to this is to exalt ritual. If you are both unable to love such men and incapable of exalting ritual, then you will only be learning a mass of jumbled facts, blindly following the *Book of Songs* and the *Book of History*, and nothing more.[39]

As has been suggested earlier, the fact that the Chinese have traditionally attached supreme importance to man's social behaviour and have geared their education to the need to improve this has made them over-optimistic about the extent to which man is mouldable through education. They have often seen a revolution in education as a cure for political and social problems. If society had gone astray, it could only be because the Confucian books were imperfectly understood; so one must go back to the sources again and extract their true meaning. Fan Chung-yen, a famous eleventh-century reformer, saw the introduction of a nationwide school system as the basic solution to the political problems of his time. Others suggested the reform of the examination system, and in the declining years of the empire officials were still making such suggestions and seeking to ward off rebellion by establishing colleges in troubled provinces to educate the people in Confucian principles. In the present century we have seen two important cultural revolutions; the first, which started in 1917, was centred on the introduction of the use of the vernacular language as the common medium of literary communication instead of the old Classical language, and the second was Mao's Great Proletarian Cultural Revolution, which started in 1966. 'Save the country by education' was a common slogan in the earlier reform movement; and in Mao's cultural revolution, the aim of which was to combat revisionism and hasten the creation of a classless society, the schools and universities were all closed down so that the educational system could be thoroughly reformed. And just as the Confucian educational system was much concerned to use the Confucian Classics to put before the student edifying models of the Confucian virtues, so 'the basic task of socialist literature and art is to create heroic models of workers, peasants, and soldiers'.[40]

VII

The development of the human personality and the improvement of man's ability to play social roles, which is seen as the task of education, is described in terms of certain desirable virtues which must be explored in order to round off this survey of the ancient Confucian tradition and its impact on later Chinese history. These virtues are not easy to describe since it is difficult to find suitable English equivalents for the terms used.

The most important events in human life are births and marriages, which place a man in the centre of a network of relationships; and deaths, which cut off some of the threads. Although in our civilization we tend to place much greater stress on the rights of individuals, the Chinese lay emphasis on the duties imposed by these relationships, which bind individuals to each other. In early Chou history such bonds were extremely important, for the rulers had to rely very heavily on the support of fief-holding relatives to ensure the administration and security of the state; and ancient literature frequently reflects a sense of the importance of the ruling family sticking together to repel dangers from without. Mencius set out the five basic relationships as the love between father and son, the duty between ruler and subject, the distinction between husband and wife, the precedence of the old over the young, and good faith between friends. This list he attributed to a mythical Minister of Education in the remote past. Generally Mencius describes the link between father and son in terms of the benevolence of the former and the filial piety of the latter, while loyalty is the conventional term for the attitude of the subject towards his ruler. In later convention the five relationships include three family ones, the elder brother–younger brother relationship replacing the precedence of the old over the young.

Much space is given in the ancient Confucian texts to describing and interrelating virtues. For example, *jen* (goodness, benevolence) has a wide range of description in the *Analects* and *Mencius*. Confucius said that one who was *jen* was 'in private life courteous, in the management of affairs respectful, and in relationships with others loyal'.[41] Mencius said that, if he lacked this quality, 'the Son of Heaven could not protect all within the four seas, the feudal lord could not protect the altars to the gods of earth and grain, the high official could not protect his ancestral temple, and the knight or commoner could not protect his four limbs'.[42] Such characterizations abound, and the relationships between virtues could be described in different ways without any sense of the need for consistency. They were all attempts at approaching the ineffable truth of human relationships. The virtues of benevolence, righteousness, propriety, wisdom, and good faith were commonly grouped together as the 'five constants'. These virtues were not thought of as having vices in opposition to them. They were regarded as elements in the structure of the universe, not unrelated to earth, wood, fire, metal, and water, which were known as the 'five elements'. Indeed, in the Han period there was a theory that these five elements were the corporeal essences of the five constant virtues, and an attempt was made to show that these five constant virtues also corresponded to the 'five viscera', benevolence being linked with the liver, righteousness with the lungs, propriety with the heart, wisdom with the kidneys, and good faith with the spleen. Although the argumentation which supported these equations was bizarre, the theory shows how firmly the ancient Chinese believed that these virtues had as much reality as the material world about them.

To practise the Confucian virtues was not a straightforward matter. There were inner inconsistencies within the tradition which led to problems of behaviour and interpretation, but it was only under such a wide umbrella that Confucians of whatever temperament and in whatever times could take shelter. The virtue of loyalty, which belonged to the relationship between subject and ruler, could be interpreted as abject surrender by a minister anxious to save his skin in autocratic times, but this would be to ignore the minister's duty to remonstrate with his sovereign which had been urged by Mencius. Filial piety presented similar problems: should a son meekly accept everything his father did, or should he remonstrate with him and even inform on him if he were guilty of a crime?[43] But despite the difficulties of interpretation in some circumstances, filial piety developed into one of the most important of the virtues. In the *Book of Filial Piety* it is the 'root of virtue and the source of all teaching'[44] and is treated as a major principle of the universe. Throughout Chinese history it went hand in hand with ancestor worship, the common religious practice of the Chinese, and provided the stimulus to ambition in a career, which must both provide for the needs of aged parents and establish a reputation which might bring glory to the ancestors. At the same time it stressed the need for male children so that the family line might continue and the future of the family sacrifices might be assured. Conspicuous examples of filial piety became popular themes in literature and in art, which helped to indoctrinate the people with the right attitude towards the social virtues. The parallel virtue of loyalty was overshadowed: the Chinese emphasis on personal relationships is further illustrated by the fact that loyalty remained entirely a matter of personal fealty to superior or sovereign and was not transformed into patriotism. The fifth of the five Confucian relationships, that between friends, also remained important, notably, as we have seen, in the very special ties which existed between those who had graduated in the same year.

Apart from the social virtues, necessary to maintain the harmonious structure of society, certain words were also appropriated to describe the ideal human being who was fit to govern and organize this society. Of these *sheng* (sage) was the highest, for it was the sages who were the supreme examples of men who were able to preserve the Way. *Chün-tzu* (literally 'ruler's son') was next in importance, particularly for Confucius: it meant the ideal member of the ruling classes, the ideal gentleman. There was deep concern in the early Confucian writers about the misuse of language. Words like *chün-tzu* and *wang* (meaning 'king') obviously had moral content, since only an expert on human relationships could fulfil these important roles in such a way as to ensure that the Way prevailed. So what was needed to restore order in society was to introduce what became known as the 'rectification of names', the theory that if names corresponded with realities, all would be well in the world. If the king behaved not simply as one who had naked political power, but as one who had political responsibilities and duties – if he behaved as a true king – then all would be well. Similarly, it was important for the member of the ruling elite to behave like a true gentleman in the moral sense, not just in the class sense. Other terms used to describe men of virtue were *hsien* (worthies), men with both administrative ability and moral qualities who were fit to be employed as ministers, and *shih* (knights), originally members of the lower aristocracy who fought in chariots, but later the class of educated people employed in specialist occupations, to which Confucius and other philosophers belonged. Because these men were educated, they were expected to behave morally even if they suffered hardship.

There is another important group of virtues which do not belong to specific relationships (like loyalty and filial piety), but have a much wider relevance. *Jen* (benevolence) and *i* (righteousness), used by Mencius to refer specifically to the father-son and ruler-subject relationships, also have this wider connotation, being two out of the four Mencian virtues deriving from natural shoots or growth-points in human nature. Among other such virtues are *li* (propriety, observance of the rites), and *te* (virtue, moral power).

Although the word *te* is often translated 'virtue', it must not be thought of as the opposite of vice, for in the ancient Chinese view of the world as a kind of organism in which all parts must function harmoniously, there is no room for vice or sin as a positive element. The failure of this organism to work properly is ascribed to lack of virtue or lack of harmony: it is a situation in which the Way does not prevail in the world. *Te* was sometimes used as a general term for virtues but normally it meant something like moral force or influence, and so it was often contrasted with *li*, meaning physical force (a different word from *li* meaning ritual). This moral force may belong either to institutions or to people (the *Analects*, for example, refers to the *te* of the Chou Dynasty and also the perfect *te* of T'ai-po, an ancestor of the Chou rulers who renounced sovereignty three times).[45] It may be described as the quality of personality which enables a ruler to rule morally and benevolently. For example, Mencius was asked by a ruler to explain what sort of moral force was needed to enable one to become a true king, and in reply he equated it with the ability to protect the people and proved that his questioner had the requisite innate qualities of heart.[46] Moral force may be accumulated by the performance of moral acts and may pervade all-under-Heaven if the Way prevails. If the Way does not prevail, moral power declines. The concept of the close relationship between the human and natural order is reflected in the belief that *te* (moral force) and *jen* (benevolence) pervade the universe in a quasi-physical manner.

Another pervasive virtue is *i* (righteousness, rightness, justice, duty), which appears basically to mean what seemed just to the natural man before concepts like *fa* (law) and *li* (ritual) clothed it with cultural associations. Mo Tzu, for example, posits a state of nature, 'before there were laws or government' in which every man had his own *i*, so that there was total disagreement among men which could only be reconciled by placing some in positions of superiority and then adopting the principle of identification with the superior, so that men must approve everything which the superior approves.[47] In Mencius it comes near to the meaning of 'duty', and is taken as the development of the shame-feeling aspect of the heart.

The third of the Mencian fundamental virtues, *li* (propriety, observance of the rites) had a much more important part to play in Chinese culture. The original meaning of the word was 'sacrifice', which later broadened to include all the ritual appropriate to religious ceremonies. Then, since there was no sharp division between the religious and the secular, the rules of ritual conduct naturally spread first to such dignified secular activities as behaviour at court, and thence gradually permeated the whole of life; so that as society became more concerned with the welfare of man than with the worship of gods, ritual developed into a device for bringing order and restraint to the conduct of individuals in society and for giving a touch of ceremony to the ordinary activities of life. This development had its disadvantages, for an excessive regard for ritual proprieties could easily decline into an empty formalism. The Confucius of the *Analects* was already acutely aware of the dangers: he declared that a man without virtue had nothing to do with *li*, and that he could not bear to see the forms of *li* gone through by men without reverence in their hearts.[48] Ironically Confucius was depicted in some later texts, and even in material which has found its way into the *Analects*, as a pedantic stickler for details in ritual behaviour; and this gave authority to those petty Confucians of later times who thought it all-important to follow the form, since they were incapable of appreciating the essence. When even in the *Analects* Confucius was reported to have enjoined his disciples 'not to look at what is contrary to propriety',[49] it is not surprising that later inferior Confucians should have appeared to their adversaries to be heavily shackled by the demands of ritual.

The increasing application of the concept of *li* to all human activities could make men forget its religious origins and see it mainly as an ornament to man's social life; so that even the conduct of sacrifices could be seen in terms of the moral value to mankind of the performance of aesthetically pleasing rituals, regardless of whether or not the ritual was effective in moving the spirits. In antiquity Hsün Tzu was an extreme sceptic about the efficacy of prayer, saying 'if you pray for rain and it rains, it would have rained anyway',[50] but he believed very strongly in the social value of the rites. He said that sacrifice was considered by the gentleman (*chün-tzu*) to be a practice beneficial to human beings but by the common people to be a serving of the spirits; and this view was upheld throughout Chinese history by the more sceptical among the intellectuals. In Hsün Tzu's chapter on military affairs it is rites which are the 'highest means of organizing and making distinctions, the basis for strengthening the state, the way of making conduct authoritative, and the essence of achievement and fame'.[51] They are more important than stout armour, sharp weapons, high walls, and deep moats. He also sees the rites as being created by the ancient sage kings to reform man's evil nature. In fact Hsün Tzu thought that *li* was so important to human society that he elevated it to a cosmic principle; for, despite his scepticism, he shared his contemporaries' profound belief in the interaction of the human and natural worlds. 'Through rites,' he declared, 'Heaven and Earth join in harmony, the sun and moon shine, the four seasons proceed in order, the stars and constellations march, the rivers flow, and all things flourish, men's likes and dislikes are regulated and their joys and hates made appropriate.'[52] Three works on ritual found their way into the *Thirteen Classics*, and of these the *Record of Rites* in particular provided a source book on correct ritual practices which was closely followed throughout Chinese history, thus having a profound influence on social life. So *li* gave a distinctive quality to the Chinese experience and in European eyes ceremoniousness has seemed to be a most prominent feature of Chinese behaviour. But it was not only *li* which survived until recent times, for the language of nineteenth-century official discourse was full of Confucian virtues, while the foreigners were condemned, as Mencius condemned the rulers of his own day, because they talked only of profit, and never had a word to say about benevolence and filial piety.

This extreme tenacity of early Confucian attitudes in later Chinese history is one justification for dealing at length with the world of early Confucian thought. Another justification is the profound influence on later Chinese culture of the view that the world of man and the world of nature will work harmoniously if the virtues based on human nature are properly cultivated; for both education and government were geared to the creation of harmony based on these virtues. Very fundamental, too, is the conception of the pattern of human relationships as a series of concentric circles moving outwards from the inner self, to all within the four seas, or all-under-Heaven; with all it implies for the political viewpoint of the Chinese, who saw their country as the Middle Kingdom bound together at the centre by a web of close family relationships having increasingly tenuous links with the more remote barbarian periphery. This survey has mainly concerned itself with the world-view which the ancient thinkers had in common rather than the differences between them, which are less important when seen in the context of 2500 years of Chinese history; but some space must now be found to deal with the major rivals of the Confucian school in antiquity.

CHAPTER 5

THE RIVALS OF CONFUCIANISM

I

The late Chou period was an age unrivalled in Chinese history for the variety of its philosophical ideas, so that the thinkers of the day were described as the Hundred Schools; but this chapter is restricted to three ways of thought which were in direct conflict with Confucianism and represented a challenge to three of its major characteristics. Firstly the Confucian interest in family relationships stimulated the Mohists into responding with their doctrine of Universal Love, with which they opposed the graded love of their adversaries; secondly the Confucian concern for rule by good men was in conflict with the Legalists' advocacy of the rule of Law, a clash which reverberated down the centuries; and finally the Confucian preoccupation with man as a moral being was confronted by Taoism, which dismissed the ethical concerns of the Confucians as worthless and embraced nature rather than man.

But although Taoism poked fun at Confucianism, it was not just a response to that philosophy, but an entirely independent growth with its roots deep in antiquity. Lao Tzu, its reputed founder, is a very insubstantial figure. The rival mythmakers did characteristic jobs on the two great founders; for while Confucian piety made of Confucius a supreme ritualist, unshackled Taoist imagination believed that Lao Tzu (literally 'the old child') was given that name because his mother's pregnancy was so protracted that he emerged from the womb as an old man with a long white beard. Apocryphal stories were told of meetings between the two great men, and Lao Tzu's name was also linked with the Buddha, for he was alleged by Taoists to have taught the founder of the foreign religion after he disappeared on a long journey to the West. It was therefore possible for Taoists to maintain that Buddhism was an imperfectly understood and inferior version of their own doctrine, just as Christian missionaries much later considered that ancient Chinese religion was an inferior version of Christianity spread about in antiquity. About the famous book associated with his name, the *Tao Te Ching* (which Waley translated as the *Classic of the Way and its Power*), there is much dispute, some even thinking that its fundamental philosophy could have been put together as early as the time of Confucius; but it is plainly a composite work, which was probably not assembled until the third century BC. But although Lao Tzu is wrapped in mystery, Chuang Tzu, the other important Taoist figure of antiquity, was a genuine historical character roughly contemporary with Mencius. However, the book named after him is also not a unified piece of work, but a collection of Taoist material mainly featuring Chuang Tzu and sheltering under his name.

It is not easy to give a fully coherent account of Taoism, partly because of inconsistencies arising from the anthological nature of the writings and partly because the central doctrines concerning the nature of the Tao are essentially ineffable; but it is possible to give a schematic impression of the philosophy, which will be sufficient to illustrate its general impact on the Chinese experience. From this point of view it is perhaps more important to linger and cull the anecdotes which cover the foothills of the climb towards truth rather than attempt to scale the unconquerable peaks, for these stories have richly coloured the Chinese imagination.

In contrast with Confucianism, then, Taoism does not regard man and his ethical relationships as of central importance. Instead it tries to see man as a part of nature of no special significance. From the point of view of the Tao nothing in the universe is more important than anything else, and the human value judgements which single man out for special attention are subjective and ephemeral. Thus the harmony with the Tao which the Confucians saw as the goal of man's conscious ethical conduct could, in the Taoist view, only be achieved through the totally unconscious and unintellectual process whereby everything else plays its part in the natural order. In other words, the social disorder of the times could only be cured by a complete abandonment of the idea of social order and a return to a primitive state of nature.

A second fundamental contrast between Confucianism and Taoism concerns man's longing for permanence in a world of constant change. The late Chou period was a time of unprecedentedly violent political, social, and economic upheaval. The Confucian response to this crisis was to seek a return to the Way of the sage kings, the restoration of an ideal and unchanging political order. The Taoist response was meta-physical: they assumed that something permanent underlay that state of flux which disturbs all mortal men if only because of their own mor-tality. In early Taoist thought it is the Tao itself which constitutes the permanence which is present in all things. Man must cling to the fact that all the changes which occur in nature and affect him have a per-manent pattern which he should adapt himself to, so that instead of grieving over loss he sees birth and death as mere incidents in this con-stant pattern of change. Man should not be disturbed by transitory phenomena, but should seek enlightenment about the essence of the Tao which underlies all things, and adapt to the ever-recurring pattern of change as one adapts to the changes of the seasons. The Confucians had wanted to stop the world and fix it in a certain pattern, as their doctrine of the rectification of names illustrated; but the Taoists were content to let themselves float freely on the current of change, which man could not dominate but could adapt to. Even the death of a dear one should not bring grief, so Chuang Tzu was said to have sung when his wife died. His friend, the logician Hui Tzu, reprimanded him: 'You live with someone, she brings up your children and grows old. And then when she dies, you don't weep! Surely that's going far enough, but to drum on a bowl and sing really is going too far!' Chuang Tzu replied that the changes which brought her to life and have now taken her away are like the sequence of the four seasons. 'She will sleep peacefully in the Great Abode. If I were to weep and wail after her, I should be behaving as if I did not understand destiny, and that is why I refrain.'[1]

The central concept of the Tao is not apprehended by reason, but ultimately arrived at by mystical experience. It cannot be explained in words, which can only serve to point one in the right direction. The *Tao Te Ching* describes the Tao as 'existing before Heaven and Earth' and elsewhere as the 'Mother of the Ten Thousand Creatures'[2] (i.e. of all living creatures), but such metaphysical descriptions can be no more than vague clues to the true experience of comprehending and adapting to the Tao, which is described in the very beginning of the *Tao Te Ching* as ineffable: 'A Tao that can be told of is not the permanent Tao.' A commentator on this passage wrote that the 'Tao which can be told of' referred to the Confucian teachings and values, which the Taoists re-garded as artificial. The word Tao in Taoism is by contrast used to serve as name for what is really nameless, the Principle of the Universe, and the Way of living which consists of adapting to it. This Way of living also cannot be described in words, just as a swimmer cannot really describe what he does to keep afloat. Adapting to the Way is a return to natural spontaneous action.

Ordinary knowledge and speech are therefore not adequate tools for dealing with the supreme Principle, but in Taoist writing they are also condemned for another reason: the universe is too vast for the narrow range of human perception. As the *Chuang Tzu* says, 'Our life is limited, but knowledge is limitless. To pursue the limitless by means of the limited is dangerous. To strive for knowledge in spite of that is dangerous indeed!'[3] The only effective kind of knowledge, then, is intuitive, not the kind of partial knowledge which is all that can be gained by the senses. Taoism pursues this line of argument to the conclusion that perfect knowledge is of a mystical kind which ultimately effaces the distinction between the self and the objects of knowledge, so that 'Heaven and Earth were born with me, and the ten thousand things are one with me.'[4]

The mysticism of the Taoists involved going into a state of trance, as we know from the *Chuang Tzu* book. In one passage Confucius finds Lao Tzu in such a condition. 'Did my eyes deceive me or was it really so?' he asked. 'Just now, sir, your body was like a withered tree, as though you had abandoned things, taken leave of men, and were standing in total solitude.' 'Yes', replied Lao Tzu, 'I was letting my mind wander at the origin of all things.'[5] The third great Taoist book, the *Lieh Tzu*, which probably dates from the third century AD, gives a view of the experience from the inside. Lieh Tzu tells how, after many years of initiation, he was no longer aware of any right or wrong or usefulness or harmfulness that could concern himself or others, nor of having a master or a fellow disciple.

Outside and inside were one, and my eyes were like my ears, my ears like my nose, my nose like my mouth – all my senses were alike. I felt as if my mind were solidifying, my body coming apart, and my bones and flesh dissolving. I did not notice what my body leaned against, nor what my feet trod, but let myself be borne east and west by the wind, like a leaf or dry wood-shaving; and finally I could no longer tell whether the wind rode me or whether I rode the wind.[6]

This kind of mystical experience did not bring a vision of the true reality hidden behind the veil of illusion so much as an intuitive awareness of right action in accordance with the Way. Similarly the ordinary commonsense knowledge which the Taoists condemned is primarily knowledge concerned with moral action. Learning for the Taoists as for the Confucians was learning what one ought to do, so in condemning learning they were mainly condemning the moral values held dear by the Confucians. Such concepts, they claimed, did not exist in Nature, which has no concern with man's moral principles. This explains the harshness of the *Tao Te Ching*:

> Heaven and earth are unkind;
> They treat the myriad things as straw dogs.
> The sage is unkind;
> He treats the people as straw dogs.[7]

As Chuang Tzu put it, 'from the point of view of the Tao, things do not have nobility or baseness. From the point of view of things, each considers itself noble and others base'.[8] Just as ideas of size are purely relative, so that 'Heaven and Earth may appear as a tiny grain and the tip of a hair as a mountain',[9] so value judgements are also purely relative. It is only when man forgets about such ephemeral and subjective notions as *jen* (benevolence) that he rediscovers the Tao, and conversely it is only

When the great Tao is abandoned, benevolence and righteousness arise.
When intellect emerges, the great fabrication begins.
When families are in discord, dutiful sons appear.
When the State falls into anarchy, loyal subjects are to be found.
Banish wisdom, discard knowledge, and the people will benefit a hundred-fold.
Banish benevolence, get rid of righteousness, and the people will return to filial piety and kindness.
Banish ingenuity, eschew profit, and there will be no more thieves and brigands.[10]

So it is only when the notion of good is introduced that evil comes along too. One must abandon these distinctions and return to the Tao.

The refusal to make qualitative judgements went hand in hand with a belief in the natural equality of all things, since from the point of view of the Tao everything had its own proper place and function. The Taoist must treat king and beggar alike and must be tolerant of all men and ideas, and all things. This contempt of value judgements meant that the Taoists in their personal lives despised what the world held dear. Stories were told of Chuang Tzu's refusal to become embroiled in worldly affairs as minister in the state of Ch'u.

A thousand pounds of gold [he told the messenger] is a substantial reward, and ministerial rank is an honourable position. But have you alone not seen the ox used for the sacrifice outside the city walls? After being fattened up for several years, it is decked out in embroidered trappings and led into the great temple. At that moment, even if it wanted to change into an orphan piglet, it would be quite impossible. Go away! Do not defile me! I would rather enjoy myself by frolicking in the mire than be haltered by the ruler of a state. To the end of my life I will never take office. Thus I will remain free to follow my own inclinations.[11]

Such stories inspired the long Taoist tradition of staying aloof from public life and living as a recluse. In this matter, it will be remembered, they were not in total opposition to the Confucians, who also advocated withdrawal from office if the Way did not prevail.

The main rule of conduct for Taoism is summed up in the expression '*wu wei*', meaning 'without doing' or 'absence of action', and so often translated as 'non-action'. This paradox is easier to understand when it is remembered that *wei* in ancient Chinese often meant 'act for the sake of', so that 'absence of purposive activity' is a legitimate rendering of the words '*wu wei*'. Action in accordance with the Tao is, as we have already seen, natural and spontaneous rather than conscious and purposeful action. As the *Tao Te Ching* says, 'The Tao never acts, yet there is nothing it does not do.'[12] Everything in nature comes about of itself without conscious action (no creator divinity being presupposed), and the Taoist should behave in accordance with this universal pattern. This applies even to the ruler, indeed it is to the ruler that the *Tao Te Ching* is primarily addressed, as are most of the ancient philosophical books. 'Ruling a large kingdom is like cooking small fish'[13] – for the less interference and stirring up the better – is but one expression of the view that the ruler should not intervene, but let all creatures develop according to their own nature.

The Taoists' regard for spontaneity meant that they had a special appreciation of the kind of skill which is unknowingly applied, like that of the swimmer, or of the butcher who has an unconscious awareness of the Tao of the meat he is chopping and so spontaneously cuts it along the right line. At the same time the concern with non-intervention and non-interference with spontaneous action in accordance with the Tao causes yielding and adaptability to be highly prized qualities. It is only if we are assertive and aggressive rather than adaptable that we can be injured by things outside ourselves.

In the *Tao Te Ching* water is symbolic of the strength of this yielding-ness: 'nothing in the world is softer or weaker than water, yet nothing can surpass it for overcoming the hard and the strong'.[14] Valleys and low-lying places are also symbolically used to represent the Tao, because in them the waters converge. For similar reasons femininity was also highly regarded in the *Tao Te Ching*, despite the values of the feudal society in which it was written.

The total rejection of conventional standards of value implies that useful and useless are the kind of complementary ideas that should be dismissed, but Chuang Tzu ascribed a positive value to uselessness since it ensured survival. He was fond of quoting examples like the tree 'whose trunk is so deformed that one cannot put a measuring line to it, and whose branches are so twisted that one cannot use the square and compass on them. . . . Axes will never shorten its life and nothing will ever harm it. Since there is no use for it, how can it come to grief or pain?'[15] Elsewhere the *Chuang Tzu* says: 'All men know the use of the useful, but they do not know the use of the useless.'[16]

So the Taoist ideal state was a primitive and blissful world unspoilt by value judgements and purposive action, a world before writing was invented, a world in which people

> find their food sweet and their clothes beautiful, are happy with their way of life, and contented with their abodes. Though neighbouring cities are within sight of one another, and the sound of dogs barking and cocks crowing in one can be heard in another, yet the people of one place will reach old age and death without having any dealings with those of another.[17]

For the individual the ideal condition was that of the Taoist sage whose life was so much in tune with the Tao, who participated so fully in the infinity and immortality of nature, that he was completely free of the handicaps of ordinary biological life. Such a person felt as if he were riding on the wind. Those who did not understand the mysteries would take it that the Taoist adept could literally ride on the wind, and so later Taoism would decline into a system of magic practices; but for the initiates this was a way of describing a high degree of attainment of the desired state of unity with the Tao. The journey was really a journey of the mind and the destination was to be free of everything, even the wind, as one was borne aloft on the principles of the universe.

So life and death are just stages in this infinite progression and one should not rejoice at one and mourn at the other. Indeed life itself may be a dream, and once Chuang Tzu claimed not to know whether he was Chuang Tzu dreaming that he was a butterfly or whether he was a butterfly dreaming that he was Chuang Tzu.[18] Man must calmly accept his place in this eternal order, and should no more expect to escape his lot than can metal leap up and insist on being made into a special kind of sword.[19] Man's place in the universal order is not to be seen in the kind of hierarchical terms enamoured of the Confucians, but as described in the *Chuang Tzu* book:

> Your own body is not your possession. . . . It is the form lent to you by Heaven and Earth. Your life is not your possession; it is a harmony granted you by Heaven and Earth. Your nature and destiny are not your possessions; they are the course laid down for you by Heaven and Earth. Your children and grandchildren are not your possessions; Heaven and Earth lent them to you to cast off from your body as an insect sheds its skin. Therefore you travel without knowing where you go, stay without knowing what you are holding to, eat without knowing what you are tasting. You are the breath of Heaven and Earth, so how can you ever gain possession of anything?[20]

This does not mean that human life is futile, but rather that it shares in the magic of the universe.

Thus Taoism confronted the prosaic and conventional moralizing of the Confucians with the weapons of poetry and mysticism. It became the philosophy of privacy and of withdrawal from the cares of that public life for which Confucianism provided the rules. The language of the Confucian Classics is in general earthbound, except for occasional rhetorical passages in which moral qualities are given cosmic importance, but the Taoist writings are full of poetry and paradox, wit and mysticism. It was one of the strengths of Chinese civilization that the Confucian quality of *gravitas* was tempered by the unconventional spirit of Taoism, so that the one could serve man in his public life while the other could console him in his retirement, the one could sustain him at court while the other could inspire his pleasures in painting and poetry, the one could support him in his sober moments while the other could keep him company in his drinking.

Taoism not only gave much to the enrichment of the human personality in China, but also contributed greatly to the history of art and letters. Its concern for nature rather than man also provided a climate conducive to the growth of the natural sciences. The early Taoist writings continued to be read, and in the T'ang Dynasty, which gave official blessing to the philosophy since the royal line claimed descent from Lao Tzu, Taoist literature was even used for a time for the official examinations, Lao Tzu being honoured with the title of Very Noble Celestial and Primordial Emperor. But after a resurgence in the third century AD, when the *Lieh Tzu* book was written, there were no new and original contributions to the high tradition of Taoism. Instead there developed a Taoist religion based on a crude vulgarization of some of the noblest aspirations of the philosophy, since literal-minded men sought means to prolong the physical life instead of seeking the spiritual immortality preached by Chuang Tzu. This they did by special breathing techniques, and gymnastic and sexual practices, all designed to store up the vital energies. Others sought special medicines and food-stuffs to prolong life, and the alchemists busily tried to produce long-life drugs from cinnabar and gold. Lao Tzu came to be generally thought of as an adept at long-life practices. He was also deified and, according to one version, after his death,

his left eye became the sun, his right the moon; his head became the Kunlun Mountains; his beard became the planets and mansions; his bones became the dragons; his flesh became the four-footed animals; his intestines became the serpents; his belly became the sea; his fingers became the Five Peaks; his body hair became the trees and grasses; his heart became the (constellation) Flowery Canopy; and his two kidneys joined together to become the Father and Mother of the Real.[21]

The Taoist contribution to Chinese religion was rich and imaginative but disorganized. It broke up into a multiplicity of sects and also became intermingled with an amorphous popular religion borrowing from many different sources. It followed Buddhism in adopting a monastic system, and in the T'ang there were already over 1600 monasteries in existence.

II

Confucianism and Taoism were poles apart, but a close examination of Mohism shows that it shared many more attitudes with Confucianism than their confrontation in the late Chou period would seem to suggest. Indeed in the Han Dynasty, when the Mohist school no longer posed a threat to the Confucians, the two philosophies were often grouped together.

Nevertheless the *Mo Tzu* book does contain bitter attacks on Con-fucius and the Confucians. The chapters entitled 'Against Confucians' criticize those petty rite-peddling Confucians who 'corrupt men with their elaborate and showy ritual and music and delude relatives with lengthy mournings and fabricated grief'.[22] As for Confucius himself, his broad learning cannot be used to decide what is right for the age, and his laboured thinking cannot assist the people. One could live to a ripe old age and still not master all his learning, and in a long lifetime one could not carry out all his rites; while a massive fortune could not finance his music. With his elaborate showmanship and depraved practices he got control of the rulers of the time, and with his lavish musical performances he corrupted the ignorant people. His doctrines cannot be used to instruct the age, and his learning cannot be used to guide the multitude.[23]

Mo Tzu, a shadowy figure who flourished in the late fifth century BC, is thought by some to have been of plebeian origin, which would explain the frugal and radical tenor of his philosophy.

The central core of the book named after Mo Tzu consisted of eleven doctrines given each in three different versions, possibly representing three different sects within the Mohist school. Several chapters are missing and the text of others is extremely corrupt, but at least one version of each of these doctrines has survived. The content of the anti-Confucian chapters is different in tone from the very general messages conveyed by the other ten doctrines, which can conveniently be divided into three groups, covering the philosopher's attitudes to Heaven, Earth, and Man, the trinity which dominated the ancient Chinese world-view. Or, to put it in modern terms, his philosophy comprised religious, economic, and ethico-political aspects. Mo Tzu's is a well-integrated philosophy, sometimes extraordinarily radical and original, but sadly lacking, as his ancient critics felt, in understanding of the subtleties of human nature. Despite the many attitudes the Mohists shared with the Confucians, it was this lack of understanding which caused Mohism to fail and Confucianism to survive.

The three doctrines concerning Man are entitled Honouring the Worthy, Identifying with Superiors, and Universal Love, the latter being the most famous of the Mohist teachings. The first of these doctrines was in tune with a typical Confucian attitude, and similar arguments are quoted in its support: rulers know they must employ a tailor to make their clothes and a butcher to slaughter animals, but when they see the state in danger, they do not know that they should honour the worthy and employ the capable to deal with the situation, but instead employ relatives, or the wealthy or good-looking. The starting-point for 'Identifying with Superiors' is a Hobbesian state of nature in which every man has his own standards of right or justice (i), which causes mutual recrimination and necessitates the establishment of a Son of Heaven to unify these discordant standards. A hierachy of feudal lords and officials is also established, but these are not to act independently, but must 'identify with their superiors' right up the hierarchy to the Son of Heaven. The way this is to work is proclaimed by the Son of Heaven:

Upon hearing of good and evil a man shall report it all to his superiors. What the superior approves must be totally approved by his subordinates, and what the superior condemns must be totally condemned by his subordinates. If the superior commits any faults, his subordinates shall remonstrate with him, and if his subordinates do good, they shall be commended. Identifying with one's superior and not uniting with subordinates is conduct which shall be rewarded by those above and praised by those below.[24]

This could serve as a text for the more authoritarian Confucianism of imperial China, with its strong condemnation of factionalism and its vision of government as a process whereby advice in the form of memorials is fed to the Son of Heaven, who then takes a decision which all must accept. As to the awkward question of how the most worthy and able man in the world is selected for the job of Son of Heaven, the answer is left vague.

The Mohist doctrine of Universal Love, the last of the three which relate specifically to human relationships, has often been regarded as the principal point of conflict with Confucianism, but the gap between the two philosophies' attitude to love has been exaggerated. Although the Confucians thought that it was natural for a man to show most affection for those nearest and dearest to him, they at the same time felt that the ruler's benevolence should not be reserved for his own kin, but should embrace all within the four seas, and that the virtues which he practised within the family should have their counterpart in his administration of the state. The language in which Mo Tzu talks about universal love is often very Confucian. If we are to be filial sons, we must first make a point of benefiting other men's parents, and then those other men will certainly benefit our parents. So the principle is not 'we must love all equally', but rather 'we must love other men's parents, or families, or states, as our own'.[25] The reciprocal advantages of this are reminiscent of the Confucian doctrine of *shu* (reciprocity), defined in the *Analects* as 'Never do to others what you would not like them to do to you.'[26] So ironically universal love can be seen as a Mohist application of a general Confucian moral rule to family relationships which have seemed to be the concern of the Confucians rather than of the Mohists.

The doctrine of Universal Love is what commended Mo Tzu to the interest of Christian missionaries in nineteenth-century China, but what makes it less than noble as an ethical teaching is the fact that Mo Tzu insisted on the benefit to the doer of practising it. He even went so far as to say that rulers should stimulate universal love by means of rewards and punishments. The utilitarian nature of the doctrine and the way it is advocated in terms of the Confucian relationships is well illustrated by the final paragraph:

The principal of universality is the way of the sage kings, the means of bringing security to rulers and officials and of assuring ample food and clothing to the people. Therefore the best thing for the true gentleman is to study it and strive to put it into practice. If he does, then as a ruler he is bound to be gracious, as a subject loyal, as a father kind, as a son filial, as an elder amiable, and as a younger brother respectful. So if the true gentleman wishes to be a gracious ruler, a loyal subject, a kind father, a filial son, an amiable elder brother, and a respectful younger brother, he must put into practice the principle of universality. It is the way of the sage kings and a great benefit to the people.[27]

The benefit of the people is also to the forefront in a group of chapters which deal with use of the Earth's resources. These are Against Offensive Warfare, Moderation in Expenditure, Moderation in Funerals, and Against Music. Warfare is condemned both because of the waste of resources involved and because of the inconsistency of praising the great unrighteousness of offensive warfare when minor acts of unrighteousness are always condemned. 'Moderation in Expenditure' argues that in the case of houses, clothing, weapons, boats, and carts the merely decorative should be dispensed with and only that which contributes to the basic purpose should be permitted, so that 'wealth is not wasted, people's resources are not exhausted, and yet many are the benefits procured'. 'Moderation in Funerals' also argues that lavish mourning wastes resources and takes people away from their productive occupations. Benevolent men, planning the welfare of the world, seek to enrich the poor, increase the population, and bring order to the world. Elaborate funerals and lengthy mourning will not do any of these things, so they are not in accordance with benevolence and righteousness, and are not the duty of filial sons. Similarly in 'Against Music', this activity is held to be wrong because it uses up resources and manpower and has no purpose in the sense that boats and carts have a purpose. In these doctrines Mo Tzu was completely at odds with the Confucian tradition; for, although Confucius believed in frugality, he also acknowledged the value of the adornments of life, while Mencius took the line that the ruler's pleasures were only wrong if he did not share them with the people, or if they took people away from their work on the land when they could not be spared. It was Mohist extremism that thought they could never be spared, and which caused Hsün Tzu to voice the apposite criticism: 'Mo Tzu was blinded by utility and did not understand culture.'[28]

Finally, in his group of doctrines concerning the supernatural, Mo Tzu differed markedly from Confucius in that he regarded religious sanctions as necessary to ensure correct human behaviour. This aspect of his teaching is covered in three sections entitled the Will of Heaven, Explaining Ghosts, and Against Fatalism. The first of these sections features a loving and all-providing Heaven. It loves the world universally, and seeks to bring benefit to all people. Man must accept the Will of Heaven because Heaven desires righteousness and hates unrighteousness, while man desires good fortune and prosperity and hates misfortune and calamity. To avoid the latter one must do what is right. 'Explaining Ghosts' contains a long attempt to prove from reported instances that ghosts do exist. As often, Mo Tzu starts from the same position as the Confucians: since the ancient sages passed away the world has gone into decline, chaos reigns, and the feudal lords regard might as right. The world remains in disorder because 'people are in doubt whether ghosts and spirits exist, and are not clear that ghosts and spirits are able to reward the worthy and punish the wicked.'[29] If people realized this, how could there be any disorder in the world? Finally, in 'Against Fatalism', Mo Tzu attacks belief in destiny for taking away human incentive and initiative. The Confucians did have a certain belief in fate, but they did not go so far as the advocates of fatalism mentioned in the *Mo Tzu* book, who held that 'if fate decrees that the state will be wealthy, it will be wealthy; if it decrees that it will be poor, it will be poor.'[30]

This section 'Against Fatalism' is noteworthy for describing Mo Tzu's three tests of a theory – its origin, its validity, and its applicability. 'Origin' would be acceptable to the Confucians because it means that one must compare the theory with the deeds of the ancient sages. 'Validity' refers to the evidence of the eyes and ears of the people. A Han Dynasty writer made the apposite criticism that the Mohists indiscriminately believed what they heard and saw and did not exercise judgement on it with their minds. The third criterion, applicability, is judged according to whether a thing brings *li* (profit, benefit) to the state and people. *Li* was an emotive word in antiquity. Mencius sometimes contrasted it with righteousness, but *li* in Mo Tzu did not always mean the kind of selfish concern for advantage that Mencius was attacking, but often the profit of the people in general. This utilitarian spirit does pervade the Mohist philosophy, and indeed it would be true to say that ancient Chinese philosophy in general was about what had utility for society. The rift between the Confucian and Mohist attitudes is that Mo Tzu believed that Heaven rewarded goodness and punished evil, while the Confucians were aware that good is not always rewarded, but believed that this should not distract one from acting morally.

In the end Mohism fizzled out because many of its doctrines were close enough to Confucianism not to warrant a separate existence (and the extent to which Mo Tzu did sponsor Confucian virtues rather than mere utility is often ignored), while his more radical un-Confucian ideas showed an un-Confucian ignorance of human nature. As the *Chuang Tzu* put it:

> Though men sing, he condemns singing. Though men weep, he condemns weeping. Though men enjoy music, he condemns music. Is this truly in accord with man's nature? A life full of toil and a mean death! Such teaching is too harsh. It makes men grieve and sorrow. To practise his teaching is difficult indeed, and I fear it cannot be regarded as the Way of the Sage.[31]

So Mohism faded away until modern times when Christians uncritically admired it for its 'universal love' and revolutionaries thought it preferable to that family-centred Confucianism which seemed to be a great obstacle in the way of social change.

III

Another philosophy too radical and extremist to survive as the creed of a great empire was Legalism, which provided the ideology of the harsh and short-lived Ch'in Dynasty, and was consequently so execrated that it could rarely be advocated in its own right, although it added much to the more authoritarian wing of Confucianism. Confucian philosophers had spoken up for the promotion of men of worth and ability, but had still shown reluctance to turn their faces completely against the hereditary aristocracy. Legalists, in the dark period of the third century BC when the Chinese states were struggling with each other for survival, looked towards the complete displacement of the old ruling classes. As Han Fei Tzu said, 'When scholars versed in the arts of government and competent in the law are employed, powerful ministers of noble birth will inevitably be done away with.'[32] These attitudes had had their antecedents in the introduction in various states of codes of law to replace the old systems of ritual, which implied that aristocrats could do as they liked as long as they did not infringe the ceremonials and conventions. Already too the need to administer conquered territories for the benefit of the state had hastened the replacement of the feudal system by centralized bureaucracies.

The main books which openly advocated these attitudes, and which were later classified as belonging to the Legalist school, were those which went under the names of the seventh-century BC statesman Kuan Tzu, chief minister of Duke Huan of Ch'i, the first of the paramount princes (*pa*); Lord Shang, who reformed Ch'in by Legalist methods in the fourth century; and Han Fei Tzu, of the royal family of the state of Han, who lived in the last decades of the Chou period. The *Kuan Tzu* and *Book of Lord Shang* were late Chou compilations sheltering under those worthies' names, but the text of the *Han Fei Tzu* largely came from his own pen. He was stimulated to composition because he was prevented from putting across his ideas orally by a frustrating stutter, a grave handicap at a time when eloquent advisers were much in demand to help restore order to a chaotic world. His book provides a fairly comprehensive survey of Legalist ideas. Legalist writings are intended specifically for the ruler, to enable him to preserve and strengthen the state. They reject the traditional Confucian virtues, and advocate that the state be ordered by an exhaustive legal code, impartially administered and sanctioned by severe punishments and generous rewards. To strengthen the state they stress the promotion of agriculture, and openly support aggressive warfare.

The impact of Legalism on the Chinese experience may most conveniently be considered under two headings: its attitude to the traditional culture, and the methods it advocates for the control of the state. Its hostility to Confucianism and indeed to culture in general showed that Legalism, rather like Mohism, had too shallow an understanding of human nature to have much impact on the history of a state with a high civilization; but its methods of state control never lost their relevance in later Chinese history, since Confucianism, whose message made most sense in the family and small community, could not hope to administer a great empire without the admixture of a powerful dose of Legalism.

Many of the favourite Confucian ideals are attacked unmercifully in the Legalist writings. 'If the ruler employs only worthy men, then his ministers will depend on their worthiness to intimidate him'[33] is a sentiment which must have struck a chord in the hearts of many an autocrat faced with a powerful minister self-righteously mouthing Confucian platitudes. In any case the principal Confucian virtues do not get one very far, for Confucius

> perfected his conduct, illuminated the Way, and thus journeyed about the world, but those within the seas who were delighted by his benevolence, and attracted by his righteousness, and who served him as his disciples were only seventy. . . . Yet when scholars of the present time counsel a ruler, they say that he must not rely on wielding authority, which is sure to bring success, but instead that he must devote himself to the practice of benevolence and righteousness before he can become a true king. This is, in effect, to demand that the ruler must reach the standard of Confucius, so that all the ordinary people of the time are like Confucius's disciples. Such a policy is bound to fail.[34]

Elsewhere Han Fei Tzu berates the Confucians because they do not praise measures which will bring order today, but talk only of the achievements of men who brought order in the past. Benevolence and righteousness served in ancient times, but are no longer relevant today. They may be all very well for the private individual, but they are against the interests of the state.[35]

So the Legalists coldly disregarded all moral values. They accepted the low view of human nature which Hsün Tzu, who was once Han Fei Tzu's teacher, had seemed to hold; but unlike the Confucians they had no regard for the power of education to transform it. They took the view that man is totally self-seeking, and cited as evidence for this view parents' attitude to children of different sexes: because they thought only of their later convenience, boy children were always welcomed but girls were sometimes put to death. Men could only be motivated towards desirable ends by fear of punishment and eagerness to obtain reward, so these must lie at the heart of a ruler's method of controlling the population.

Naturally Yao and Shun were also dismissed as irrelevant, since the Legalists were only interested in how an ordinary ruler of the day could control his state. A Yao might turn up once in several centuries, but to tell people in their present plight that they must wait for a Yao was like telling a drowning man to wait for an expert swimmer to come from a distant state. Yao and Shun were also to be condemned for surrendering their thrones to mere common people. In any case, as the *Book of Lord Shang* put it, 'Former generations did not adopt the same doctrines, so which antiquity should one imitate?'[36] Like other early Chinese thinkers, Han Fei Tzu speculated about the original state of nature and the ancient sages who provided mankind with those inventions which were basic to human needs or who performed great feats in the service of mankind, like Yü who cleared the floods. But he argues that one must not revere these past achievements. They were right for their own age, but the sage of today has to deal with the affairs of today. In any case, if order prevailed in antiquity it was not, as the Confucians maintained, because the ancient sages knew the Way, but because there was a much smaller population. 'In ancient times,' said Han Fei Tzu, 'husbands did not till the fields, for the seeds of grass and the fruit of trees were enough to eat. Wives did not weave, for the skins of birds and beasts were enough to wear. They got enough to live on without effort. The people were few and there was an abundance of resources, so they did not compete with each other for them.'[37] This all contrasts sharply with the Confucian conception of a rather static world whose problems can be solved by looking back to the Way of the ancient sages. As the *Book of Lord Shang* put it, 'there is not just one Way to govern the world and there is no need to imitate antiquity in order to benefit the state.'[38] It was rare indeed for such bold hostility to historical precedent to be expressed later in Chinese history. The anti-evolutionary view is put at its most absurd in the words of a ninth-century commentator on Hsün Tzu: 'The oxen and horses of today are not different from those of antiquity. Why then should it be only when we come to man that there should be a difference?' In matters of political philosophy it took an exceptional spirit to swim strongly against the Confucian tide; and even out-and-out reformers had to pretend that Confucius was himself a radical in order to get their ideas accepted.

Han Fei Tzu's hostility to culture was partly stimulated by reaction against the people in the state who were not engaged in the productive occupations which kept it strong, and especially the large class of travelling scholars who thronged the courts of the day. 'Those who talk about agriculture are many, but those who hold the plough are few,' he said. His great antipathy to culture is explained in a passage which runs:

Now if one cultivates literary pursuits or becomes practised in the art of persuasive speaking, then one has the fruits of wealth without the labour of ploughing, and one has the honour of high rank without the danger of battle. In that case who will not take up such pursuits? Thus there will be a hundred men engaged on wisdom for every one who makes use of his physical strength.

If those engaged on wisdom are many, the laws will be defeated, and if those who make use of their physical strength are few, the state will be poor; and this is how the age becomes disordered. Therefore the state of an enlightened ruler has no books written on bamboo slips, but treats law as the source of instruction. It has no sayings of the former kings, but treats officials as teachers.[39]

So, like the Taoists, Han Fei Tzu goes in for primitive simplicity as opposed to culture, but in his case it is advocated for the harsh purposes of state control rather than as the logical consequence of a profound conception of the universal order. Moreover the state of simplicity would not be shared by the rulers, who would manipulate the people rather than share in their conformity with the universal Way. There is also something in common with Mohist utilitarianism, except that Mo Tzu, wisely perceiving his own vulnerability to the argument against indulging in intellectual activities rather than physical labour, did put the case in favour of being a teacher and teaching men to plough, since if one man ploughed and did not teach others to plough, this would not do much towards feeding the world's hungry.[40]

To turn now to the positive aspects of the Legalists' teaching, the first matter to discuss is the concept of Law, which gives them their Chinese name, which literally means 'School of Law'. In English the word 'law' has benevolent connotations. We think of the law as something which safeguards the rights of the individual. In science the Western tradition used to assume the existence of a celestial law-giver laying down the laws of nature, which the scientist had to decipher. In China, on the other hand, law was seen as a harsh and unbending system of control, which needed mitigating by the humane and flexible qualities of Confucianism. This is partly because of the oppressiveness of the Legalist-inspired Ch'in regime, but long before that, when law codes were first introduced in the Chinese states, the mechanistic and inhuman conception of law they enshrined was being bitterly opposed by Confucian sentiment, which believed in making allowance for circumstances. The essence of the Legalists' policy was to make law so rigid and detailed that no element of personal decision was left to the implementer. A fallacious analogy which often occurs in ancient Chinese writings is that between craftsmanship and social organization. 'Though a skilled carpenter is capable of judging a straight line with his eye alone, he will always take his measurements with square and compasses,' says Han Fei Tzu. 'Though a man of superior wisdom is capable of handling affairs by native wit alone, he will always look to the laws of the former kings for guidance.'[41] He goes on later: 'The law does not lean towards men of high station any more than the plumbline bends to fit a crooked place in the wood. What the law has imposed the wise man cannot dispute nor the brave man dare to contest.' Han Fei Tzu's answer to the Confucians' advocacy of virtue was: 'Those who rule must employ measures that will be effective with the majority and discard those that will be effective with only a few. Therefore they devote themselves not to virtue but to law.'[42]

So the great weakness of the Legalist conception of law was the belief that human beings could be manipulated by the law just as easily as weights and measures were standardized in the Ch'in Dynasty. To a surprising degree the Legalists had alienated themselves from the concept of human society as an organism which needed nurturing and keeping in a balanced, healthy state, which is characteristic of the ancient Chinese world view; and, having abandoned that, they were lost without any true guidelines to an understanding of human behaviour. Also their faith in the possibility of introducing a system of law so detailed and precise that it could apply itself without the ruler having any more to do conflicts strangely with their radical belief that the constant evolution of human society implied the need to look for solutions for today rather than to rely on antiquity. However, the Legalists had reached this position by reflecting on the increasing complexity of administration. As Han Fei Tzu put it, 'If the ruler of men personally checks all the various offices of his government, he will find the day not long enough and his energies insufficient.'[43] They found ready to hand the Taoist doctrine of non-action (*wu wei*) which they were able to adapt for their political purposes: 'The ruler firmly bars his inner door, and from his room surveys the courtyard; he has provided the rules and yardsticks, so that all things know their place. Those who merit reward are rewarded, and those who deserve punishment are punished. Reward and punishment follow the deed, and each man brings them upon himself.'[44]

Another important concept in the Legalist philosophy is *shu*, the art or method of governing, the ruler's means of administrative control. The Legalists recognized that the ties of blood, loyalty, and the rites, which had bound ruler to minister under the old system which they wished to destroy, had to be replaced by other means of controlling the growing bureaucracies needed to administer large states; and it is these means which are referred to as *shu*. An important ingredient in this concept is the old idea of rectification of names, which had interested ancient

Chinese thinkers from both the ethical and the logical points of view, and was now being adapted to the needs of politics. As the *Kuan Tzu* put it, 'When names and actualities are in accord with each other, there is good government. When they are not in accord with each other, there is disorder.' In the Legalist context, actualities meant the acts performed by an individual in office, and names the name of the office and the duties he was expected to perform. The two had to correspond exactly if good order were to be maintained. The Legalists also emphasized the *shih* (power, authority) which derived from the ruler's position as ruler, and enabled him to deal out appropriate rewards and punishments.

Han Fei Tzu referred to the 'two handles' of reward and punishment whereby the ruler controls his ministers, and emphasized the need for severe punishment and generous rewards. 'In bestowing rewards,' he wrote, 'the enlightened ruler is as benign as the seasonable rain, and all men profit from his bounty. But in inflicting punishment, he is as terrible as the thunder.'⁴⁵ Again the policy lacks understanding of human psychology. 'The ultimate goal of penalties is that there shall be no penalties,'⁴⁶ as the *Book of Lord Shang* puts it. The doctrine is closely related to the 'rectification of names'. If name and actuality tally precisely, then a man is to be rewarded; if not, even if he has done more than required of him, he shall be punished.

The Legalists were also responsible for inventing the system of mutual responsibility, which in later ages became an important method of social control. In the words of Ssu-ma Ch'ien, the state of Ch'in introduced legislation

> that the people be organized into groups of families, which should be mutually responsible for each other's good behaviour and share each other's punishments. Anyone who did not denounce a culprit would be cut in two at the waist; anyone who denounced a culprit would receive the same reward as if he had cut off the head of an enemy soldier; anyone who harboured a culprit would receive the same punishment as if he had surrendered to the enemy.⁴⁷

These methods were all designed to help the ruler to control the state. To strengthen it, the Legalists laid stress on agriculture and warfare. They firmly insisted on the priority of agriculture, and had no use for scholars, merchants, and artisans, who did not engage in the primary tasks of producing food and clothing. Han Fei Tzu picked out five groups as the 'vermin of the state': scholars who praised the Way of the ancient kings, speechmakers who propounded false schemes, swordsmen who gathered private bands of followers about them, evaders of military service, and merchants and artisans, who exploited farmers by waiting for the best time to sell.[48] Confucianism agreed in regarding agriculture as the primary pursuit and in being hostile to the merchants. But Legalists did not have the traditional low opinion of soldiers. Indeed the *Book of Lord Shang* glorified warfare in the most forthright fashion:

The people that looks to warfare as a ravening wolf looks at a piece of meat is a people that can be used. In general fighting is a thing that the people detest. A ruler who can make the people delight in war will become king of kings. In a country that is really strong a father will send his son, the elder brother his younger brother, the wife her husband, all saying as they speed him: 'Conquer, or let me never see you again!'[49]

In peacetime the 'six maggots' of Rites and Music, the *Book of Songs* and the *Book of History*, and the various Confucian virtues would thrive and the state would be ruined. Such attitudes eventually helped to bring Ch'in out on top in the struggle between the Warring States, and in 221 BC it was able to complete its conquest of the other states, and inaugurate the Ch'in Dynasty. Its ruler, Ch'in Shih Huang Ti, set about creating the vast bureaucratic empire Han Fei Tzu had dreamed of. He introduced harsh laws, standardized weights, measures, and the writing system, suppressed other philosophies, devoted huge resources to public works, including the Great Wall and the magnificent palaces which enabled him to hide himself away with the air of aloofness appropriate to the Legalist concept of an enlightened ruler. The Ch'in Dynasty, its ruler boasted, was at last a time when actualities had been put into strict correspondence with names.

It was not long before the Chinese people rejected the harshness of the Ch'in regime and its over-hasty attempt to remove all traces of the old feudalism. *Li* (ritual) gradually regained its importance and, although law codes were necessary, they were modified in practice by the concept of *li*. But Legalism later had a big and lasting influence: the bureaucratic principle on which the empire would operate had already been stated firmly and unequivocally in the *Book of Lord Shang*: 'Neither in high nor in low grades should there be hereditary succession to the offices, ranks, lands, or emoluments of officials.'[50] The Legalists also contributed a strong awareness that, with the growing complexity of government, specialist knowledge and skills were required, and that virtue was not enough, as the Confucians seemed sometimes to suggest. The dominant ideology of the Chinese state was a mixture of Confucianism and Legalism, but because of the Chinese experience under the Ch'in, the Legalist contribution could not be acknowledged.

CHAPTER 6

BUDDHISM

I

To complete this survey of the foundations of China's philosophical experience it is necessary to give some account of Buddhism, the only foreign system of thought which made a profound impact on Chinese civilization before modern times. In the T'ang period, which was the time of its greatest influence, it coloured many aspects of life in China; and, even after it waned, its influence on the beliefs and practices of the Chinese people remained strong. It was spoken of as one of the Three Doctrines, the three great systems of thought which dominated Chinese society, the other two being Confucianism and Taoism. Chinese Buddhist literature is vast and little known in the West, and no volume like this can possibly do justice to its profound insights. But in the context of this book this does not greatly matter, since the subtleties of Buddhist thought, although deeply influencing intellectuals like the poet Po Chü-i who lived at the time of its apogee, did not become a normal part of the intellectual furniture of the literati in later ages. We shall see something of the confrontation between Buddhism and the rival systems of Confucianism and Taoism; but the importance of Buddhism for this study lies also in non-philosophical areas of the Chinese experience, such as the conflict of Buddhist monasticism with the interests of the state and the story of how followers of a religion which believed in withdrawal from the world were made to accept state control just as they accepted state patronage; and the influence of Buddhism on art, literature, social and economic life, and popular religion. But first we must see how this alien religion was able to take root in Chinese soil.

The first signs of Buddhism in China date from the first century of our era. The Former Han Dynasty had adapted the Confucianism of pre-imperial times by incorporating other beliefs into a system which provided an ideology appropriate to a confident and successful empire, but it was ill-suited to a period of social disintegration such as occurred in the declining years of the Later Han. By that time the economic development and political expansion of the Former Han had fostered widespread external trade, and merchants from the predominantly Buddhist areas of Central Asia found themselves living in the Chinese capital and other major cities. The Buddhist faith gradually spread from these foreign communities to the Chinese, and this development gathered pace as increasing social and political disintegration left a vacuum for new beliefs to provide consolation in times of suffering. When the Han finally collapsed neither of the three succession states was able to impose its will on the others, and eventually the whole of the north of China, including the Yellow River basin – the ancient home of Chinese culture with its great cities like Changan and Loyang – was completely overrun by non-Chinese tribesmen; while a series of feeble exiled dynasties reigned in the Yangtze Valley, which at this time was still a sparsely populated frontier area. In these circumstances, Confucianism survived mainly because it was the only suitable ideology under which the empire could conceivably be re-established; but for personal consolation many were drawn to Taoism and to this new foreign religion, whose very foreignness was an attraction to the barbarian rulers of the various competing north Chinese dynasties, who preferred an alien faith to the danger of being swamped by Chinese ideas.

On the surface no culture could seem more alien to China than the Indian culture from which Buddhism emerged. The languages are poles apart, for Sanskrit is alphabetic, highly inflected, polysyllabic, and has a very complicated grammatical system; while Chinese is written in ideograms, is basically monosyllabic and uninflected, and has an extremely economical grammatical system. Chinese literature, despite Taoism, is comparatively earthbound, while Indian takes off in flights of imagination; China was this-worldly, while the Indian tradition pursued other-worldly goals; China dealt with historical timespans, India with cosmic eons; and China was concerned with family ethics, while India was devoted to universal salvation. How was this great gulf to be crossed?

The initial success is partly explained by the fact that the Chinese who first became interested in Buddhism regarded it not as a foreign religion so much as an offshoot of Taoism; and the religion's domestication was further assisted by the fact that Taoist terms had to be used to translate the key concepts of Buddhism. At the same time Buddhism at this early stage appealed to the general human desire for salvation and the protection of powerful gods, instead of attempting to propagate very specific Indian ideas. The Neo-Taoist influence was very effective in preparing the way for Buddhism in the Chinese-held south; but in the north, as has been said already, the barbarian rulers preferred to lend an ear to foreign proponents of a foreign religion rather than become too dependent on Chinese advisers. Buddhist monks also (like eunuchs at the imperial palace or clerics at European courts) had the attraction of having no family attachments to provide another focus of loyalty, and so they seemed likely to prove trustworthy servants. Consequently these proponents of an unwordly religion were soon drawn into politics, which they were glad to embrace for the opportunity it gave them of securing patronage for their faith.

The credulous barbarian chieftains were not, of course, won for Buddhism by the exposition of metaphysical subtleties, but by the monks' apparently magical powers. The performance of miracles persuaded the superstitious rulers not only of the efficacy of their Buddhist counsellors but also of the power of the Buddhist deities to protect the state, which remained the important reason for imperial patronage of Buddhism even in the more sophisticated era of the T'ang. Magical practices were also a feature of Buddhism in its Indian birthplace; and great pilgrims, scholars, and translators did not abide permanently on the higher plane of doctrine, but descended to perform their various party tricks. The famous monk and translator Kumarajiva, for example, was an adept at swallowing needles, a skill he often displayed before hosts of awed spectators. And when the pilgrim Hsüan-tsang went to India he saved himself from being killed by pirates by concentrating his thoughts on Maitreya in the Tushita Heaven, with the miraculous consequence that a great wind arose, and the waters of the Ganges mounted and capsized the pirates' ships, which made them repent and become lay members of the Buddhist community. Performances of magic were featured among the entertainments at the great Buddhist festivals, and this interest in magic stemmed naturally from the fact that Buddhist philosophy considered the world to be an illusion.

In addition to attracting state patronage, magic also had a powerful appeal for the common people. In troubled times monasticism was also a great attraction; for it meant renunciation of the cares of the world, and freedom from the obligation to pay taxes and do compulsory labour or military service. At their lowest the monasteries became havens for draft-dodgers, but at the highest level the monastic vocation – withdrawal from the world's cares to a life of contemplation, scholarship, and devotion amid remote mountain scenery, with the aim of working in accordance with the Mahayana ideals for the salvation of all creatures – was a vocation which attracted men of lofty scholarship and fine personal qualities, the kind of men who in better times would have worked within the Confucian tradition.

In the very early development of Buddhism in China the Hinayana (Smaller Vehicle) teaching had predominated. This was closer to the original heart of Buddhism as founded by the Indian prince Gautama Sakyamuni, who lived in the sixth and fifth centuries BC. Abandoning his luxurious existence for a life of religious devotion, he attained a state of enlightenment and was henceforth known as the Buddha (the Enlightened One). The central belief of his teaching was that life is suffering, that suffering is caused by desire, and desire can be banished by following the Buddhist rules for right living. Those rules are summed up in the 'noble eightfold path', consisting of right views, right intentions, right speech, right action, right livelihood, right effort, right mindfulness, and right concentration. According to the doctrine of *karma*, living beings go through an endless cycle of rebirths; and the state into which they are born in the next existence (whether deity, man, animal, hungry ghost, or denizen of hell) depends on their conduct in the present existence. The final goal is to break the endless chain of existence through the ending of all desires. This is the state known as *nirvana*.

Hinayana Buddhism thus stresses the individual's pursuit of his own salvation as well as the remoteness of this goal, for an individual has to go through countless existences and rebirths before attaining *nirvana*. It was only with the development of the faith in its Mahayana (Greater Vehicle) form, which preached pity for all creatures and salvation for all humanity as the only possible means of achieving personal salvation, that Buddhism in China could be transformed into a mass religious movement which reacted to the disillusion of the times by uniting all men in a dream of universal salvation. This universalized faith could be made to seem much warmer than Confucian family-based ethics and could give great solace at a time of social disintegration, while the belief in the endless revolution of the wheel of *karma*, which implied reward in the next life to make up for undeserved suffering in this, could give comfort at a time when nothing seemed just and nothing seemed enduring. In time salvation became too easy for some, for according to the popular cult of Amitabha Buddha it was only necessary to invoke his name to achieve this goal, the opposite extreme from the eons which had originally seemed necessary.

The growth of understanding of Buddhist doctrine was dependent on the production of good translations of the voluminous scriptures. Early efforts were crude and unsatisfactory because the missionaries knew little Chinese and their Chinese collaborators knew no Indian language, so that the ideas of founders of Chinese schools of Buddhism have to be understood largely in the context of Chinese intellectual history. But some remarkable translations were achieved by such men as Kumarajiva, who in the early fifth century headed a huge and highly structured translation team; and the seventh-century pilgrim-translator Hsüan-tsang, one of whose projects was said to be eighty-four times the length of the Bible, (frightful nightmares, in which he was on the edge of an abyss being attacked by wild animals, warned him that he must not make a single cut). Hsüan-tsang was exceptional in having a knowledge of Sanskrit; but however skilful and conscientious such work was, the process of translation was bound to be an adaptation of Buddhism to Chinese ideas, for Buddhist terms had to be translated into indigenous Chinese ones, so that, for example, *wu wei* (the Taoist 'non-action') was used to stand for the Buddhist *nirvana*.

But what happened in the case of the hard core of essential Buddhist beliefs which were diametrically opposed to Confucian attitudes and so completely unacceptable to the indigenous culture? For example, monasticism must be completely hostile to the ideals of filial piety, which taught that one must stay at home to care for one's parents and must procreate children to continue the family sacrifices. Even the tonsure could be considered unfilial, because it was wrong to mutilate in any way the body a man has received from his parents. On the other hand the apologists for Buddhism could counter such arguments by pointing to ancient heroes who had not married but had been praised by Confucius for their wisdom and benevolence.

To show that Buddhism positively favoured filial piety, the Buddhists drew special attention to canonical writings which laid stress on that virtue. One such work was given a commentary which tried to show that Buddhism as well as Confucianism regarded filial piety as the highest of virtues. 'That which began during the primordial chaos and now saturates heaven and earth, unites man and deity, connects the high and the low, and is revered alike by the Confucians and the Buddhists, is none other than filial piety,'[1] says this commentary, which also refers to the Buddha himself as having left home to cultivate the Way and having become enlightened to pay for the love and kindness of his parents. Another sutra claimed that the Buddha, after attaining enlightenment, spent three months preaching the law to his deceased mother in the Trayastrimsa heaven before descending to earth to resume his mission among men. In addition to the use of genuine material, some sutras stressing filial piety were forged to help commend Buddhism to Confucian sentiment.

Chinese Buddhists also maintained that their concept of filial piety was superior to the Confucian one because, whereas the Confucians merely attended to the physical needs of their parents and strove to be a credit to them, the Buddhists aimed at converting their parents to Buddhism with all the blessings which that would involve. Moreover the Buddhist monk was aiming at salvation not only for his parents but for all living creatures. Because of the cycle of rebirth, which means that living beings are continuously being reborn in various modes of existence, all beings must be looked on as equal; and therefore the Buddhist must aim at universal salvation, for success will mean that his own ancestors, whatever their present mode of existence, and the ancestors of others will be saved. Thus, rather like Mo Tzu in antiquity, the Buddhists considered that this universalization of the sentiment of filial piety was vastly superior to the graded love of Confucianism. As a Chinese Buddhist text put it, 'Buddhism teaches filial piety in order that its followers will reverence all parents under Heaven. It teaches loyalty in order that its followers will reverence all the ruling princes under heaven.' (So much for the Buddhist belief in withdrawal from the world and denial of duties to earthly rulers!) The Buddhists thought they were teaching a more extended and nobler view of filial piety than the Confucians; and, on a more practical level, despite their withdrawal from family life, they did make concessions to Confucian susceptibilities by taking part in the rituals of ancestor worship. Buddhists also tried in various ways to correlate the five cardinal precepts of their religion with the five Confucian virtues. These were not to kill, not to steal, not to commit adultery, not to tell lies, and not to drink intoxicating liquor; so it took much ingenuity to match them with benevolence, righteousness, propriety, knowledge, and good faith.

As the religion gathered large numbers of adherents, not only those who took the vows, but also laymen whose pious gifts contributed to the increasing prosperity of the monasteries, so the state was bound to become increasingly concerned about the presence within its iurisdiction

THE CHINESE EXPERIENCE

of large groups of people claiming exemption from the ordinary
duties of the population and apparently contributing nothing to the
economic well-being of the community. Moreover Buddhism, like
Christianity in the Roman empire, presented the novel phenomenon of
a religion of foreign origin privately and voluntarily embraced by
individuals, as opposed to the traditional concept of state religious
ceremonies under the ultimate authority of the Son of Heaven.

At the same time, despite Buddhist attempts to plead innocence,
monasticism was charged with violation of the kinship system which was
at the very heart of Confucian morality; so that, for example, in the
Ch'ing Dynasty it was a punishable offence to become a monk if one
came from a family with less than three males. The growth of the
monasteries also got completely out of hand, for huge numbers of peasants took their vows in order to escape the crushing burden of taxation
and conscription, while the rich and powerful also took shelter in
monastic life to shed the burdens of taxation or their public responsibilities. Officials complained bitterly of the sumptuous life of the
monasteries, grown fat as the state became impoverished. Such a situation was seen as a threat to the state, and indeed Buddhist-inspired
armed rebellions frequently occurred during the Six Dynasties period,
and later in history large monasteries remote from secular influence
were often suspected of concealing caches of arms. Ideologically, too,
Buddhism had doctrines which could lend support to rebels. Worshippers
of Maitreya, the future Buddha, thought that the end of the world was
at hand and that his descent would inaugurate a new heaven and new
earth. This was not conducive to contentment with existing temporal
regimes; and there were other subversive doctrines which helped to
inspire popular rebellions, which were often characterized by an ideal
of universal salvation which was obviously inspired by Buddhism. All
these were powerful reasons why the state should seek to control the
foreign religion.

Looking at it from the Buddhist point of view, when one joined the
sangha or monastic community and undertook the vows of celibacy,
poverty, subsistence on alms, and the cultivation of monastic discipline,
one felt no longer obliged to pay homage to the ruler. Indeed in India
it had been the custom for secular rulers to pay homage to the cleric,
as the pilgrim Hsüan-tsang found when the powerful King Harsha,
emperor of all India, kissed his feet. Such a practice was totally at odds
with the Chinese view that homage to the emperor was part of the
ethical system which underlay the universal order. Monks might argue

122

that their religious lives were of benefit to the state, and that they must flee the attachments of the world if they were to be rid of desire and suffering and work out their salvation and that of all living beings, thereby bringing great benefit to all-under-Heaven; but in the end the Chinese view that all-under-Heaven was part of an integrated universal order would ensure that Buddhism was absorbed into that order just as surely as, on the more pragmatic level, the state could not afford the large-scale tax-evasion which Buddhism implied. After a long controversy the Buddhists in 662 won their claim not to pay homage to the ruler, but in the meantime the true independence of the Buddhist *sangha* had been eroded in several ways, so that this appears as a mere concession to their *amour propre*.

Because uncontrolled entry into the *sangha* meant that too many took the vows, the state had gradually taken over the supervision of ordination, which in India had always been a matter solely for the individual and the Buddhist community. At the end of the fourth century the Northern Wei Dynasty had already established a government bureau to supervise the monastic community, when the monk in charge defended his acceptance of this innovation by claiming that he was not paying homage to the emperor, but was honouring one whose wisdom and adherence to the Buddhist faith entitled him to be regarded as a Buddha incarnate. Under these bureaucratic arrangements ordinations were limited and monks and nuns had to be registered. Although it was specifically condemned by the Buddhist scriptures, registration was also enforced under the T'ang; and the state also took responsibility for certifying the ordination of monks, which might be granted either by imperial grace or as the result of examination. This policy was nullified when ordination certificates were sold as a means of hurriedly raising revenue after the An Lu-shan rebellion. The state also took upon itself the power to defrock monks, and many purges took place to get rid of undesirable elements and of those who had no serious knowledge of the religion they professed. In the T'ang Dynasty, supervision of the *sangha*, which had previously been in the hands of monks, passed into the control of government offices run by lay officials, and bureaucratic supervision by the state was to persist until modern times. The construction of temples and monasteries, which had previously been a matter of individual piety, also began to be regarded as a matter for the state. Such buildings were given official charters, and increasingly the Chinese rulers, especially those of the Sui and the T'ang saw the value of establishing temples under imperial auspices in order to harness

Buddhism to the service of the state by means of their patronage. At the same time the monks became increasingly subject to secular laws rather than to their own code of conduct, and restrictions were placed on their movements and activities.

Finally, members of the Buddhist community found themselves playing an overtly political role in the service of the state. Installed in chapels within the palace, they were required both to minister to the royal family and to recite the scriptures for the protection of the state against disasters. The Japanese monk Ennin who visited China in the ninth century reported that in one of the imperial palaces three sets of seven monks were picked out and 'assigned in rotation to perform devotions there each day without cease, both day and night'.[2] To justify this standing precaution against mishap the Chinese government was able to quote a sutra which had a section 'on the protection of the state' in which the Buddha had advocated such means of warding off disaster.[3] Thus the monks served as the religious arm of the government to ensure that the spiritual forces would work for the benefit of the empire. At the same time monks served in the national Buddhist monasteries established for the celebration of the imperial cult, in which memorial services for the departed imperial ancestors were conducted. This kind of activity really had nothing to do with Buddhism, but followed from the policy of Sui and T'ang rulers to harness the powerful deities of Buddhism in the service of the state and at the same time claim credit among many devout Buddhists for their patronage of the religion.

Special use of this device was made by the Empress Wu, who, needing justification for female rule, which certainly could not be found in the Confucian canon, sponsored the establishment of Great Cloud Monasteries throughout the country, named after a sutra in which Buddha predicts that a certain female deity will be reborn in a future age as a universal monarch. The monks of these monasteries assiduously fostered the claim that the Empress Wu was a reincarnation of the Buddha Maitreya, come down to earth in accordance with this prediction. In earlier times, during the Six Dynasties period when Confucianism was in eclipse, the rich Buddhist store of legend had provided a new model of royal conduct in the Cakravartin king, who ruled well through devotion to the Buddha. This model not only appealed to the shaky courts of this era, but also strongly influenced the Sui founder, who was born in a Buddhist temple and cared for in his early years by a nun, and who later patronized the foreign faith as well as the revived Confucianism specifically needed as an ideology for the more mundane aspects of imperial government. The most famous of Buddhist monarchs, however, had been Emperor Wu of the Liang Dynasty, who reigned throughout the first half of the sixth century. He took Buddhist vows and was called such names as Emperor Bodhisattva and Bodhisattva Son of Heaven in recognition of his attempt to combine the Buddhist and traditional Chinese ideals of kingship.

By the time of his reign, Buddhism had gained a hold on the lives and thoughts of people of all classes. For the rich there was an opportunity to display their wealth and work for their own salvation in the construction of splendid temples, and for the poor there was a chance to escape from the harshness of reality whether in the haven of the tax-exempt monastery or in the comfort of the layman's belief in easy salvation through calling on the name of the Buddha. For the intellectuals there was a rich literature and scholarly tradition to which they could apply themselves with the traditional techniques of Chinese scholarship, as well as a faith to meet their disillusionment with a world in which the Way seemed to be lost for ever. In the T'ang too the religion grew in strength until the great persecution of 845, which permanently weakened it. It is now necessary to understand the impact of Buddhism on various aspects of Chinese life at this period of its greatest influence, and visualize the long-term effects of Buddhist teachings on the Chinese experience.

II

In the development of its teachings Chinese Buddhism predictably owes very much to native Chinese intellectual traditions. One of the main problems facing the Chinese was that an enormous corpus of literature embodying a great variety of doctrines emanating from numerous different sects was translated into Chinese; so it was difficult to see how all this could have been preached by one man. But the strong historical sense inherent in the native tradition enabled scholars to work out a means of assigning the scriptures to different periods in the life of the Buddha, bearing in mind not only the evolution of his doctrine, but also the need to adapt his teaching to different types of audience. It was the T'ien-t'ai school, founded in the sixth century, which undertook this task of forming a comprehensive school of Buddhism which would incorporate the diverse teachings attributed to the Buddha.

Another process in the sinicization of Buddhism, which ran contrary to this comprehensive, encyclopaedic approach, was the development of a characteristically Chinese form of scholasticism, whereby a sect would devote itself entirely to the exposition of one particular text and regard it as the authoritative word of the Buddha. This approach derived naturally from the Chinese tradition of commentary on the Confucian Classics and other works of basic importance. The third important development in Chinese Buddhism was a growth of faith in the benefits which might be conferred by the Buddha and the bodhisatt-vas, whose favour could be won by building temples, copying sacred texts, paying for images to be made, and by other methods of accumu-lating merit.

The excessive concern for the external trappings of religion, whether in the form of the construction of temples and images or of devotion to textual criticism, prompted a reaction in the shape of a school which wanted to go back and seek the original essence of Buddhism. This was the Ch'an or meditation school (Zen in Japanese), which argued that the essential component of Buddhism was meditation, which was how the Buddha himself had attained enlightenment. Through meditation we can awaken the Buddha nature that is in all of us and achieve enlightenment. This hostility to learning and scriptural studies had its roots in the native Taoist tradition. And just as the Taoists had tried to shock their opponents, as when Chuang Tzu played and sang after his wife had died, so the Ch'an masters paradoxically tried to shake their followers out of excessive reliance on external support in achieving spiritual progress by declaring that the Buddha was a barbarian devil and the bodhisattvas dung-heap coolies. Artists also gave vivid expres-sion to this attitude, as in Liang K'ai's picture of the patriarch Hui-neng tearing up the scriptures.

The Ch'an doctrine had a strong appeal for lay intellectuals, and T'ang poets often referred to their relations with Ch'an masters and their retreats in Ch'an monasteries. The literature of the time clearly reflects how profoundly Buddhism in general affected the lives and thoughts of the scholar class despite their Confucian education. Po Chü-i's poems are full of incidental allusions to his devotion to the faith, which show clearly that Buddhism had become his predominant religious conviction. He made gifts to monasteries and declared that he was incapable of the monastic life himself because, as a poet, he had to express his emotions whenever they overcame him and could not suppress them as a monk should. When he grieved for the loss of his greatest friend, he hoped they would meet in a future reincarnation. Other poems express his desire to escape the rounds of rebirth, or conjure up the atmosphere of a great monastery:

> To the east there opens the Jade Image Hall,
> Where white Buddhas sit like serried trees.
> We shook from our garments the journey's grime and dust,
> And bowing worshipped those faces of frozen snow
> Whose white cassocks like folded hoar-frost hung,
> Whose beaded crowns glittered like a shower of hail.
> We looked closer; surely spirits willed
> This handicraft, never chisel carved![4]

On the life of the people as a whole the most dramatic impact of Buddhism was made by the great religious festivals which brought all classes together in a sense of community born of the Mahayana emphasis on compassion and salvation for all sentient beings, a feeling of togetherness which was alien to both the Confucian and the Taoist traditions. These festivals relieved the monotony of life with their carnival atmosphere, for on the fringes of religious celebration there were story-tellers, magicians, and other entertainments, and the curfew was relaxed for the occasion. At the same time religious hysteria could reach fever pitch, especially when relics of the Buddha were reverenced. Such relics were usually bones or teeth of the Buddha, but on his pilgrimage to India Hsüan-tsang was shown the Buddha's eyeball and walking-stick, and even a place where the Buddha had 'left his shadow'. In Changan there were four teeth of the Buddha, each kept in a different monastery, and Ennin tells how he took part in the adoration of one of these teeth, reverently holding it, and how the various monasteries offered all kinds of medicines, foods, fruits, and flowers to the Buddha's tooth. The common people rushed to make donations to the relic, 'tossing cash like rain' towards the building where it was stored.[5]

The most hysterical outbursts occurred on the occasions when a fingerbone of the Buddha was taken from a monastery just outside Changan, said to have been originally built by the ancient Indian emperor Asoka, and presented to the imperial palace. When it was finally returned to the monastery, the frenzy reached such a pitch that many were reported to have mutilated themselves in their ecstasy. Other great occasions were the celebrations of the Buddha's birthday, when Buddha images were paraded through the streets. There is a vivid description of the celebrations at Loyang when it was capital of the Northern Wei Dynasty in the sixth century:

The images were paraded through the streets in the direction of the imperial palace. When the procession arrived there, the Emperor personally appeared above the gate to welcome it and scatter flowers. The procession itself was a gala affair. Some of the participants carried flowers made of gold that sparkled in the sunlight. Others carried ornamental parasols and brilliantly coloured banners and pennants. Along the course of the procession, so much incense was burnt by the devoted populace that the incense fumes blanketed the street like mist. All the while, the skies resounded and the earth trembled with the music and the chants given forth by the exuberant throngs, who decided that the occasion was to be one of joyous abandon and spirited play. With troops of monks and elders milling about, and with the ground covered by flowers dropped by the people, a magnificent confusion was the predominant order of the day.[6]

It was not only on festive occasions that Buddhism affected the social life of the ordinary people. Since as individuals they could not afford to match the rich people's conspicuous expenditure on their religion, Buddhist laymen formed societies and clubbed together to finance acts of piety. In the Northern Wei period the predominant activity was the making of statues and images but later the copying and recitation of the scriptures was commonly financed by laymen. These Buddhist lay societies involved themselves closely with the monasteries' attempts to spread the faith among the people by such means as lectures, and they also helped to establish a sense of comradeship between the monasteries and the lay community which ensured the integration of Buddhism into Chinese society.

Another way in which the monks were drawn closer to secular life was through their sponsorship of philanthropic activities in the community. Originally Buddhist monks, who made a vow of poverty and so had to support themselves on alms, were the recipients of charity, and the layman who presented gifts to the monastery was thereby storing up merit which could count towards his own salvation. But the orgy of generosity which this doctrine engendered brought great wealth to the monasteries, which consequently had the resources to sponsor charitable institutions themselves, for the monks in theory could not benefit since they were sworn to poverty. At the same time the old concept of withdrawal from the world to seek one's own salvation had been overshadowed by the Mahayana doctrine with its emphasis on compassion and universal salvation, which gave inspiration to these philanthropic activities. These included the establishment of hospitals within the monasteries, as well as the provision of facilities for the community at large, such as maintenance of inns for pilgrims. Po Chü-i enlisted the aid of benevolent monks to widen and deepen a dangerous river channel near Loyang, and celebrated it in the following poem:

A seventy-three year old man like me, at the twilight of his life,
Vows to change a dangerous defile into a free-flowing thoroughfare.
The ships passing here at night will no longer be overturned.
In the early morning chill the people wading across from now on will suffer
  no more.
Ten li of roaring rapids will become as peaceful as the Milky Way,
The eight cold hells will be converted to sunny springs.
Although my body will die, my spirit will live for a long time,
Invisibly bestowing my compassion to all people after me.[7]

Thus well-to-do individual laymen like Po Chü-i as well as Buddhist societies could support the local monasteries both in their propagation of the faith and in their sponsorship of those philanthropic activities which were the concrete manifestation of the compassion at the heart of Mahayana Buddhism.

The accumulation of wealth in the monasteries had a definite impact on economic history, for it stimulated the development of capitalistic enterprises and the establishment of pawnshops and other usurious activities. As we shall see later, Chinese craftsmanship was also stimulated by the demand for Buddhist images and paintings of Buddhist scenes, and literature was influenced by the use of stories in the propagation of the faith.

From time to time even during the heyday of Buddhism the voice of Confucian reaction was heard complaining of the economic burden of the monasteries and the impropriety of adopting this alien creed. This naturally intensified after the An Lu-shan rebellion in the middle of the T'ang Dynasty had gravely weakened the regime and made the country introverted and xenophobic instead of expansive and outward-looking. The most famous expression of this hostility to Buddhism was a memorial to the throne written in 819 by Han Yü, a most famous man of letters, who was particularly nauseated by the excesses of self-mutilation which accompanied the periodic presentations of the Buddha's finger bone, for such conduct outraged filial sentiment. In this memorial, which resulted in his banishment, Han Yü specifically mentioned those who 'make the rounds of temples and cut off their arms and slice their flesh in the way of offerings'. In antiquity, he claimed, before Buddhism was introduced, the empire was at peace and the people were contented and happy. At the heart of the memorial there is a direct attack on the Buddha. He

was of barbarian origin. His language differed from Chinese speech; his clothes were of a different cut; his mouth did not pronounce the prescribed words of the Former Kings, his body was not clad in the garments prescribed by the Former Kings. He did not recognize the relationship between prince and subject, nor the sentiments of father and son. Let us suppose him to be living today, and that he came to court at the capital as an emissary of his country. Your Majesty would receive him courteously. But only one interview in the audience chamber, one banquet in his honour, one gift of clothing, and he would be escorted under guard to the border that he might not mislead the masses.

How much the less, now that he has long been dead, is it fitting that his decayed and rotten bone, his ill-omened and filthy remains, should be allowed to enter in the forbidden precincts of the Palace?[8]

Not long after this came the great persecution of 845, which aimed at the destruction of numerous monasteries, the melting down of their images because of the shortage of metal for coinage, and the return of large numbers of monks and nuns to lay life. There had been other acts of persecution in 446 and 574, but this was far more serious for, although the anti-Buddhist policy was soon reversed by the next monarch, the damage done to Buddhism was permanent. An imperial edict excused the persecution in familiar Confucian terms: in antiquity there had never been any talk of Buddhism, and only since the Han had this idolatrous religion come to flourish:

In recent times its strange ways have become so customary and all-pervasive as to have slowly and unconsciously corrupted the morals of our land. The hearts of our people have been seduced by it and the masses are all the more led astray. From the mountains and wastes of the whole land to the walled palaces of the two capitals the Buddhist monks daily increase in number, and their monasteries daily grow in glory. In exhausting men's strength in construction work, in robbing men for their own golden and jewelled ornaments, in forsaking ruler and kin to support their teachers, in abandoning their mates for monastic rules, in flouting the laws and harming the people, nothing is worse than this religion. Now when one man does not farm, others suffer hunger, and when one woman does not weave, others suffer from the cold. At present the monks and nuns of the empire are numberless, but they all depend on agriculture for their food and on sericulture for their clothing. The monasteries and temples are beyond count, but they are all lofty and beautifully decorated, daring to rival palaces in grandeur.[9]

So Buddhism, partly because it was not the Way of the Former Kings and partly because of prejudice against those who consume but do not grow food expressed in the familiar ancient cliché, had at last suffered the severe persecution which had been foreshadowed earlier in the dynasty by large-scale defrockings. But the lives of the people could not be washed clean of the colouring which Buddhist beliefs and practices had given them. The Mahayana Buddhist concept of compassion gave a new dimension to the Confucian ideal of universal benevolence and of devotion to duty regardless of consequence, while among the populace at large the concept of *karma* and of rebirth in a new existence depending on the merits accumulated in one's previous life had made its indelible mark, with beneficial effects on moral standards. The participation of Buddhist monks became a regular feature even of ancestor worship at the very heart of the classical tradition, and Buddhist masses were said for the dead at intervals after the funeral. The Buddhist practice of cremation also became quite common during the Sung period. Philanthropic activities were continued in reduced circumstances, but more importantly the charitable nature of Buddhism had infected official attitudes, so that in the Sung period the state itself began to organize public clinics, homes for the aged, and similar institutions.

Chinese religious belief was also permanently enriched by the takeover and sinicization of many Buddhas and bodhisattvas of the Mahayana tradition, which were eventually incorporated into the amorphous and eclectic religion of the common people, to whom all gods were acceptable as long as they were effective. Maitreya was one who underwent a typical transformation. Originally he was the future Buddha waiting to be reborn on earth to purify the religion and introduce a glorious new era. So in the Chinese context the cult of Maitreya came to figure in the messianic beliefs of seditious movements among the people; and it was also, as we have seen, enlisted in the cause of Empress Wu's usurpation. Much later, however, this same divinity had been transformed into the Laughing Buddha, often depicted as a pot-bellied figure with a swarm of children climbing over him, signifying prosperity and a large family, two of the very mundane blessings which the Chinese expected their gods to provide. The moustachioed bodhisattva Avalokitesvara even underwent a change of sex and emerged as Kuanyin, the Chinese Buddhist Goddess of Mercy and bringer of children. Also extremely popular in China was Amitabha, the Buddha of the Western Paradise, or Pure Land, where all who have faith in him will be reborn to remain in perfect bliss until the moment of *nirvana*. This desirable end was achieved merely by perfect faith in Amitabha's miraculous power, expressed by a simple invocation of his name.

Such a belief marks the decline of a religion as surely as the revolving bookcase which Ennin described, one turn of which was thought to confer as much merit as the reading of the voluminous literature it contained. After the resurgence of Confucianism, which had its origins in the T'ang and came to maturity during the Sung, there was no room for Buddhism to recover its old sway. A much more secular society began to flourish in the thriving commercial cities of the Sung empire. Men of quality found scope in bureaucratic careers, and the shrunken Buddhist monasteries became places of retreat for the poor and destitute. By the late sixteenth century, when the Jesuit missionaries first reached China, the faith was deeply despised by the Confucian literati; and the Jesuits shared their feelings of contempt, seeing in the celibacy, the tonsure, the ritual, the chanting of the scriptures, and the masses for the dead what seemed like an evil and degraded mockery of their own religion. Nevertheless it did continue to survive, partly because of the colour and hope it had given to the religious and ethical lives of the Chinese and partly because at heart it was a religion of withdrawal and contemplation, so that in hard times it could be allowed to continue on a reduced scale without being resented as a challenge to the state as at the time of its greatest success. In modern times it was even seen as one answer to China's need to seek within its own traditions a solution to the moral problems of twentieth-century society, while later the Japanese, for imperialistic reasons, tried to set up Sino-Japanese Buddhism as a common faith for their new East Asian order.

Attempts were also made in the twentieth century to use Confucianism as a state religion for China, but these were bound to fail since Confucianism was nothing if not a universal system, which had as an essential ingredient the concept of the Son of Heaven as ruler of all-under-Heaven, a concept which could not survive the Middle Kingdom's nineteenth-century humiliations. Confucianism was also discredited since it was the ideology of a system which had manifestly failed, and its final abandonment may really be dated from 1905 when the old-fashioned civil service examinations were abolished.

The first chapter of this section concentrated on the original teachings of the Confucian school and their profound influence on later Chinese thought and society. But during the course of Chinese history these ancient texts were subjected to an immense burden of scholarship and commentary, and in the Sung period the Neo-Confucians, influenced by both Buddhist and Taoist concepts, provided the ancient ethical ideals with a metaphysical basis.

Confucius himself became a regular object of worship. He became in effect the patron god of scholars, and consequently received official worship in view of the importance of the scholar class to the state. Regular worship of Confucius in government schools started in the Later Han Dynasty, and it was in the T'ang Dynasty that temples to Confucius were erected throughout the empire. At that time he became the patron of officials, and so an important figure in the state pantheon. In the Confucian temples the chief disciples and other distinguished Confucians of later times were also honoured. The family temple at Ch'ü-fu was also occasionally visited by emperors for worship and sacrifice, but the ceremonies held there were generally the ancestor worship conducted by Confucius's descendants, who continued in unbroken line until the present century, a signal example of the extraordinary continuity of the Chinese family, which is the first topic of the following chapter.

Grand audience at the imperial palace, Peking, in the 18th century.

Court portrait of the K'ang-hsi emperor.

An emperor on tour.

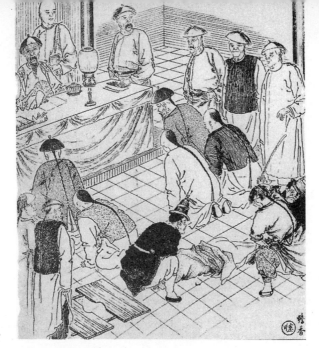

Official as punisher of wrong-doing. Note the cangue, the wooden collar used as a punishment.

Official as 'father and mother' of the people, advising peasants.

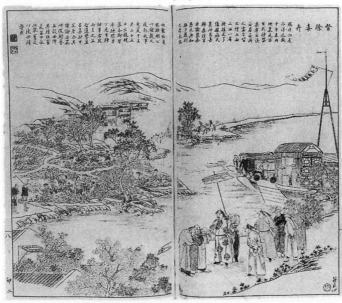

Confucian rectitude: a portrait of the sage himself.

Taoist non-action: *Hermit fishing*, by Ma Yüan

Buddhist compassion: a Yüan Dynasty porcelain figure of Kuanyin.

Door god: deified general of the T'ang Dynasty.

A farming family returns thanks for the harvest.

Plumpness was favoured in the
T'ang Dynasty.

Young girl attendant in
submissive pose: Han tomb
figurine.

Palace garden with noble lady and her servants.

Women as entertainers: a T'ang palace concert.

Picking mulberry leaves.

Planting out rice.

高轉筒車

Raising water to
irrigate a paddy-field
at a higher level.

Brine being raised
from the bottom of a
salt well.

汲鹵

Variety of transport in Sung Dynasty Kaifeng. Note the crowds round a street-corner story-teller.

In the north donkeys were a common means of transport: a painting by Ma Yüan.

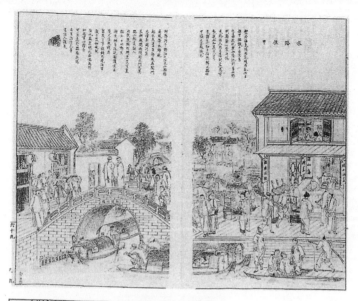

And in the south
boats: Soochow, city
of canals.

Barbarian envoys
presenting tribute.

Kaifeng: the city gate of the Sung capital.

長板橋頭天飲祭天歲買金陵四十餘寺丁秦淮陸棄合秦淮陸棄全

Nanking, capital of the early Ming Dynasty.

The earliest Chinese writing: a Shang Dynasty oracle bone.

Calligraphy of the Sung emperor Hui-tsung.

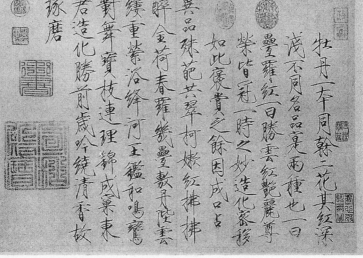

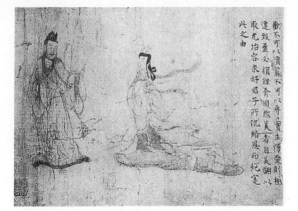

The old master Ku K'ai-chih: detail from *Admonitions of the Instructress to the Court Ladies*.

Duke Wen of Chin: from a Sung handscroll.

Detail from *Night Entertainment of Han Hsi-tsai*.

Economical portraiture: *Li Po* by Liang K'ai.

A quasi-kinesthetic experience: *Two Minds in Harmony*.

Buddhist Temple in Snowy Hills, by Fan K'uan.

Woods and Valleys of Yü-shan, by Ni Tsan.

Communing with nature;
Ma Yüan: *Scholar by a
Waterfall.*

An example of the bird and
flower tradition of court
painting.

Detail of bamboo painting with calligraphy.

The traditional blend of painting, poetry, and calligraphy in a modern painting.

Elephant-shaped bronze vessel of the Shang Dynasty.

Bronze vessel showing *t'ao-t'ieh* mask.

Pottery water pitcher. Neolithic.

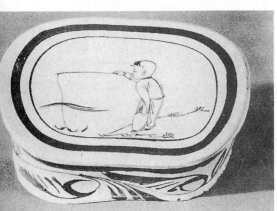

Tz'u-chou ware porcelain pillow, Sung Dynasty.

Blue and white bowl, with men playing *wei-ch'i*.

Jade pendant showing a tiger crouching over a man, Chou Dynasty.

Green jade brush-pot.

The pleasures of a
Chinese garden.

A Soochow garden
today.

Inside the house: note
especially the book-
case.

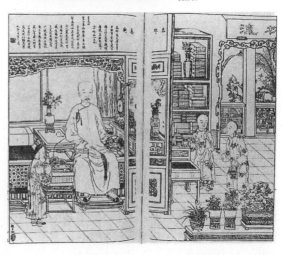

An ancient comedian.

Plays were often staged in outdoor theatres.

The first railway in China through Chinese eyes.

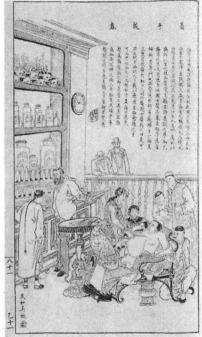

A lady surgeon at work.

PART THREE
THE SOCIAL AND ECONOMIC EXPERIENCE

CHAPTER 7

THE SOCIAL EXPERIENCE

I

Our study of Confucianism in Chapter 4 showed how traditional Chinese moral philosophy stressed the proper observance of family duties and responsibilities. Apart from the virtues of filial piety and brotherly affection, which all men must display, the princely man or ideal gentleman (*chün-tzu*) had a special responsibility for cultivating his own personality so that he could properly administer his family and state. In the traditional Chinese world-view there is no concept equivalent to our 'society': man was envisaged as functioning in two spheres – within the family ('inside') or within the state ('outside'). Other forms of social organization, like guilds or secret societies, modelled themselves closely on clan or family groupings. The family has been regarded not only as the basis of the moral order, but also as the fundamental unit in the political order; so that taxation, ownership of property, and maintenance of law and order have tended to be family rather than individual responsibilities. Often, too, the family has functioned as the basic economic unit: peasant families tilled the soil together, and craftsmen and shopkeepers ran small family businesses. So a consideration of the nature of the family must be at the forefront of any chapter devoted to the social and economic experience of the Chinese. Through the study of the family we can understand Chinese attitudes to the important milestones of birth, marriage, and death, and become acquainted with ancestor worship, which has been the most enduring and universal feature of Chinese religion. Families were grouped in larger kinship units known as lineages or clans, which will be described later.

The word *chia* in Chinese has a much wider range of meanings than 'family' in English. It is used for 'house' as well as 'family', and the earliest form of the character is a pictogram of a pig under a roof. The *chia* included not only the group of family members living in the house, but also the animals and property involved in the exploitation of the *chia* as an economic unit, which was envisaged as a trust which ought eventually to be equally divided among the sons; although if there were several sons and the family's land were small, it would be economically impossible to conform with this ideal. The word *chia* also has powerful moral associations because of the great importance attached to the Confucian family virtues. At the same time it implies a deeper sense of continuity than the word 'family' bears: people were profoundly aware of the presence of the ancestral spirits and of their participation in great family occasions, and they constantly desired to build up an inheritance for un-born generations who would in their turn maintain the ancestral sacrifices.

Ideally the Chinese *chia* consisted of the paterfamilias, his wife, and their sons and grandsons, each surrounded by their own families, all living together; but this was not at all typical, although Chinese inter-preters of their own civilization, coming from the wealthy stratum of society in which such families were possible, have sometimes given the impression that it was the normal pattern. As in many other aspects of Chinese society, the ideal was not often approached in reality. The pursuit of the ideal was officially encouraged by award of honours to those who had conspicuously attained it; and families did expand whenever economic conditions permitted, so as to include not only the family as increased by proper marriages but concubines and their children as well. Such a development is shown in the career of Wang Lung, the poor peasant in Pearl Buck's *The Good Earth*. When he became rich, his establishment expanded so that it comprised his wives and concubines, his sons with their wives and children, his unmarried daughters, and several slaves. Normally, however, the peasant had only enough land for mere subsistence, and a division of his smallholdings between sons would mean intolerable poverty for all of them; so it was generally necessary for younger sons to leave the family and become agricultural labourers or seek other work. Consequently the typical household consisted of the stem family, in which only one son continued to live with the parents after marriage. The average number of people in a family was as low as five, and the big family living in an establish-ment with several courtyards was the privilege of the few and the stuff of novels such as *Dream of the Red Chamber* and *Golden Lotus*, in which the jealousies and intrigues inherent in a family with several wives provide rich material for the plot.

The importance of the family is shown by the ways in which individuals were subordinated to it. Surnames were of very ancient origin in China, and the surname comes before the given name, indicating that it is of prior importance. Within the family it was often the custom for the children of several brothers living in one household to be numbered in accordance with their ages, regardless of the seniority of their fathers. For example, one of the main characters in the eighteenth-century novel, *The Scholars*, was known as Mr Tu XVII. Relatives were also addressed by number, e.g. Third Brother, instead of by name. This use of kinship terms rather than personal names as forms of address within the family symbolized the importance of the family as compared with the individual and the priority of kinship obligations over personal feelings. The practice also carried over into the world outside the family, so that, depending on his age, a friend might be addressed as brother or uncle. The family not only had priority over the individual; it also sometimes took priority over the state. The state was remote, but family discipline dominated a person's life. Traitors were forgiven or their sentences severely reduced by emperors in some cases where they were motivated by family concerns, and armies were sometimes reduced in number by sending home one son from each family so that there should be someone at home to care for aged parents.[1] The ideal Confucian view was, of course, that a man who practised filial piety within the family could not be disloyal to the state, since these were the manifestations of the ideal gentleman's character appropriate to those separate spheres. On the other hand, the solidarity of the family in the face of the outside world was prescribed in such classical tags as 'Brothers may fight within the house, but will join hands to resist insults from without.' Those who were without a family were regarded as deeply unfortunate because in this life they had, as Mencius put it, 'no one to tell their grievances to',[2] and in the after-life they would have no descendants to sacrifice to them.

The solidarity of the family group is also reflected in the traditional design of the large Chinese house which has walls screening it from the outside world, in contrast with the European house which is generally much more exposed to the community at large. Within the house, on the other hand, rooms lead into one another and there is much less privacy than in the modern European house. The brick platform known as the *k'ang*, a common feature of northern Chinese houses, also promoted togetherness. In winter it could be heated from underneath and, being furnished with cushions and low tables, it could be used by several persons to eat, work, or relax on in close proximity to each other during the day, as well as providing a very commodious bed at night.

Although the close-knit family group was a source of strength to its members, it was also a convenient unit in the government's traditional system of control. Taxes were demanded of families rather than individuals, and this followed naturally from the fact that ownership was a family rather than an individual matter. In criminal matters too there was a long tradition of mutual responsibility inspired by the Legalist philosophy; so that, especially in antiquity, but also in the late imperial period, whole families were wiped out for the serious political crimes of one of their members. On the other hand family connections also brought privileges even under the bureaucratic system, because in the early empire in particular office was open hereditarily to the sons, grandsons, and sometimes the younger brothers of those who had held appointments.

Relationships within the family were never between equals but were always marked by the distinction of superior and inferior, which we have seen to be characteristic of the Confucian moral philosophy. This even applied to the brotherly relationship, although sons were supposed to inherit equally. There is not even a single word for brother, but instead separate terms for elder and younger brother, so that if one wants to refer to brothers collectively, one has to say 'elder and younger brothers'. Similarly there is no single word for uncles, aunts, or cousins. The most important relationship is, of course, that between father and son. This is the essential link which joins the living family with the ancestors and also guarantees the continuity of the family line, so the filial piety which is meant to characterize this relationship is a solemn and awesome matter. The obedience and devotion of filial piety was required of the children both for the ordinary reason that the parents had done much for them, but also because it was regarded as an eternal principle, inherent in human nature. Breaches of filial piety which amounted to crimes against the parent were treated much more seriously by the law than crimes when committed against a non-parent, and for scolding or striking a parent a man could even be sentenced to death. The character for father, in its most ancient form, seems to show a hand holding a stick. Traditionally a stern disciplinarian, he was entitled to beat his sons unmercifully even after they were grown up and married, and there are recorded cases of officials being beaten by their sires.

The father, on the other hand, had duties towards his son. He had to provide him with a moral example, support him, and train him in his occupation. Later he had to ensure the continuance of the family line by providing him with a wife and an inheritance. The mother's attitude towards her son was more affectionate, as was natural not only because of maternal instinct but also because the birth of a son to continue the family line brought her status and a greater sense of acceptance within her new family. Over two thousand years ago the *Record of Rites* foreshadowed the essential contrast between paternal and maternal attitudes:

As for the father's affection for his sons, he shows affection for the worthy and places on a lower level those who lack ability. As for the mother's affection for her sons, if they are worthy, she does show affection for them, but if they lack ability, she feels sorry for them. The mother treats her sons with affection rather than respect, and the father treats his sons with respect rather than affection.[3]

II

Although the father-son relationship was regarded as of primary importance, the conjugal relationship was also necessary to ensure the continuance of the family line. It was a family concern, rather than an affair between two individuals, and the Chinese character for 'to give a daughter in marriage' is composed of the characters for 'woman' and 'home'. As so often in these matters, the *Record of Rites* has the classical statement which remained appropriate right through to the twentieth century: 'Marriage is a bond of affection between two surnames, so as to serve the ancestral temple on the one hand and continue the family line on the other.'[4] To ensure that the proper purposes of marriage were fulfilled the matter could not be left to the two individuals most closely concerned, but had to be arranged by the parents. In some cases girl children were even adopted with a view to later marriage to one of the sons of the family. The quotation also makes it clear that people of the same surname should not marry. Although this taboo was later often ignored, ancient texts recorded the view that marriages between those of the same surname would not be fruitful.[5] In traditional Chinese society marriage was considered to be the natural and inevitable situation in adult life, although in reality many men had to stay unmarried through being unable to afford a wife. It was marriage that made a person complete; and the most unfilial act, as Mencius had said, was to be without descendants.[6] But girl descendants were not much use to their own family. As the proverb said, 'A boy is born facing in; a girl is born facing out.' She was destined to leave her family at an early age, and would later be worshipping somebody else's ancestors.

The status of the ideal wife was seen in terms of 'three subordinations', firstly to her father before her marriage, secondly to her husband, and thirdly to her eldest son after her husband's death. She was also supposed to have four virtues, those of fidelity, cautious speech, industriousness, and graceful manners. Clan rules have much to say on wifely virtues, and give detailed instructions on demeanour, such as that she must not sit with her knees crossed or stand with her legs wide apart. To choose a bride and arrange a match the family – as the *Record of Rites* insisted – had recourse to a go-between;[7] for the delicate negotiations, which could result in much loss of face if the union proved unsatisfactory, could not be conducted without the intervention of a third party, as also happened in other kinds of important negotiations between different families. Necessary though they were, the proverb said that 'go-betweens must know how to lie'; and the unscrupulous match-maker, whose smooth tongue could persuade the prospective bridegroom's family that the girl was a veritable goddess and then cut twenty years from the man's age in her dealings with the prospective bride's family, is a stock figure of fun in Chinese literature. Go-betweens were bound to get a bad name because they acted as safety valves and could be blamed for the disappointments of an ill-starred wedding.

The events leading up to marriage were ultimately based on the sequence laid down by the *Record of Rites*.[8] Firstly enquiries were made in a girl's family by a go-between acting on behalf of a family seeking a bride. Then horoscopes were sought by the go-between. Then the girl's horoscope was matched with the boy's, to see whether the marriage was made in Heaven (which also meant that Fate rather than the judgement of the parents could be blamed if the marriage went wrong, just as Fate was held responsible in the case of failure in examinations). Next the betrothal was clinched by the transfer of gifts (which in one sense completed the marriage, for if the bridegroom died afterwards, the ceremony might still go through, with the bride entering her betrothed's family as a widow). Next the date of the bride's conveyance to her husband's house was fixed, and finally the bride was transferred.

Although the betrothal was the first point at which it might be said that the marriage became effective, there were several different stages to be gone through before the marriage could be regarded as finally consummated. The first necessary ingredient was the dispatch of the red bridal chair from the bridegroom's home to fetch the bride to her new home. This was a heavily symbolical journey: the red of her bridal chair was a joyous and auspicious colour; and, as she passed from the family of her birth to the one in which she would spend the rest of her days, she was protected with all possible devices to ward off evil spirits. She never touched the ground from leaving the one house to setting foot in the other, for movement in space was an essential dramatization of the basic reality of marriage, so essential that it persisted after the establishment of the People's Republic, with bicycles serving instead of sedan chairs. The second ingredient was the homage paid by the husband and wife to Heaven and Earth, to ensure that the marriage was sanctioned by gods as well as men. A ceremony also took place before the ancestral tablets to ensure that the ancestors were duly informed. This presentation of the bride to the ancestors might be regarded as the real moment of introduction of the woman into her husband's family. Then, after the marriage feast, the bride and groom, who traditionally had not set eyes on each other before this day, retired for the night, having submitted to the ordeal of the 'disturbance of the room', which meant that they had to be on show in their bedroom and put up with such teasing as their relatives thought appropriate to the occasion. Other important acts remained for the morrow, for it was then that the bride was introduced to her domestic duties under the supervision of her mother-in-law. Marriage was colloquially known as taking a daughter-in-law, and the bride's domestic service was an important part of the deal, for it was the concrete expression of that filial piety which was at the heart of family life. Even after this her incorporation into the family was still not quite complete, for barrenness was a ground for divorce, and the object of the marriage was not fulfilled until she had given birth to a son and presented him to the ancestors. The final event which would confirm her membership of her new family would be her death and the inclusion of her tablet in the ancestral shrine.

All this took place in the husband's home, and was a matter entirely for his family. The marriage was not registered with the civil authority, nor did the bride's family take any part in the ceremony or jollification, although the couple did go a few days later to pay a formal visit to the bride's home. The rites of marriage symbolized the fact that the bride's body, fertility, domestic service, and loyalty had been handed over by one family to another. They also provided an opportunity for the groom's family to display its affluence and glory in its prestige in the community. The splendour of these occasions was a severe burden on a family's resources, but they served not only to impress the neighbours but also to make the young couple feel properly indebted and dutiful. An additional expense was the gifts to the bride's family, the betrothal presents, which were a thinly disguised price for the person of the daughter-in-law and a clear indication of her total subservience to her new family.

In her new family the bride's life was not easy, for she was a total stranger entering a close-knit community. With luck a genuinely affectionate relationship might develop between her and her husband, but until she presented him with an heir her status in her new family was very lowly. The law, too, emphasized the wife's disadvantageous position. Husbands who beat their wives were punished less severely than ordinary cases of beating. The penalty for beating a daughter-in-law to death was three years' imprisonment, but this only applied if the beating were unprovoked or cruelly administered. Even if she were severely ill-treated, there were few grounds on which a woman could obtain a divorce. The marriage might be dissolved if the husband severely mistreated members of his wife's family. It was sometimes dissolved by mutual consent if the parties wished to separate. But in general the wife's bond to her new home was meant for life and was not even dissolved on the death of her husband. The marriage was fated and she was adjured to accept Fate however difficult things might be. She might escape back to her own family, but sentiment was strongly opposed to this; and the remarriage even of widows was frowned on by society, although practised among the common people. Suicide was the most obvious solution to an intolerable marriage.

For the man, however, the situation was quite different. The woman had been taken into the family for specific purposes and, if she did not come up to scratch, she could be dismissed, and the fatedness of the marriage would be conveniently forgotten. The seven traditional grounds for divorce, which obtained for more than two thousand years, were: disobedience to the husband's parents (for one of the most important objects of marriage was the acquisition of a filial daughter-in-law); barrenness (for another was to continue the family line); adultery (which if it led to offspring was intolerable, because it would muddy the clear channels of the ancestral cult); jealousy (particularly of the barren wife who was opposed to her husband taking a concubine – indeed according to the common belief there was a special place in hell for women who were jealous when their husbands took a concubine); incurable disease (for the chronic invalid was not a fit person to prepare an ancestral sacrifice); loquacity (for this could disturb the essential family harmony); and theft. Nevertheless the wife had some protection in law. She could not be divorced if she had no close relatives to receive her, if she had endured poverty with her new family but they had later become rich, and if she had already been long enough in the family to have worn three years' mourning for her husband's parents. Divorce was in fact quite rare in traditional Chinese society.

There were other kinds of marital relationship in addition to the orthodox marriages described above. Widows remarried, girls married in families into which they had previously been adopted, and occasionally a man married into the house of his father-in-law, if the latter had no son of his own to continue the family line. Also, among the upper classes who could afford it, polygamy was practised. In rare cases a second wife was taken into the family with full ceremony, to enjoy equal status with the first wife, but a much more convenient and common arrangement was concubinage. This institution was perfectly acceptable in the eyes of society, especially if the wife were barren; and indeed for a man to have several concubines was a not disreputable sign that he had reached a certain position in life which might be represented in present-day Western society by the possession of more than one house or car. A lady in *Dream of the Red Chamber* encouraged her husband in an affair with the words: 'Lots of men in well-to-do families like ours have *troops* of concubines. Why should it be so shameful only in our case?'[9]

Although arrangements were made by go-betweens, the concubine was taken into the house without formal wedding ceremony or ritual recognition, so her place in the family was insecure and she could be dismissed without the traditional grounds for divorce being invoked. Her position in the family was lowly: she was not addressed with kinship terms, and her status was little better than that of the maidservants. Her children, though regarded as legitimate, did not enjoy the same status as the wife's children and did not inherit equally with them. Often she was totally excluded from the ancestral rites, although some clans did allow the possibility of her having an ancestral tablet and receiving sacrifices. Before the law her status was inferior to that of the wife, so that she suffered heavier penalties for crimes committed against the husband; and likewise the husband was more lightly treated by the law for harming his concubine than for harming his wife.

These discriminations against the concubine were obviously essential in order to preserve family solidarity and traditions. The absolute necessity of continuing the family line opened the way to concubinage, and this institution then gave the opportunity for the dominant males to indulge themselves in relationships which were alien to the family's social and religious role; but it was possible for this to be done without radical disturbance to family harmony if these women had low status and did not interfere with the kinship system. If their sons had had equal rights of inheritance, this would have been a severe cause of friction. Moreover, concubines were generally bought from poor families and even from the ranks of prostitutes, so these women of low social origin had to be prevented from achieving too powerful a position in the proud households of the upper classes. Respectable families would not allow their daughters to go into concubinage except into the imperial palace or into families of extremely great wealth or prestige, although from antiquity right down into the twentieth century it sometimes happened that a younger sister accompanied a bride to her new home and became her brother-in-law's concubine.

Prostitution was accepted by traditional Chinese society, and until this practice was stamped out by the present regime, houses of prostitution were used by officials and merchants as places where they could entertain their colleagues, and poets drew inspiration from them. The only harm in it was if a man wasted his substance at such establishments. The talented courtesan was a common character in popular literature and often provided the love interest, because respectable women were generally less free to move about in society on their own. Prostitutes were usually recruited by purchase from the families of the poor, but often in the literary version a girl of respectable family trained at a very early age in all the desirable arts is forced into prostitution by the loss of her parents or some other disaster. The Flower Queen in *The Oil Vendor and the Courtesan*, a tale of poor boy winning prostitute with a heart of gold, was the daughter of a grocer, who could write poetry at ten, and at the age of twelve was an accomplished lyrist, chess player, calligrapher, painter, and needlewoman. As a result of the Jürched invasion in the twelfth century which brought the north of China under the domination of the Chin Dynasty, the family became refugees. In the confusion the Flower Queen was lost, and she was eventually sold into a bawdy house and forced into prostitution; but her many talents brought her to the top of her profession, so that she was able to enjoy the social round of parties, boating expeditions, poetry meetings, chess tournaments, and the like. Another extremely successful girl is described in a story written in the twelfth century called *The Scholar and the Courtesan*:

She had a clear skin and a delicate figure, her hair was glossy and her eyes large, her graceful hands were slender, and her exquisite waist yielding: she was outstanding in her time. Carriages and horses went to her house in crowds, and her gates were as busy as a market. Moreover she was intelligent and quick-witted, she was accomplished in music, and she excelled in poetry and painting. The young men about town would pay thousands of pieces of gold for a smile from her, and they competed for her love, only fearing to fall behind. When the government officials of the area held banquets, they would ride out to escort her to them.[10]

Women's inferior position in traditional Chinese society was not simply a matter of custom but of deep-rooted belief about the nature of the universal order; for in the dualism of Yin and Yang males were ranged on the side of Yang, brightness and warmth, and women on the side of Yin, darkness and cold. In the popular literature a female character might say that in her previous existence she had been a man but to punish her for her misdeeds in that life she had been reborn a woman. The character for woman was originally composed of elements illustrating a female and a broom, symbolizing her domestic role, and in ancient literary sources even the wives of princes are shown doing menial tasks.[11] The *Record of Rites* argued that women's great power inside the house compensated for her exclusion from public affairs, and those who have liked to paint a romantic picture of Chinese society in more recent times have echoed this view. But a woman could never be the head of a household, and was only delegated to run the domestic side by her husband. Her subordinate position is clearly demonstrated not only by the nature of marriage and divorce and concubinage but also by her lack of opportunity to prepare herself for any other role or career than the domestic, and her enforced seclusion and inability to move freely in society, which was a feature of Chinese manners from the Sung period onwards.

These were burdens of a kind borne by all women in all traditional societies, but in China from the Sung period onwards there was the additional hardship of submitting to the excruciating experience of footbinding. This was the practice of binding girls' feet tightly in cloth so that they assumed a deformed hoof-like shape. The custom is said to have begun in imitation of an imperial concubine of the Five Dynasties period who was required by her royal master to dance with her feet bound in white cloth. Small feet came to have powerful erotic appeal and the practice of foot-binding survived until the present century. Add to all these other misfortunes the fact that girl children were valued less than boys because they did not stay in the family and contribute to it economically and ritually, so that in harsh times far more girl children were left to die than boys, and it will be clear why story-tellers often introduced female characters with the words 'unfortunately she was born a woman'.

In spite of these disadvantages a few females did achieve distinction in traditional Chinese society. Women were not entirely denied the opportunity of cultivating their literary talents, and there were several distinguished women poets; but the most notable woman of letters was Pan Chao, who was especially famous for completing her brother Pan Ku's work, the *History of the Former Han Dynasty*. There are also fictional portraits of beautiful and talented girls much loved by their fathers. One such was the daughter of Compiler Lu in the eighteenth-century satirical novel *The Scholars*, who, given such an education as a boy would have received to train for the civil examinations, so that her dressing-table was stacked with examination essays while she spurned poetry and gave it to her maids to read, was married off to a young man who was supposed to have similar interests; to her enormous disappointment he turned out to have much more frivolous preoccupations. A few women even succeeded in wielding political power. When the Han founder died, his successor was only a child, so his mother the Dowager Empress became the effective ruler of China. Some later Dowager Empresses also had a powerful influence at court, the last being the notorious Dowager Empress Tz'u-hsi, who achieved power when her young son became emperor in 1861. When he died in 1875, she further entrenched herself by putting a four-year-old nephew on the throne and, except for a decade spent in retirement, was effectively ruler until her death in 1908. But the only woman to hold the throne in her own name was the formidable Empress Wu of the T'ang Dynasty. She obtained great political power because of the infirmity of her husband, the Emperor Kao-tsung; and soon after his death in 683 she usurped the throne from her son and reigned for twenty years before being forced to abdicate.

It is not surprising that one of the most powerful forces in the modern revolutionary situation has been the demand for women's rights. In traditional China there were already those who refused to accept the conventional women's role. In Kwangtung there was a women's movement which started early in the nineteenth century among workers, particularly in the silk industry; they refused to have anything to do with marriage, and lived in so-called 'Girls' Homes'. Large numbers of women fought in the Taiping Rebellion, and they were also allowed to take part in the civil service examinations and to hold office in the Taiping administration. These remarkable innovations foreshadowed the sweeping changes of the twentieth century when foot-binding and other symbols of women's inferiority were eventually swept away, until under the People's Republic the old marriage rituals have been replaced by the simple process of registering the union with the authorities.

III

In the normal course of events, marriage was soon succeeded by the next great crisis in the family history, birth, which was such a hazardous business that it was naturally fraught with superstition. Horoscopes were consulted to see whether the child was born at a lucky time, and magic was used to ward off evil if the horoscope proved to be unfavourable. Boy children were often given names which reflected the parents' hope that their sons would prolong the family's prosperity, or their wishes that their children would enjoy health and longevity, and develop appropriate talents. What was important for girls, however, was that they should have beauty and the virtues desirable in a wife; so Jade or Pearl or the names of birds or flowers expressed hope that the girl child would turn out to be beautiful, and appropriate virtues like Chastity, Diligence, and Thrift also often occurred among girls' names.

The young child was schooled early in the virtues appropriate to his situation, especially through stories from the famous twenty-four examples of filial piety. These recounted the self-sacrifice of such heroes as Wu Meng, who let himself be eaten by mosquitoes in order to divert them from his parents, and Lao Lai-tzu, who in adult life still dressed as a child, and played with his toys to make his parents happy. A story which most clearly indicated the proper priorities was the tale of the Kuos, who could not afford both to nurse their sick mother and to look after their three-year-old son. So, saying to each other, 'We have only one mother, but we can always get another child', they decided to bury the child. When Kuo started digging, he struck gold, for the gods had decided to reward his exemplary filial piety.

At the age of five or six the peasant boys were already accompanying their fathers into the fields to do light tasks and the girls were beginning to learn to take part in the various household chores. For those who received schooling, whether from private tutors or in schools sponsored by local officials, wealthy individuals, or clan organizations, or established by the state, the education was heavily biased towards the Classics, and there was much emphasis on rote-learning and little concern for whether the books were understood. The following is a description of an old-fashioned school in the early Republican period:

The walls were dark and the windows were pasted over with grimy old paper so that the lighting was very bad. The tables, benches, and stools were brought by the pupils from their homes. Boys ranging in age from six to twenty years were herded together in one room. The teachers' quarters were partitioned off from the schoolroom and here the teacher sat all day, except when he had calls to make, went to the market town, or was invited out to entertain a guest or write documents for a village family. At school his chief function was to maintain order.

The students were sent to school before the sun was up in the morning, about an hour before the teacher arrived. Each boy was expected to use this time in reading his assignment at the top of his voice and to memorize what he was reading. When the teacher appeared, another hour was spent in reviewing the textbooks. Then the boys were called upon to recite one by one. Each boy as his turn came placed his books on the teacher's desk, turned his back, and recited all or part of the assignment. All of this took place before breakfast. Both pupils and teachers went home to eat. When they returned from the morning meal, they practised calligraphy and tried their skill at filling in couplets and composing poems. Occasionally there were lectures on good manners and on the ethical doctrines of Confucius. The teacher gave out the new assignments to each pupil individually, as there was no class system.[12]

After lunch school continued again in much the same way and the hours were very long. There was no physical education: an important teaching of filial piety was that the body was a precious gift from one's parents which had to be preserved from harm, so violent and dangerous physical exercise ran contrary to the requirements of the traditional morality.

That the young should be taught to respect the old was natural in a conservative and relatively unchanging society. It was the old who had lived longest and therefore had the most experience of the various crises and problems of birth and death, of seed-time and harvest, and knew what to do. Furthermore they formed the closest link with the revered ancestors. In traditional China the old were free from worry, so long as they had sons to provide for them, and their advancing age was celebrated as great cause for joy, especially at the milestones of the sixtieth, seventieth, and eightieth birthdays. The state honoured the aged by providing special banquets for them, and preferential treatment was also given to elderly candidates in the civil service examinations.

Mencius long ago recognized that of the three universally respected things, nobility, age, and virtue, age was what was most highly regarded in local communities; and this has had a marked effect on social life.[13]

Lao meaning 'old' is a common honorific prefix, while *hsien-sheng*, meaning 'born earlier', is a polite form of address which came to be used as
the equivalent of the English 'Mr'. Kinship terms, as we have already
noted, reflected relative ages, there being different words for 'elder
brother' and 'younger brother'; and brothers normally wedded in order
of seniority, as could easily be managed in a system of arranged marriages. Age was also worthy of respect in the eyes of the law, for it was
more serious to assault an older than a younger relative. As the old
neared death and the day when they would join the ancestors approached, the gift of a coffin marked the son's filial concern that this
great transformation be attended by rites which befitted the occasion.

The full duty of filial piety was often described in the words 'supporting the living and bidding farewell to the dead', so the proper management of a parent's funeral and of the period of mourning which ensued
was considered just as important as lifelong devotion to the task of providing him with care and sustenance. In fact, mourning was considered
primarily as a duty of the young towards the old, and there was little
ceremony involved in the burials of those who were young and unmarried at the time of death. Mourning was not worn for a son or grandson. This did not mean that grief was not felt and informally expressed,
but rather that there was no formal recognition of the occasion. A
Chinese sociologist writes that, if a baby died in his village, its body was
not deeply buried and could easily be dug up by wild dogs or wolves.[14]
But, for the adult, the completion of life was burial in one's native place;
and there are many stories in Chinese literature and even in recent
history of people's bones being interred in a temporary grave far from
home and later being dug up by son, close relative, or devoted friend
and restored to the ancestral village for burial.

Apart from the expression of grief and loss which to us are the obvious
reasons for funerary ceremonies, the rites which took place at a person's
death had two other distinct purposes – to ward off the evil influences
associated with the dreadfulness of death itself, and to see to the welfare
of the departed in the next world. To secure the well-being of the deceased, the first act was to report the event to the appropriate authority
in the underworld, just as births and marriages had to be reported to
ancestors. Reporting the event to the appropriate god, which varied
according to local tradition, facilitated the admittance of the departed
into the spirit world.

The next important task was to equip the departed for his sojourn in
the other world, by dressing him in fine clothes, placing useful articles

in his coffin, and filling his mouth with gold, silver, pearls, or other precious objects. In the Shang period rulers were buried with slaughtered horses and servants to attend them in the next world as well as vast quantities of treasure for their use; and in antiquity a loyal henchman might commit suicide at the time of his master's death to be able to accompany him and serve him in the hereafter. But in later periods mortuary figurines of pottery were used, and in most recent times the practice has been to burn paper images of houses, furniture, servants, and everything needed for the comfort of the departed; these were felt to be sufficient to symbolize belief in the continued existence of the deceased and his need for earthly comforts. Every seventh day for the next seven weeks after the funeral those families which could afford it had scriptures chanted by Buddhist and Taoist priests to aid the spirit in its travels. But side by side with these rites designed to see the departed off on his journey, there were others provoked by the sheer horror of death and the need to frighten off the evil influences associated with it. A propitious hour had to be chosen for the burial, mourners were tabooed from entering other people's houses, and the corpse had to be placed with feet towards the door, so that if it rose as a vampire it would walk straight out of the house.

As in many other societies, grief was conventionalized so that the mourners knew precisely what was expected of them. Coarse food was eaten and coarse mourning garments worn, and periodically the entire family group gathered before the mourning altar to wail in chorus, giving expression to their family cohesion at this time of sorrow. Genuine lamentation was submerged in ritual pretence, as when the chief mourners were supported at the funeral procession as though incapacitated by grief; and much of the proceedings reflected not just the family's sense of loss, but also the solidarity, respectability, and regard for the rites which they wished to exhibit at this time of crisis by putting on a good show before the world. The extravagance of the funeral arrangements, the assembly of large numbers of relatives and friends, the honorific titles bestowed by the imperial government, the mourning arches built for the occasion in front of the house, the bands playing funeral music, the procession of monks, the decorated sedan-chair for the spirit tablet, and the splendid coffin all served to impress the neighbourhood and to reassure the family of its status at a time when it had suffered loss.

At the same time as mourning displayed a family's solidarity to the outside world, the grades of material and colours of mourning dress, of which there could be as many as a hundred variants representing the different relationships to the deceased, served as a visible reminder of the internal structure of the family. The children of the deceased were naturally expected to weep the most bitter tears, eat the coarsest food, wear the roughest garments, and endure the most protracted period of mourning. Officially this went on for twenty-seven months, which was conventionally described as the three-year mourning period. Members of the civil service had to resign from office, and there was strong sentiment against those statesmen who were granted exemption from this rule on account of their indispensability. The degrees of mourning also had their impact on the law, for punishment for adultery, and for assault and theft involving relations was graded according to a scale which corresponded with the degrees of mourning; and mourning charts were consequently included in the Ming and Ch'ing Dynasty law codes.

But the law not only used the mourning system as a guide to the severity of penalties that should be imposed for various crimes, it also laid down firm rules concerning the mourning itself. The quality of the coffin, grave clothes, and utensils buried with the deceased, the number of bearers, and the size of the grave and graveyard were strictly regulated. But just as sumptuary laws for the living were often ignored, so these regulations were frequently disregarded, especially as it was difficult to condemn the filial piety which led a poor man to give his father a grander burial than the law allowed.

Another matter which deeply concerned the Chinese was the siting of graves, for it was believed that it was possible to site a tomb in relation to the conformation of the landscape and the vicinity of watercourses, in such a way that a mysterious fecundity was drawn from the earth and transmitted to the descendants of the deceased. The science of discovering suitable sites was known as *feng-shui* (wind and water), and people who could afford it would employ expert geomancers to seek the most propitious sites for their family graveyards.

After death the departed ancestors became the recipients of worship. The ancestral rites may be regarded as the essential and universal religion of the Chinese. Even the Buddhists, who abandoned the ties of kinship, were required by Ch'ing law to worship their ancestors. Ancestor worship had been an essential ingredient of Chinese religion since the dawn of history just as surely as the family had been an essential element in the social structure. From the point of view of the state it was a good thing, for it cemented the kinship system which was the main bulwark of the social order. It was not always taken at its face value by

Confucians, some of whom sympathized with the view which had long ago been expressed in the *Record of Rites*, that it was 'simply the expression of human feelings'.[15] Consequently the Jesuits who introduced Christianity to China were able to accept ancestor worship as a ceremony which was without deep religious significance and not incompatible with their own faith. But ancestor worship was seen by the mass of the people as a reciprocal arrangement between the dead and the living, in which the latter looked after the supposed physical needs of the former, while in return the ancestors benignly participated in the affairs of the living, receiving news of important events such as births and betrothals, and advising and conferring benefits upon their descendants. They were still thought of as part of the family in the same way as the bureaucratically organized gods of the popular religion were an extension of the political order reigning on earth.

The focal point of ancestor worship was the domestic shrine which contained the ancestral tablets. These tablets, made of wood, normally represented one individual. They were inscribed with his name, with one dot omitted from one of the characters. This dot was filled in at the graveside rites, preferably by a scholar or man of high status, and this act consecrated the tablet, and made it the resting place of the individual soul. The tablets housed on the domestic altar were subject to the same considerations of hierarchy which affected the living. They included all men and women who had attained social completeness by being married, but young men and women of marriageable age who were single at death might be included through the fiction of posthumous marriage. Children who had committed the unfilial act of dying young were less likely to be retrieved in this way. After three or four generations the tablet was removed and either burnt or buried near the deceased's grave, so the tablets on the domestic altar normally only related to persons who had died within living memory. If there were several brothers in a family, which consequently divided into separate households, the tablets normally remained with the elder brother; so that the other brothers' families had to return to the old home to take part in ancestor worship until deaths in the newly established family furnished a new series of tablets. Alternatively the new household, especially if set up at a distance from the ancestral home, might start with a general tablet recording details of all the ancestors it had left behind. Routine care of the ancestral tablets was generally left to the women, who had to see to the daily offerings of incense, as well as the special sacrifices on the first and fifteenth of the month and also on the death dates of the various ancestors. They were merely delegated to do the routine jobs in the same way as they were delegated responsibility for running the household.

If a clan or part of a clan was rich enough to be able to maintain an ancestral hall, then the removal of the ancestral tablet from the domestic altar might not mean that the deceased passed into oblivion. A new tablet might be made for him and housed in the ancestral hall, where it would remain as long as the hall survived. Here ancestor worship was conducted in a very different atmosphere. The rites were performed twice a year, with only men participating, and they were grander occasions conducted by scholars in accordance with the ritual Classics, quite unlike the intimacy of a woman's prayer in the little domestic shrine. They were also festive occasions which gave the gathering of descendants a chance to glory in the achievements of their ancestors and at the same time reflect on how their own prosperity and distinctions had brought credit to them.

Apart from the domestic shrines and the ancestral halls, worship also took place at the graves, particularly at the Ch'ing Ming (Clear and Bright) festival in the spring, when family parties went out to the ancestral graveyard to tend the graves and make offerings. So the Chinese traditionally thought of the soul of the departed in three different ways. It was located in the ancestral tablet, but it also inhabited the grave, where it was sacrificed to at Ch'ing Ming. Thirdly there was the soul which passed on and was judged by the nether bureaucracy, punished for its crimes on earth, and reborn again in a form which depended on the merits accumulated in previous existences. The group of ancestral tablets reflected the importance of the kinship system in Chinese society, just as the concept of the soul being judged in the underworld mirrored the magistrate's court and the practices of the bureaucratic state.

Through ancestor worship the Chinese evolved a method of transforming the biological links between them into something more enduring, and developed the short-lived memories and affections of mortal life into an organization embracing both the dead and the living, which was hallowed by religious feelings. It gave great cohesion and solidarity to the kinship group, which depended for its success and prosperity on this earth on all the prestige and co-operation it could achieve. But although it was the most important feature of the religious life of the family, there were other objects of devotion. The kitchen god acted as a kind of inspector of the family on behalf of the nether world, and there were door gods to protect the family, wealth gods to bring it prosperity, and even the privy was presided over by its own special deity. Every home was therefore a centre of intense religious activity, in which the ritual which united the family on all important occasions and made it seem a strong, divinely inspired, and immutable institution, was one of the supremely conservative features of the Chinese experience.

IV

The wider kinship unit, which we shall call the clan, has also played an important role in the development of Chinese society. Although there had been powerful noble clan organizations in antiquity, these had later declined; but the clan has flourished (although latterly only among overseas Chinese) since it was revived in the Sung Dynasty as part of a policy of social reform. It was thought that it could provide moral teachings which would parallel and support the function of the law enforced by the state. The newly modelled clan institution was not to be confined to the privileged class but was to permeate the whole of society. In the event the clan system was cherished much more by scholar-officials than by the ordinary people, and it became more deeply entrenched in the south where the better climate and longer growing season produced the kind of prosperity which could finance the clan institutions. Here there were many villages consisting entirely of members of one clan. In the north, by contrast, the frequent floods and droughts resulted in much greater poverty and insecurity, and there were many population movements brought about by barbarian invasions, so the clan system was not able to take such deep root.

The clan consists of all persons of the same surname who can trace their descent from a common ancestor. Consequently it often comprised several thousand members and contained a cross-section of people of all classes, the leadership in clan affairs being taken by members of the scholar-gentry class. Clans normally met twice a year, once in spring, round about the time when the graves were visited, and once again in the autumn. The meetings were held at the ancestral hall, and the proceedings were initiated with a lecture or readings on ethical behaviour delivered by a clan member who was respected for his moral standards. Then sacrifices were made to the ancestors, and afterwards the clan held a business meeting dealing with financial and disciplinary matters. All adult male members were obliged to attend the meeting, but normally only the more distinguished and elderly members took part in the feast which concluded the proceedings. In some clans all attended the feast, and the denial of one's share of the sacrificial meat was used as a sign of excommunication for offences against the clan rules.

These great gatherings deeply impressed the participants with the traditions and moral purposes of the clan and, as members kotowed in order of seniority in the sacrificial ritual, they were imbued with that sense of hierarchy which the ancestral rituals within the family also helped to instil. A Chinese writer's description of the ancestral hall and the tablets within it brings out the impressiveness of this institution:

The heart of the ancestral temple lay in the ancestral altar in the main hall. The altar consisted of one or more elevated, open cases built of intricately carved wood decorated with gold leaf or gold paint. Inside each case were tiers of ascending wooden steps, and on these steps were rows of spirit tablets, each representing a departed ancestor. The centre of the highest tier was occupied by the tablet of the founder or originator of the clan. On the sides and on the lower tiers were the tablets of his descendants, arranged according to the seniority of their generational order. . . . As one case was filled, another would be built to house new tablets. On the altar the hundreds of spirit tablets constituted a visible representation of the long continuity of the clan and stood as a tangible reminder that not living members alone, but the roles of the living and dead together, made up the clan organization.

The spirit tablets were not mere mute blocks of wood, for the members' accomplishments and aspirations were inscribed in wood and stone to resurrect their past. Standing along the walls, hanging under the eaves and on the pillars were carved wooden plaques bearing official ranks, imperial academic degrees, public honours, and citations bestowed upon the clan's illustrious sons by the Imperial and Republican governments and public organizations. Other plaques carried mottoes and exhortations left by the forefathers to inspire ambition and moral quality among their posterity. Looking at the mass of spirit tablets and then turning to the plaques of honorific titles and moral admonitions, one could almost hear the voices of the dead speak out from the altar, recounting their exploits, urging the living to respect the foundations built by the predecessors and to achieve even greater glories.[16]

Apart from these periodic meetings the clan also had a powerful instrument of moral guidance and social control in its genealogy. Genealogical records had been a feature of ancient historical writing, in which the descent lines of royal and noble houses were recorded. In early imperial times the government ran a genealogical bureau, for it was important to keep a check on such matters when civil service appointments depended on descent rather than on merit. But the modern genealogy dating from the Sung period was a private document for the edification of the clan only and it was conceived as a means of promoting Confucian morality within the clan. In addition to the routine genealogical material concerning the ancestors, genealogies might contain prefaces on the illustrious origin of the clan, essays on clan solidarity, information on clan ritual, a description of the ancestral hall, information on the clan property, and citations from government records and other sources referring to the distinguished achievements of famous members of the clan. Many genealogies also provided a code of conduct to govern the personal behaviour of members, administration of the clan organization and property, relations with other clans and with the government, and the treatment of criminal offences.

The clan rules often stipulated punishments, which were more lenient than those provided by the law, so that the clan was in effect protecting its member from the harshness of the state legal system. The clan head was entitled to administer justice in accordance with the clan rules, and to judge the case as he thought fit if there were no written law. Many misdemeanours were therefore punished without the intervention of the state legal process. Litigation was avoided if possible because it was costly, and only when the clan leader could not settle the problem did it get into the courts. The government recognized the clan head's responsibility for administering punishment within the clan, which was in effect an institution for the administration of law at the lowest level. Penalties inflicted by the clan head included fines, corporal punishment, forfeiture of clan privileges, and expulsion from the clan and exclusion from its genealogy, but crimes serious enough to warrant the infliction of penal servitude did not come within the clan head's jurisdiction, and nor did crimes which involved members of other clans, which would have to be taken to court if the cases could not be settled by arbitration or agreement between the clans. In a few cases the death penalty or order to commit suicide are mentioned in the clan rules, although the law did not officially recognize the clan head's power of life and death.

Clan genealogies were revised every generation or so, and copies were normally printed and distributed to each family. Undoubtedly the clan rules did much to spread the Confucianization of society to all classes, although unfortunately they did not reflect the noblest of Confucian ideals. They tended to favour the wealthy and educated who formed the backbone of the clan organization, so the clan's charitable resources did not extend to the poor and humble as effectively as they might have done. Idealistic Confucianism saw the family as a training ground for individuals who might give leadership in the wider sphere of community and state, but clan rules tended to look inward and emphasize the family and clan interest to the exclusion of broader concerns.

The practical manifestation of this self-interest was to be seen in the social welfare schemes financed by the clan's economic resources. Many clan rules stress the virtue of thrift, which was a necessary foundation of group prosperity (although members must not be miserly over provision for a parent's funeral). Collectively owned ancestral estates were also essential to the development of strong clan organizations. Poorer members of the clan could hope to rent corporate property at more favourable rates and with greater security of tenure than in the open market, while for the wealthier members there was great attraction in the building of large estates which were not subject to rapid disintegration within a few generations like family properties divided between sons. The revenue from these estates could be used for the maintenance of the ancestral hall, that symbol of clan solidarity. It could also be used for the maintenance of clan schools and for other charitable purposes, especially the provision of scholarships and travelling expenses to secure success in the examinations for promising members of the clan who would later repay the debt by bringing distinction to it. These charitable estates had first been developed in the Sung period, probably on the model of the Buddhist monastic estates, which accumulated large corporately administered resources as a result of the charity of the faithful.

The clan therefore did provide an effective means of low-level social control, and the under-manned bureaucracy did not normally expect to meddle in its affairs. But there were sometimes violent inter-clan clashes which did cause concern to the state, while the inward-looking clan mores imposed conflicts of loyalty on the more important clan members who had themselves seen service in the bureaucracy. These conflicts of loyalty were, however, minimized by the sensible rule that civil servants could not hold office in their own home locality, so that relations between local officials and clan gentry, harmonious to some extent through shared class ideals, retained a certain necessary aloofness.

It is impossible to exaggerate the extent to which the individual was dominated by family and clan in traditional Chinese society. His upbringing, the formation of his attitudes, his vocation, his public career, his social life, his material security, and his emotional life were all closely bound up with the family. Many of his outside contacts were made through the channels of kinship. There were few associations outside the family to help cater for his needs, and these generally modelled themselves on the family pattern, and used the language of kinship. Bureaucrats were often referred to as 'father-mother officials'. Friends and neighbours addressed each other with kinship terms, although they were not related. Apprentices were solemnly admitted to a relationship with their masters in which they were expected to show the same reverence as a son for a father. Secret societies regarded their founders as 'ancestors' and conducted appropriate rites to them; and literary societies and guilds of craftsmen and merchants were similarly coloured by the predominance of the family institution.

The simplest of such groupings was the sworn brotherhood or sisterhood, which consisted of a small group of friends with identical interests and common aims who, if their purposes were really serious and dangerous, might sip each other's blood to symbolize the tie between them. Sisterhoods were sometimes formed, as we have already seen, by spinsters working away from home and spurning the marriage tie. These groups kept the spirit tablets of deceased members and offered sacrifices to them, just as if they were true families.

The secret society, a very common phenomenon in Chinese history, may be regarded as a kind of expanded version of the sworn brotherhood group, the simulated kinship tie being again symbolized by the mutual sipping of blood by members. The Triad society organization was referred to as a family, the initiation ceremony taking place before an altar which included the spirit tablets of prominent deceased members arranged in order of seniority. The first vow made by the initiate said:

Your parents are the same as my parents; your brothers and sisters, my brothers and sisters; your wives, my sisters-in-law; your sons and nephews, my sons and nephews. Any violation of this rule or any disregard of this sentiment means desecration of this vow, and will bring punishment of death and elimination by thunder.[17]

This simulated family relationship was taken so seriously that a member could not marry or have sexual relations with the widow of a fellow-member, just as if he were truly a brother of that fellow-member.[18]

Some secret societies were primarily religious in character and some were primarily economic and political, using religious rites as a means to secure loyalty and unity of purpose. Religious sects which did not get the legal recognition afforded to Taoism and Buddhism were forced underground, where they faced constant risk of suppression, although they were sustained by the belief that their particular deity would bring universal salvation.

Secret societies became most powerful and rebellious at times of hardship and in places where economic disaster most regularly struck. Often they flourished and broke out in rebellion in the declining years of a dynasty, and the great Taiping Rebellion, which cost many millions of lives and nearly brought down the Ch'ing, was also the climax of a long series of religious uprisings which had plagued even the flourishing days of the Ch'ien-lung emperor's reign. Secret societies eventually helped in the final overthrow of the imperial system. They flourished too in the chaotic early days of the Republic, and the leader of one known as the Single-hearted Celestial Principle Dragon-flower Sacred Religion Society set himself up briefly as emperor. Throughout Chinese history secret societies gave men hope in desperate economic circumstances, and faded into the background when conditions improved. In times of distress they could offer the immediate benefits of belonging to a mutual-aid brotherhood, and often the promise of universal salvation of a kind which owed much to Buddhist inspiration. The leaders were often credited with magical powers and special relationships with the supernatural, and so were able to win the allegiance of the gullible masses who were in need of desperate remedies for their plight. The secret societies were abhorrent to the government not only because of the threat to order and security they represented, but also because they were voluntary groups which fell outside the natural pattern of social organization which they felt to be essential to cosmic order.

V

In this discussion of family and clan and non-kin associations in Chinese society, law and religion have often been mentioned, so it will be appropriate to conclude this survey of the social experience of the Chinese by giving a general impression of the way in which these two important determinants of social behaviour have operated in the Chinese context.

It will have become apparent that the sphere of law was comparatively limited in traditional Chinese society. The law was primarily a penal code set up for the punishment of serious crime. It told the people what not to do, and what would happen to them if they disobeyed. It did not much concern itself with civil matters such as marriage, adoption, and inheritance, which were dealt with in accordance with custom and *li* (propriety) or in conformity with the rules of behaviour adopted by clan or guild or other organization to which a person belonged. Furthermore Confucius had expressed his hostility to litigation, so litigation was where possible avoided. It was an expensive and disagreeable business, for the litigants were exposed to the cruelty and dishonesty of government runners and were dealt with in court in a humiliating manner. There were no professional lawyers to plead one's case and no jurymen to decide its merits, for everything was done by the magistrate himself. Again the vastness of the country and the paucity of officials meant that it was impossible to attempt to enforce the law as effectively as in modern states. Many things were strictly forbidden by law, but widely accepted custom tolerated them. Local communities ran themselves according to their own traditions, and the law stayed in the background as a harsh reminder of what severe penalties could be invoked if the state so wished.

In less developed societies it is the function of authority to declare the law rather than to enforce it, for it does not necessarily have the power to do so. In these circumstances taking the law into one's own hands to avenge a crime is recognized as justifiable. In traditional China the law continued to be a model to aim at rather than a system to be rigidly applied. Hence law codes underwent remarkably little change over the centuries, especially after Confucian values had attained their domination over law and society.

In antiquity there was strong opposition to the impersonal law advocated by the Legalists and it was certainly not thought by the Confucians to be an appropriate sanction for the gentleman. His conduct should be guided by *li* (propriety) and if he erred, he should be censured and his sense of shame should be sufficient to bring him to heel. In the ancient texts actions are often condemned for not being in accordance with *li*. If punishment were necessary, exile, an extreme form of social ostracism, was an appropriate penalty for a gentleman to suffer. The death penalty was not applicable to the gentleman, so in the case of heinous crimes he was given the opportunity to commit suicide in response to the sense of shame which someone with his status and upbringing was bound to feel, instead of being executed and exposed in the market-place like a common criminal. The practical necessities of maintaining law and order in a large empire conspired with the Legalist philosophy to cause a big movement away from these Confucian attitudes. In fact even Hsün Tzu had admitted that legal principles had an important place and in the *Record of Rites* the function of punishment was discussed, so these new attitudes found their way into the Confucian tradition at an early stage.[19] But when they recovered power in the Han

Dynasty and later, the Confucians increasingly breathed the spirit of *li* into the law, and so in the long term they brought about its Confucianization.

Thus the Confucian contrast between superiors and inferiors meant that the noble and the mean received different punishments; and since, according to *li*, clothing, houses, marriages, funerals, and sacrifices must all reflect social status, sumptuary laws came to be written into the codes. The importance of preserving the family system and hierarchical relationships within it also came to be reflected in the law's differential scale of punishments linked to degrees of relationship.

In fact the Confucian family ethic influenced the law in a variety of ways. The father's role was so dominant that not only could he beat his sons unmercifully, but he could also have them flogged by the court on charges of disobedience brought by him. Similarly filial piety was so strongly regarded that sons were sometimes pardoned for killing their father's murderers, and thus the old right of vengeance was sometimes admitted even in modern times. Again the law allowed one to conceal the crime of a close relative and not testify against him in court, except in the case of rebellion, where duty to the state took priority. Sometimes a criminal was pardoned or had his sentence reduced if his son, grandson, or younger brother volunteered to be punished in his place. For a period such substitution even became compulsory in the case of criminals who were over eighty or were seriously ill.[20] From the T'ang period onwards a criminal sentenced to death might be pardoned by the emperor if he had to look after aged or sick parents or grandparents. We have already seen that crimes committed against relatives were punished more severely than crimes against strangers. The exception to this was the case of theft, for it was considered less serious to steal from a relative, since relatives were under obligation to help each other in case of need. The mourning system, as we have also seen, played an important role because it provided a basis for calculating sentences in accordance with relationships. Moreover, the rules of propriety concerning the three-year mourning period for parents found their way into the law: sons could be punished for holding office or marrying when they should have been in mourning, and the T'ang code even prescribed the death penalty for anyone who conceived during the mourning period. So in the end the Confucian ethical principles which did much to stabilize Chinese society were supported by the sanctions of both *li* and law, which came into harmony with each other. Thus law was closely involved with ethics and customs and did not develop its own independent existence. It was always simply an instrument of government, and part of the ordinary routine of administration.

VI

Religion also did not attain that separate and independent status which a powerful church has sometimes achieved in European society. Despite the existence of major religions like Buddhism and Taoism, each with its own independent institutions and activities, the religious experience of the vast majority of the Chinese has not revolved about one of these to the exclusion of everything else. Instead, all of life's activities have been coloured and enriched by religious attitudes derived from a variety of sources, and Buddhism and Taoism have made their own characteristic contributions to the general stock of religious experience. Religion was part of family life through worship of ancestors and household gods, it affected community life through temple festivals, it permeated working life through the worship of the patron deities of craft guilds, it conditioned political life through the doctrine of the Son of Heaven, it entered local affairs through the religious duties of district magistrates, and it influenced education through the reverence paid to Confucius. Because of its diffuse nature, it has to be described in terms of its impact on various facets of the Chinese experience rather than in a separate chapter, but now that the religious experience of the Chinese has forced itself upon our attention in various contexts, it is possible to make some general observations about it.

The nature of Chinese religion was blurred by early Western missionary scholars, who often concentrated on the three systems of Confucianism, Taoism, and Buddhism in their more philosophical manifestations to the exclusion of the teeming folk religions of the country. In the late imperial period Confucianism's rivals were to be seen only in decadent form, and in the light of the Master's own beliefs Confucianism itself could be represented as a doctrine which was concerned with this world rather than the next, so some modern Chinese intellectuals have been glad to think of their society as superior to the West because it was not dominated by ecclesiastics and did not tear itself apart for religious reasons. Many Western sinologists have similarly over-emphasized the agnostic character of Confucianism.

In fact religion coloured all aspects of Chinese life. The countryside teemed with temples, which the ordinary Chinese patronized according to the needs of the moment. If money was wanted, there were many gods of wealth, and if children were wanted, the local temple to Kuanyin might be the solution to one's problems. For the common people the purpose of religion was to obtain happiness and ward off evil, and to this end they sought the aid of the most efficacious gods. People were not concerned with the boundaries between various faiths, and country priests sometimes did not even know what religions their temples belonged to, for the gods had got themselves mixed up into a common pantheon. A man's morality might be derived from Confucian ideas with an admixture of Buddhism, but the role of the generality of gods and spirits was to punish him if he erred and reward him if he behaved morally. The moral order was heavily dependent on these popular religious beliefs as a deterrent to deviation from its rules. People were conscious of ever-present divinities inspecting their conduct; for instance, the kitchen god made yearly reports on the conduct of the family to the Jade Emperor, who presided over a bureaucracy of deities who would eventually be called upon to judge one's performance and determine one's future in the afterlife.

This eclectic attitude to religion meant that there were no such things as church membership or regular congregational worship. The ordinary people did not derive their religious beliefs from sermons or from readings of sacred scriptures, but mainly from mythological lore in which moral behaviour was supported by supernatural forces. As deterrents to unethical behaviour there were vivid and detailed descriptions of the hells appropriate to various types of misdeed, which became part of the folklore and were vividly depicted in temple paintings and book illustrations.

To see how this situation came about it is necessary to try to envisage the historical development of religion in China. In the most ancient known form of Chinese religion the two important elements were already ancestor worship and the worship of Heaven and subordinate nature deities, such as the gods of mountains and streams. In the ruling families of the states, ancestor worship had great political significance, since the ancestors were protectors of the state, and 'to preserve the ancestral temple' was a term often used to mean 'to preserve the integrity of the state'. In imperial times the emperor's ancestors also had this protective role. In Shang and early Chou times, divination was very important, and rulers constantly consulted the oracles about their proposed actions. Hence political decisions, if supported by the oracle, acquired a sacred character, and this was an early example of how political power could exploit religion. When the Han Dynasty sought to consolidate the unification of China, it was possible for it to absorb local religious beliefs into an empire-wide system by the simple process of incorporating local divinities into the pantheon of deities subordinate to the supreme power of Heaven.

However, the early period of empire saw the growth of religious Taoism and Buddhism, both of which were not part of the universally accepted Chinese tradition (like ancestor worship and the worship of nature deities), but were religions voluntarily accepted by individuals. Buddhism was also a foreign religion, and its growth in China posed the same kind of problems as Christianity in the Roman Empire. At first it gained strength through political patronage and through the appeal of its foreignness at the courts of the barbarian rulers of north China, but ultimately it posed an economic and political problem by drawing people off into the tax-free havens of the monasteries. Consequently, although the early T'ang rulers had tried to win support by patronizing the religion, the late T'ang government, weakened and xenophobic after the catastrophe of the An Lu-shan rebellion, eventually resorted to persecutions after which the faith never regained its old strength as a separate institution. Later it continued to survive but the size of the priesthood was carefully controlled by the state. In the long run there were many reasons why Buddhism, despite its impact on Chinese mores, could not become a powerful institution in its own right: Buddhist renunciation of the world could not provide a totally satisfying ethic for the secular life; and unlike their Christian counterparts in Europe, the Buddhist priesthood never found a part to play in the educational system, nor did Buddhist literature, which was too closely concerned with propagation of the religion, seem to have any general educational relevance. Lacking a central organization and restricted in size by the state, it suffered also from the eclecticism of the Chinese attitude towards religion, which went so far that many Buddhist monasteries were given names which had a Confucian ring to them. Since the sixteenth century there has been a tendency towards the harmonization of the three great religions, so that images of Confucius, Lao Tzu, and the Buddha have appeared side by side in the same temples. Harmony between the three religions is a prominent feature of religion in Taiwan today.

So in recent centuries the impact of Buddhism on the Chinese people has not been in the form of doctrinal developments nor have the monasteries and temples played an essential role in its influence, although the monastic life did continue to fulfil an important social function as a haven for those who lacked the all-important support of family and clan. Rather it is to be seen in the diffusion throughout society of certain key ideas and the general influence they had on Chinese culture—for example, Buddhist compassion lent support to Confucian benevolence. The most powerful and invasive concept was *karma*, the cycle of rebirth in which the deserving were reborn to a higher existence and the undeserving to a lower or more unfortunate life. Its profound influence is testified to by frequent references in short stories and novels. Characters often say things like, 'The reason I have no son is because I did not do enough good in my last life.' Animals are constantly thought of as human beings receiving punishment for sins committed in a previous existence, and the whole idea of *karma* is a profound consolation for those who have acted virtuously but failed to get their deserts in this life. The effect of this doctrine in particular was that Buddhism, instead of being a threat to the state, came to play a humble role in securing order among the people and served as a means of moral education for the masses. At the same time the deities of both Buddhism and Taoism tended to merge into an amorphous popular religion. Both religions even made their impact on the ancient indigenous practice of ancestor worship, for their priests participated with their own rites in funerals and sacrifices. So, although as separate institutions these two religions with their hostile messages could have been a threat to the state, in the end they were tamed by it, and Buddhist beliefs in particular helped to maintain the stability of social institutions.

In the last centuries of the imperial period the government exercised an increasingly firm control over religious behaviour. The persecution of heresy which had helped to reduce Buddhism to a servant of the state and society continued, so that sectarian religious movements were still being suppressed in the present century. Religions came under the administration of a government department, the Board of Rites, and no new monasteries, temples, or other religious buildings could be put up without government permission. This prohibition does not seem to have been very sternly enforced, but the number of priests was rigidly controlled by licensing. Although in earlier periods the government had sold ordination certificates in order to raise revenue, these now had to be surrendered on the deaths of their holders. The purpose of government policy was to ensure that religion was a force for political stability and to prevent the growth of independent religious groups which might prove to be a threat to the administration by offering the people an instant cure for their misfortunes.

The government not only exercised negative control, but also provided a positive stimulus to approved religious practices, by classifying temples as either for official sacrifice or for the people's sacrifice. The temples for the people's sacrifice were mainly those to which people went to pray for their personal needs. Official cults were those which satisfied the definition which was given in the *Record of Rites* two thousand years ago, but which still applied in the twentieth century:

> According to the regulations of the sage kings about sacrifices, they should be offered to those who bestowed laws upon the people, those who gave their lives in the fulfilment of their duties, those who stabilized a country through their labours, and those who were capable of warding off great disasters. . . . The sun and moon, the stars and constellations are what the people look up to; and the mountain forests, river valleys, and the hillsides are the places whence people obtain materials for their use. Only such men and things are included in the sacrificial canon.[21]

The local official had to sacrifice at the appropriate times to all officially recognized gods within his jurisdiction, on the one hand the gods of earth and grain, of the local mountains and rivers, and of the forces of nature (wind, thunder, rain, etc.), and on the other hand the spirits of sage monarchs, brilliant princes, loyal officials, and heroic martyrs whose temples lay within his district. In other words they had to worship not only divinities symbolizing natural forces, but also those related to political leadership and civic virtues.

From antiquity it had been the practice to offer sacrifices to men who had distinguished themselves for their moral and civic qualities, and occasionally a temple was even erected to a prominent man while he was still alive. But just as men were treated as gods, so gods behaved like men; and as Chinese civilization became more bureaucratic, so this was reflected in the common belief in a divine bureaucracy which was modelled very closely on its human counterpart. This divine bureaucracy was presided over by the Jade Emperor, and it rewarded the good and punished the evil both in this life and in the hereafter. It had the same paraphernalia of filing systems and red tape associated with the earthly bureaucracy, and the same kind of rules of protocol. Men had to go through the proper channels when approaching the gods, so the common people could only appeal to subordinate deities. City gods, who filled a role in this divine bureaucracy comparable with that of the district magistrate among living bureaucrats, were graded according to the size of the territory they administered; and they occupied what were envisaged as official posts, which were filled on a short-term basis by a series of meritorious deceased officials. The divine bureaucracy was not all superior to the earthly bureaucracy, so living officials could instruct, reward, or punish divinities of inferior rank. Indeed there were even cases of district magistrates thrashing city gods in time of drought to try to make them send down rain. The emperor had authority over all but the highest gods, and temples throughout the country bore tablets indicating the titles and honours conferred by him on deserving deities, so that people got the impression that he held power over gods and spirits as well as men.

In literature gods are often depicted as behaving in a totally human fashion. There is, for example, a Ming Dynasty play about a god who is a rapist being fought and wounded by a soldier, and later demoted by the emperor at the soldier's request. Another story about the nether world has reference to a house of ill repute patronized by clerical workers, and another tells of civil service examinations in the nether world taking place at the same time as they do on earth. Another describes how an ex-bandit nominated as successor to a god whose image he has smashed as a punishment for immorality is himself so moral that he does not wish to inherit the wife of the god he has replaced, so that her statue has to be moved to another part of the temple. In late imperial China gods were routine figures, who had all the vices, and even some of the virtues, of human beings.

CHAPTER 8

THE ECONOMIC EXPERIENCE

I

In considering the social experience of the Chinese we have been mainly concerned with the individual family, with the relationships within it, and with its manner of coping with birth, marriage, and death, which are the main crises in its life. The family is also important as a basic unit in the economic organization of China, for at least in the late Ch'ing and Republican periods the typical family was the peasant household working its scattered three or four acres outside the village. But whereas the story of the social experience of the Chinese is the story of how a certain pattern was followed in innumerable individual families throughout the length and breadth of China, the story of the economic experience of the Chinese must concern itself less with how the individual peasant household tilled its tiny plots of ground than with the cumulative effect of all the hard work, ingenuity, and thrift of these families (and of their brethren involved in craft and industry, trade and commerce), in bringing about the economic development of China, using the resources which nature and climate had put at their disposal. All the palaces and temples and refinements of life depended ultimately on the thrift and labour of these sturdy peasants.

An important part of any country's history is its struggle to provide itself with the economic resources necessary to survival and progress; and this is dramatically true in the case of China, for the major theme is the gradual occupation of the land by generation after generation of farming people, spreading far and wide from the early nucleus of Chinese civilization in the Yellow River valley. History shows how this ever-increasing area of settled agriculture needed to be protected from the nomadic peoples on the northern frontier, and how more and more land had to be exploited by better and better methods to support the huge and ever-growing population. Dynasties rose and fell in accordance with their effectiveness in organizing these toiling masses and providing tolerable conditions for survival. The story is not yet complete, for large areas of China are still peopled with aborigines of non-Chinese stock whose lands have not been entirely absorbed by the dominant Han race, while the last quarter of a century has seen an attempt to provide for the now mammoth population by means of land reform and technological development in agriculture.

The vital importance of agriculture was recognized in antiquity, when farming was referred to as the 'root' or basic occupation. Farmers were treated as second of the four traditional social categories, coming after scholars, but before craftsmen and merchants, the latter being disesteemed because they were thought not to create wealth but merely to exploit it. This simple ancient class structure was remarkably persistent. In remote antiquity literacy in the form of ability to interpret oracles and compile state annals was a basic essential to political authority, and consequently throughout Chinese history the scholar-bureaucrat was dominant. Of vital importance to the members of that class were the peasants who provided the wherewithal to keep them alive, so they were admitted by the scholar-bureaucrats to be second in importance to themselves and were entitled to move up into their own ranks. The only other two significant classes, the craftsmen and the merchants, were viewed as servants of the ruling elite, for whom they provided less essential goods, and so were thought of as engaged in 'branch' activities as contrasted with the 'root' occupation of the peasants. Merchants and craftsmen continued to be underprivileged, although less so from the Sung period onwards, when closer liaison between ruling and commercial interests gradually became more common. Despite its irrelevance to the complexities of the late imperial period, the fourfold class system survived, for in Chinese society, classical models often persisted long after they matched the reality. It is noteworthy that the model consigns no place to scholarly activity except in the government service. It also allows no recognition in the scale of social esteem to other criteria such as wealth, military valour, or holiness. These four traditional categories will form the basis of this survey of the economic experience of the Chinese, which will deal in turn with agriculture, industry, and trade (the occupations of the three lowest classes) and conclude with an account of how the scholar-bureaucrats in the government tried to secure economic control and exploitation of the other three classes.

The success or failure of the peasants to perform their fundamental role in the state depended on various factors: what crops they grew, what animals they kept, what tools they used, and how satisfactorily technological improvements and the increase in the area of land under cultivation could keep pace with a population which was always large by world standards. It also depended on the nature of the system of land tenure. Traditional China did attain high standards in many aspects of agricultural practice, such as the intensive application of human labour, the development of irrigation devices, the use of marginal lands by terracing, and the development of improved strains of rice; but land tenure was one important area in which it was impossible to reach a satisfactory solution. The basic trouble was that although the state depended on the grain-tribute which accrued from the labour of those who tilled the soil, there was a recurring tendency for impoverished peasants to have to give up their land, which then accumulated in the hands of powerful landlords who were able to avoid the payment of tax. Although fair distribution of land was a traditional ideal, the state was never able to find a means to securing this end; and the nineteenth and early twentieth centuries saw such extremes of wealth and poverty in the countryside that it is not surprising that at last a regime has appeared which has made drastic attempts to ensure that the land is used for the general benefit.

The ancient ideal was the 'well-field' system, which late Chou thought attributed to the golden age at the beginning of that dynasty, and which had a powerful impact on the imagination of later agrarian reformers. The system takes its name from the Chinese character for 'well', which looks like a noughts and crosses pattern, and the idea was that an estate should be divided up along the lines of such a pattern, and that the eight outlying sections should each be cultivated by a single peasant family to supply its own needs, while all eight families combined to cultivate the central square for the support of the lord (or for public purposes, as Mencius put it).[1] This plan has generally been dismissed as an idealization which cannot have been put into practical effect; but on the other hand it was found possible, as we shall see, to operate a system of equal distribution of land at a much later time in Chinese history. Certainly in the early stages of Chinese agriculture, when there was much completely undeveloped land to be exploited, it would seem natural to have some method of allocating equal portions of land to peasant families. Indeed the ancient belief that the sage king Yü divided the land into nine provinces on the same pattern could perhaps have originated as a reflection of this simple method of land allocation.

The early Chou peasants did not, of course, own the land on which they worked. They farmed temporary clearances and their status was serf-like, but after the seventh century BC permanent fields came to be established, so that land became a saleable commodity, in which a brisk trade was being done by the fourth century BC. The process of change from the early Chou manorial type of economy towards a system of free peasants who paid taxes and rendered services to the state was hastened by the rise of the radical and anti-feudal Ch'in; but in the Former Han more and more of the unsuccessful lost their lands and became tenants of the prosperous, and the disease worsened as fewer and fewer free tax-payers remained to pay heavier and heavier taxes while vast areas of the country turned into latifundia. This crisis toppled the Former Han, and led to a vain attempt by the usurper Wang Mang to solve the problem by nationalization of the land. The Later Han also suffered from not being able to keep the powerful families under control, and few peasants succeeded in remaining independent. The typical great families of this period controlled vast tracts of land, including numerous villages and various industrial enterprises, and the wealthy landowner's entourage would include hundreds of dependents and slaves, as well as a large private army. Recent tomb excavations give some indication of the enormous riches which these families enjoyed. When the Later Han collapsed, these powerful independent barons made it impossible for any strong dynasty to emerge as its successor; and the invasions of non-Chinese people from the north merely confirmed the trend, for the tribal chieftains adopted the same pattern of great family estates which reduced the peasant population to serfdom.

The Northern Wei was the first dynasty powerful enough to attempt a solution of these problems, which they did by introducing the 'equal fields' system. This radical innovation implied a reassertion of the doctrine that all land belonged to the state, so that it was only held for the lifetime of the tenant, except for small plots needed for the mulberry trees essential to silk production, which had to be retained on a long-term hereditary basis. The amount of land allocated varied according to the number of males, slaves, and oxen in the family. To make this new system acceptable to the local chieftains with large estates, their revenues from these estates were now treated as salaries, so they were no worse off although the state had formally taken over their lands.

A similar system was adopted by succeeding northern dynasties and practised quite extensively and successfully in the early part of the T'ang. Under the T'ang system each male between the ages of sixteen and sixty was granted 100 *mu* (about thirteen acres) of land, twenty of which were to be held in perpetuity. His allotment dropped to forty *mu* at the age of sixty, but he was no longer liable to taxation. Where there was not enough land for the full entitlement smaller amounts were given. Officials were given large areas in accordance with their rank, but a serious flaw in the system was that, unlike the peasants, they held their concessions in perpetuity. What made things worse was that emperors could not restrain themselves from making presents of large tracts of untaxed land to their favourites. Inevitably also the privileged and powerful infringed the rights of the unprivileged peasant, and lands were illegally sold, so that large estates again began to accumulate. In some areas the equal fields system could never have been successful. It was not suited, for example, to rice-growing regions, where constant efforts were needed to maintain irrigation ditches for the long-term benefit of the crops, so that length of tenure was necessary if productivity was to be maintained. Finally the An Lu-shan Rebellion dealt a severe blow to the system, which could only work in settled times because of the need for very careful registration of land. By the tenth century China had moved into another period in which few independent peasants remained and the bulk of the land was held in the form of large estates worked by tenant-serfs.

An eleventh century description says 'rich commoners have vast properties, the fields of which stretch out in unbroken lines. They recruit migrants, and assign the cultivation to them. They drive them to work under the lash of the whip, treating them as serfs'.[2] But although the home farm would be under the close supervision of the proprietor or his manager, the outlying tenants would probably be free from day to day interference, although they were bound to the land and to service. Conditions for the peasants became even harsher in the Yüan period, when large tracts of land were confiscated for the use of the Mongol army and aristocracy. The Ming also made no attempt to keep landlordism within bounds.

Land was valued because of the social prestige attached to it, and also because of its security. As one early Ch'ing writer put it,

Only land is a commodity that is continually new, even after a hundred or a thousand years. . . . From of old until the present there has never been any anxiety that it will rot, decay, crumble, or be destroyed, nor any worry that it will run away or get less. . . . Always when goods are gathered together in this world there is fear of floods, fires, and robbers. The rarest of precious objects easily attract the swiftest misfortunes. . . . Only with land do we not worry about floods, or fires, or robbers and do not exert ourselves to protect it. If there is fighting or drought or floods, we can leave our place of residence, coming back when the trouble has passed.[3]

Nevertheless land was not the most lucrative of investments, and from the sixteenth century onwards the greatly increasing commercial activity inevitably attracted the wealthy land-owning class so that they began to diversify and invest their resources in more profitable activities such as trade and money-lending. Consequently commercial activity became respectable and merchants ceased to be discriminated against. Also, tenant uprisings in the seventeenth century had done much to undermine the institution of serfdom. Many of the great land-owners moved their residences to live in town, and rarely came out into the countryside, so their hold over the peasants weakened. Great estates were being fragmented on inheritance, and there was no longer the same incentive to build them up again now that better opportunities of investment were available. Gradually land tenure was transformed until by the early nineteenth century the Chinese countryside was largely farmed by smallholders and petty landlords who owned little more land than the peasants.

II

This brings us to the typical Chinese peasant family of the first half of the twentieth century, trying to eke out a living from a mere three or four acres of land, which, to make matters worse, was often in small, widely scattered parcels. It was not enough to support an adequate standard of living, although they wasted not a scrap of anything, using grain stalks for fuel and human as well as animal excrement for fertilizer. Even in good years survival was their only hope, and for the future all they had was the nagging fear that flood or drought would bring death or misery to hundreds of thousands of their kind. There was such intense pressure on the land that no improvement in their lot could be achieved by traditional agriculture, and modern technology was very slow to penetrate the countryside. Rural decline was speeded by the import of foreign manufactured goods, a disaster for the handicraft industry which had brought supplementary income to the peasant families; while the turbulent political situation in the early twentieth century and the devastation caused by the Japanese occupation and civil war meant that a drastic agrarian reform would be necessary once the country returned to stable government.

The depressed state of the countryside in the early twentieth century was the final defeat in the struggle of traditional agriculture to keep pace with a population which had grown at a high rate during the eighteenth and nineteenth centuries. To understand the development of agriculture in China it is necessary to remember that the north and south of the country have radically different types of climate. The north has very cold winters and hot summers (in Peking, for example, the average temperatures range from $-5°$ Centigrade in January to $25·6°$ Centigrade in July). Rainfall is limited and unreliable, so droughts frequently occur. The landscape is flat and brown, and donkeys have always been a common means of transport. The main crop in antiquity was millet, and later other dry-land crops such as wheat were grown. South China has plenty of rainfall and a lush green landscape and much smaller variations in temperature. The main crop is rice, and a great abundance and variety of fruit is also grown. Countless boats ply along the rivers and canals and across the lakes. Until the T'ang period the weight of political and economic strength had been in the north, but the development of canal communications with the south caused that area to develop rapidly, especially during the Southern Sung, when the north of China was under foreign control. North–south migration was a constant feature of Chinese history, which was intensified in the periods when the north was under barbarian control. As early as the Sung period, the hillsides in the Lower Yangtze region and Fukien began to be terraced for rice cultivation because the lowland space was getting crowded, and from Ming times northern dry-land crops were grown in the southern uplands.

There were two main periods of technical development in traditional Chinese agriculture. The middle and late Chou period saw the introduction of the first extensive irrigation schemes and the earliest use of iron tools. The animal drawn plough also came into use, and fallowing and the use of fertilizer became common. In the Sung Dynasty there was a further period of advance, characterized in the south by the development of more sophisticated methods of water-control, such as the noria and the treadle water-pump, which hereafter became common features of the rural scene. There was also a big improvement in strains of seed, so that they became more drought-resistant, yielded more heavily, or came to maturity more quickly. These quick-maturing strains made double cropping common, and even triple cropping was possible in some areas. Unprecedented development of a commercial network meant that there was much more scope for the farmer to specialize in the crops most suited to his own land. All the new techniques were widely disseminated, since the development of printing encouraged the publication of practical handbooks on agriculture; and, for the benefit of the illiterate, pictures illustrating farming methods were painted on the walls of government offices. In the north at this time there was also some progress, for better milling machinery led to widespread cultivation of wheat, but it was in the south that progress was made on several fronts at once. However, after this period of rapid development the pace slowed down dramatically, and innovation in farming techniques almost came to a halt, so that the increase in population could only be catered for by exploiting virgin lands and by extending the best farming techniques to the more backward areas.

In the early twentieth century the Chinese were slow to take advantage of modern farming techniques. Energetic young Chinese with an interest in technology were attracted by the importance of building up industrial power, so little happened to bring about improvements in the countryside, which continued to suffer deeply from the social and economic disintegration which followed the breakdown of the old order. Large-scale mechanization, massive use of chemical fertilizers, and a huge programme of irrigation projects would be necessary before China could keep pace with her rapidly growing population and hope to give her people modest increases in their standard of living. One striking example of the task awaiting the present regime is that, in spite of the long history of water control in China, it was claimed that in 1957 and 1958 more land was brought under irrigation than in the whole of previous Chinese history.

Apart from cereals and vegetables, the peasant family also reared chickens and pigs for food. It was profitable to keep pigs because they were a valuable source of fertilizer as well as meat. In antiquity dogs were also reared for food, and sheep and cows were common in earlier periods, but in the small-scale garden-type farming which was characteristic of the nineteenth and early twentieth centuries there was obviously no space for grazing animals.

The peasant family also traditionally produced its own clothing, the other great basic necessity of life. According to Mencius's injunction, the homestead of a mere five *mu* should keep mulberry trees for the feeding of silkworms.[4] Sericulture had been practised in China back in neolithic times, and it continued to be of fundamental importance, so that the equal fields system of the Northern Wei and T'ang periods allowed the retention in perpetuity of land for the planting of mulberry trees (fruit-trees not even being mentioned in the legislation). Silk had a very important part to play in the Chinese experience, for it was not merely used for clothing. Before paper was invented two thousand years ago it was also commonly used for writing on and it continued to be used by painters as an alternative to paper. It was a valuable export commodity, and it was sent to the Roman Empire in such quantity that the Roman economy was harmed by the eastward drain of silver. The Latin name for the Chinese was Seres, which was derived from the Chinese word for silk, and the transcontinental route across Eurasia came to be known as the Silk Route. Silk was also known in Egypt in the first century B C and was worn by Cleopatra. Later, in China, it had a long history of being used as a currency in large-scale transactions: for example, the Sung Dynasty paid tribute to its northern neighbours, the Liao and Hsi-hsia states, in the form of bolts of silk. Internally silk was a status symbol, for in general in imperial times the wearing of silk of the finest quality distinguished the official classes from the ordinary people, who could not wear any but the poorest qualities of silk. In the late imperial period officials were distinguished from commoners by the fact that they wore satin boots.

The common dress material in antiquity was hemp, which also dated from neolithic times, but from late Sung onwards cotton became the normal cloth for ordinary wear. Cotton was not native to China, but by the Former Han the plant had spread to Central Asia from Western India where it was indigenous. Cotton cloth entered China as tribute from the Han to the T'ang and may have been manufactured in China as early as the T'ang period. By the end of the Ming cotton manufacture was very widespread, occurring in four-fifths of the counties of China. Again the industry was generally organized round peasant households, which made sufficient cotton cloth for their own use and sold small quantities of surplus cloth in the market. In the town, families sometimes had more than one loom and took in a few hired weavers, but production tended to remain on a small scale. Although cotton manufacture was widespread, the growing of cotton was restricted to certain small areas.

Textile technology early reached a very high level, and a water-operated spinning machine, illustrated in a manual of 1313, was very widely used, but it had completely gone out of service by the seventeenth century. In fact there was no great incentive to technological progress in textiles. The British cotton industry was able to expand rapidly because vast resources of the raw material had been found in the West Indies and South America, but China could ill spare the diversion of more land to cotton production. Surplus labour was also readily available on the farms during the slack seasons. Nor was the silk industry capable of rapid expansion, because its size is dictated by the number of mulberry-trees, which have to be brought to maturity. The merchants who dealt in textiles did not themselves become directly involved in production, for there was no need for them to tie up their capital by financing it. There were big undertakings, such as the imperial silk factories and the large-scale private enterprise in Soochow, Hangchow, and Nanking which was also closely linked with the needs of government, but the combination of circumstances which might lead to an industrial revolution failed to materialize despite the early technological breakthroughs which the Chinese had made in various fields.

III

It is only since the Second World War that Europeans have begun to be aware of how the world has been transformed by Chinese inventiveness. It used to be held by Europeans that the Chinese race lacked scientific and technological understanding, and even a distinguished Chinese philosopher could write an article called 'Why China has no science';[5] but the researches of Joseph Needham have now shown that the mandarin robe was not out of place in the laboratory. Many Chinese inventions ultimately transformed the world, without having a similarly dramatic effect on China itself. Of these, four are generally given pride of place because of their truly epoch-making impact: paper, printing, gunpowder, and the magnetic compass. Paper was originally made from tree bark, hemp, old rags, and other materials, and the traditional date of its invention was AD 105, but archaeological discoveries have shown that it was in use in the second century BC. As a writing material of remarkable cheapness it was to have a profound effect on the history of education and literacy, but it was not until the eighth century, when some Chinese paper-makers were captured by Arabs at the Battle of Talas, that a military engagement brought this civilizing material across to Western Asia and thence to Christian Europe, which it eventually reached in the thirteenth century. Before the invention of paper the Chinese had written on silk or on strips of wood or bamboo tied together.

The invention of printing supported this innovation and helped to ensure that learning would henceforth be widely disseminated instead of being merely the privilege of the few. The technique of printing developed out of the early use of seals with characters carved on them to authenticate documents. The Buddhists found this device particularly useful because a method of reproducing large numbers of religious charms or even of texts was a valuable means of religious propaganda, which at the same time ensured that the person responsible accumulated a large store of merit. (It will be remembered that according to the debased belief of the Pure Land School the repeated enunciation of the name of Amitabha was sufficient to secure eternal bliss, so repetition in writing was thought to bring similar benefits.) From the printing of charms it was not too great a step to the reproduction of whole books from woodblocks, and very fine standards of craftsmanship had already been achieved before the end of the T'ang, as can be seen from the oldest extant datable printed book, the *Diamond Sutra* of 868 which is now in the British Museum. The development of printing was also stimulated by another traditional practice apart from seal-carving. From the Later Han Dynasty onwards it was thought to be the solemn duty of government to give permanence to an accurate edition of the Confucian Classics by having it engraved on stone tablets from which rubbings could be taken by individuals needing a copy of the authentic version. The transition from this practice of taking rubbings to block printing merely required that the characters be carved in relief instead of incised and cut back to front so that they came out the right way round on the printed copy. Nevertheless, the first woodblock printing of the Classics, produced by one of the short-lived Five Dynasties, was regarded as rather a makeshift way of recording a new edition of the Classics by comparison with the engraving in stone which the imperial dignity properly demanded. It was not until the fifteenth century that this invention passed to Europe, although even movable type printing, much less suited to the Chinese language with its innumerable characters than to an alphabetic script, had already been in use in the Far East as early as the eleventh century.

The third of the great world-shaking discoveries was magnetism, which eventually, when knowledge of the magnetic compass reached the West, provided an indispensable tool for European exploration and colonization. Although magnetism was known to no other people in the ancient world apart from the Chinese, a primitive compass was in use in the Han Dynasty. At that time it was only used to determine auspicious sites for buildings or tombs, and it may not have been employed in navigation before the tenth century.

The fourth of these most influential discoveries was gunpowder, which eventually enabled Europeans to dominate the world they had explored by means of the compass, although in China its use did not make a similar revolutionary impact. There had been a long tradition of chemistry in China, and pieces of bronze apparatus dating from the Han period have survived. Such researches were inspired by the Taoist quest for an elixir of immortality, which encouraged experimentation with all kinds of chemical substances. These activities stimulated major advances in medical knowledge, but gunpowder was the most formidable product of medieval Chinese alchemy. At first it was used mainly for fireworks, but in the tenth century it came into military use.

Among weapons the crossbow is believed to have been used thirteen centuries earlier in China than in Europe. Also important for its effect on warfare was the development of the foot-stirrup, the earliest evidence of which appears on tomb figurines dating from about AD 300: by welding the rider to his steed it enhanced the efficiency of the cavalryman and helped him retain his supremacy in warfare right through to the Mongol domination of the Euro-Asian landmass in the fourteenth century. The Chinese also led the world in making the horse more efficient in its civil capacity – as a draught-animal – by developing improvements in harness. In ancient times they used a form of breast-strap harness which was much superior to the harness used in ancient Europe, and they even used the modern type of collar harness in the fifth century AD, about three hundred years before it came into use in Europe. Before railways and motorcars came on the scene, the efficient use of horse-power had an important effect in Europe, not only in the development of transport, but also in social changes due to the availability of easy long-distance carriage of goods. In China, where the water buffalo is the main plough-animal, and rivers and canals the main means of transport for much of the country, the impact was not so great.

In agriculture, as we have already seen, the main technological advances in antiquity were in the development of water control and in the introduction of cast-iron tools. Cast iron was invented in China eighteen centuries before it came to be known and used in Europe. Iron technology continued to improve, especially after the invention of piston bellows operated by water power in the first century AD, which was the earliest application of water power to industry in China. A notable use of this metal, as early as the beginning of the seventh century AD was in the construction of iron chain suspension bridges, which replaced some of the old bamboo cable suspension bridges used to cross ravines in south-west China. It was more than a thousand years before such bridges were constructed in Europe. In the Northern Sung Dynasty the iron and steel industry reached heights of technical achievement and of productivity which were not surpassed in China until the nineteenth century. Good iron and coal deposits were available in close proximity to the capital, Kaifeng; and large-scale undertakings turned out huge quantities of the tools of war and peace – swords, bows, arrows, spades, hoes, and ploughshares. Much iron was also needed to supply the rapidly expanding shipbuilding industry of the time with anchors, nails, and armour. Iron was also used for bridges, gates, pagodas, Buddhist images, and the heavy pans needed by the salt industry. Iron currency was put into circulation in some border regions to try to prevent copper cash from flowing out of the country. The Northern Sung was in general a period of remarkable industrial expansion: the use of coal both for domestic and for industrial purposes reached a peak which was not surpassed until modern times; and such industries as shipbuilding, printing, and paper-making operated on a greater scale than anywhere else in the world before the late eighteenth century.

Shipbuilding in China was characterized by another group of inventions, which helped to make water transport more efficient. Water-tight compartments were not used in the construction of European shipping until the early nineteenth century, although they were invented in China more than a thousand years before. The stern-post rudder existed in China in the first century BC, but was not used in Europe until the twelfth century. Paddle-wheel boats were first referred to in the literature of the fifth century AD; and treadmill-operated paddle-wheel boats, which had taken part in important military campaigns in earlier centuries, were still in operation in the Opium War (1839–42), when the British thought they were imitations of their own paddle-steamers, although the history of the paddle-boat in Europe does not go back beyond the sixteenth century. Canal lock-gates were another ancient Chinese device, but they were not used in Europe until the fifteenth century.

The technique of deep drilling was in use in Szechwan province from the Han Dynasty onwards. Boreholes were drilled down to two thousand feet for the extraction of brine by techniques unknown in Europe for another eleven centuries. In bridge construction the Chinese were far ahead; for not only did they have suspension bridges much earlier, but they also constructed segmental arch bridges which were not known in Europe until seven centuries after their first appearance in China at the beginning of the seventh century AD. At a much lower level of sophistication, the humble wheelbarrow had already appeared in China by the third century AD, although another thousand years elapsed before it came onto the scene in Europe. And, in the world of art, porcelain was made in China twelve centuries before Europeans knew the secret of its manufacture.

IV

The development of technology and the growth of industry generated the thriving commercial life which Westerners from Marco Polo onwards saw as one of the most conspicuous features of Chinese civilization. In the traditional fourfold class system the merchants were in the lowest position, but this largely resulted from late Chou ideas. Earlier, in the Shang and early Chou periods, merchants did not form an independent class, but were, like craftsmen, in the employ of the ruling elite, serving to provide them with goods which could not be supplied from their own resources. But the economic development and consequent social changes of the late Chou period brought the growth of an independent merchant class, some members of which grew extremely wealthy.

Both the Confucians and the Legalists were hostile to the merchants, the Confucians on the ground that profit was an ignoble goal which led to contentiousness rather than the social harmony which was their ideal, and the Legalists because merchants were not making any contribution to the power of the state but were drawing off resources which should have gone to its benefit. In the Han Dynasty they were discriminated against, not being allowed to wear silk, ride in carriages, or carry weapons; and they were not officially permitted to own agricultural land. Later on there were rules against their sons taking part in the civil service examinations and holding official appointments. Like many other features of Chinese society this discrimination was a social ideal rather than a policy which could be rigidly adhered to; nevertheless, during the first half of the imperial period there was a powerful anti-commercial ethos.

The great expansion of the Han empire and the trade both internal and international which accompanied it naturally brought great wealth to some merchants, so that moralists of the Later Han period bemoaned the fact that the fundamental occupation of agriculture was being neglected in favour of this more frivolous pursuit. One writer declared that at the capital there were ten times as many traders as farmers, while loafers were ten times as many as traders. The commercial spirit of the age is reflected in another writer, who refers to rich merchants as having

thousands of male and female slaves, as well as followers counted by tens of thousands. Engaging in commercial pursuits in every corner of the country, their boats ply on all waters and carts roll on every road. Cities are full of their warehouses with stored commodities. Jades and other precious articles in their possession are beyond the capacities of even big rooms; and as for their horses, oxen, sheep, and pigs, there is no pasture large enough to graze them. Bewitching boys and beautiful concubines fill up their decorated chambers, and singers and entertainers attend on them in deep halls. . . . All these are either the enjoyments that properly belong only to lords and marquises, or the privileges that are exclusively granted to kings and princes. But today they can be obtained by those who just know how to use guile and practise fraud![6]

The ideological antipathy to commerce could never seriously impede cases of dynamic economic growth, which were the result of technological improvements and other forces outside the government's control. And after the economic transformation of the Sung period, the profit motive gained greater respectability. Within the Chinese political framework the merchants could never attain to the kind of independent power that they achieved in Europe, and they were always liable to be exploited by the state, as for example when goods were requisitioned for the palace at less than the commercial price; but gradually from the Sung period onwards the legal and social discrimination against them was dropped. By the nineteenth century merchants were even acquiring official degrees, some by purchase and some by examination; and as large landholding declined and the official classes needed to diversify their sources of wealth, especially in families with many sons which could be impoverished by the system of equal inheritance of landed property, so the distinction of classes gradually broke down.

Fabulous wealth was amassed by some merchants, and especially notorious were the salt merchants of Yangchow in the eighteenth century. They vied with each other in conspicuous consumption. A contemporary guidebook describes how one erected wooden nude female statues in front of his inner halls, all mechanically controlled, so as to tease his guests.[7] Another, who wished to get rid of ten thousand taels (ounces of silver) in a single day, bought pieces of gold foil and scattered them in the wind from the top of a hill. Another, who was a megalomaniac, designed for himself a huge bronze urinal five or six feet tall which he had to climb up to. While some squandered their money on such eccentricities, others built famous libraries and art collections and patronized scholars and poets, in the hope that through conspicuous spending on cultural activities they could win their way to the kind of prestige and esteem which was denied to all who were beyond the pale of the traditional high culture. Some became serious men of letters, like the renowned poet and salt merchant Chiang Ch'un, who was so rich and famous that he not only entertained literary figures from all over the country, but even gave hospitality to the Ch'ien-lung emperor on no fewer than six occasions.

As commercial life became more respectable, so it became possible to find within the Confucian tradition beliefs which were more favourable to the merchant class. The Ch'ing Dynasty officials' basic attitude towards commerce was 'not that it was a necessary evil, but that it was a necessary good likely to turn evil unless properly controlled'.[8] They were often personally interested in the active promotion of commerce.

The convenience of markets was also something which had been recognized by the canonical writings. Mencius wrote that in antiquity markets were set up so that people could exchange what they had for what they lacked, and that the taxation of merchants only originated because of someone wanting to net all the profit of the market.[9] In the Golden Age the simple business of barter had ensured the sensible distribution of goods. As the *Commentaries* of the *Book of Changes* (the *I Ching*) put it:

When the sun stood at midday, the Divine Husbandman held a market. He caused the people of the world to come together and assembled the riches of all-under-Heaven. These they exchanged with one another and then returned home, each having found its appropriate place.[10]

The *Chou Ritual* gives authority for the establishment of official marketplaces within the cities and along the main roads.[11] Restriction of commerce to specific areas was sometimes harshly enforced in antiquity, and there is even reference to unregistered merchants and artisans being buried alive in the Han period;[12] but gradually, as trade increased, controls slackened. Within the cities shops were set up all over the place, rather than in the official market quarters, so that by the ninth century the pattern of urban marketing was transformed. In the countryside unofficial markets sprang up to cater for local needs, and these are already referred to in literary sources of the third century AD.

These rural markets became a basic feature of the economy for the last thousand years of Chinese history, and were the nuclei from which many small market towns developed. An essential feature of the rural markets was that they were only held periodically and for a short time. This suited both the peasants and the small tradespeople, for to be commercially viable a permanent market would have had to draw on far too large an area for the convenience of the peasants, who needed to be within walking distance of it; and at the same time the tradespeople were able to enlarge their area of business by travelling from market to market. These markets arose naturally out of trade based on exchanges between peasants. The goods were often bartered rather than sold, and the main commodities available were such things as rice, wheat, millet, firewood, vegetables, fish, poultry, pigs, fruit, salt, wine, and tea. Some markets developed in conjunction with periodic religious celebrations: they were sited near monasteries and temples, and incense, candles, and other such commodities were sold in addition to ordinary goods.

The small market town not only provided for the material needs of a small sharply defined area of the country, but also served as the centre of society for most peasants in traditional China, supplying all their social as well as their economic needs. Journeys to the market town were not complete without visits to the teahouses and wine shops to catch up with the latest gossip and enjoy the sense of community experienced in such places. The market town was also almost the only source of entertainment for the peasants, with its story-tellers, jugglers, theatrical troupes, and acrobats; and many voluntary associations, formed for such activities as crop watching or irrigation, would find the community linked by the local market town the natural area within which to function. This was also the area from which families would normally take their new brides. It might also show slight cultural differences from the neighbouring communities, whether in dialect, folklore, or religion. It would be the centre of its own distinctive little tradition, pulling against the standardizing force of the great tradition sponsored by the central administration.

But it was not only local trade which flourished, spawning the development of market towns. By the Sung period the long-distance trade too had expanded greatly. In the early T'ang the new long-distance canals had mainly served to convey tribute grain to the capital and luxury goods to the court; but in the Sung there was much interregional traffic even in such essentials as rice. Regions were already specializing in the products most suited to the local conditions, particularly in the south-east, where cheap water communications made interregional trade very practicable. Peasants did not have quite the same tradition of self-sufficiency as their European counterparts, but for the past thousand years, at least in regions of easy communications, they have tended to gear their production to the needs of the market, assessing the relative profitableness of different crops and also taking into account the value of income from rural handicrafts. Rice was generally the heaviest yielding crop, but it required a high concentration of labour; so in double-cropping it was necessary to decide whether to produce another crop of rice or combine it with another grain, and natural conditions and especially the availability of water would be one of the determining factors. When markets expanded sharply over a relatively short period, they brought changes throughout the economy, and cropping patterns, local handicrafts, and land values were all affected. At the same time the addition of wealth to the community would buy the leisure to produce a measurable increase in examination success.

By the Sung period all this commercial activity had resulted in the development of a sophisticated and complicated structure of business relationships. The trader no longer carried his own goods, for transportation had become a specialized concern; so that the activities of shipping brokers in connection with the chartering of transport and the loading, carriage, and sale of goods became commonplace. There were also specialist firms dealing with storage; and in Hangchow, for example, there were specially built warehouses surrounded by water to give greater protection from thieves and fire, which provided a lucrative source of income for the empresses and eunuchs of the imperial harem who had them constructed. There was also a great variety of types of business association; and, while rural markets developed into small market towns, cities began to turn into commercial and industrial centres instead of being predominantly headquarters of the administration.

Although internal trade naturally developed as a result of spontaneous economic forces, foreign trade was much more conditioned by the purposes of state. This happened not only because the state could seek to prevent it, or monopolize or secure the bulk of the profit from it; but also because Sino-barbarian relations in antiquity had had a large economic component, out of which had developed the tribute system, a system of political and economic interchange which characterized China's foreign relations for the remainder of the imperial period.

Obviously there was a long-term community of economic interests between the sedentary Chinese and the nomadic peoples beyond their northern frontiers; for the latter desired more of the movable commodities which they did not themselves produce, while the former were more interested in retaining or acquiring land which they could cultivate. There was an ancient tradition which brought respectability to the practice of buying off the threat of barbarian invasion; for the venerable King T'ai, grandfather of that King Wen who had paved the way for the Chou Dynasty, had sought to appease invading barbarians with gifts of skins and silks, horses and hounds, pearls and jades.[13] Even the powerful Sung Dynasty, which spent much on military preparedness, bought peace from its northern neighbours, the barbarian Liao Dynasty and the Tangut tribesmen of the Hsi-hsia state, with annual gifts of bolts of silk. But what the Chinese tried to impose on their neighbours was a system whereby emperors presented gifts to them in return for tribute. This was in effect an attempt to impose a relationship on neighbouring peoples which was comparable with the internal political order; for within China itself the emperor rewarded meritorious officials with gifts while tribute came in from the provinces to the capital. The rare luxuries which came from the remote provinces of the empire as well as from beyond its bounds enhanced the emperor's prestige and at the same time symbolized the submission of provinces and foreign peoples alike. In imitation of the court the aristocrats sought similar exotic luxuries, and a mood of fashionable extravagance pervaded the ruling class during the Han period when the tribute system came into being.

The tribute system under the Han, which established a pattern for later dynasties, was shaped by relations with the Hsiung-nu, a powerful barbarian people identified with the Huns. A defeat at their hands suffered by the founding emperor of the Han caused him to offer substantial annual gifts and the hand of a royal princess in marriage in return for a pledge that the Hsiung-nu ruler would stop raiding border areas. However, the economic demands of the Hsiung-nu continued to grow while they only made token gifts to the Chinese in return, so that it became increasingly obvious that it was the Chinese who were tributaries of the Hsiung-nu, despite their belief that the Son of Heaven should rule all under Heaven. Much as they would have liked to do so, it was not possible for them to adopt the dominant role until the Hsiung-nu were weakened by fratricidal wars in the middle of the first century BC. Eventually the Hsiung-nu submitted, on the understanding that their leader or his representative would come to China to pay homage, and that a Hsiung-nu prince would be kept hostage in China as a guarantee of their submission, and that they would present tribute to China in return for the favour of imperial gifts. Chinese gifts to the Hsiung-nu were on an enormous scale, but what mattered to the Chinese was the submission represented by the tribute and by the sending of a hostage to China. This was a pattern which characterized Han relations with other non-Chinese peoples within their sphere of influence, and formed the basis of Chinese foreign relations through to the middle of the nineteenth century. On the Chinese side the tributary relationship had great political and ceremonial importance, prostrations being expected as a matter of routine from the members of the tribute mission (as members of the Macartney Embassy discovered to their embarrassment when they too were treated as tributaries). On the barbarian side these missions were valued more for the trade they brought, for merchants accompanied the tribute missions and sometimes the envoys themselves took part in trade.

Outside the tribute system there was a big expansion of foreign trade in antiquity. China's interest in the Far West (the region of the Tarim basin and beyond) derived from the need to separate the Hsiung-nu from their military and economic resources in that area, and a famous embassy under Chang Ch'ien went in 139 BC to seek allies among the Hsiung-nu's enemies there; and trading relations developed when the people of that region proved to be greedy for Han goods. This part of Central Asia eventually came within the Former Han tributary system, and was again part of it for a period during the Later Han Dynasty; but far beyond this region lay the countries of India, Parthia, and Rome, with whom non-tributary trading relations were established, silk being one of the chief commodities.

Silk reached Rome by sea as well as by the overland route. Overseas trade between China and South-east Asia and India began before the Christian era, and there is evidence that an overseas silk route from China to Rome was of considerable importance in Han times. Canton already flourished as a centre of overseas trade early in the Former Han Dynasty. Navigation in the East China Sea is of very ancient origin, and in the Han period China established close relations with Korea and also had contact with Japan and other islands.

In later ages foreign trade continued to be restricted and controlled by the government; and frontier markets under state supervision were the regular means whereby the Chinese traded with their neighbours, in addition to the traders included in diplomatic and tributary missions. The Chinese tried to prevent the export of weapons and strategic materials. Their aim was to trade in surplus consumables like silk, and in return they were mainly concerned to get horses, which they needed for military purposes. During the T'ang, when Chinese influence in Central Asia was restored, a great deal of trade again came in along the silk route, whereas the Ming by contrast was very isolationist, and reluctant to allow frontier trading. The loss of northern China to barbarians under the Sung meant that the old transcontinental trade routes were closed and China had to look to overseas trade for a greater proportion of her revenues, so superintendencies of maritime trade were established in the main southern Chinese ports to ensure that the state obtained its share of the profit from these ventures. Before the Sung, during the T'ang period, long-distance overseas trade had been in the hands of foreigners from the Near East, many of whom were long-term residents in the Canton area; and this was one route via which Islamic influence entered China. The early Ming was notable for long-distance sea voyages under the eunuch admiral Cheng Ho, when fleets of huge vessels reached the eastern coast of Africa and brought back exotic creatures such as giraffes, zebras, and ostriches to court, as well as captive rulers from Sumatra and Ceylon. For a time tribute missions came from Bengal and other distant places, but soon the navy, which had flourished since the Southern Sung period, went into a decline and never again regained its strength and importance. A contributory factor in its deterioration was the construction of the new Grand Canal from Peking to Hangchow, which meant that the grain tribute could go north by inland waterway rather than along the coast.

The growth of trade obviously depends heavily on the standard of transport and communications. In antiquity the Ch'in and Han Dynasties put much effort into building a highway system worthy of a great empire, and the Ch'in founder even introduced standardization of axle gauges, because in the loess country near his capital ruts easily formed in the roads. The T'ang and Sung regimes also tried to maintain and improve the chief land routes, and in T'ang times it was possible to travel on fast horses from the capital at Changan to Canton, the furthest important city in the country, in eight days. But there was no real development in the quality of roads and no improvement in land transport from antiquity until the coming of the railways. Even before the unification of China in the third century BC the various feudal states had major roads lined with trees, with inns situated at convenient points; and the Han founder constructed a tree-lined Imperial Highway, which the *History of the Former Han Dynasty* describes as being fifty paces wide and stretching from the ancient states of Yen and Ch'i in the north to Wu and Ch'u in the south.[14] In contrast with this a nineteenth-century European traveller commented on the good quality of the roads, 'considering that they are not made for the passage of two-wheeled carriages and only for foot-passengers, with occasionally a wheelbarrow, and a few animals'.[15] It is only under the present regime that China has begun to develop a really extensive highways network.

The writer quoted above was travelling in the south-east, where water transport was much easier and cheaper than land transport, so that the latter was neglected. As the old proverb said, 'In the south go by boat, in the north take a horse.' In water transport there had been great progress. Canal construction had started in the pre-imperial period, and much work had been done during the Ch'in and Han Dynasties; but all earlier achievements were dwarfed by the great Sui and T'ang canal network which linked the capital at Changan with both the Peking area in the north and the Yangtze Valley and Hangchow in the south. Later the famous Grand Canal constructed during the Yüan period linked Peking and Hangchow in a more direct north–south route over a distance of eleven hundred miles. The invention of lock-gates several centuries before this device reached Europe also facilitated the development of the canal network. But such enterprises entailed an enormous outlay of human effort, especially in stretches where silting provided a constant problem, so the efficiency of this service varied according to the political situation. But the flatter areas of central and southern China were eventually covered by an intricate network of waterways, which gave a great boost to interregional trade.

Shipping also developed, until in the Sung period Chinese junks achieved supremacy and replaced foreign vessels on the overseas trade routes. They were extremely sophisticated. They had water-tight bulkheads, buoyancy chambers, bamboo fenders at the waterline, scoops for taking samples from the sea floor, sounding lines for determining the depth of water, magnetic compasses for navigation, and small rockets propelled by gunpowder for their self-defence. The sheer volume of Chinese inland shipping from the T'ang period onwards was also impressive. For example, a T'ang official had two thousand boats built for service on the Yangtze, and it has been calculated that their capacity was equal to almost a third of that of the British trading fleet in the middle of the eighteenth century. Marco Polo was astonished at the shipping he saw on this great river: 'I assure you that this river runs for such a distance and through so many regions and there are so many cities on its banks that, truth to tell, in the amount of shipping it carries and the total volume and value of its traffic, it exceeds all the rivers of the Christians put together and their seas into the bargain.'[17] Much of the shipping was carried on by family groups, often of peasant origin, driven by poverty into abandoning the fields. The whole family of three generations would live aboard, taking their few household possessions with them.

The great upsurge of commerce and industry meant progressively greater freedom from government interference. State control of markets could no longer be imposed, and by early Sung times shops were to be found all over the cities. With greater freedom of action the merchants and artisans formed themselves into guilds so as to reach agreement among themselves on conditions of trade. Workers employed in the same occupation tended to congregate in the same areas of the cities, so that in late imperial China whole streets would often consist of shops selling the same goods.

Towards the end of the empire merchant and artisan guilds had developed into institutions capable of playing many of the parts performed by modern trade unions. The main functions of the guilds were to maintain monopolies for their members, so that no outsider could ply his trade within the area of the guild's jurisdiction; to control the distribution of work so that members did not entice customers away from other members; and to determine prices and wages so as to avoid cut-throat competition between practitioners of the same craft. Guilds also organized social services, such as the provision of free medicine and funeral expenses. Merchant guilds also collaborated to provide provincial hostels in the capital or other major commercial centre, where merchants from their own province could receive accommodation and assistance on their business trips. Guilds held periodic meetings for a combination of business and religious activities, and in this way they behaved very much like clans.

Such associations still existed in Peking in the early Republican period. The porters' guild was known as the Public Welfare Enduring Righteousness Holy Tea Association and, in the words of its leader, its purpose was 'to prevent outsiders from carrying goods'.[18] Membership of the guild was hereditary, and the leadership was the prerogative of certain families. The guild fixed minimum wages and exercised discipline over members, the gravest punishment at its disposal being expulsion from the guild. Meetings were held twice a year in temples, and on these occasions guild patron saints were worshipped, reports on past activities were presented, lectures on proper conduct were given, and the badly behaved were reprimanded or punished.

The carpenters' guild was known as the Sacred Society of Lu Pan. Lu Pan was a deified craftsman who lived in the third century BC and was adopted as a patron god by many skilled trades. The purpose of the guild was stated as 'to worship the master and thus express gratitude to the founder for originating the craft'. The privileges of membership were described as 'to receive the standard wage, to have a proper place for burial, and to inspect the affairs of the guild'.[19] At the general guild meetings the religious activities were the most prominent part of the proceedings. As they arrived the members registered and paid their fees for the year and worshipped Lu Pan. Later a play was given for the entertainment of Lu Pan by a troupe of professional actors, and business was conducted both between the acts and after the play was finished. Portraits of prominent deceased members of the guild were put on the wall on both sides of the effigy of Lu Pan, and offerings were made to them as well as to the patron deity.

The religious ceremonies conducted by the guild were very similar to clan worship, and guild discipline is also very reminiscent of clan discipline. Like the clans, too, the guilds had the demerit of being inward-looking. They were concerned only with the lot of their own members, so no nationwide network of trade unions could develop out of them. Nevertheless they constituted a powerful device for protecting the interests of their members, and they appreciably improved the lot of the merchant and artisan classes in late imperial China.

V

Despite the upsurge of private enterprise Chinese governments in imperial times did not generally allow private individuals to make vast fortunes out of essential commodities. Many of the state's needs were satisfied by the establishment of state enterprises. For example, armaments were made in state munitions factories, naval vessels were constructed in state shipyards, palaces were built and canals excavated as state undertakings, and silks and porcelains needed by the court were provided by state workshops and potteries. At the same time the market in essential goods such as grain, salt, and iron was controlled. Under the 'ever-normal granary' system government agencies throughout the country bought up surplus grain and sold it again when it was in short supply, in order to stabilize prices. This system, introduced in the time of Emperor Wu of the Former Han Dynasty, became a regular feature of government economic policy. State monopolies in salt and iron were also introduced under the same emperor, so that these commodities could only be manufactured under government licence, and excessive profiteering was brought to an end. An attempt was also made to introduce a liquor monopoly, but this failed because the manufacture of liquor is much easier to conceal than the manufacture of salt and iron.

The salt monopoly played an important part in the policies of later dynasties. At one time during the T'ang it was so successful that it provided more than half of the central government's revenue; and in the Ming Dynasty the government used the salt monopoly as a method of provisioning the troops on the northern frontier, for they granted certificates of entitlement to deal in salt only to those merchants who would supply the army. Despite government control salt merchants became extremely wealthy during the Ch'ing Dynasty, as we have already seen.

For the government to monopolize certain areas of the national economy is comparatively easy, but to invent a system of taxation which operates fairly and efficiently seems to be almost beyond human ingenuity. In the early Han period the tax on peasants amounted to only a fifteenth of their crop and later this was reduced to a thirtieth, but there was also a head tax on each member of the family, and compulsory military and labour service; so with all these demands on their resources the small farmers' living was precarious, and many found themselves compelled to sell their lands and become tenant-farmers or even sell themselves and their dependents into slavery. Thus land got into the hands of powerful people who were themselves able to avoid paying tax. Land could never be fairly taxed because the landowners were themselves the ones who formulated and administered government land policy. This was an inevitable law and all who attempted to break it were doomed to failure. Wang Mang, the usurper whose short-lived Hsin Dynasty separated Former from Later Han, attempted to nationalize the land and break up large estates for distribution to the poor, but he was forced to abandon his plan almost immediately. Under the 'equal fields' system of the Northern Wei the wealthy landowners retained their properties in the guise of official salaries, and the same happened under the T'ang, when large estates were also given to imperial favourites. Improvements were introduced, as when taxes were made fairer by grading land according to its quality, and when the very complicated taxation system was reduced during the Ming Dynasty to one single tax, and compulsory labour service was replaced by a money payment. But throughout imperial Chinese history the same weakness remained: officials were exempt from taxation, and wealthy landowners were often able to avoid tax and encroach on the property of the less well-to-do with impunity. The government was powerless to remedy the system, and in hard times it could only resort to relief measures, such as tax remission and the resettlement of landless peasants in undeveloped areas, providing them with free seed and tools.

Compared with landowners merchants were much more vulnerable to the exactions of the state. From ancient times they had to pay taxes for setting their wares out in the market-place as well as customs duties on goods in transit. In late imperial times there was a huge network of internal customs stations. When overseas trade started on a very large scale in the Southern Sung period high tariffs were exacted by the government, and these soon constituted as much as twenty per cent of state revenues.

Taxation under the Han had consisted largely of payment in kind, in the form of both agricultural produce and labour service, but later the growth of a money economy was naturally accompanied by a trend towards monetary taxation. But although money made its debut early in Chinese history, strong elements of a barter economy persisted right down to modern times. The earliest form of money used by the Chinese was strings of cowrie shells, which were presented to their followers by Shang and early Chou kings; but generally in the early Chou period wealth was measured in terms of commodities, such as jade, pearls, silk, grain, dogs, and horses. A more genuine currency first appeared in the fifth century BC, or perhaps earlier, when bronze coins in the shape of knives and spades were in circulation. These were increasingly stylized versions of the knives and spades which had previously been used for barter. The state of Ch'in introduced the round coins with the square hole in the middle which were to remain the standard form of Chinese coinage for over two thousand years; and they were used throughout China after Ch'in succeeded in conquering its rivals and inaugurated the Ch'in Dynasty. These coins were often issued in only one denomination, but they could be strung together to form larger monetary units.

Although copper money circulated in large quantities in the Han period, its use declined during the subsequent period of division. The

T'ang Dynasty was plagued by a shortage of copper for money, so it was compelled to forbid its use for other purposes, and when Buddhism was persecuted images and utensils had to be melted down. For large transactions gold had been used in the Han period, and after that bolts of silk were used, as for example in the payment of tribute by the Sung Dynasty to its northern neighbours in the twelfth century. Paper money also came into use at about this time, but it did not work well for long, and after its failure silver ingots were generally used when large sums of money were involved.

Paper money developed out of the 'flying money' used by tea merchants in the T'ang Dynasty. They were able to make payments at the capital and receive certificates from the government entitling them to draw equivalent sums from a provincial treasury, thus avoiding the dangers inherent in conveying large sums of money over long distances. The first true paper money developed in Szechwan in the early eleventh century. Iron coinage circulated in this area of China and, because of its heaviness, people began to place it in 'deposit houses' and use the receipts in financial transactions. But it was not until 1260 that there appeared the first really universal paper money, which circulated throughout the country and was convertible into silver or copper without a time limit. Marco Polo was very much impressed by Mongol paper money, for in his innocence he attributed the amazing wealth of China to the fact that the Great Khan could simply print as much money as he liked. Unfortunately, although Chinese officials under the Mongols did appreciate the need for paper money to have proper backing, severe inflation accompanied the decline of the dynasty. Paper money became almost worthless, and although attempts were made to reintroduce it during the Ming period, it was not satisfactorily re-established until the issue of modern banknotes by the Honkong and Shanghai Bank in 1866.

So in spite of the early appearance of coinage in China, the economy was never fully monetized in the pre-modern period. Even in the late empire silver ingots were used for large transactions and for smaller deals pieces of the metal were cut up with silver-scissors and weighed out; and at grass-roots level, barter of essential goods continued to be practised. Throughout most of Chinese history taxes in kind formed a large part of government revenue and rents in kind were what generally constituted the landlord's income. The wealth and leisure which these rents and taxes produced enabled some of the Chinese people to enjoy those refinements of civilization which are the subject of the next chapter.

PART FOUR
THE AESTHETIC EXPERIENCE

CHAPTER 9

THE ARTISTIC EXPERIENCE

I

So far this book has tried to give an impression of how men lived, thought, and were governed in a part of the world which seems almost as remote as ever; but unlike all the other aspects of Chinese culture already discussed, the remarkable works of art produced by the Chinese have found their way into our museums and even into our homes, so that we are able to judge for ourselves the quality of their achievement in this realm of the human experience. In Britain grand occasions like the Burlington House exhibition of 1935–6 and the display of recently excavated objects loaned by the People's Republic in 1972, the impact of which was increased by the additional exposure that television now brings to such events, were landmarks in the progress towards widespread appreciation of Chinese art.

Before this lay a long history of growing foreign awareness and appreciation of the works of Chinese artists and craftsmen. Chinese silks had reached imperial Rome in such quantities as to hurt the economy, and ancient Chinese bronzes have even been unearthed at Canterbury and recovered from an ancient Roman vessel wrecked off the Italian coast. In the Han period artefacts were also to be found as far afield as Indochina, Afghanistan, and Siberia, and during the T'ang large quantities of ceramics were shipped to the Near East as well as all over South-east Asia. Medieval European travellers to China were much impressed with the work of Chinese craftsmen, but it was not until the Jesuit missions became well established in China early in the seventeenth century that accurate accounts of Chinese bronzes, sculpture, and architecture were brought to Europe. In the eighteenth century Chinese porcelain had a powerful appeal in the West, where it stimulated the development of *chinoiserie*. The highly decorative contemporary wares which were exported were supreme products of the potter's craft, but together with the intricate ivory carvings and miscellaneous crinkum-crankums which came to Europe in the last phase of the imperial period, they gave an impression of a rather effete and effeminate civilization; and it was not until the collapse of the empire that the consequent impoverishment of some of the wealthy collectors brought onto the market the full range of treasures, including the ancient bronze ritual vessels, the superb jades of all periods, and the earlier ceramics, which had more restrained and classical qualities of form and decoration than the later wares. Most notoriously the last emperor, P'u-yi, during those twilight years in the Forbidden City which were described at the beginning of this book, disposed of a large proportion of the magnificent Imperial Palace collection. As a result of this outflow of art objects great private collections were built up in Europe and America during the early part of this century, and many of these have since been passed on to museums.

The arts which were slowest to find appreciation and recognition in the West were painting and calligraphy. Although some Chinese paintings found their way to Europe as early as the seventeenth century, it was not until much later that serious attempts were made to understand the unfamiliar aesthetic which underlay them. Influences were also slow to penetrate in the opposite direction. Jesuit painters at the Chinese court at first aroused intense interest, but their ultimate effect on Chinese artists was very slight. They were regarded as artisans, rather than painters, for they lacked the brush technique which was the hallmark of the true artist. Conversely Ricci, the founder of the Jesuit mission, and many later Western writers condemned Chinese painting for its apparent lack of perspective. Although the beauty of Chinese jade and porcelain has immediate appeal and even the ancient bronzes with their outlandish decoration make a dramatic impact on the European imagination, in order to appreciate Chinese painting (and more especially calligraphy) it is necessary to understand the intellectual world in which its underlying aesthetic developed. The predominant genre of painting is landscape, and to come to terms with Chinese landscape painting it is necessary to have a lively awareness of the Chinese attitude to nature, the origins of which lay deep in ancient Chinese thought. It is also necessary to be acutely conscious of the profound implications of the close relationship between painting and calligraphy, which is rooted in the fact that for both arts the same brush is used. For the calligrapher the pictographic nature of the characters he writes is never entirely forgotten, so they are felt to be beautifully condensed symbols of something far more complicated, essentially a kind of shorthand which gives intense aesthetic satisfaction. The same skills which the calligrapher develops to bring out the beauties of the Chinese script are transferred to the craft of setting down on paper or silk the shorthand versions of nature which is what Chinese landscape painting consists of. Painting is, in a sense, a kind of calligraphy.

The development of calligraphy as a fine art was a long process culminating in the Han Dynasty. It derived naturally from the practical need to compose the disparate elements out of which characters were formed into orderly symbols which could fit together neatly into a series and follow each other on the page with an appearance of symmetry and uniformity. Each character in itself presented a problem of composition before it could become an aesthetically satisfying element in an aesthetically satisfying whole. But the relationship between characters on the page was equally important, and the only effective solution was that, no matter how simple or complicated they were, they should all occupy imaginary squares of the same size. The transition from the untidy and disorderly oracle bone inscriptions to the orderly scripts of the Han period, the immediate precursors of the modern script, is a masterly achievement.

The earliest writings which used the language of art criticism and contained aesthetic theories were concerned with calligraphy.[1] This was natural since it was not only a most demanding art, but also one which every literate person necessarily practised. Admiration of fine calligraphy has continued into the present, and it has been a common practice to decorate the home with scrolls bearing moral maxims in fine handwriting. The beauty of the script can be seen very clearly when one compares a passage written with the brush with the printed version of the same characters. The latter possesses a dull and pedestrian symmetry and immobility, but the brush-written characters have an appealing asymmetry; and the individual strokes, skilfully yet spontaneously executed, broadening or narrowing, getting heavier or lighter on the page, give an air of vigour and mobility to the writing. The printed characters are like figures in a Victorian photograph, standing stiffly to attention; but the brush-written ones dance down the pages with the grace and vitality of the ballet. The beautiful shapes of Chinese calligraphy were in fact compared with natural beauties, and every stroke was thought to be inspired by a natural object and to have the energy of a living thing. Consequently Chinese calligraphers sought inspiration by watching natural phenomena. The most famous of all, Wang Hsi-chih, was fond of watching geese because the graceful and easy movement of their necks reminded him of wielding the brush, and the monk Huai-su was said to have appreciated the infinite variety possible in the cursive style of calligraphy known as grass-script by observing summer clouds wafted by the wind.

Since the Han Dynasty calligraphy has also been thought to reveal the nature of the writer. For example, according to Chiang Yee, the calligraphy of the emperor Hui-tsung of the Sung Dynasty, a famous painter and patron of artists, shows him to have been a well-built, handsome figure. The sample illustrated shows the beauty and vigour of the strokes, and reveals how a sense of movement is given to characters by making horizontal strokes tilt slightly, by making the brushline thicken or grow thin, by running informally from one stroke to the next, in a display of virtuosity which no simple alphabetic language can ever match, and which makes Egyptian hieroglyphs look static and graceless by comparison.

Although an aesthetic of calligraphy developed early in China, there are few references to painting in the ancient literature. The brush had already been used in neolithic times for painted decoration on pottery, but the ancient literary sources of the Chou period still treat painting as a craft rather than an art. The six arts of antiquity were ritual, music, archery, charioteering, calligraphy, and numbers, and so did not include painting, although later writers emphasized the close relationship between calligraphy and painting and their common divine origin. Although painting had a somewhat lowly status, a craft which employed the same tool as the scholars used was bound ultimately to rise in general esteem. It was ink-brush painting which became the predominant form of painting in China, and everyone who became an ink-brush painter had first been a calligrapher, so ink-brush painting was automatically a craft of the educated elite.

The influence of calligraphy on this art may be seen in several ways. Firstly, the brushline was considered all-important, and what critics looked for in paintings more than anything else was that vigour of brushstroke which was the consequence of the artist's calligraphic training. Another highly prized aspect of skill with the brush was the method of rendering third dimension by varying thickness in the brush-stroke. This technique was already in use as early as the second century AD, and it was to become one of the important devices for indicating depth, another being variation in the ink tone, so that paler, more watery ink was used to render hazier, more distant objects. Rapidity, indeed spontaneity, in the brush-stroke was another ideal which sprang from painting's close kinship with calligraphy, for just as we write automatically, without thinking of the strokes as we form them, so it was thought that ideally one should be able to paint spontaneously. This rapidity and spontaneity of execution could make the appreciation of Chinese painting a 'quasi-kinesthetic experience', as Cahill calls it when describing the painting *Two Minds in Harmony*, in which the vigorous movements of the painter are clearly reflected in his work, with black blobs where his brush has rested, and trailing streaks from the separate hairs of the brush as it moves swiftly across the paper.[2] Because the brush-stroke was considered of primary importance, painting in colours came to be regarded as inferior.

Secondly, the very satisfying sense of composition which is characteristic of much Chinese painting may also spring from the painter's initial training in disposing elements in space in the writing of characters and in placing them in relationship to each other.

Thirdly, certain subjects and motifs obviously lend themselves more readily to calligraphic treatment than others. As the eleventh-century art historian Kuo Jo-hsü wrote in his *Experiences in Painting*, 'in depicting drapery folds and trees one's use of the brush will be of exactly the same sort as in calligraphy'.[3] Later, especially in the Yüan Dynasty, bamboo painting became a major genre, in which the resemblance to calligraphy is most clearly marked. Eventually there were traditional brush-stroke conventions, categorized in calligraphic terms, which became standard elements of the repertoire of Ming painters and were listed and illustrated in painting manuals in the seventeenth century, the most famous of which was called the *Painting Manual of the Mustard Seed Garden*. The publication of such manuals inevitably gave the false impression that Chinese painting is a matter of assembling stereotyped formulae.

Fourthly, there is in Chinese painting a strong tendency to abstraction conditioned by the abstract nature of the calligraphy which is so closely related to the painter's art. This seems to be in conflict with the powerful basic motivation of depicting nature realistically, to make it seem as if one were actually there, which many painters and critics expressed; but this realistic purpose itself naturally developed into a desire to go beyond producing a likeness of one particular mountain and capture on paper the essence of mountainness. The important Ch'ing Dynasty painter and art historian Tung Ch'i-ch'ang did much both in his writings and in his art to turn painting into an abstract medium like calligraphy. His attitude is summed up in the maxim: 'If one considers the uniqueness of scenery, then a painting is not the equal of real landscape. But if one considers the wonderful excellence of brush and ink, then real landscape can never equal painting.'[4] But at the same time this abstraction was not felt to be a move away from realism. Rather the painter achieved a greater sense of realism because in the very act of painting he felt the physical energy of the things he was painting; and instead of merely seeing and describing trees and rocks, he acts out their characteristics as he works. Chinese painting never totally abandoned reality for abstraction. Just as the written character, in however bizarre a hand, must bear some resemblance to the standard script, so the painting would have appeared totally meaningless if it had been completely divorced from reality.

Once paintings had become as strongly calligraphic as they were in the Yüan period, it was a natural development that real calligraphy should play a fully integrated part in the picture. Calligraphy appears on the earliest extant Chinese paintings to describe what is being illustrated but it was only gradually that the subtle technique of making it an integral part of the composition was developed. The cultured amateurs who dominated the painting tradition in late imperial times were poets as well as painters, so it was natural that they should reinforce the sentiment of the painting with an appropriate poem written in beautiful handwriting which fitted in well with the composition as a whole. The empty space in the composition ceases to be sky or rock, but is an area which can be filled by a poem just as legitimately as by any other creation of the calligraphic brush which the Chinese painter wields.

So the history of painting in China is not so much a matter of the exploration of the physical world as the development of a brush repertoire for exploring that world. The brush-stroke is the central theme in Chinese painting, and one theoretical treatise opened by saying that the single brush-stroke was 'the origin of all existence and the root of the myriad phenomena'.[5] Just as it was believed that the hexagrams in the *Book of Changes*, which were widely used for purposes of divination, were abstractions of natural phenomena, so it was felt that brush-strokes were not merely a depiction of an object's external appearance, but were an abstraction of its essential vitality. Brush-strokes seemed to stand for the inner structure of rocks as well as to imitate their outward appearance.

II

The two main categories of painting in China have been figures and landscapes. Figure painting was the more important of the two in earlier times, but from about the eleventh century landscape painting went ahead and became the supreme expression of the Chinese artistic genius.

The main influence on the rise of figure painting was Confucian. As we saw in an earlier chapter the imitation of exemplary characters of antiquity was at the heart of the Confucian concept of learning, so it was natural that the portrayal of ancient worthies should become an important ingredient of Chinese art. This happened at least as early as the Han period.

Confucian influence on the arts has generally been considered slight in comparison with the obvious impact of Taoism on landscape painting and the ubiquitous manifestations of Buddhist art, but there are various ways in which the philosophy did have a strong influence on painting and connoisseurship. In the first place, painters were generally Confucian scholars and, however much they might also be attracted by Taoist ideas, their writings invariably betrayed their Confucian education. The examination system ensured the existence of a bureaucracy full of men who were imbued alike with Confucian sentiment and love of painting; and Confucian officials inevitably became the main arbiters of taste, as well as forming the largest group of art patrons the world has ever known. This meant that Confucian principles like *li* (propriety) were reflected in artistic taste in the restraint and harmony which is characteristic of Chinese painting. Another important feature of the Confucian ethos which has had a profound impact on Chinese painting is the belief in achieving the gentlemanly ideal through self-cultivation. From the Confucian point of view, as we shall see in more detail later, art is to be valued as a revelation of the artist's nature; so, provided he had a modicum of talent, the cultivated Confucian gentleman was in a sense to be regarded as a better artist than a man of low moral qualities. Art therefore had educational value in that it embodied the responses of the superior man. But, characteristically, the very summit of Confucian praise was to give painting a role in the cosmic order, as in the opening words of the ninth-century *Record of Famous Paintings of Successive Dynasties*, the first history of art ever written:

Painting perfects the process of civilization and brings support to human relationships. It penetrates the divine permutations of Nature and fathoms the mysterious and subtle. Its achievement is the equal of any of the Six Arts and it moves in unison with the four seasons. It proceeds from Nature itself and not from human artifice.[6]

From this point of view the painter actually takes part in the creative processes of nature, just as the ancient folk dances were thought to aid the fertility of nature in spring. In the ideal creative act the painter creates as Heaven does, spontaneously.

To revert to figure painting, which was originally much inspired by Confucian attitudes, there are basically two kinds – firstly the portrait of an individual which exudes moral qualities, and secondly the illustration of morally enlightening episodes from life or literature. From the Confucian viewpoint the contemplation of portraits of worthies was morally inspiring. As the poet Ts'ao Chih put it:

There is none who in front of a picture of the Three Kings and Five Emperors would not raise his head in thankfulness, nor any that before a painting of the depraved monarchs of the decadence would not heave a sigh. There is none who contemplating the picture of a good and honest man would not forget his meals, nor any that on coming on the image of a licentious husband or abandoned wife would not hastily avert his gaze.[7]

Kuo Jo-hsü wrote of the need for appropriate characterization in painting:

In the case of Buddhist monks, the faces should tell of good works and practical expedients to gain salvation. In the case of Taoist figures, the cultivation of purity and other-worldliness is the standard which must be satisfied. In the case of monarchs, it is proper to honour their appearance of supreme sanctity, like the very orb of Heaven. In the case of outer barbarians, one must catch their mood of respectful obedience and devotion to the Flowery Kingdom. In the case of Confucian worthies, one makes visible their reputation for loyalty, faithfulness, correct conduct, and sense of right.[8]

A sceptical voice had long before spoken out against this whole idea, asking why such a fuss should be made of portraits when the words and deeds of virtuous men provided much more satisfactory models to emulate.[9] It must be mentioned, too, that portraits were painted for much less lofty purposes, even in antiquity. The Han emperor Yüan was said to have had his court painters portray the members of his harem because it had grown so large that he no longer had time to receive all his ladies personally. Portraits of eligible Chinese ladies were also sent to Hsiung-nu princes so that they could select one for marriage. But the tradition of uplifting portraiture can still be seen in one of the earliest extant paintings, a majestic scroll of thirteen emperors traditionally attributed to the T'ang artist Yen Li-pen, which commands great skill in depicting the different personalities of the rulers.

In addition to the moral value of individual portraits of men of worth, instructive lessons could also be drawn from the interplay between human beings in famous scenes from literature; and recorded lists of early paintings indicate that the Confucian Classics and the histories were frequently illustrated.[10] None of these ancient scrolls still exists, but interesting examples of the kind of message which could be put across survive from the reign of the emperor Kao-tsung, who established the Southern Sung Dynasty after the whole of the north of China had fallen to the Chin tartars. For him the theme of dynastic revival was of special importance, so he sponsored a scroll based on the story of a famous seventh-century BC ruler called Duke Wen of the state of Chin, one of the famous paramount princes of that era. He had spent a long period in exile before returning triumphantly to rule his homeland and raise it to the leading position among the feudal states of the time. It is a horizontal scroll, which is gradually unrolled to reveal a series of episodes showing how he was received in the various states he visited during his exile.[11] The illustrations alternate with relevant passages from the *Tso Tradition* transcribed by the emperor himself, and the final scene shows the Duke's triumphant return to Chin as his stately procession moves towards the palace gate. The emperor Kao-tsung was a keen calligrapher, who believed that one should practise one's calligraphy by copying out the Classics, thus engaging in two worthy cultural activities simultaneously. He copied out the Thirteen Classics in their entirety and had them engraved in stone from his calligraphy. He also commissioned a series of handscrolls illustrating the *Book of Songs*, one of the most treasured of Confucian books, a project which was intended as a conspicuous reaffirmation of the values of civilization at a time when the country was under threat of barbarian conquest.

The beautiful figure compositions of the Duke Wen scroll are reminiscent of work attributed to Ku K'ai-chih, who lived in the fourth century and has been admired as the first great genius of Chinese painting. The famous scroll in the British Museum entitled *Admonitions of the Instructress to the Court Ladies* has generally been ascribed to him, although there is no certain proof. This is another painting in the didactic tradition, based on a third-century literary work of high moral tone where a typical scene shows a lady being admonished by her husband. Paintings of groups of figures were of course not always done for didactic purposes. Sometimes they were purely illustrative, and this was a tradition which went back to Han Dynasty reliefs showing scenes of everyday life, and which has in more recent centuries found its most common expression in scenes, painted on porcelain, of ordinary family life, often set in a garden. Other frequent themes of such paintings on porcelain were sages and old men, or bands of worthies like the Seven Sages of the Bamboo Grove, a famous and convivial group of men of letters who lived in the third century AD. Such scenes were generally depicted with a Confucian dignity and restraint, the classic example being the famous painting *Night Entertainment of Han Hsi-tsai*, which was an official artist's record of the nocturnal revels at the house of a high-ranking minister, which would seem to have been conducted in a surprisingly composed and seemly manner.

This sense of restraint also marked the technique of portraying the features and personalities of individuals. Faces tend to be shown as impassive, the expression being only very slightly and very subtly depicted. Another means of characterization is the very subtle sense of composition, which enables the artist to reveal much about the individuals he portrays by showing their relationships and the attitudes they adopt towards each other. As much care was generally lavished on the detail of the clothing as on the features, and special attention was given to any attributes or insignia thought to be appropriate to the subject. One artist painted creases so faithfully that it was said that his 'clothes looked as if they had just come back from the wash'.[12] The depiction of garments with long bands of cloth seemingly fluttering in the breeze, with the hem curving away from the vertical as if caught in the wind is used to give movement and vitality to the portrait. Interest in the human figure was always slight, except for the time when Buddhist influence brought a certain sensuousness into sculpture. The head of the Chinese male is often shown at a strange angle to the body, to indicate the kind of scholarly stoop which was much admired. Another convention was that rulers were often portrayed bigger than their subjects and sages bigger than their disciples; and human beings, especially men of importance, were often much too large for their steeds. Yet realism was regarded as the ideal, and hence Han Fei Tzu's complaint that dogs and horses were harder to draw than ghosts and spirits, for in the case of the latter it was much more difficult to check whether the likeness was faithful.[13] Complete realism was certainly required by the T'ang emperor T'ai-tsung, who had portraits of two famous generals painted to stand outside his door and protect him at night. This was so successful that the fearsome pair were later worshipped as door gods. Portraits had

to portray, but ideally the features should wear proper Confucian sentiments and be serene and thoughtful. And if the painter could achieve
not only convincing portraiture but also use a brush technique which
could be admired for its calligraphic qualities, like Liang K'ai in his
portrait of the poet Li Po, this was even more admirable.

Although Confucian ideals were an important incentive to the realistic
portrayal of the human figure, Buddhism provided fresh impetus both
in individual and in group portraiture; for on the one hand figures of
Buddhas and bodhisattvas, whether painted or sculptured or wrought
in metal, were needed for devotional purposes, while on the other hand
the art of depicting readily understood moral situations was needed for
the illustration of scriptural stories in order to propagate the faith.
Reproductions of Buddhist paradises or episodes in the life of the Buddha
had great propaganda value, and gave much scope to artists. The most
famous works produced were the stone carvings at the great sites of
Yünkang and Lungmen and the cave paintings at Tunhuang, where
the Western Paradise of Amitabha was one of the most popular themes.
The style of painting and sculpture was naturally very strongly influenced by the Indo-Iranian tradition; for, although in Buddhist literature the process of adaptation to native systems of thought is immediate
because translation is necessary before it can be understood at all, and
key terms in translation automatically carry nuances which are proper
to the native culture rather than to the imported religion, Buddhist
styles in painting and sculpture could be transported to China without
modification, and it was some time before native Chinese aesthetic
values reasserted themselves and fought back. Thus in the earliest paintings at Tunhuang there is a powerful influence from the Central Asian
tradition, which was colourful and quite uncalligraphic; and the technique of shading to give a sense of volume was introduced, although it
was alien to Chinese methods and was much deplored many centuries
later when the Jesuit court painters used it. Similarly the Indian portrayal of the human body was full and sensual, in contrast with the
restrained and linear treatment of the Chinese.

The earliest Buddhist figurines, few of which predate AD 400, were
very much in the Gandharan style, but the first great relics of Buddhism
in China, the enormous figures carved out of the cliff-face at Yünkang
in the late fifth century, have lost that style, and are colossal, solid,
awesome, and somewhat Sphinx-like in atmosphere. The earliest figures
at Lungmen, created after the court of the Wei Dynasty had moved to
Loyang in AD 494, reject foreign models: the Chinese aesthetic reasserts

itself with rhythmic lines of draperies, and the human body is de-emphasized. Later, however, fresh inspiration came from the sources of Buddhism, so that T'ang images became much more sensuous again, and a critic even accused the Buddhist artists of making bodhisattvas look like dancing-girls.[14] At the same time as the two aesthetics wrestled with each other, the expressions on the faces of the figures become more tender and merciful as the doctrine became less austere. Indeed the sculptors' ability to portray in stone a whole range of appropriate expressions from the aloof and awe-inspiring down to the gentle and compassionate was a remarkable achievement which gave an accurate reflection of the development of the religion.

Like Buddhist sculpture, Buddhist painting also stood apart from the main tradition of Chinese art. The temple walls of T'ang China were undoubtedly covered with frescoes of the kind which have survived until the present day in the Tunhuang caves, but Buddhist painting was thought of as a special kind of foreign art practised by specialists; and Wu Tao-tzu, the greatest painter of Buddhist subjects, in fact abandoned foreign techniques as soon as his own style had matured. Many of these temple frescoes were destroyed during the persecution of AD 845, although some were removed and preserved in private houses. The foreign style had no lasting impact on the austere and self-contained standards of the indigenous painting tradition as far as technique was concerned. The paintings are magnificent and colourful, and are also interesting because they provide contemporary evidence of the architecture of the period, little of which has survived; but, as far as China is concerned, they are a self-contained manifestation of artistic genius, right outside the mainstream of the tradition.

Where Buddhism did infringe on the main territory of Chinese painting was through the impact of Ch'an. Its influence was felt in technique as well as in subject matter. As far as technique is concerned, the essential style of monochrome ink painting, in which the brush moved in a flash to give immediate response to the painter's inspiration, was ideally suited to the Ch'an temperament. It was by a sudden flash of intuitive knowledge that the Ch'an master became one with the Supreme Unity. This fleeting experience cannot be described in words, but an attempt can be made to capture it with the brush. The Ch'an master's desire to experience this sense of oneness with the world was at the root of his intense interest in nature. Since the Buddha nature was thought to be present in everything, the subject matter of Ch'an paintings was varied, and included economically executed portraits of Ch'an patriarchs, abbreviated landscapes, or strange, shocking pictures like *Two Minds in Harmony*, designed to jolt the viewer into awareness. A further influence on subject matter was this sect's attitude to cult objects and holy texts: pictures were painted of Ch'an masters using images of Buddha as firewood or tearing the scriptures to shreds.

The Ch'an influence was temporary, and if one seeks to identify the lasting impact of Buddhism on Chinese art, the main contribution was the ability to transform blocks of stone into serene, dignified, and compassionate embodiments of the Buddha ideal. Apart from these individual manifestations of profound religious feelings, Buddhist art also brought to China a new style of composition, the symmetrical pattern of central Buddha flanked by disciples or bodhisattvas, which is even thought to have had an influence on the arrangement of mountains in landscape painting. It also brought, temporarily at any rate, a more realistic and sensuous depiction of the human figure; and it had a long-term effect over the whole range of Chinese art by introducing such motifs as the lotus and a general use of vegetable ornamentation, which is especially to be seen on later porcelain.

III

The essential features of Chinese landscape painting and the theory of it had already been established by the seventh century. Although figure painting had been more important in earlier periods, by the ninth century there had been a big shift of interest from man to nature, and by the eleventh century this shift was complete and was never reversed. Appreciation of landscape painting had developed during the period when the collapse of the Han had induced a widespread Taoistic desire to withdraw from the troubles of the world and contemplate the beauties of nature. It was at this time that the concept of the artist as an individual pursuing his own ideals independently of the state came to maturity. The great justification of landscape paintings, stated for example at the beginning of Kuo Hsi's important essay on the subject, was that they served as substitutes for the real thing. Confucius said: 'Wise men find pleasure in water, and the virtuous find pleasure in mountains'; and the Chinese word for landscape is literally 'mountains-and-water'.[15] Kuo Hsi opened his essay by asking why the virtuous take delight in landscapes. The reason given is that the good Confucian scholar-bureaucrat is too busy at his desk to take time off to wander in the mountains, and so has to nourish his spirit by means of imaginary journeys through landscape paintings. Writers on painting endlessly repeated their wonder at the artist's ability to encompass so much in such a small space: 'In a sheet of paper is contained the infinite. And evolved from an inch-sized heart, an endless panorama.'[16] Indeed, as we saw earlier, the great painters were credited by the critics with powers akin to natural creation. But landscape painting attained its supreme place in the arts of China, not merely because of the great technical virtuosity achieved by the artists and the wonderful observation and analysis of nature which went into their work, but also because communion with nature came to fulfil the loftiest spiritual needs of the Chinese, especially after the powerful appeal of the Buddhist creed had faded.

Since the artist considered the enjoyment of landscape painting to be a substitute for the pleasure of wandering amid beautiful scenery, it is not surprising that he developed devices to enable the viewer to enter the picture in spirit. Often a tiny figure is to be seen, dwarfed by the towering mountains; and the viewer naturally focuses on this little figure, identifies with him, and sets out with him along the paths and over the bridges; and as his eye wanders through the landscape he is awed by its grandeur, as if he were really there. A time dimension enhances the experience of enjoying the three-dimensional space represented in the painting. Two other distinctive features of Chinese landscape painting followed from this encouragement to the viewer to travel through the landscape. The first of these is the invention of the long horizontal handscroll, which is unrolled on a table from right to left so that the viewer only sees a small part of the painting at a time. In this way the viewer is drawn through the landscape, and his eye is compelled to follow the path through it, viewing the scenery on either side as it goes. Secondly, the one-point perspective with which we are familiar in European art is unsuitable for such painting. A shifting perspective is necessary in order to convey the sense of movement through the landscape. Many European writers, from the Jesuit missionaries onwards, criticized the Chinese for not understanding perspective, but as Rowley put it: 'We restrict space to a single vista as though seen through an open door; they suggest the unlimited space of nature as though they had stepped through that open door.'[17]

What is this nature which the landscape painters depicted? In view of the literal meaning of the Chinese word for landscape, mountains and water are naturally the almost invariable components of landscape painting. Often too there are rocks and trees in the foreground, and trees also lining the slopes of the mountains. Often the painting is ascribed to a particular season, and skilfully portrays winter snow and summer heat with the limited means at the artist's disposal; but there is no sign of rustic toil, and even less of horror and violence, for only spiritually refreshing themes are appropriate. The painting is not generally of a particular place. The landscape painter's pictures were the product of meditation on his stored up memories and images. He transformed his visual impressions into a balanced and coherent pattern, which would convey a profound conviction of the underlying order and integrity of nature. This abstraction from reality, this imposition of a sense of order and coherence, this interpretation of the whole scene by means of a uniform calligraphic technique has the uncanny effect that the sage or fisherman, the huts, pavilions, and temples in the picture all seem to be integral parts of nature and do not stand out as different in kind from mountains, rocks, trees, and water. Human life and activity are not singled out, but are all part of the Tao, just as the ancient Taoist philosophers held. At the same time the presence of a human being in the picture did sometimes, for example in the finest works of Southern Sung artists, convey a sense of communion with nature reminiscent of the Taoist's mystical response to it. By this time the experience of being emotionally moved by nature could itself become the subject of a work of art, so that man was surrounded in the picture not by nature but by an impression of his emotional response to it.

As the phenomena of nature were thought of as visible manifestations of the workings of the Tao, it was also natural that their representation in art should be abstract and generalized, and that there should be generalized mountains rather than particular mountains. And just as the phenomena of nature were manifestations of an inner order, so too they were vibrant with the change which was an essential part of the Tao. Just as the universe was in a state of flux, so the world of nature was intensely alive. Mountains and streams, trees and rocks, as well as all the creatures which dwelt in the landscape, were all permeated by the same cosmic force represented by the concept *ch'i*, which literally means 'breath'. It was thought that this *ch'i* had a physical manifestation in the form of clouds, which appeared to be exhaled by the peaks of mountains. Kuo Hsi felt the vibrant life of nature intensely, and expressed it by writing: 'Watercourses are the arteries of a mountain, grass and trees its hair, mist and haze its complexion. Therefore with water a mountain becomes alive, with grass and trees beautiful, with mist and haze charming and elegant.' Elsewhere he declared that: 'Stones are the bones of heaven and earth ... water is the blood of heaven and earth.'[18] So the forms of nature visible to the artist's eye are outward manifestations of the workings of the Tao. The artist is uniquely endowed with the faculty of apprehending these forms and representing them in such a manner that their cosmic vitality is not lost, but is transferred to the paper.

The landscape painter made use of various devices to create an illusion of recession in space. In the middle distance he used bands of mist and haze, which seemed to remove the mountains behind them to a greater distance and also made them appear higher. He also used paler ink washes to depict the fainter, more distant parts of the scene, and in contrast he placed in the foreground large rocks and clumps of trees executed in darker ink. With the aid of these devices the painter was able to make his work appear as if it were at three removes from the viewer: the foreground would be occupied by trees and rocks, and in the middle ground there would be a lake or bank of mist, out of which the mountains would soar in the distance. In the early landscapes there was often a dominant mountain in the centre, and indeed Kuo Hsi saw the link between the hierarchic arrangement of mountains and of human figures which we have referred to earlier: 'A great mountain is so stately', he wrote, 'that it becomes the master of multitudinous others arranged round it in order. ... Its appearance is that of an emperor sitting majestically in all his glory, accepting the service of and giving audience to his subjects.'[19] Later there was a shift of interest from the dominant mountain to a microcosm in which one little scene would speak for all, and even further to the style of 'one-corner' Ma, who pushed his simple and economical compositions to one corner so that the philosopher sitting in the picture could gaze out into the limitless space of the rest of the paper. But whatever style the painter adopted, it always reflected the fastidious sense of design which flowed naturally from his calligraphic training.

Landscape painting, then, was something which grew out of the very primitive signs with which the Chinese people first communicated with each other and developed into an art of great sophistication. In remote antiquity mountains and rivers were worshipped, and these were the dominant topics of the later landscape painter. The art itself started slowly, serving merely as background to human action, as on funerary tiles of the Han period. It was the increased interest in Taoist philosophy, with its belief in mystical communion with nature, which was the great source of inspiration for the development of landscape painting as we know it. The practice of seeking out places of scenic beauty first became popular in the school of Taoist painters and poets of the Six Dynasties period. But it was not until the T'ang that the problems of landscape painting were truly mastered and its great age began. At this time there were, according to later Chinese art historians, two main schools of landscape painting. One was characterized by precise outlines and the predominant colours were blues and greens, and the other was the familiar monochrome ink landscape, which soon gained the upper hand because its calligraphic nature made it the more congenial mode of expression for the amateur scholar-painters, who naturally began to dominate taste as the scholar-bureaucrat class became dominant in politics and society. The more precise and less imaginative style naturally became the province of professional and court painters. The T'ang was a period of towering mountains and vast panoramas, peopled with tiny figures. The Sung turned to more intimate and more romanticized scenes; and under the Mongols, when the tradition was maintained by scholars who were in retreat from the world, the style became more withdrawn, abstract, and calligraphic. As the centuries passed, the range of expression achieved during the history of monochrome ink landscape painting was truly amazing in view of the apparently limited scope of the materials at the artists' disposal and the conventions within which they worked.

IV

In contrast with the lofty mountains dwarfing human beings and human habitations there is also a style of painting which goes to the opposite extreme and delights in the intimate detail of nature. Already in the time of Ku K'ai-chih bird and animal painting was classed as one of the four major categories, the others being portraits, landscapes, and architectural drawings. Later Chinese critics made bird, flower, and animal painting one of the three major categories, together with landscapes and portraits, although they considered this category trivial compared with the other two. The most famous centre of bird and flower painting was the Sung court, in the time of the emperor Hui-tsung, who was himself a renowned exponent of the art. From that time onwards bird and flower painting was especially associated with court artists. A strong influence on the minute inspection of nature seen not only in this kind of painting but also in the more intimate scale of landscapes character-istic of this period was the philosophy of Neo-Confucianism, which was deeply concerned with close examination of the physical world. However, the art of flower painting which Hui-tsung and his academicians practised was not wholly Chinese in origin, for Buddhist paintings had been richly adorned with flowers, and the Chinese art of flower painting also owed much to that tradition.

The academy style was characterized by most careful precision and attention to detail, and Hui-tsung would reprimand his painters for the most trivial lapses from accuracy. But at the same time these artists were not seeking photographic fidelity to nature. The compositions were too orderly, too perfect and clear in detail, too timeless, and too lacking in spontaneity to be realistic. In other words these artists, just like the landscape painters, were really seeking to capture the essence, and to portray the general and timeless rather than the ephemeral and particular. This style could easily lapse into mere prettiness, and eventually it evolved into the kind of highly decorative art which was long thought by Europeans to be the most characteristic expression of the Chinese artistic genius.

Another category of painting, which came into prominence during the Yüan period, was bamboo painting. In the *Book of Songs* the grace and strength of the bamboo is compared with the elegance of the *chün-tzu*, the ideal gentleman of the Confucian tradition.[20] So bamboo was later used to symbolize the qualities of the superior man, who is upright and enduring, who may yield to the winds of circumstance, but does not break or become permanently bent. It became especially popular as a subject among the literati of the Yüan period, when the symbolism became even more apt as they maintained their integrity by refusing to collaborate with the Mongol court.

A further impetus to bamboo painting at this time was the growing interest in the calligraphic nature of painting which went hand in hand with the development of the amateur scholar-painter tradition. In bamboo painting exactly the same kinds of stroke are used as in calligraphy, and it is closer in technique to Chinese writing than any other kind of painting. The leaves broaden and then narrow to a point again, following the natural rhythm whereby pressure on the brush increases near the beginning of the stroke and then decreases again as it leaves the page; while the subtle curves of the leaves are very reminiscent of calligraphic strokes. The spacing also, both as between individual leaves and between clusters of leaves, requires a refined taste and skill in composition, which comes from being steeped in the similar problems of composition in calligraphy. The gradation from the darker inks of the foreground to the paler shades of the furthermost leaves must also be most skilfully managed for a satisfying and harmonious composition to be achieved. The symbolism of bamboo paintings could be exaggerated, for it was clearly the calligraphic skill required which mainly appealed to the artist. Some artists spent their whole careers on bamboo, but one said that he painted bamboo when angry and orchids when happy, since the brush-strokes required in each case were appropriate to those particular moods.[21]

V

It will have become evident that quite early in their history the Chinese developed an interest in aesthetics and art criticism, and an appreciation that works of art are not necessarily produced for moral, magical, symbolical, or propaganda purposes, but can be admired simply because they give aesthetic satisfaction. Early traces of this sophisticated belief may be seen even in Hsün Tzu, who took the view that ritual was to be appreciated for its beauty as well as for its moral and social significance. The new works of literary criticism which appeared in the Six Dynasties period must have been influential on the thinking of artists. For example, *The Literary Mind and the Carving of Dragons* says that 'when a literary masterpiece is produced, there is nothing in it which is not the artist's temperament';[22] and the *Anthology of Literature* was of great importance because it introduced to literature the notion of aesthetic criteria in addition to moral judgements.

Nevertheless the powerful philosophical associations of art meant that purely aesthetic considerations did not dominate, and the idea of painting being mainly a matter of self-expression did not come to the fore until much later. The earlier attitude was intensely imbued with the desire to understand nature, commune with it, and reproduce its inner life as well as its outer form. There was even a feeling that the painter actually identified his inner self with the object, an idea inspired by the mystical contemplation of the Taoists and their sense of becoming one with the universe. Indeed the famous poet-painter Su Tung-p'o spoke of this quite literally: 'His body was transformed into bamboo.'[23] Another poem tells of the trance state through which the artist achieved spiritual communion with the object:

> When a wild goose sees people,
> Its expression changes before it rises up.

From what place did you look
To get this natural attitude?
Could it be that you became like dry wood,*
So that both man and bird were at ease with each other?[24]

With such attitudes to painting, artists naturally prepared themselves carefully for their work. The great early Sung landscape painter Fan K'uan, who lived as a mountain recluse, would sometimes spend a whole day gazing at a configuration of rocks. Tseng Ping described his experience as follows: 'By living in leisure, by nourishing the spirit, by cleansing the wine glass, by playing the lute, and by contemplating in silence before taking up the brush to paint, although remaining seated, I travel to the far corners of the world, never resisting the influence of the heavens and for ever responding to the call of the wild, where the cliffs and peaks rise to soaring heights, and the forests are shrouded in clouds that stretch as far as the eye could reach.'[25] As for Kuo Hsi, on a day when he was going to paint, he would seat himself by a bright window, put his desk in order, burn incense to right and left, and place good brushes and excellent ink beside him; then he would wash his hands and rinse his inkwell, as if to receive an important guest, thereby calming his spirit and composing his thoughts. Not until then did he begin to paint.[26]

It was in about the year AD 500 that a painter called Hsieh Ho drew up a famous set of six principles by which a painting should be judged, and these have served as the cornerstone of art criticism in China. These principles are 'animation through spirit consonance', 'structural method in use of the brush', 'fidelity to the object in portraying forms', 'conformity to kind in applying colours', 'proper planning in the placing of elements', 'transmission of the experience of the past in making copies'. The first principle is the most difficult to understand. The word translated as spirit is *ch'i*, that cosmic spirit or energy which was thought to vitalize all things, both animate and inanimate, and was seen as being physically exhaled by mountains in the form of clouds and mist. It was thought that human beings could nurture this *ch'i* and that the artist must attune himself to the cosmic spirit, so that his own *ch'i* may flow through his arm and brush in order to vitalize the painting as he works. The presence of *ch'i* ensures that the painter reproduces the quintessential nature of his subject. The second principle, 'structural method in use of the brush', refers to the need to establish the correct forms by means of the brush, and indeed expresses the central importance of the

*In a trance a man's body was thought to look like dry wood.

brush-stroke in Chinese painting. These first two principles were essentially ones which had earlier been prescribed for calligraphy. The next three principles refer to the more obvious matters of securing fidelity in form and colour and satisfactory composition, and the final principle stresses the need for a painter to learn his art by studying and copying old masters.

Since corrections were impossible, Chinese painting required high standards of technical accomplishment, which had to be acquired by much practice and copying. The painter had to develop a technique as demanding as that of a musician in our society, so the constant repetition of familiar themes was no more plagiarism than are repeated performances of the same symphony. What the painter sought was not originality, but a feeling of identity both with nature and with the traditional ways in which it was represented. In China age always took precedence over beauty, so imitation of the past was naturally the painter's first concern.

Paradoxically this stress on practice and copying does lead in the end to spontaneity, just as in calligraphy after much practice the most complicated characters are written as spontaneously and unthinkingly as an alphabetic script. As Su Tung-p'o's friend Wen T'ung put it, 'Suddenly I forget that the brush is in my hand, the paper in front of me. All at once I am exhilarated, and the tall bamboos appear, thick and luxuriant. How is this in any way different from the impersonality of creation in nature?'[27] Conscious effort will produce an artificial result, so the act of painting must parallel natural creation, with forms emerging naturally as if they are second nature to the painter.

The cult of spontaneity did, however, lead to the opposite extreme from the attitude to painting which I have been describing. The T'ang painters had needed solitude, concentration, and spiritual preparation to enable them to complete their monumental works. But in the Sung period people like Su Tung-p'o took part in convivial gatherings at which paintings were improvised. Now that painting was part of general scholarly culture, the earlier institution of poetry meetings was paralleled. Su frequently improvised paintings when drinking with his friends, just as he produced poems spontaneously. People also took part in co-operative painting games similar to the literary games in which each person contributed a couplet to a poem of combined authorship. Wine was thought of as a source of inspiration for painting as for poetry; and it is reported that Su would drink several cups of wine at a party, fall asleep, and later get up and write or paint with great verve.

This more casual attitude also harmonized with the idea – which grew with the increasing dominance of Neo-Confucianism – that painting was an embodiment of the artist's feelings rather than a representation of nature. From this viewpoint art served to express the thought and feeling of the individual man, in addition to or even instead of any descriptive or philosophical statement it made. An expression often used was that the painter 'lodged' his feelings in a work of art. In other words, art serves as a kind of catharsis, a release of pent-up emotions, so that the painter can preserve his composure. It was an outlet for what could not be put into words, and was sometimes referred to as 'soundless poetry'. The old naive Confucian idea that painting should be valued for the morality of its subject matter could be discarded in favour of the view that the value of a painting depends not upon the subject matter, but upon the mind of its creator. The painting is a revelation of the nature of the man who painted it; and therefore, assuming that he has a modicum of technical proficiency, a man of learning, refinement, and nobility of character will paint superior paintings.

In this way painting becomes a worthy activity of the educated man. On the one hand it is a means of self-cultivation which fits in very well with Confucian ideas, and on the other hand it is a way of making manifest the virtues of cultivated individuals so that they can have a civilizing influence on others. Hence painting joins literature, calligraphy, and music as an activity appropriate to the superior man. Like calligraphy, painting was described by Kuo Jo-hsü as the gentleman's heart-print,[28] and from the Yüan Dynasty onwards it was only scholar-painters who were thought to be capable of painting poetically and imaginatively, court painters being regarded as inferior by the dominant Confucian scholar-bureaucrat class. From the end of the Sung the characteristics of Chinese painting had been shaped by scholar-artists. This was seen both in the taste for painting in subdued colours and in the practice of writing poems or colophons on pictures. The culture of the literati became the backbone of Chinese painting and art criticism. In the Yüan period scholar-painting reigned supreme, for it was one means of symbolizing the scholar's personal virtues and integrity at a time of social collapse. 'Anyone who talks about painting in terms of likeness', as Su Tung-p'o had written, 'deserves to be classed with children.'[29] For it was no longer the purpose of the artist to make the viewer feel that he was in the very place depicted. Instead the viewer comes face to face with the artist, for it is the mind of the artist which is the real subject of the picture. In Western art this is a comparatively modern attitude, but it existed long ago in traditional China.

VI

To give an impression of the very special role of painting and calligraphy in China it has been necessary to deal with general trends and give minimal attention to individual painters, but we should not neglect to pay tribute to those geniuses who shaped the tradition in their own times. In the pre-T'ang period the most important figures were the court painter Ku K'ai-chih and Hsieh Ho, famous for his six principles; and we have already met Yen Li-pen, the most celebrated court artist of the proud early years of the T'ang Dynasty. Later in the T'ang the active period of the great wall-painter Wu Tao-tzu, who overshadowed all others in this field, coincided with the reign of the famous emperor Hsüan-tsung in the second part of the eighth century, the most glorious period of T'ang culture. He painted his numerous frescoes with such energy that crowds gathered to watch him as he worked, and his Buddhist hell-scenes were said to be so lifelike that they terrified the butchers of Changan into seeking other employment. Almost exactly contemporary was Wang Wei, equally famous as a poet, who was traditionally regarded as the father of monochrome landscape painting in ink.

In the Northern Sung the massive peaks of Fan K'uan excited the wonder and admiration of his contemporaries, but later the tradition was pushed in a novel direction by the impressionistic work of Mi Fu. He was an eccentric who always wore T'ang Dynasty costume and addressed a favourite rock in his garden as 'my elder brother'. He was so obsessed with cleanliness that he was always washing, and he would not let anyone else touch his pictures. In his painting he used what came to be known as the 'Mi-dot' technique, which was in strong contrast with the calligraphic style, for dabs of ink were laid on with the flat of the brush. This technique was also used by his son Mi Yu-jen, and was well suited to his own particular locality, where it was said that the vaporous landscapes looked like clouds and the clouds looked like landscapes. The 'Mi-dot' technique was not approved by the emperor Hui-tsung, whose court painters were required to turn out the kind of bird and flower paintings he himself produced so expertly.

When the court moved to Hangchow, the grandeur of Northern Sung landscape in the Fan K'uan tradition was the inspiration of Li T'ang, but an entirely new mood was set by Ma Yüan and Hsia Kuei, who were responsible for a style which has had great appeal outside China, characterized by a most successful use of the bare silk, either to create a sense of space by pushing the landscape to one side of the picture, or by a sensitive concentration on the mere essentials within the composition itself in a way which suggests a deep sense of communion with nature. For example, a tranquil evening by the lake is depicted by showing a grey misty shoreline in pale ink and a few matchstick boats very slightly disturbing the calm surface of the water. At the same time Ch'an Buddhist masters like Liang K'ai were working in their own very different styles in the hills just outside Hangchow.

In the Yüan period the great painters abandoned the brilliantly economical styles of their immediate predecessors and sought inspiration in the full and detailed compositions of the tenth and eleventh centuries. Five painters from the period are especially famous. Chao Meng-fu, a member of the Sung royal house who collaborated with the Mongols and was a successful courtier, made a great reputation as a painter of horses, a theme especially dear to his Mongol masters; but he also paved the way for the four leading landscapists, Huang Kung-wang, Ni Tsan, Wu Chen, and Wang Meng. Although these artists differed much in style, they all displayed great austerity and concern for detail, and lacked the romantic and decorative qualities which belonged to their Southern Sung predecessors. Wang Meng's work is a congested tapestry of trees, rocks, cliffs, and peaks; but Ni Tsan, who spent years drifting in a houseboat amid the varied scenery of the lakes and rivers of Kiangsu, nevertheless devoted his whole painting career to one basic landscape, consisting of a few trees standing on a river bank, with a distant view of mountains on the opposite shore. It is an empty landscape, with no boats or human figures to enliven the scene; and if there is a human habitation, it is empty. During the Yüan period, too, many artists spent their whole careers painting nothing but bamboo.

During the Ming Dynasty the tradition of bird and flower paintings was continued by court artists, who also produced landscapes in the style of Ma Yüan and Hsia Kuei. Outstanding among the amateur painters of the early Ming was Shen Chou, who was steeped in the work of the Northern Sung masters. Living the enviable life of a scholar in comfortable retirement, he produced works which were a warmer and more human version of Ni Tsan's. A little later came Ch'iu Ying, a painter of humble birth whose pictures of palaces and pavilions idealized the leisured life of the gentry. Towards the close of the dynasty lived the great philosopher of painting Tung Ch'i-ch'ang, who was himself a fine landscapist. He proclaimed the superiority of the amateur scholar-painter, whose wide reading gave him an understanding of the nature of things which the professional artist could never aspire to, and who was free to paint as he liked because he was subject neither to academy control nor to the necessity of earning a living. Indeed landscape painting, thought Tung, was the scholar's chief means of expressing his understanding of the operation of natural principles as well as displaying his own spiritual worth. His analysis of the history of Chinese painting, which confirmed the distinction between the scholarly amateurs with their free spirit and calligraphic virtuosity and the court and professional painters with their precise and decorative but inferior talents, gave much reassurance to the literati painters at the time when the Ming Dynasty was in decline.

In the Ch'ing Dynasty there are far too many artists working on far too long a tradition for easy generalization. At the beginning, four artists all surnamed Wang and working under the influence of Tung Ch'i-ch'ang's historical approach produced exquisite landscapes in the manner of the Sung masters; but there were also many original talents, like Kung Hsien, whose eerie landscapes resemble nothing else in the Chinese tradition and may show the influence of Western engravings. This was in general a period of great vitality and variety in painting, before the long decline of the Ch'ing was accompanied by a steady loss of artistic vigour.

Apart from these orthodox painters China had its share of eccentrics. There was one who faced in one direction and painted in another, waving his brush in time to music. There was also a famous dragon painter who would get drunk, drop his cap in the ink and smear it around to make a rough picture, which he later completed with the brush. Some did not even use the brush at all. One would spread pools of ink on silk laid out on the floor and drag an assistant round on it, seated on a sheet. One painted with his braided hair dipped in ink, and others used their fingers or toes instead of brushes. Even the great Mi Fu was said to have sketched with twisted strips of paper, sugarcane husks, or lotus seed pods. Indeed the action painters of today had their traditional Chinese equivalents.

VII

Most of the great Chinese painters were gentlemen amateurs, but there was also, as we have seen, a long tradition of court patronage. Already during the Former Han period, when several emperors were enthusiastic art collectors, a special bureau in charge of paintings and books had been established. In the Later Han Dynasty the emperor Ming formed the Academy of the Great Metropolitan Gate in which to gather rare works of art. Emperor Ling surrounded himself with writers, painters, and calligraphers, and his patronage did much to inspire the later palace tradition in Chinese art. During the post-Han period of division court patronage did continue (Ku K'ai-chih himself being a court painter), but the greatest benefactors of art were the Buddhist monasteries. In the T'ang, people presented large numbers of writings and paintings to the emperor to obtain office and rank, and there was a member of the bureaucracy entitled Imperial Commissioner for the Searching out of Writings and Paintings; but at the Hanlin Academy, which was founded in 754, painters were still included among artisans rather than being classed with the scholars.

An official search for works of art was also launched by the second Sung emperor. Other sovereigns of this dynasty were enlightened patrons of the arts, and at the end of the Northern Sung Hui-tsung was a voracious collector. Early in the Sung period separate academies of painting and calligraphy were established, and later a system of examinations for academy painters was introduced, modelled on the literary examinations. Candidates were required to illustrate lines from poems. Academy painters were also expected to study literary texts, and they were gradually given many privileges, although their status never seriously approached that of the scholar-bureaucrats.

Imperial patronage also flourished during the Southern Sung, but after the collapse of that dynasty the court was no longer an effective cultural centre. During the Ming period court painters were honoured with high military titles, but were governed by strict rules and regulations, which they broke at risk to their lives. In general throughout both the Yüan and the Ming Dynasties serious painters kept clear of the capital and formed coteries in which they painted for each other's pleasure, while patronage increasingly came not only from the literati themselves, but also from members of the wealthy merchant class who aped their culture. The Ming was an age when fine collections of paintings were built up by private individuals and connoisseurship developed. The survival of many old paintings until today is largely due to these Ming connoisseurs, whose treasures found their way into the imperial collection during the Ch'ing period and have thus survived to reach their present home in the National Palace Museum on Taiwan.

The emperor mainly responsible for accumulating these treasures was Ch'ien-lung. Unfortunately he could not forbear to stamp the paintings which came into his possession with huge seals and adorn them with specimens of his own inferior poetry in his own handwiting (for, as well as incorporating some of the artist's own calligraphy, perhaps describing the scene or explaining why he painted it, a painting could be inscribed by a friend or collector with an appraisal of the work). The inscription of a famous critic and connoisseur discussing the artist's work in the light of the tradition has an equivalent in the field of literature in the shape of commentaries on classical texts. Chinese paintings were not once-for-all artistic statements: they gained an accretion of fresh commentary and new associations over the years. And emperors who took their cultural role seriously left their own accolade on the fine works which they had removed from private collections and installed in the palace.

The acquisitiveness of Ch'ien-lung did preserve for posterity much that might otherwise have been scattered and lost, but in other cases imperial greed meant ultimately that priceless masterpieces were lost in dynastic cataclysms. The burning of the Ch'in palace in 206 B C was the first of many historic occasions when accumulated imperial treasures were destroyed. When the Han Dynasty petered out, a similar disaster occurred: the capital was sacked and burned in AD 190, and silk paintings were used to make tents and knapsacks or carried off by the cartload and ruined by exposure to the weather. A self-inflicted disaster was that of the Liang emperor Yüan who, upon his abdication in AD 555, set fire to vast quantities of art treasures and prepared to cast himself on the flames with the words 'Verily the line of Hsiao at last has come to this! The Way of art and learning shall not survive this night.'[30] Similar tragedies punctuated the T'ang, especially at the time of the An Lu-shan rebellion and the ¹Buddhist persecution of AD 845, and Hui-tsung's greed helped to ensure further heavy losses in the disastrous events which terminated the Northern Sung Dynasty. China's emperors thought that the good things of the world should come to them as tribute, so when dynasties fell or palaces were sacked the loss to posterity could be immense.

VIII

The patronage of Chinese emperors also helped to make possible the very high standards attained by Chinese craftsmen throughout the ages.

From the time more than three thousand years ago when the Shang royal workshops yielded bronzes which have not been surpassed either in technical excellence or in vigour of design, via the centuries when the great imperial potteries and silk factories turned out elegant porcelain and gorgeous robes for the palaces, right through to the eighteenth century, when fine furniture and magnificent objects made of ivory, jade, enamel, glass, bronze, gold, and lacquer were produced in workshops set up by the K'ang-hsi emperor within the palace itself, China was always a place unrivalled for the excellence of its craftsmen. Although Chinese painting is not easy to understand, fine porcelain touches a common chord of human appreciation, and no special knowledge or training is required to respond to the elegant shapes, lustrous glazes, and exquisite decoration on Chinese wares; and the techniques used in their manufacture are part of the common fund of human skills rather than peculiar attributes of the Chinese experience. A detailed survey of this and other Chinese crafts would therefore be out of place in this volume, nor would it be possible to provide adequate illustration of such a treatment. Nevertheless there are certain very general observations which should serve to underline the special nature of the Chinese experience in the minor arts.

First of all, how does one account for the very excellence of the Chinese achievement? Three factors spring to mind. Firstly there is the remarkable technological progress which gave sophisticated bronze-casting techniques to the Shang people 3500 years ago, saw the early development of iron (which could be used to make jade-carving tools, so that high technical levels could be established in this craft more than two thousand years ago), and perfected the manufacture of porcelain more than a thousand years before the discovery of the secret in Europe as late as the eighteenth century. Secondly, imperial patronage (imitated, of course, by wealthy and fashionable families) meant that the thousands of man-hours needed to carve a Buddhist scene out of the living rock or produce an especially prestigious piece of jade were readily available. Finally, the supreme sense of balance and harmony which is often such a pleasing feature of the decoration on Chinese art objects is something which lies deep at the heart of the Chinese experience and may derive partly from the sense of harmony prevalent in the ancient Chinese world-view and partly, as we saw in the case of Chinese painting, from long practice in disposing elements pleasingly in space which the early experience of solving the problems of calligraphy gave to the Chinese at the dawn of their history; so that the decoration on Chinese objets d'art is rarely jumbled or crowded. But in the last analysis supreme excellence is beyond explanation. All one can do is enjoy it and be thankful.

Of the various crafts one must give pride of place to ceramics for the enormous range of its products, from huge earthenware storage jars out of neolithic hovels through to dainty eggshell wine cups used by an emperor. As the centuries passed new technical achievements kept the tradition fresh: the T'ang, for example, saw the perfection of porcelain and the introduction of polychrome glazes to replace the plain greens and browns of the Han; the Sung gave us above all a classical purity of form, and very famous wares like the lustrous green celadon (much in demand by Near Eastern potentates because poison was thought to make it crack or change colour), the fine creamy-white *ting*, with its delicate patterns carved or impressed in the paste, or the more robust *chün* with its lavender-blue glaze splashed with purple. In the Yüan period came the technique of underglaze painting in cobalt blue which made possible the blue and white wares which are the best known and most imitated in Europe, decorated with flowers and birds and other motifs derived from the courtly painting tradition. Finally during the Ch'ing, while the blue and white tradition still continued, bequeathing a distant legacy in the *chinoiserie* willow pattern which brought a touch of the orient to many Victorian dressers, there appeared the ornate masterpieces of *famille verte* and other enamelled wares, as well as a beautiful range of monochromes and the milky white *blanc de Chine*, which was also extremely popular in Europe.

Apart from the familiar bowls, wine cups, teapots, vases, and the like, the Chinese made pottery pillows, which raised a woman's head from the bed so that her headdress remained unspoilt. Barrel-shaped pottery stools were also a common item of garden furniture; and brush-rests, brush-pots, and other articles for the study were also made of pottery. But perhaps the most interesting products of the potter's craft were the grave goods which survived in great quantities from the Han through to the T'ang period. More recently, models of all the impedimenta needed for the next life – which in the present century included aeroplanes and motorcars – have been made of paper, but fortunately the ancients used more durable material. The toy-like houses, farmyards, servants, dancers, musicians, and animals which they supplied for the departed gave much information on ancient architecture, agriculture, and social life. The cosmopolitan air of the T'ang is reflected in the figurines of Armenian merchants and Bactrian camels, while the gaiety and richness of social life is revealed in models of musicians, dancers, and polo players.

It is worth mentioning at this point that the T'ang figurines are the high-water mark of the Chinese achievement in small-scale modelling, reached at the same time as they were doing their best work in large-scale stone sculpture, at the great Buddhist sites. In traditional China there was not much tradition of secular sculpture in stone, and none of commemorating human beings by erecting statues to them; so, apart from some of the sublime Buddhist monuments, the Chinese genius for modelling best expressed itself in small-scale work, not only in the tomb figurines, but also in objects made of jade, ivory, wood, and bronze.

The most important centre of the porcelain industry in China wsa Chingtechen in Kiangsi, which had the monopoly of palace wares from the Yüan Dynasty right through until the end of the Ch'ing. Even in the late Ming period large quantities of its huge output were already being transported to Europe, but the heyday of this centre of the industry came in the first half of the eighteenth century, when over a hundred thousand men were employed there. By that time there was such a degree of specialization that one piece might have to go through the hands of as many as seventy men. The place was known as the 'town of year-round thunder and lightning',[31] and a Jesuit description speaks of 'volumes of smoke and flame rising in different places, so as to define all the outlines of the town; approaching at nightfall, the scene reminds one of a burning city in flame, or of a huge furnace with many ventholes'.[32]

Rivalling the ceramic art both in the beauty of its products and the length of its history is jade-carving, which has been practised by the Chinese with unique skill ever since neolithic times. The true jade which has been highly valued since the dawn of Chinese civilization is nephrite, which is not found in China proper but had to come all the way from the Khotan region of Central Asia, a striking testimony to the length of neolithic trade routes. Nephrite can be white, green, blue, yellow, red, brown, grey, or black. The brilliant green jadeite, from which much jewellery is now made, comes largely from Burma, whence it was first imported by Chinese jade-carvers in the eighteenth century.

The appeal of jade lies not only in its beauty but also in its hardness. This added to the value of the finished product, for it is an extremely difficult and time-consuming material to work; but, more importantly, it was thought by the ancient Chinese that jade's indestructible quality was transferred to anything which came into contact with it, so that it was their custom to protect the bodies of the deceased with various jade ritual objects. The orifices of the corpse were also plugged with jade so that noxious influences should not escape from within, and there were cases of the whole body being enclosed in a jade suit (including a head mask) made of countless thin squares of jade sewn together with gold thread.

The extreme hardness of the material made it unworkable without the use of an abrasive on the cutting edge of the tool, but the development of iron tools in the late Chou and early Han made it possible to carve three-dimensional figurines and hollow out bowls. Jade-carvers also began to exploit flawed and multicoloured pieces of stone, so that a dull-coloured pebble with a blotch of red on it might be made to look like a dagger dripping with blood, or a brown patch on a white stone might become a dragon soaring among the clouds.

The qualities of jade were thought of as moral as well as physical, as the ancient dictionary description makes clear: 'Jade is the fairest of stones. It is endowed with five virtues. Charity is typified by its lustre, bright yet warm; rectitude by its translucency, revealing the colour and markings within; wisdom by the purity and penetrating quality of its note, when the stone is struck; courage, in that it may be broken but cannot be bent; equity, in that it has sharp angles which yet injure none.'[33] Implying moral as well as physical beauty, the word for jade has been commonly used in girls' names and, more generally, as a complimentary epithet denoting pure or chaste.

The fact that it did not simply appeal to the senses of sight and touch but also carried an aura of morality and purity meant that jade had an especial appeal for the Confucian gentleman, who also relished its antiquarian associations. Although during the Shang and early Chou its main use had been for ritual and mortuary objects, in the latter part of the Chou period, when articles of great beauty were already being made, it was commonly used for purely ornamental objects. In late imperial times it continued to be used for religious objects, such as altar furniture, but it was also in constant everyday use at court and among the wealthy. It was made into jewellery, such as hair-ornaments and pendants; dress accessories, such as belt-hooks; and items of personal adornment, like the sheaths the scholar used to protect his long fingernails. At banquets jade vessels and chopsticks might grace the table, and in the study the accoutrements of scholarship, like inkstones, brush-pots, and brush-rests were often made of jade.

The third material in which the Chinese have done magnificent work is bronze, for their creations of three thousand years ago are unsurpassed not only in China, but anywhere else in the world. In the Shang period bronze was an aristocratic material, used by people of high rank for weapons, chariot and harness fittings, bells, incense-burners and the like; but its main use was in the manufacture of vessels for offering food and wine to the ancestral spirits. There were over thirty different types of vessel, some for cooking the sacrificial food, some for serving it, some for heating or mixing wine or pouring libations, and some for ritual ablutions. The fascination of these vessels lies in the stylized animal decoration, which gives them a terrifying vitality such as naturalistic animal decoration could hardly surpass. The most mysterious of these animals is the *t'ao-t'ieh*, a composite creature which has elements of bird, tiger, and snake in its make-up, but the predominant feature is the bulging eyes, as of an angry bovine creature about to charge. The earliest explanation of the *t'ao-t'ieh* in Chinese texts describes it as one of the four devils who were driven away by the mythical sage-ruler Shun, and were subsequently made defenders of the land from evil spirits.[34] It certainly looks as if the function of these designs might have been to frighten off the evil spirits from the precious sacrificial food and wine contained in the vessels, although some have suggested that the monster itself represents a deity. These vessels show in a unique way how superb craftsmanship and advanced technology can co-exist with a deep awe of the supernatural, and reveal the intensity of feeling which makes the human sacrifice of the period more intelligible. Bronzes of fine quality were also made in the Chou period, but with the growing humanism of that age the terrifying creatures of the Shang bronzes dwindle into purely decorative motifs; while the vessels themselves are used as commemorative pieces to mark the promotion of meritorious officers, and are appropriately inscribed to mark the occasion.

There was a strong tradition that the sage emperor Yü had nine bronze tripod vessels cast in metal brought as tribute from each of the nine provinces. They were thought to have magic properties, and the prosperity of the land was held to depend on their being kept on Chinese soil, but at the end of the Chou Dynasty they were lost. This tradition survived, and in the T'ang period Empress Wu had a set of nine tripods made as part of her campaign of self-legitimization. Ancient bronze vessels have been collected for centuries, the Sung emperor Hui-tsung being a notable early connoisseur. Ever since his time they have been not only collected, but also studied, copied, and forged.

Copies were made because of the reverence for antiquity which was characteristic of the Sung, in exactly the same spirit as the Neo-Confucians tried to revive the country by seeking the truth enshrined in the ancient texts. Hui-tsung was concerned to have identical reproductions of the ancient ritual vessels for use in his own imperial ceremonies, so authentic pieces were sought throughout the empire to serve as models. Illustrated compilations of ancient bronzes were published, and archaistic pieces began to be modelled on these illustrations rather than on the ancient bronzes themselves. Later this archaistic style spread from the palace and invaded the lesser arts in general, joining the general repertoire of themes which also included the birds and flowers which had similarly emanated from courtly art. Craftsmen continued to use this new addition to their vocabulary, now deprived of all religious significance, throughout the remainder of the imperial period. We have noticed how painters also repeatedly sought their inspiration by going back to the styles of much earlier ages; but their object was not so much to copy earlier masters as to evoke the past, to compose variations on a theme, to make skilful stylistic allusions, and to display erudition, just as the literary man makes subtle use of literary references.

In this brief account of Chinese craftsmanship something must be said about the textile arts, the chief glory of which was the kind of silk tapestry known as *k'o-ssu*, a technique of Central Asian origin which was perfected by Sung weavers. The work was so fine that it was and is used for copying paintings, but the best-known examples were the dragon robes worn by emperors and officials in the Ming and Ch'ing periods. Dragons were generally regarded as beneficent creatures who dwelt in the waters or up in the clouds, and caused the rain to fall. From the Sung period onwards they were the main symbol of the emperor. As chief among the animals the dragon was supposed to be composed of outstanding features of other animals. The traditional description gives it the horns of a stag, the forehead of a camel, the eyes of a demon, the neck of a snake, the belly of a sea-monster, the scales of a carp, the claws of an eagle, the pads of a tiger, and the ears of an ox. The imperial dragon had five claws to distinguish it from the dragon worn by lesser mortals, which only had four.

The dragon appears on the breast of court robes, surrounded by a design made up of the three elements of which the universe is comprised, the Sky (indicated by an all-over cloud pattern), the Sea (shown as a hem of parallel lines topped by storm-tossed waves), and the Earth (in the guise of rocky land-masses emerging from the sea). The robe also features the Twelve Symbols, which had an association with the emperors going back to the Chou period. These Twelve Symbols originally represented elements in nature, but during the T'ang period they were reinterpreted as symbols of imperial virtues, so that, for example, the sun, moon, and stars now stood for enlightenment. By the Ch'ing Dynasty they were simply regarded as an ancient mark of emperorhood.

The study of symbols and decorative motifs on Chinese art objects and paintings throws much light on Chinese attitudes and values at various periods. The fearsome *t'ao-t'ieh*, for example, was reinterpreted by Sung antiquarians as the representation of a glutton, put on food and wine vessels as a warning against over-indulgence. The symbols of Buddhism also lost their religious force and degenerated into lucky charms and finally into mere ornament. Important Buddhist symbols included the lotus, a sign of purity because it looks clean against the muddy waters in which it grows; and the wheel of *karma*, symbolizing the eternal round of transmigration. Popular Taoism was especially concerned with means of prolonging life, so special reverence was paid to a group of Eight Taoist Immortals, but eventually the attributes associated with these also declined into mere symbols of good fortune.

The most prolific source of symbolism in Chinese art was nature itself. The Chinese felt a special affinity with plant and animal life, not only because of the Taoist belief that the Way lay in living in harmony with nature, but also because the Buddhist doctrine of reincarnation disposed man to feel a sense of community with the animals, birds, and flowers around him. Consequently, as we have seen, the Chinese have been especially successful as painters of plant and animal life. But there is often more in these paintings than meets the eye. As we saw in the case of bamboo paintings, animals, birds, and plants often have symbolical significance. This either stems from the characteristics associated with the creature concerned, as in the use of the crane to symbolize longevity; or from some mythological association, as when peaches stand for immortality because the immortal Queen Mother of the West had peaches which took three thousand years to flower and mature; or because of a pun, as when bats mean happiness, because both are pronounced *fu*.

Common bird and animal symbols include the deer which, by a pun, represented official emoluments; and fish, which stood for abundance, both by a pun and because they are naturally prolific, so that a pair of fishes made of jade would be an auspicious wedding gift, expressing a hope for the fertility of the match. Pairs of mandarin ducks also symbolized happy marriage, because these birds were reputedly devoted to their mates. Carps, because of the tenacity with which they had to swim against the current to reach their spawning grounds, became a symbol of examination success. Swallows, by a pun, represented the banquet given to successful candidates. The domestic cock was a symbol of the Yang principle because it crows at dawn to welcome the sun. Symbols could appear in incongruous combinations to convey more complicated messages. For example, a bat carrying a swastika in its mouth meant 'ten thousand happinesses', because the swastika is used to write 'ten thousand'. Similarly a bat, a musical stone, and two spotted catfish mean 'May you have happiness and good fortune from year to year'.

The Chinese have always been very fond of flowers, and the Flowery Land is a common name for their country. The Flowers of the Four Seasons (peony, lotus, chrysanthemum, and prunus) are frequent subjects in paintings and on porcelain. Among trees the pine and cypress are symbols of endurance because they are evergreen; and among fruits peaches represent long life, as explained before, while the pomegranate, with its numerous seeds, was an obvious symbol of fertility.

Mention of flowers brings us to thought of gardens, but Chinese gardens were not designed for the mundane purpose of displaying flowers or cultivating fruit and vegetables. In fact the task of the Chinese garden-designer was akin to the aim of the landscape painter – to create a landscape in miniature through which the imagination might wander freely. Hence the importance of rocks and water, for rocks did service as miniature mountains, so that the two main elements of landscape were prominently featured in the traditional Chinese garden. Hence too the importance of tiny bridges, from which to view these elements to best advantage, and winding walks to take one through the landscape and enable one to see it from different vantage points, just as the eye follows and explores the pathways of a landscape scroll. Hence the moon-gates, through which the wanderer can see the next landscape composition before walking through into it. Here too are bamboo, willow, and pine, and other plants rich in symbolism which are shared with the painter's brush. Here too are little pavilions, inscribed with appropriate names skilfully culled from poetry or classical literature, where scholars can sit and paint or write poetry, or sip wine, or play the lute. Gardens were immortalized by their association with gatherings of famous poets or painters, such as the Orchid Pavilion, where Wang Hsi-chih and his friends assembled to compose poems, timing themselves by floating their wine cups down a winding stream.

Gardens were to be enjoyed and lived in, so buildings were an essential part of them; and the architecture of curved roofs with glazed tiles and of painted pillars and balustrades is perhaps at its best in such intimate and pleasurable surroundings. Yet the same basic elements are used with surprising success in the monumental precincts of the imperial palace, which have already been described in the chapter on capital cities. There the viewer is captivated by the beauty of the materials, the magnificent symmetry of the buildings, and the awesome sense of history which pervades the whole place. But it is a solid and conservative architecture compared with the more adventurous use of the basic themes which T'ang architects seem to have used. And compared with the multiplicity of styles and movements in the European tradition, Chinese architecture only had the Buddhist introduction of the pagoda to relieve its relative monotony; so perhaps, despite its obvious beauty, it has less of interest to offer than all the other arts of China to the European with his rich heritage of palace, castle, cathedral, college, and stately home – upon which the arts of China themselves, despite the great distances over which they had to travel, once exerted a very considerable influence.

CHAPTER 10

LITERATURE

I

The core of the preceding chapter was the written word, composed of those brush-strokes which were the very essence of the Chinese style in the visual arts, even communicating linear rhythms to the three-dimensional art of sculpture. The core of this chapter is the same word in the context of speech and understanding, which imparts qualities to thought and literature which are just as distinctive as the impact of the written character on the visual arts.

In the spectrum of languages Chinese is at the opposite end from Latin being totally lacking in inflexion. Even in English, which has some inflexions, like -ed and -ing, word order is extremely significant. In Chinese it is of vital importance, although there are devices for changing the normal subject-verb-object pattern for the sake of emphasis. Only context tells one whether a word is functioning as noun, verb, or adjective, so the reader is constantly aware of words' relationship to each other instead of seeing them in isolation. Parallelism is also an extremely important device, for if one sentence follows another which has exactly the same construction, their juxtaposition may resolve problems of interpretation which would be formidable if one of those sentences appeared in isolation.

Occasional signposts are provided in the form of conjunctions like 'if', 'because', 'although', or 'but' relating clauses to each other; but these are used most sparingly, since such relationships between clauses are often clear without being specified – as in the saying 'more haste, less speed', in which 'if' is implied but not expressed. Most languages overdo the use of words or grammatical forms indicating tense: indeed they have to express tense whether it is relevant or not. Chinese does not have to express tense, although words meaning 'finish' or 'experience' can be put in front of a verb to indicate that the action is over and done with, while the idea of 'to be about to' can also be expressed if it is really necessary to do so. Similarly nouns may be either singular or plural, but grammatical number can be indicated by the use of words meaning 'some', 'many', 'all', 'one', and the like. 'More haste, less speed' gives an impression of the pithiness which is characteristic of Chinese. It dispenses not only with 'if', but also with number, person, and tense, all of which are unnecessary. Indeed, to say 'if we are more hasty' or 'if you had been more hasty' would be to weaken the statement and deprive it of its universality. The saying also exemplifies the irrelevance of parts of speech, because it uses two nouns ('haste' and 'speed') in a context in which the more normal English idiom would operate with verbs.

A good example of the versatility of a single Chinese word is i, meaning 'one', which is written with a single horizontal stroke. In different contexts this can be used as equivalent to the adjectives 'one', 'first', and 'whole', to the nouns 'one', 'unity', and 'unification', to the word 'once' functioning both as an adverb and as a conjunction ('he did it once' and 'once he had done it'), and to the verb 'to unify' (which alone has a large array of variant forms in Latin).

The paucity of grammatical words and the ability to dispense with words indicating person, number, and tense unless they are relevant gives the language a magnificent economy, which is its main characteristic. This shows itself in the penchant for pithy sayings which is characteristic of Chinese literature and thought from the *Analects* of Confucius to the modern political slogan. The lack of person, number, and tense also brings the impersonality, universality, and timelessness which are the great qualities of Chinese poetry, enabling it to achieve the same abstractness as the painter achieved in his generalized portrayal of the essence of mountains. The device of parallelism can add force to prose through its rhetorical effect, and delight to poetry through the skilful juxtaposition and cross-reference of images. As a vehicle of philosophical thought it is plain that it is not the kind of language which could have nurtured some of the problems which have preoccupied Western thinkers through the ages.

The language I have had in mind so far in this description is the literary or Classical language, the medium in which was written everything seriously regarded as literature in pre-modern China. This literary language gradually grew apart from everyday language during the early centuries of our era. The separation of the two was intensified by the cultivation of a very artificial prose style during the sixth century, and the divorce was completed when the originators of the Neo-Confucian movement in the T'ang Dynasty sought a return to the style of the ancient Classics. The everyday language eventually evolved an armoury of grammatical words and constructions which were quite different from those of the Classical language, and also developed into a language in which most 'words' were not represented by single characters, but by compounds of two or more (a feature which is reflected in pidgin English equivalents like 'look-see'). This change was accompanied by such phonetic impoverishment that today the Classical language cannot readily be understood if read with a modern pronunciation, because of the number of words which now sound the same. It was in this vernacular language that most novels and short stories were written, and consequently they were considered unworthy of serious consideration by traditional scholars. It was not until the cultural revolution of 1917 that this kind of literature became a respectable object of study and the Classical language was replaced by the vernacular language as the medium of education and literature.

The Chinese language continues to be written in characters which are direct descendants of those used on oracle bones in Shang times. Many simplifications have been adopted, but the total abandonment of this script in favour of an alphabet will not happen in the foreseeable future. The pictographic nature of the language makes no substantial contribution to the pleasures of reading Chinese literature. Ezra Pound believed that an added dimension was given to Chinese poetry through awareness of the components of characters. For example, he rendered a word meaning 'lovely' as 'lady of silken word', simply because the character is a complicated one which does include elements meaning 'lady', 'silk', and 'word'. But such ideas are fanciful, and in fact the great majority of Chinese characters incorporate elements which were originally pictographic solely for their phonetic value (just as if, for example, we were to write the past tense of the verb 'to see' by drawing a picture of a saw). Of course, the vast majority of people who have used the Chinese language have been illiterate, and so totally unaware of the composition of the characters which represent the words they are using; but even the scholarly, through the habitual and hurried use of characters, are no more conscious of their make-up than one is fully alive to the etymology of English words as one uses them hurriedly. Instead of registering that the word *jo* (compliant, conform to, accord with, resembling) was originally written as a kneeling man with hair standing on end and hands upstretched in an attitude of surrender, one's mind is fully occupied with nuances of meaning, so that one can select the interpretation appropriate to the context.

II

The quantity of literature written in this language is enormous, the range is wide, and the problems of translation are daunting; and therefore any kind of potted history of Chinese literature is bound to be indigestible. So after a few introductory remarks on the general characteristics of Chinese literature, I shall devote the rest of this chapter to giving some impressions of how the literature reflects the Chinese experience as recounted in the earlier chapters of this book.

Since the third century AD the Chinese have used a fourfold system of classifying their literature for library and bibliographical purposes. Classics came first, followed by history, philosophy, and *belles lettres*. Only literature written in the Classical language was included, since novels and short stories in the vernacular were beyond the pale. The Classics section consisted of the Confucian Thirteen Classics, most of which we have met before, put first because they were considered the chief repository of truth. They consist of the Four Books (*Analects*, *Mencius*, *Great Learning*, and the *Mean*); the *Book of History*, a collection of documents containing speeches and conversations of early kings; the *Book of Songs*, China's most ancient poetry collection (reputedly compiled by Confucius); the *Spring and Autumn*, the annals of Confucius's native state of Lu (also allegedly compiled or used extensively by him in his teaching), together with the commentaries which were later attached to this work; three collections of writings on ritual (including the *Chou Ritual* and *Record of Rites*, which have both been quoted in these pages); the *Book of Filial Piety*, which we have also encountered; a manual of divination (the *Book of Changes*); and a glossary of difficult words which occur in the Classics (the *Erh Ya*) – the whole forming quite as odd and unlikely a collection of reading matter as the Bible to serve as the repository of the ultimate truth.

Under Confucian influence all serious literature was bound to be didactic, and it was literature which provided the models of behaviour which Confucian education taught men to imitate. Apart from the Classics the other three branches of literature also had a didactic function, for the histories provided models of virtuous or evil conduct for future generations to emulate or avoid, the philosophers were especially concerned with the behaviour of man in society, and poets were conditioned by the didactic role assigned to the *Book of Songs*, in which the simplest folk-song could be given a solemn allegorical interpretation. Confucius was on record in the *Analects* as advocating the educational value of this work, which was quoted frequently in ancient Chinese literature to make moralistic points, often by stretching the meaning of the text and totally ignoring the context.[1] So in Chinese literature aesthetic excellence was generally held to be secondary to moral values, although in the Six Dynasties there was a new consciousness of literature as an art which could be pursued for its own sake, and obviously much Chinese poetry pursues no nobler aim than its own excellence. But Po Chü-i, for example, frowned on this, holding that in the sixth century AD poetry was mere 'sporting with wind and snow, toying with grasses and flowers'. He criticized Li Po and Tu Fu for lack of satire and criticism in their work and wrote that 'the duty of literature is to be of service to the writer's generation; and that of poetry to influence public affairs'.[2] The Confucian purpose was to give literature, like art, a grander role than the mere provision of pleasure. This role was described by Lu Chi in the third century AD:

> The use of literature
> Lies in its conveyance of every truth.
> It expands the horizon to make space infinite,
> And serves as a bridge that spans a myriad years.
> It maps all roads and paths for posterity,
> And mirrors the images of worthy ancients.[3]

In addition to Confucian didacticism, Chinese literature is also largely characterized by a Confucian sense of decorum. Like landscape painting, it is on the side of calm rather than frenzy, friendship rather than passion. In contrast with European literature it is more secular in tone and lacking in grand religious themes and inspirations. It does not share the Western concept of tragedy, inexorably resulting from a flaw of personality in a great human being. In Chinese literature calamities occur when the virtuous and innocent come into conflict with the evil forces in society. At the end of the story the reader expects the satisfaction of the good triumphing over the bad, or solace in a sign that the good did not suffer in vain. Chinese literature – or rather that part of it written for an educated elite by an educated elite – is also characterized by an assumption that the reader knows the great literature of the past, so there is much of both skilful allusion and obscure pedantry. It is also more self-contained than any of the other great literatures, being very little touched by outside influences until the modern impact of the West.

Turning to the main fields of literature as seen from the Western viewpoint, I shall first make some general comments on poetry. The technicalities of prosody will mean little to the uninitiated, so I shall merely say that all traditional Chinese poetry rhymed; and that because of the relative phonetic poverty of the language, it rhymes easily, so that the same rhyme can be maintained over long stretches, which in English verse would seem monotonous. The *Book of Songs*, as we have seen, was the great early classic of poetry. Some of its pieces have a freshness and directness which later poetry could hardly recapture. Tradition maintained that officers of state toured the countryside to collect folk-songs which would inform the ruler of the mood of the people, and this particular collection was allegedly compiled by Confucius himself. Later in Chinese history the T'ang Dynasty was the greatest age of poetry, and for a time the composition of verses became an examination requirement, since the Confucian revival of the time meant a renewed sense of the moral purpose of poetry. The great poets Li Po, Tu Fu, and Wang Wei (who was a master landscape painter as well) all flourished during the reign of the emperor Hsüan-tsung, and Po Chü-i lived shortly afterwards.

As poetry became a common occupation of educated people, it was naturally used on many trivial occasions as well as for more serious purposes. Outings to places of natural beauty, excursions to admire the flowers in season, farewell parties for friends posted to distant regions, and convivial gatherings of all kinds were suitable occasions for verse composition. However trivial the event, poetry was the natural medium through which to express one's feelings, and much of the work even of major poets consisted of slight occasional pieces.

Poetry as a social activity led to poetry as an elegant pastime indulged in by societies whose members met to compose in competition with each other, being set the same subject, metre, and rhyme. This kind of literary competition may seem trivial, but since most educated people wrote poetry and poets were not thought of as a separate group of geniuses, there was no inhibition against dabbling in the trivial, any more than a great prose writer in our society would hesitate to write commonplace everyday letters.

This attitude strongly contrasted with the didactic view of poetry expressed in the preface to the *Book of Songs*, which was traditionally attributed to a disciple of Confucius: 'The ancient kings used it to regulate the tie between husband and wife, to perfect filial piety and respectfulness, to deepen human relationships, to beautify moral instruction, and to transform the customs of the people.'[4] Poets of the T'ang period at least paid lip-service to this doctrine. They felt that poetry should be a means not only to influence personal morality, but also to expose social evils and reflect the people's attitude towards the government.

There was, however, a contrary school of thought, which could equally find support in ancient scriptures. As the eighteenth-century poet Yüan Mei put it, 'Poetry is what expresses one's nature and emotion. It is enough to look no further than oneself for the material of poetry. If its words move the heart, its colour catches the eye, its taste pleases the mouth, and its sound delights the ear, then it is good poetry.'[5] A slightly different attitude, influenced by Ch'an Buddhism, was that poetry was the embodiment of the poet's view of the world, which he achieved after attaining a calm and contemplative state of mind. This attitude admits the need for inspiration rather than mere study or technique. So although poets in general were ordinary people engaged in an ordinary activity, rather than geniuses possessed by inspiration, there was some room for the concept of inspiration in Chinese poetry.

The special flavour of Chinese poetry owes much to the peculiar characteristics of the Chinese language which have already been described. Since there is a dearth of grammatical words and the language has a great capacity for concise and economical expression, poetical images flash before the reader with the minimum of interruption or padding. The lack of person, number, and tense automatically provides the air of universality for which the Western poet has to strive. Translation always spoils the effect. The introduction of the word 'I' converts the universal to the autobiographical, and opens the doors of self-praise or self-pity, self-righteousness or self-condemnation. The past tense closes the door on what should stand for all time. With his acute sensitivity to nature the Chinese poet is skilled at capturing a moment's vision in a few short lines, at giving commonplace incidents and experiences a timeless and immemorial quality, at sketching a farewell or a lonely night with superb economy. He uses words with great subtlety and knowledge of tradition. Although his work may lack the noble conceptions and sustained grandeur of some of the great masterpieces of European poetry, it has calmer beauties which have drawn the Western reader to it, even through the mists of translation.

Classics and philosophy have been discussed elsewhere, so the only one of the four major categories of literature which still needs introducing is history, which was very highly regarded for its moral and political importance and therefore placed second to Classics. The Chinese have always been a people with a strong historical consciousness: the historical record they have kept is unrivalled in magnitude anywhere in the world, and their non-historical literature is also very rich in historical references. This deep concern with history originated with ancestor worship, which not only necessitates the keeping of genealogies, but also involves the reporting to the ancestors of important family events such as births, marriages, and deaths. In the case of royal ancestors, their worship was on a grander scale; and, since in life they cared for both state and family and in death they still afforded protection for both, important state affairs such as victories in battle would doubtless be reported in addition to purely domestic matters. All this would need to be written down for the sake of reference, and so too would oracular responses need to be placed on record. Out of such material emerged the rudiments of the chronicle and the beginning of history writing in China.

What ensured that there would be a long historical tradition was the next stage, when the petty feudal states of the Chou period produced their own annals. One of these compilations, the chronicle of the state of Lu, known as the *Spring and Autumn Annals*, attained canonical status because of a tradition that Confucius had put it together, employing subtleties of terminology to praise or blame the characters for the parts they had played in history. The terse, unvarnished narrative permits no such interpretation, so Confucius's criticisms must have been expressed in the form of comments on the text which has been handed down to us. But this tradition concerning the *Spring and Autumn Annals* is the seed of the didactic view of history which flourished in China, the idea that history was to be regarded as a 'mirror' in which later generations could see themselves and judge their own conduct – a concept of history which was to be one of the cornerstones of the Confucianization of China.

The earliest historical work to have literary appeal as well as historical value was the *Tso Tradition*. Ostensibly it is a voluminous commentary on the sparse text of the *Spring and Autumn Annals*, but it also incorporates other material including a history of the times from the viewpoint of the state of Chin, based partly on romantic stories about the major historical figures. The *Speeches of the States* contains similar material at a further stage of fictionalization and dramatization, and the only other surviving work of a historical character from this period, the *Intrigues of the Warring States*, uses historical episodes to illustrate what is in effect a manual for political advisers. The philosophers of the Chou period also regarded references to historical precedent as compelling evidence for their theories, so schematized history is a common ingredient of *Mencius* and other philosophical writings.

The sudden breakthrough to genuine historiography came with the composition of the *Historical Records* by Ssu-ma Ch'ien, completing the work of his father Ssu-ma T'an, who preceded him in the hereditary office of Grand Scribe, which involved working with the official archives. Living at a time in the Former Han Dynasty when China seemed to have achieved a settled goal after centuries of turmoil, Ssu-ma Ch'ien and his father formed the grand conception of gathering within a single work all extant information about Chinese history from the beginning until their own time. They also departed from the format of a single narrative and evolved a most sophisticated scheme for looking at history from different angles; and perhaps it was only in China, a society in which men were especially conscious of the manifold relationships governing the lives of individuals, that such a multidimensional view of history could have been devised at that early time.

The work is divided into five sections: the Basic Annals, chronological tables, monographs (which deal with the history of various matters appertaining to government, such as ritual, the calendar, rivers and canals, and food and money), the Hereditary Houses (an account of the history of the pre-Ch'in states), and the memoirs (consisting mainly of biographies, both individual and collective, but also including accounts of foreign countries). One great merit of the book is the conscientious preservation of sources. Ssu-ma combines them into a skilful narrative, but keeps his own judgements on events carefully separate, instead of using them to make an imaginative reconstruction of the past. A further virtue is the consummate literary skill he devotes to the biographical chapters and other sections in which he is obviously recounting oral tradition rather than submitting written sources.

The general scheme devised by Ssu-ma Ch'ien was copied by another great historian, Pan Ku. Living in the first century AD, he devoted his history solely to the Former Han Dynasty. But he kept the separate sections of monographs (which he increased in number) and biographies, and imitated Ssu-ma's objective use of sources. Pan Ku's work was the prototype of the dynastic histories, which were the standard-bearer of the Chinese historiographical tradition right through until there were no more dynasties to record. From the T'ang Dynasty onwards the dynastic histories were written by teams of scholars working under the History Office, which was set up to gather materials and compile them into histories of single reigns, known as *Veritable Records*, which could later be used in their turn as sources for the dynastic histories. These later dynastic histories suffered from the disadvantages as well as the advantages of being huge impersonal compilations, so the height of literary achievement attained by Ssu-ma Ch'ien was never approached in later dynastic history writing; and for signs of genuine historical imagination one has to turn to the individual writings which existed side by side with the official histories. Apart from its greatness as a work of history, Ssu-ma Ch'ien's book filled a place in the Chinese experience similar to that occupied by the major novelists in our own literary tradition. Long before novels were written in China, his gifts as a story-teller gripped men's imagination, and he was as much an inspiration to writers of fiction as to historians.

Indeed the historical writings of antiquity – and the philosophers as well – are a rich source of anecdote, fable, and legend, indicating that a lively art of story-telling already existed at that time. Collections of stories were recorded in the bibliographical chapter of Pan Ku's history, which already uses the title 'small talk' (*hsiao-shuo*), which later served as the general word for fiction, although it was more appropriate to the kind of anecdotal material which was covered by the term at that time. The earliest extant stories date from the fourth century AD, but it was not until the *ch'uan-ch'i* (tales of the marvellous) written in the T'ang period that a short-story literature of high quality was produced. These stories were written in the Classical language by men of letters, and they dealt mainly with love, chivalry, and the supernatural. They were peopled with merchants, craftsmen, beggars, courtesans, and other urban characters. They were just one manifestation of the general eighth-century flowering of letters, and they were considered respectable enough for examination candidates to include them in the specimens of their writings which they submitted to the examiners by way of introduction. The tradition of short-story writing in the Classical language continued in later centuries.

At the same time a quite different kind of short story was developing. This was born in the market-place rather than the study, for it was the kind of story which was told by professional story-tellers as a public entertainment. The story-tellers were already in existence in the eighth century, and probably had their origin much earlier than that. They flourished during the Sung period, when story-telling was a popular form of entertainment in the amusement parks of Kaifeng and Hangchow, where the people jostled to watch acrobats, jugglers, puppeteers, clowns, and entertainments of all kinds. Story-telling was also popular in high places, and a well-known practitioner of the art might be called upon to leave his booth to go and perform at an imperial banquet. The tradition of oral story-telling has persisted in China right through to the present day, but at the same time these popular oral entertainments gradually began to be written down. Eventually during the late Ming Dynasty the vernacular short story reached the heights of achievement in the collections published by two men of letters called Feng Meng-lung and Ling Meng-chu. Centuries of interaction between performer and audience had doubtless helped to make plot water-tight and characterization lifelike, and in the hands of Feng and Ling this type of story was an extremely polished and intricate work of literature. Some of these stories were adaptations of earlier works, but others are clearly their original compositions; and their contribution made this kind of writing acceptable to the literary world of the time, while the prosperous cities of the Lower Yangtze area provided a ready market for such publications, which had a wide appeal because they vividly portrayed the social and commercial life of the age. Unfortunately the conservative and puritanical Ch'ing regime suppressed this literature, which was frank and realistic in its subject matter. Despite their sophistication, the stories retain some of the devices which belong to the story-teller's technique; such as the short curtain-raiser on a similar theme, which arouses anticipation and ensures that those who arrive a few minutes late do not miss any of the main offering; recapitulations of the action for the benefit of those who arrive after the main story has started; regular appeals to the audience for its attention; and occasional bits of verse to point a moral.

The story-telling tradition had a powerful influence on the novel. Chapters end with a form of words appropriate to the conclusion of a story-telling session, and the style is loose, rambling, and episodic, as if the author is prepared to go on and on as long as he can keep an audience. The subject matter of the early novels also derives from the story-telling tradition.

There are half a dozen novels which tower above all others, and the earliest of these is *The Romance of the Three Kingdoms*, by a fourteenth-century writer called Lo Kuan-chung. It is based on material about the history of the third century AD which had already been circulating in the form of short stories or plays. At that time China was divided into three kingdoms contending for the succession to the great Han Dynasty, and the chief participants in this struggle later acquired legendary characteristics – especially the kind and generous Liu Pei, ruler of the kingdom of Shu; the loyal, righteous, and brave Kuan Yü, who was later deified as God of War; the wizard and arch-strategist Chu-ko Liang; and Ts'ao Ts'ao, the personification of evil. Written in the literary rather than the vernacular language, the novel is akin to historical narrative and shows history unfolding from year to year; but the view of history which it presents derives from folk attitudes, and it served further to popularize such conceptions of history.

Lo Kuan-chung also revised *The Water Margin*, which was written by a contemporary called Shih Nai-an. This novel (which is also known as *All Men are Brothers*, after the Pearl Buck translation) is based on stories which had long been circulating about a rebellion which took place in Shantung early in the twelfth century. It is mainly concerned with events which led individual heroes to flee the injustice of the age and form an outlaw band which had its lair in the marshy and mountainous country of Liangshanpo, whence they surged forth to prey on the wicked and tyrannical and help the poor and distressed. The heroes have colourful and appropriate nicknames, and the leader of the band is an ex-magistrate's clerk called Sung Chiang, known as the Opportune Rain. A reluctant rebel, he looks forward to the day when he can redeem himself by loyal service to the government. Written in the living language of the day, the book is full of violence as well as adventure and humour.

The third of the great novels, *Journey to the West* (part of which was translated by Arthur Waley under the title *Monkey*), is also based on an existing story-cycle. It was written up as a novel by an unknown author in the sixteenth century. In it Hsüan-tsang's pilgrimage to India in the seventh century in search of Buddhist scriptures is built up into a fantastic adventure story in which the hero runs the gauntlet of an assortment of monsters, magicians, and temptresses. He is supported in his enterprise by the resourceful and mischievous Monkey, who possesses miraculous powers, including the ability to somersault 108,000 *li* and the trick of pulling out his hairs and turning them into thousands of little monkeys, and the sensual Pigsy, a most unlikely pilgrim who sadly misses the fleshpots of his former existence.

Golden Lotus is the first of the famous novels to be essentially a new creation, although its unknown author incorporates some material from existing plays and stories and fits popular songs into the narrative. Indeed the main characters, the lustful businessman Hsi-men Ch'ing and Golden Lotus, the fifth of his six wives, had already appeared in *The*

Water Margin. Golden Lotus removed the obstacle to her union with Hsi-men Ch'ing by murdering her dwarf husband, and in *The Water Margin* the latter is speedily avenged by his brother, Wu Sung, an out-law renowned for having slain a tiger with his bare hands. In *Golden Lotus* the act of vengeance is postponed until the reader has had a chance to savour her lechery and cunning, and her ruthless determination to win the chief place in Hsi-men's affections. The hero himself dies of his debauches when Golden Lotus plies him with aphrodisiac pills and thrusts her attentions upon him although he is exhausted after a long period closeted with the wife of one of his store managers. The characters are varied and lifelike, and develop as the book progresses, and the book's other great merit is that it skilfully documents the corruption and decadence of urban social life in the late Ming period.

Again, in *Dream of the Red Chamber*, the innumerable denizens of a great eighteenth-century household are very skilfully drawn. Here the thoughts and feelings of the characters are explored in a manner un-paralleled elsewhere in traditional Chinese literature; for the outside impinges only slightly on this enclosed world, in which the main action is the series of internal social occasions and casual encounters, which stimulate the jealousies, intrigues, and affections of the main characters. Typical major events are the creation by one Horticultural Hu of a new garden in preparation for the visitation of a daughter of the family who has become an imperial concubine, and the establishment of a family poetry society called the Crab Flower Club. But tragedies inter-vene and the scene darkens as the family goes into decline, echoing the experience of the author Ts'ao Hsüeh-ch'in, impoverished grandson of a favourite of the K'ang-hsi emperor. The author's concern for the thoughts and feelings of his characters did not distract him from provid-ing a most detailed and sensuous portrait of the physical surroundings of this great family and a most vivid description of the trivia of everyday life.

The last novel which must be mentioned was written a few years earlier than *Dream of the Red Chamber*. It is *The Unofficial History of the Literati* (translated by Yang Hsien-yi and his wife Gladys as *The Scholars*). It was written by Wu Ching-tzu, an intellectual who chose to stay out of the scholar-bureaucrat rat-race under the Manchus. He satirized not only the examination system and the scholar-bureaucrat class, but also lower-class snobs, literary upstarts, and many other categories of people. He saw virtue only in scholarly recluses and men in humble walks of life who retained their integrity.

The story-cycles used by the authors of *The Romance of the Three King-doms*, *The Water Margin*, and *Journey to the West* were also rich sources of material for dramatists, who in general did not invent their own plots but were content to convert existing ones into the theatrical idiom of the day. The theatre in China sprang largely from the court entertainments of antiquity. These were mainly provided by clowns, jesters, acrobats, and dancers; but by the T'ang Dynasty a dramatic art had developed, and Changan had a famous training centre for actors called the Pear Garden, as well as schools for court singers and dancers. In the Sung Dynasty the theatre spread to the masses; so, as well as entertaining in palace or yamen, troupes of actors appeared in permanent theatres set up in the amusement quarters of the big cities and even toured the countryside. Puppets and shadow-plays also became popular at this time.

The first dramatic literature of high quality dates from the Yüan Dynasty. The authors were men of talent deprived of political opportunities by Mongol rule and so given leisure for such work. They drew much inspiration from the lives of the common people, and their writing had a new emotional depth. Their plays were called *tsa-chü* (mixed entertainments) and included sung verse as well as prose dialogue, and dancing and mime as well as acting. There were different styles in the north and south, but all Chinese drama has certain features in common. There are a limited number of character-types, and actors specialize in one of these; and there is a bare minimum of scenery. It is sometimes described as opera, but this is misleading since the music is not specially composed for each piece and, unlike opera libretti, the dialogue, and more particularly the poetry, are generally enjoyable as literature.

After the Yüan Dynasty the theatre declined in originality. In modern times the Peking Opera has been the most important theatrical genre, although it is only 150 years old. Its literary quality is not high, and the plays depend for their success on the brilliant costume and make-up and the skill of the stylized acting and singing. Although the Peking Opera has brought great fame to some performers, the acting profession has generally been a lowly one, entailing disqualification from the civil service examinations. Troupes of actors not only gave public performances, but also played in private houses on birthdays and other special occasions. They were also sometimes invited to enter-tain the gods, for example at annual guild meetings, when a special show would be put on for the patron deity. In *Golden Lotus* a farewell performance of plays is given in front of the coffin of the Lady of the

Vase the day before her funeral. A wealthy family might keep its own troupe of actors, as did the Chias in *Dream of the Red Chamber*.

III

Turning now to how literature treats the various subjects dealt with in the earlier chapters of this book, we find that emperors in literature are larger than life, their love affairs are grander than those of ordinary men, their sexual prowess is greater, their life-style is more luxurious, and their tragedies more heart-rending. One infinitely sad theme is the ill-fated romance between the ageing emperor Hsüan-tsung of the T'ang Dynasty and his favourite concubine Yang Kuei-fei, the most famous treatment of which is Po Chü-i's poem *Song of Everlasting Sorrow*. The emperor was so infatuated with his beloved that when

> She turned her head, a single smile,
>   A hundred charms were born –
> The beauties of Six Palaces
>   Of all their looks were shorn.[6]

This blissful affair was rudely interrupted by the An Lu-shan rebellion, when the soldiers of the imperial bodyguard, disapproving of the excessive influence exerted by the Yang family, insisted on her execution:

> The soldiers of the army stopped,
>   They would no further ride,
> Till, sinking at their horses' hooves,
>   The moth-eyed beauty died.
> Kingfisher plumes and golden pins
>   And jade-carved diadem,
> Her combs inlaid with flowers lay strewn
>   And no man gathered them.
> The Emperor could not spare her life;
>   He turned his head around.
> When he turned back, his tears of grief
>   Spattered the blood-soaked ground.
> A shrill and bitter wind sprang up;
>   The yellow dust swirled round.

After the rebellion was over he was able to return to the desolate palace, where 'the steps were heaped with crimson leaves That no one swept away', but he was constantly haunted by her memory. Eventually a magician skilled at communicating with the spirits of the departed located her soul in a Taoist paradise. But all she could do was send back tokens of their love and reminders of their vows:

> In Heaven may we become paired birds
> With wings still linked in flight!
> On Earth may we become two trees
> That in one trunk unite!

The poem ends with the lines:

> The Heavens are high, the earth is wide,
> Yet both shall end ere long;
> But time will not obliterate
> This everlasting wrong.

In the words of the poem

> Three thousand ladies at his court,
> Of beauty rare were they!
> But all the love he owed to them
> In her one body lay.

For an emperor who seems to have everything at his command, to lose what is dearer to him than all the rest of his treasures put together seems sadder than the losses of ordinary mortals. There was a special poignancy in the thought that even the all-powerful were destined to suffer the pangs of bereavement. Tu Fu had also written a poem about this tragedy soon after it took place, and the story recurs in later literature, such as the Yüan play called *Rain on the Wu-t'ung Tree*, in which the forlorn emperor's sadness is captured in the image of listening to the rain

Sometimes intense like myriad pearls falling on a jade plate,
Sometimes loud like songs and music mingled noisily at a banquet,
Sometimes resonant like a waterfall from a cold spring at the head of a blue ridge,
Sometimes fierce like the beating of war-drums below an embroidered flag.[7]

The same sense of loss pervades the Yüan play *Autumn in the Han Palace*, which deals with the sad fate of the court lady sent off to marry a Hsiung-nu prince to fulfil the terms of a peace settlement.[8] There are various versions of what happened to this lady, whose name was Wang Ch'iang. An early account has her presenting the Hsiung-nu ruler with an heir who, after his father's death, marries her in accordance with the local custom, so that she bears children in turn to father and son. A variant of this has her taking poison to avoid this incestuous fate. In this much later theatrical elaboration of the story she failed to win the emperor's favour in spite of her beauty, because she was the only one who refused to pay bribes to Mao Yen-shou, the counsellor responsible for selecting the harem, so that he had her portrait spoilt; and the emperor, who had so many women that he chose whom to favour by examining their portraits rather than interviewing them personally, remained unaware of her charms. It was not until ten years later that the emperor, attracted by the sound of her playing the lute, saw her for the first time. He was enchanted by her and, discovering how he had been deceived, he gave orders for the villainous Mao to be beheaded. But Mao fled to the Hsiung-nu and suggested that their prince should ask expressly for her to be presented to him in fulfilment of the terms of the peace settlement. When he received the request, the emperor wished to take up arms rather than submit to it; but Wang Ch'iang insisted on going to the Hsiung-nu court in order to prevent needless bloodshed, and the emperor reluctantly agreed. After a sad leave-taking she departed, but when she reached her destination she threw herself into the river rather than submit. In the end Mao Yen-shou was brought back in chains and beheaded, and his head was offered as sacrifice to the spirit of Wang Ch'iang.

The ephemeral nature of royal pomp and circumstance is also a constant theme in Chinese literature. The Ch'in founder thought he had established a dynasty which would survive for ten thousand reigns, but it soon crumbled into dust. The vanity of royal possessions is described in this piece by the fifth-century poet Pao Chao:

> Have you not seen, my lord, the Cypress Tower*
> Today a ruined mound, all overgrown?
> Have you not seen, my lord, the Ah-fang Kung*
> A cold and misty marsh where pheasants roost?
> Singers and dancing girls, where are they now?
> Flaunting long sleeves, in throngs they vied for fame.
> I would not offer now their former price.
> Take wine, take pleasure, take life as you please,
> Don't let them send you wistful to the grave.[9]

*The tower was built by emperor Wur of the Han Dynasty, and the Ah-fang Kung was a palace built by Ch'in Shih Huang Ti, the Ch'in founder.

Imperial harems are also a natural setting for more pornographic descriptions of sexual relations. Being a classic example of the 'bad last ruler', the emperor Yang of the Sui Dynasty had pornographic pictures on the walls of his palace and was capable of dealing with several tens of women each day. As was mentioned in the chapter on Sons of Heaven, he even had beautiful girls to pull his imperial barge along the canals, and the stories of his licentiousness were told in great detail. In fact pornography in China starts with reports of life in the imperial harem. *The Emperor and the Two Sisters*, dating from the Han period, is probably the first of such stories.[10] In it the Son of Heaven comes to a very sad end. He suffers a serious decline in his virility through being caught in a snowstorm while out hunting. A miraculous cure is eventually found, and one of the sisters is entrusted with the task of administering it, but one night in a drunken stupor she gives him seven pills at once, with the predictable result that he expires as a consequence of the night's excesses.

The luxurious life of the court often forms the background to such stories, but for a classic example of direct description of court life there is a *fu* by Ssu-ma Hsiang-ju of the Han Dynasty, describing the emperor's Shanglin Park. The *fu* is a term applied to long descriptive pieces written partly in verse and partly in prose. Here is a small taste of the cornucopia:

> Spanning the valleys rise his rustic Courts,
> Amid the hills, Imperial resorts.
> While storied chambers on the hilltops stand
> And porticoes surround on either hand,
> With eaves gay-painted and jade-bedizened.
> The Royal car a winding course may trace
> For many a mile; arcades his walks embrace.
> Peaks are torn down and level courts appear;
> Rank upon rank new terraces uprear.
> Deep through the hills the rocky halls extend;
> The eye retires from chasms without end.
> Yet other palaces assault the skies,
> Where shooting Star or speeding Comet flies,
> And Rainbows the astonished Guest surprise.
> From east Pavilions emerald Dragons prance,
> And ivory Carts from western Halls advance.
> On tranquil Towers guests Immortal dine,
> In southern shelters sundrench'd Sprites recline.[11]

Later we see the emperor out hunting:

> The Son of Heaven sets bound'ries to the Chase,
> Then in his ivory Carriage takes his place.
> Six Dragon-horses lead the cavalcade,
> Their harness clinking, set with precious jade.
> Before the Host, the Rainbow pennants go,
> Behind, Cloud-banners in the breezes blow.

and then when they get into the field

> First from the ridges hunters spy their prey;
> By plashy paths at last it turns at bay.
> Then through the hills, across the lowland plain,
> Like storm-clouds whirling, or like driving rain,
> The chariots and horsemen thunder forth,
> Startling the skies and menacing the earth.
> Panthers and leopards both alive are ta'en,
> But wolf and skulking jackal swiftly slain.

Emperors also play their part in the great novels. The climax of *Monkey* is when the pilgrims at last return home to Changan and are received by the Son of Heaven. They hand over the scriptures which they have brought back with them and are guests of honour at a great banquet, and the emperor enquires about their journey and looks at their passports to see how many countries they have visited. In *Golden Lotus* the hero Hsi-men Ch'ing, who despite his unworthiness holds an official position, interrupts his debauches to attend court, when

> gongs were beaten and bells rung, as the emperor came back to his palace to receive the homage of his officers. Clouds of incense streamed towards the skies. The great ceremonial fans waved to and fro. His Majesty ascended the throne, and the crack of whips gave the signal for silence. The officers, holding their tablets of office before their breasts, made five salutations and kotowed three times before the throne, doing homage to the Sacred Majesty.

A high official kneels before the throne and makes a loyal address concluding with the words 'We pray that you may be spared to live as the mountains, that the light of the sun and moon may always shine upon us. Your Majesty's graciousness is beyond our power to express; we can only enjoy the blessings that come to us through it. We offer Your Majesty our most humble congratulations and praise.'[12] By contrast with this, one treasures the irreverence of the character in *Monkey* who cries out: 'I live in a decent tiled house, not in a sickly yellow place like this, that looks as if it had got jaundice!'[13]

After Sons of Heaven the next main topic in the first part of this book was the bureaucracy, which was the target of much satire, especially as those who despised and avoided official life had more leisure to write about it. Most notable among these was the eighteenth-century satirist Wu Ching-tzu, author of *The Scholars*, who resolutely refused to have an official career under the Manchu invaders. In this novel the most famous characters are the penurious middle-aged scholars Chou Chin and Fan Chin who, after years of failure, fortuitously pass the examinations and immediately soar to great heights of success and prosperity. Chou Chin runs a village school housed in a Buddhist temple, and the unruly children make his life a misery. A recent graduate stays overnight at the temple, does not invite Chou to share his meal, but leaves the down-trodden fellow to sweep up the mess the following morning. Eventually he gets the sack for failing to flatter the snobbish but illiterate village head. His brother-in-law gives him a job as accountant to a group of merchants travelling to the provincial capital. There he has a chance to visit the examination buildings, and this experience makes him so miserable that one of the merchants suggests that they club together to buy him a rank which entitles him to enter the provincial examination. Having surmounted this hurdle, he quickly passes the metropolitan and palace examinations and becomes a provincial examiner himself. In this capacity he encounters the pallid and threadbare candidate Fan Chin, whom we have already met in Chapter 2. At first Chou thinks his papers are drivel, but after successive readings he sees merit in them and passes him. Fan Chin, who is in the market to sell a hen when the news reaches him, at first refuses to believe he has passed the provincial examination, and faints with excitement when he realizes it is true. The change in his fortunes is shown in the reaction of his father-in-law, butcher Hu, who previously bullied him unmercifully, but now boasts what a fine match his daughter has made. Fan soon achieves rapid promotion and is surrounded by untold riches, for presents arrive from far and wide as people seek to ingratiate themselves with him because of his newly acquired prestige.

Elsewhere in the novel an actor called Pao Wen-ch'ing, a man of high moral quality despite his lowly profession, is asked by his patron, who is an examiner, to go along and inspect the examination buildings, taking his son T'ing-hsi with him. Wu Ching-tzu describes the scene thus:

When the candidates appeared, some were substitute examinees, some were passers-on of cribs, and all in general threw balls of paper about, flung bricks, winked and gave each other knowing looks, and got up to all kinds of tricks. When the time came for them to grab their refreshments, they all shoved in a mass and collapsed in a heap, and Pao T'ing-hsi turned his eyes away in disgust. There was one candidate who, pretending he was going off to relieve himself, walked over to the earthen wall of the examination compound, scooped out a hole in it and was stretching out his hand to take an essay pushed through from outside when he was observed by Pao T'ing-hsi, who wanted to seize him and take him over to see the Examiner. But Pao Wen-ch'ing stopped him. 'It's just that my son doesn't know the way of the world,' he said. 'You are a respectable, book-learning fellow, young sir, so go back to your place at once and get on with your essay. If His Excellency had seen what you were up to, it would have been awkward for you.' He quickly picked up some earth to fill the hole, and escorted the candidate back to his cell.[14]

Elsewhere the book describes a graduate taking the examination as substitute for a numskull in return for payment. This graduate, K'uang Ch'ao-jen, first appears on the scene as an extremely studious and dutiful boy, who pursues his studies with diligence while looking after a bed-ridden father; but once he passes his examinations he is totally corrupted by success and takes to a life of crime.

Indeed it is quite normal in Chinese literature for a successful scholar to be portrayed as an unscrupulous opportunist, not as one whose character has benefited from his prolonged exposure to the Confucian moral teachings. Two well-known examples of this type may be mentioned. Firstly, in Feng Meng-lung's story *The Lady Who was a Beggar*, a marriage is arranged between a beggar chief's daughter called Jade Slave and a poor student named Mo Chi.[15] When Mo Chi passes his examination, he grows tired of the street-urchins calling him the beggar chief's son-in-law, so he tries to rid himself of this embarrassing connection by pushing his wife into the river when they are journeying to his first official post. She is rescued from drowning by Transport Commissioner Hsü, who adopts her as his own child. Some time later he lets it be known among his subordinates that he has an eligible daughter; and Mo Chi, whose place of employment happens to be under Commissioner Hsü's jurisdiction, is recommended as a suitable husband. At first Jade Slave virtuously refuses to remarry, although Mo Chi treated her so badly; and she only agrees to the match when she is told that it is in fact her wicked husband that she is expected to marry. On entering the nuptial chamber Mo Chi is severely beaten by the womenservants. Put to shame by what has happened, he has now learnt his lesson; so, although he has a new father-in-law in the person of Commissioner Hsü, he receives the beggar chief into his official residence and looks after him for the rest of his life. So his character is reformed by practical experience rather than book-learning. Another such character is Ts'ai Po-chieh who won top place in the palace examination when only two months married, and then deserted his bride and wedded the prime minister's daughter. But in *The Tale of the Lute* Ts'ai's conduct is excused because it was filial piety which made him take the examination and loyalty which made him remarry at the emperor's command.[16]

As well as unscrupulous careerists, the examination system also breeds dreary old pedants, like the tutor Ch'en in the Ming play *The Peony Pavilion*, who greets his fair charge with admonitions from the *Record of Rites* about the behaviour of young women and has an inept reference to the Classics ready for every possible occasion.[17] Girls were indeed sometimes subjected to the same kind of education as men. But for the male sex success in examinations was the main aim in life and took precedence over all other values. In the play *The Injustice done to Tou Ngo* the heroine is sold by her father to Dame Ts'ai so that he can afford to go and take the examinations, so the ties of parental affection are placed below the demands of examination success; and in *The Scholars* there are those who neglect even the requirements of mourning because they consider examinations more important. In that book the true heroes are men in humble circumstances who carry the torch of culture and morality which has been abandoned by the scholar class, like the impoverished teahouse keeper K'ai Kuan, who sits reading or painting while he waits for customers, with always a few flowers and a pile of books on his counter.

There are some heroic figures among the scholar class who refuse to be drawn into official life or withdraw from it later because they find there is no other honourable course. An example of the former is Tu Shao-ch'ing, a self-portrait of Wu Ching-tzu in *The Scholars*. He feigns illness when he is summoned to court. The T'ang statesman P'ei Tu is an example of the latter. He is featured in the Ming story *The Restitution of the Bride*, where he appears as the sole man of virtue amid the corruption and squalor of official life, and decides at the height of his career that he must go into retirement.[18]

A classic case of an historical figure who did not take the examinations was the poet Li Po, who spent his early years in Taoism, knight-errantry, and drinking, rather than Confucian studies. But Feng Meng-lung gives him a splendid victory over the learned Hanlin Academicians in his story called *Li Po, God in Exile, Drunken Drafts his 'Letter to Daunt the Barbarians'*. The story opens by telling how it came about that Li Po was thought to be an immortal in human guise or a 'God in Exile' and how, since drinking was his greatest pleasure in life, he never sought a career in the government. His ambition was to roam freely the whole world over, to see all the famous scenic mountains on earth, and taste every fine wine in the universe. When asked why he did not take the examinations he said that the government was in complete chaos, and that one's examination results depended on bribery and underhand dealings. The reason why he amused himself with poetry and wine was simply to avoid being insulted by blind examiners. However, he was eventually persuaded to take the examination (an uncharacteristic act, but one which suited the convenience of the story-teller). Despite his superabundant genius, he was failed by the high officials who examined his papers, who said he was only fit to grind their ink or pull off their boots. But a letter arrived from a foreign ambassador, and none of the Hanlin Academicians could translate it. Eventually Li Po surrendered to the emperor's pleas for help and rattled off a translation with a sardonic smile. The contents of the letter, which threatened a military attack if China would not cede territory, caused grave consternation among the courtiers, but Li Po offered to draft a reply which would cause the foreigners to capitulate. By now Li Po was in such favour that he was able to persuade the emperor to order those who had previously insulted him at the examination to take off his boots and grind his ink for him. Li Po then composed his reply in the same foreign script. It was a haughty and dismissive message which the foreign ambassador felt bound to accept because it was drafted by one who had the Grand Preceptor to bear his inkstone and the Grand Captain to pull off his boots for him; and one who furthermore was an immortal and so must not on any account be offended. The emperor henceforth entertained him often, stirring his soup for him, and regularly consulted him on government. Eventually he bestowed upon him a golden tally bearing the words: 'I confer upon Li Po the title of Scholar of the Empire Without Worldly Worries, the Wandering Master of Arts of No Fixed Address. Let him drink at any wine-shop he comes across, and draw money at any branch of the treasury.'[19]

The eccentric who wins great victories against the big battalions of officialdom is also to be found in the engaging personality of Monkey in *Journey to the West*, the most sustained and amusing anti-bureaucratic satire to be found in Chinese literature. What makes it even more amusing is that the bureaucrats of the story are celestial rather than terrestrial officials. In one scene Monkey inspects the files of this other-worldly bureaucracy to try to find his own entry. It is not under the heading 'Monkeys' because he has human characteristics, but eventually he tracks it down and there

under the heading of Soul number 1350 he finds his own name, Aware of Vacuity Sun; natural product; stone monkey;allotted span of life, 342 years; a peaceful death. Monkey says: 'I'm not going to put down what the span of life is to be either. I'll just strike out the name altogether, and that'll be that. Get me a brush!' The officer in charge of the dead hastily holds out a brush, heavily impregnated with thick ink. Monkey picks up the register, and strikes out every single one of the names of the monkey clan that have been written down. Then, throwing down the register, he says: 'That's settled. Now you've got no authority over us.'[20]

When the pilgrims arrive at their destination and go to get the scrip-tures, the Buddha's disciples Ananda and Kasyapa behave rather like yamen underlings, trying to get a tip out of Tripitaka* before they will hand over the scriptures to him. When Monkey threatens to tell the Buddha, they hand the scriptures over with bad grace; but later the pilgrims discover they have been tricked, for the parcels of scriptures turn out to contain only blank paper. Monkey then complains to the Buddha, who says:

Don't shout. I already knew that those two were asking you for a com-mission. But the sutra cannot be lightly given away, and cannot be collected without payment. . . . You came to get it with empty hands, and that is why they gave you a blank scroll. In fact, it is the blank scroll that is the real wordless sutra, and it is actually better. But the rabble in your eastern land is ignorant and unenlightened, so I'll have to give you the other kind.[21]

Tripitaka has to hand over his golden begging bowl as a tip after all. Aristophanes would certainly have enjoyed reading *Monkey*.

IV

The second part of this book was concerned with philosophy, and mainly with Confucianism, Taoism, and Buddhism; so we shall now see how the Three Doctrines are reflected in literature. In one sense the Confucian influence is very wide indeed in that much Chinese literature

*The religious name of the pilgrim Hsüan-tsang.

has a didactic quality. This applies not only to the four categories of literature in the Classical language, but also to novels and short stories. Both in early times and in the more sophisticated products of the Ming period the story-tellers urge their audiences to practise Confucian virtues, to accept the Buddhist doctrine of retribution, to heed the claims of sexual morality, and to believe that one's virtues will be rewarded and one's vices punished by gods and spirits.

Some of the great names in Chinese literature were Confucian moralists, and Tu Fu was one such whose work is imbued with his beliefs. A book like *The Scholars* has an obvious Confucian moral: it is primarily an argument for the Confucian view that one should withdraw from an active role in a society in which the Way does not prevail. The book is in general the story of an age in which the Way does not prevail, so that the examinations are sterile, scholar-bureaucrats are corrupt, and virtue is only to be found in private and retired individuals. Neglect of the Confucian virtues is bitterly satirized in the portrait of the father of Tu Shao-ch'ing:

He had the ability to pass his metropolitan degree and hold office as a prefect – but he was a fool. When he was an official, he failed utterly to understand that he ought to show respect for his superiors, and instead persistently schemed to secure the satisfaction of the common people. Day by day, too, he preached that nonsense about 'esteeming filial piety and brotherly respect, and encouraging agriculture and sericulture'. Such phrases are just flowery language for use in examination essays, but he took them quite literally, and as a result his superiors were moved to displeasure, and they brought about his dismissal from office![22]

The Confucian faith in the educational value of ancient ceremonial and music also shines through in the central episode in the novel, when some of the worthy scholars of Nanking finance the construction of a temple of T'ai-po, who was traditionally regarded as the founder of the ancient state of Wu (written with the same character as the author's surname). The proposer of the scheme argues that the practice of ancient ceremonies and music in the temple will have an educative influence and eventually 'produce some genuine scholars and also assist in training people to maintain law and order'.[23]

A Confucian moral is also to be found in less obvious contexts. One of the main themes of *The Water Margin* is the Confucian saying 'Within the four seas all men are brothers', which gave Pearl Buck the title for her translation of the novel. The outlaw band is depicted as a group of men who, in spite of everything, remain faithful servants of the throne; and who proclaim the ideals of loyalty and justice, although the times are so out of joint and officialdom is so corrupt that they have to take the law into their own hands. The meeting hall of the bandits is called 'The Hall of Loyalty and Righteousness'. At the climax of the novel Sung Chiang addresses the outlaws and proposes that a great mass be said to thank Heaven, Earth and all the gods, and prays that the emperor will forgive them. They unearth a stone tablet bearing the slogans 'Work righteousness for Heaven' and 'In loyalty and righteousness complete', together with the names and titles of all the 108 outlaw chiefs. Despite these labels, however, the outlaws sometimes display utter ruthlessness and the most appalling cruelty.

Quite incongruous too is the note of Confucian frugality at the end of the prose-poem on the Shanglin Park. After all the fun and gaiety of the poem the Son of Heaven instructs his ministers: 'If there are lands here in these suburbs that can be opened for cultivation, let them all be turned into farms in order that my people may receive and benefit thereby. Tear down the walls and fill up the moats that the common people may come and profit from these hills and lowlands.'[24] It is a speech which Mencius would have warmly applauded.

Many stories illustrate individual Confucian virtues, especially filial piety, but there is also a long tradition of Confucian hypocrisy, the target of some splendidly satirical and vindictive writing. It was attacked in ancient texts like *Mo Tzu* and *Chuang Tzu*, which levelled a charge of peddling rites and currying favour with rulers. 'The Confucians,' in the words of the former, 'corrupt men with their elaborate and showy rites and music and deceive parents with protracted mourning and simulated grief.'[25] The *Chuang Tzu* gives the sage a piece of eloquence from the mouth of the legendary Robber Chih:

This must be that artful deceiver Confucius from the state of Lu, isn't it? Well, tell him from me: 'You create words and fashion phrases in reckless eulogy of Wen and Wu. ... You eat although you do not plough, you wear clothes although you do not weave. You flap your lips and clack your tongue, arrogating the power to create right and wrong, so as to delude the world's rulers and prevent the world's scholars from returning to the root of all things. Although you wantonly establish ideals of filial piety and brotherly duty, you are the sort of person who curries favour with fief-holders and with men of wealth and rank!'[26]

Good specimens of Confucian hypocrisy from later literature are the Wang brothers in *The Scholars*. Their own sister was dying, but because it suited their purposes to do so, they persuaded their brother-in-law to make his concubine the legal wife without waiting for her death. They claimed the support of lofty Confucian principle even for this signal lack of brotherly affection. Having made the necessary arrangements they left 'with righteousness written all over their faces'. At the hastily arranged wedding ceremony one of the brothers 'drew on his vast erudition to compose a literary piece informing the ancestors of the match, and it was all done with extreme seriousness'.[27]

Like Confucianism, Taoism had such an all-pervasive influence on Chinese intellectual life that its echoes are to be heard everywhere. Much of the finest Chinese poetry could not have been written without consciousness of its teachings, and the language of Taoism recurs in all kinds of literature; while Taoist immortals, magicians, or teachers are routine characters, like Kung-sun Sheng in *The Water Margin*, nicknamed Dragon in the Clouds, who was 'skilled at calling winds, summoning rains, riding mists, and mounting the clouds'.[28] He joined the outlaws and put these special gifts at the band's disposal. Monkey, too, has a lesson in cloud-soaring, and his instructor reprimands him for putting his feet together and jumping instead of sitting cross-legged and rising in that position like a true immortal. The other pupils titter, and cry: 'Monkey's in luck. If he learns this trick he can become an express messenger, taking letters and reports about. He'll be sure to find a meal to eat wherever he goes.'

One of the most amusing episodes in *Monkey* is the encounter with Lao Tzu, who is depicted not as an ancient sage, but as the kind of Taoist magician into which later legend converted him. Monkey went into his alchemical laboratory and ate some immortality pills 'for all the world as though they had been a dish of fried beans'. Realizing that he had behaved stupidly, Monkey then ran away. Lao Tzu reported the theft to the Jade Emperor, and at the same time the Great Sage – for Monkey is often thus grandiosely described – was reported missing. 'Tell the Celestial Detective to get on his tracks at once,' cried the Jade Emperor. But the Great Sage, Equal of Heaven, used all his magic powers, and even a hundred thousand heavenly troops could not quell him; but he was eventually caught by Lao Tzu's magic snare. However, at the place of execution he proved impervious to axes, spears, and swords, and even thunderbolts. Lao Tzu offered to put him in his crucible and smelt him with alchemical fire. In a little while the ape would be reduced to ashes and he, Lao Tzu, would be able to recover his elixir, which would be left at the bottom of the crucible. But when he removed the lid, Monkey showed no sign of discomfiture except for red eyes – which he never lost, so that he is sometimes called Fiery-eyes. After this Monkey became so vain that he told the Buddha that he wanted to take over the Jade Emperor's job. The Buddha said that he might if he could jump off the palm of his right hand. Monkey thought that this was easy since he could jump 108,000 *li* and the Buddha's palm could only be about eight inches across; but after an enormous leap he reached five pink pillars, and was abashed to discover that these were the Buddha's fingers.[29]

In a much more serious spirit Po Chü-i has a poem about Lao Tzu:

> Those who speak know nothing,
> Those who know are silent.
> Those words, I am told,
> Were spoken by Lao Tzu.
> If we are to believe that Lao Tzu
> Was himself one who knew,
> How comes it that he wrote a book
> Of five thousand words?[30]

Li Po, on the other hand, was a genuine believer, who held a diploma certifying that he had achieved a certain stage of initiation. He probably believed in the existence of immortals, and genuinely considered himself to be a banished one. When he ascended Mount T'ai, he attributed his safe arrival at the summit to having fasted for three thousand days and written out the *Tao Te Ching* on a scroll of silk. He reported having encounters with immortals whose eyes had square pupils (a transformation which takes place when one is eight hundred years old). His poems are imbued with Taoist feelings. He wrote a poem based on the story from *Chuang Tzu* in which the philosopher dreamed he was a butterfly. The poem begins:

> When Chuang Chou dreamed he was a butterfly
> The butterfly became Chuang Chou,
> If single creatures can thus suffer change,
> Surely the whole world must be in flux.[31]

The two main facets of Taoist influence on the content of Chinese poetry are, firstly, the great sense of harmony between Man and Nature which colours the many descriptions of landscape; and, secondly, the feeling of impermanence which imbues much Chinese poetry with nostalgia and sadness. The two facets are closely connected because this keen sense of the passage of time derives from close involvement with

Nature, which makes Man acutely conscious of its eternal renewal as contrasted with the transience and decay of individual human life. As Pao Chao put it, 'The ebbing tide is certain to return; But can a face, once withered, youth regain?'[32] The true Taoist, who discards thought of self in his sense of oneness with the Tao, should not feel like that. As Po Chü-i wrote in a poem to Yüan Chen:

> The flower of the pear-tree gathers and turns to fruit;
> The swallows' eggs have hatched into young birds.
> When the Seasons' changes thus confront the mind
> What comfort can the Doctrine of Tao give?
> It will teach me to watch the days and months fly
> Without grieving that Youth slips away;
> If the Fleeting World is but a long dream,
> It does not matter whether one is young or old.[33]

But very often one encounters a strong sense of the hurried passage of time and a determination to enjoy life while it lasts, typified in Li Po's

> See the waters of the Yellow River leap down from Heaven,
> Roll away to the deep sea and never turn again!
> See at the mirror in the High Hall
> Aged men bewailing white locks –
> In the morning threads of silk,
> In the evening flakes of snow.
> Snatch the joys of life as they come and use them to the full;
> Do not leave the silver cup idly glinting at the moon.[34]

This is such a common theme that two more examples may not be out of place. The first is by the thirteenth-century poet Liu Yin:

> The time before the flowers open, I gaze at them unopened,
> Afraid that, when they open, the wind and rain will come.
> But once they have opened, wind and rain don't bother me,
> I only wonder why you are not here
> To get a little drunk beneath their blossoms.
> A hundred years of crooked deals, a thousand years of scheming?
> We do not know today what the next day will bring.
> The spring wind tries to warn me as I sit in flowers,
> And drops one petal red before my eyes.[35]

The next is by Juan Chi of the third century AD:

> Hibiscus flowering on the graves
> Makes a vivid splash of colour.

As the white sun drops through the trees,
Flowers fall fluttering to the road.
The cricket sings in door and casement,
Cicadas cry among the thorns.
Only three days the swarming may-flies
Play on their iridescent wings.
So why do we put on such finery,
Gilding ourselves for but a moment's space?
Just how long does a man's life last?
Yet we'll try hard to show some bravery.[36]

These two poems show not only this strong sense of time passing, but also the bond between short-lived human beings and the short-lived members of the animal and vegetable world, one aspect of the close harmony between Man and Nature which is the other major emphasis deriving from Taoism. From this sense of harmony with Nature flows an abundance of landscape poetry, which began to develop in the south of China at the same time and for the same reasons as landscape painting. The movement is said to have reached maturity with Hsieh Ling-yün in the early fifth century. He was brought up as a Taoist, but was later converted to Buddhism and joined a monastic community. He was fond of walking in the mountains and even invented a kind of climbing boot. His love of mountaineering, his sense of communion with Nature, and his philosophical turn of mind may all be seen in the following piece:

At dawn with staff in hand I climbed the crags,
At dusk I made my camp among the mountains.
Only a few peaks rise as high as this house,
Facing the crags, it overlooks winding streams.
In front of its gates a vast forest stretches,
While boulders lie around its very steps.
Hemmed in by mountains, there seems no way out,
The track gets lost among the thick bamboos.
My visitors can never find their way,
And when they leave, forget the path they took.
The raging torrents rush on through the dusk,
The monkeys clamour shrilly through the night.
Deep in meditation, how can I part from Truth?
I cherish the Way and never will swerve from it.
My heart is one with the trees of late autumn,
My eyes delight in the buds of early spring,
I dwell with my constant companions and wait for my end,

264

Content to find peace through accepting the flux of things.
I only regret that there is no kindred soul,
To climb with me this ladder to the clouds in the blue.[37]

His contemporary T'ao Ch'ien (also known as T'ao Yüan-ming) was one who retreated from the world of wealth and rank to enjoy the pleasures of wine and the simple life of the countryside. He even worked on the land himself, as described in one of his best-known poems, 'Returning to my Garden and Field':

I plant my beans below the southern hill,
The grass grows thick, the beansprouts all too few.
At dawn I go to clear the choking weeds;
Beneath the moon I come home with my hoe.[38]

Many nature poems, like landscape paintings, are linked to one of the four seasons, like this evocation of winter from the fifth-century poet Yü Hsin:

The season of Shadow draws to an end in silence,
Monotonous, endless clouds cover the sky.
The swarming snow swirls down like crane-feathers falling,
The flying thistledown spins past like whirling wheels.
The homing geese know well where the warm sun is shining,
While birds in their nests contrive to keep out of the cold.
On the river's twin shores, the icy sands gleam white,
And hunters' fires have turned all the mountains red.
Men with clothes like feathers on a hanging quail –
I sigh for their lives in backstreet empty rooms.[39]

Wang Wei, the father of landscape painting, is also well known for the sense of intimacy with nature which his poems reveal. The following piece, like many others, was written about his country estate:

Chilly the mountains shade to blue and green;
The autumn waters have run down all day;
Propped on my stick outside my brushwood gate,
I hear the evening crickets on the wind.
A ferry boat still bathed in setting sun;
Thin smoke from half-deserted cottages;
When shall I see you to get drunk again
And sing wild songs by my five willow trees?[40]

Liu Tsung-yüan of the T'ang Dynasty, a friend of Han Yü, portrayed landscape in prose as well as verse, and is considered to be the greatest writer of landscape essays. The following extract shows the poetical qualities of his writing, and also makes one think of a landscape in painting as much as in nature:

This mountain rises precipitously amidst a vast azure expanse, rushing straight up to the clouds for a distance of tens and hundreds of *li*. Its tail coils around desolate and distant nooks while at its head the water pours into an immense stream. The other mountains come to it for an audience like stars encircling it and bowing in obeisance. Its fantastic verdant range spreads like an embroidered silk of variegated colours and shapes.[41]

The tranquillity of Chinese poetry and painting owed something to Buddhism as well as to Taoism, but the main influence of the foreign religion on literature (as well as on life) was to provide moral terms of reference. The doctrine of *karma* explained why good men often go unrewarded in this life, and foreshadowed an unenviable destiny for villains. Buddhism also played an important part in the story-telling tradition, and from the early T'ang period onwards monks gave popular recitations of Buddhist stories. During the Sung religious tales, mostly Buddhist, constituted one of the four categories of specialization among the professional story-tellers. The faith also deeply influenced the lives of T'ang intellectuals like Po Chü-i, whose poems were full of Buddhist compassion as well as of evidence that the doctrines were included among his intellectual furniture.

However, much of Chinese literature was written by men who, whatever feelings they may have had about Buddhist ideals, looked down on monks and nuns as lower-class figures of fun; for, especially in the late imperial period, monasteries were havens for the destitute and unwanted. So in *Golden Lotus*, although the religion is treated with respect and even provides a sort of moral framework in that Hsi-men Ch'ing's evil deeds are ultimately expiated by his son's life of dedication to Buddhism, monks and nuns are treated in a most unsympathetic fashion. Nuns had a particularly bad image in traditional Chinese literature, because they made their way into the good graces of the female members of large well-to-do families and filled their minds with scandal and superstition. Often, too, they were charged with being promiscuous rather than celibate, as in this biographical sketch from *Golden Lotus*:

Actually this nun Hsüeh was not one who had taken her vows early in life. When she was young she had a husband who made a living from selling steamed buns in front of the Kuang-ch'eng Monastery. Unfortunately trade was scanty, and she took up instead with the monks from the monastery, flirting with them and making eyes at them, and hooked five or six of them. Often they came and presented her with dumplings that had been sent as offerings, they made over to her money from their gratuities to buy flowers, and gave her cloth used for the ceremonial opening of the Underworld to bind her feet. Her husband did not know a thing. Afterwards when her husband died, she was so enthusiastic about Buddhism that she became a nun. She specialized in running in and out of families of the gentry, to solicit money for the reciting of sutras, and also to involve women of permissive character in love affairs. She had heard that Hsi-men Ch'ing had a wealthy household; so, thinking that she might get some good out of it, she often paid visits.[42]

The book also pokes fun at Buddhist miracle-working, as in its account of Wan Hui the Venerable:

He really was a man of elevated virtue, and fully initiated into the mysteries of the gods. Once, before the Stone Tiger of the emperor Chao, he swallowed two pints of needles. Again, in the temple of the emperor Wu of the Liang Dynasty, he brought from his head three relics of the Buddha. So the temple of Eternal Bliss was constructed especially for him, at a cost of I don't know how much money.[43]

Another gift to the story-teller is the monk who, instead of being a saintly recluse, is a beefy wine-swilling extrovert who breaks all his vows. Such characters had a firm foundation in fact, for criminals fleeing from justice sometimes shaved their heads and sought refuge in the monastic life. A classic example is the army captain Lu Ta in *The Water Margin*, who took his vows because he was wanted for murder. The other monks mutter timidly among themselves: 'This man does not look like one who renounces the world. He's got eyes like a brigand!'[44] As they fear, he behaves in a coarse and vulgar manner. He gets drunk and terrorizes the monastery, and even attacks the images of the gate gods and smashes them to pieces. Monkish celibacy is also fair game for the humourist: the sight of Golden Lotus or Ying-ying, the heroine of the Yüan play *The Western Chamber*, drives them to distraction and puts them off their ceremonies. As soon as the monks saw Golden Lotus, 'each one of their Buddha-loving souls and pious hearts was spellbound: they could not control their ardent desires, and fell down all over the place in a state of collapse'.[45] In the *Western Chamber* episode the head monk absent-mindedly strikes the bald pate of a novice, thinking it is a musical stone, and the acolytes forget to light the candles and burn the incense.

In *Monkey* much fun is to be had from seeing gods behave like human beings. 'Today the bodhisattva is getting on with her housework again,' says Monkey of Kuanyin. 'How come she's not meditating on her lotus throne? She hasn't made up or put on her jewels, and she's not in a good mood. What is she doing in the Grove peeling bamboos?' At the centre of the whole joke is the incongruous band of pilgrims. The unethereal Pigsy bitterly regrets he can no longer satisfy his carnal appetites:

> Once I was a fine fellow – I passed my days with my diet of human flesh, and partook of odorous beef and mutton. I was really very happy. Then you would have to become a monk, and summon me to protect you while you ran around. At first you just said that I was to be an acolyte, but actually you treat me like a slave. During the day I have to carry your luggage and lead your horse, and at night I have to empty your slops and sleep at your feet to keep you warm.

At the end of the journey, after they have successfully returned with the scriptures, they are whisked away to Paradise. Tripitaka is made Buddha of Precious Merit and Monkey becomes the Buddha Victorious in Strife. Pigsy complains bitterly at only being made Cleanser of the Altars. Why cannot he be made a Buddha like the other two? 'Because,' says the Buddha, 'you are coarse of mouth and low in appearance, and you have too great an appetite. In the four continents of the world those who revere my religion are numerous, and whenever there is a service you will be called to clean up the altars. It's a job that will get you plenty of offerings. What have you got to complain about?'[46]

V

The next part of this book deals with the social experience of the Chinese and begins with a discussion of the family. One of the best sources for the study of the extended family in late imperial China is *Dream of the Red Chamber*, which has a wealth of information on the philosophy, the intrigues, and the life-style of a huge traditional household, with its concubines and servants as well as family members. *Golden Lotus* is also rich in such material. But at the opposite extreme there are many simple little poems, which convey a sense of family solidarity, such as Tu Fu's verses to his wife and children, from whom he was long separated by poverty and war. The inward-looking contentment of the Chinese family group is captured in these verses from a long poem by the T'ang poet Han-shan:

> Father and mother left me all I need,
> I do not envy others' plots and fields.
> As my wife weaves, the loom creaks steadily;
> My children, playing, chatter on and on.
> I clap my hands to make the flowers dance,

Or chin on hand I listen to the birds.
Who comes this way to have a talk with me?
A woodman often wanders down my path.

In my thatched house I live a rustic life;
Before my gate few carriages pass by.
In the deep woods, where birds come home to roost,
The creeks and pools are always full of fish.
I pick wild berries, holding my child's hand,
Or with my wife I hoe the paddy fields.
What is it that I keep inside my house?
There's nothing but a single shelf of books.[47]

Relationships within the family provide many portraits of devoted parents and filial children. The stories of the famous twenty-four examples of filial piety were known to everyone. Even the hardbitten outlaws of *The Water Margin*, true to their Confucian ideals, are very conscious of its claims. Sung Chiang is worried that his old father at home might be made to suffer because he has joined the outlaws, and when they are eventually reunited at the outlaws' mountain lair there is a great feast to celebrate the occasion. Another member of the band, the Black Whirlwind, Li K'uei, is likewise moved to go off and find his mother. Bringing her back with him through the mountains, he leaves her to search for water; and while he is away, his mother is eaten by tigers, whereupon he kills the two animals and their cubs.[48]

Devoted mothers also have a special place in Chinese literature. The widowed mother of Mencius was proverbial for having chosen carefully where she and her son would live, so that the locality would have a good influence on him. The devoted mother generally inspires her children to noble deeds (or, of course, examination success) as a result of her wise teaching or great self-sacrifice to provide an education.

The virtuous young woman of Chinese literature must also display all the ideal patterns of behaviour which derive from her role in the family. Obedience both to husband and parents-in-law and fidelity even in the face of shameless ill-treatment are prominent features of such a personality. A shining example is Miss Chao, the heroine of the fourteenth-century play *The Tale of the Lute*.[49] We have already met her husband, who was constrained to abandon her and marry the prime minister's daughter after winning top place in the palace examination. After his defection the play gives us a harrowing picture of her trying to provide for her parents-in-law in time of famine. She only has chaff to eat, and has sold or pawned all her clothes and jewellery to provide food for the old couple, but is suspected by her mother-in-law of keeping back delicacies for herself. Eventually they both die, and she can only provide for the last rites by cutting off her hair to sell it for a few strings of cash. She builds the grave-mound herself, holding up her sackcloth skirt to carry the earth in it. Afterwards she goes off, dressed in mourning white, to seek her husband in Changan, playing the lute and begging to support herself on her journey. So as not to neglect her dead parents-in-law, she had painted their portraits to take with her so that she can burn incense and offer sacrifices to them. When she finds her husband again, he is full of remorse – primarily, of course, for having abandoned his parents and only secondarily for having deserted his wife. He returns with both his wives to pay his respects at his parents' graveside. So Miss Chao is a supreme example of that filial duty to the husband's parents which traditional Chinese marriage involved.

Just as harrowing is the story of Tou Ngo, a paragon of filial piety and chastity in widowhood, celebrated by the famous Yüan Dynasty playwright Kuan Han-ch'ing in his play *The Injustice done to Tou Ngo*.[50] Tou's father, as we saw earlier, sold her to Dame Ts'ai for the wherewithal to take an examination. She marries Dame Ts'ai's son and at twenty is already a widow. Old Chang and his son Donkey Chang present themselves as suitors for the hands of the two women, insisting that they should be thus rewarded for a good turn Old Chang had once done to Dame Ts'ai. Tou Ngo refuses to have anything to do with Donkey Chang, so the latter attempts to poison Dame Ts'ai. With her out of the way, he expects to have his will with the younger woman. But Old Chang drinks the poison by mistake and dies, and Donkey Chang then accuses Tou Ngo of murdering his father. At the trial the magistrate threatens to beat Dame Ts'ai; and, rather than see her mother-in-law suffer, Tou Ngo makes a false confession. On the day of her execution she calls on Heaven to prove her innocence by making the snow lie three feet deep although it is summer, by bringing three years of drought, and by causing her blood to flow up into a strip of white silk instead of spilling on the ground. Heaven grants her requests. Tou Ngo's father, now a high official, visits the district on a tour of inspection. Her ghost appears to him and asks for redress, and she is eventually cleared of guilt. Both these heroines pursue their ideal of total loyalty with indomitable courage, although they have been badly treated by those who should have given them most care and protection. Unthinking and uncomplaining devotion to duty is part of the feminine ideal.

But in Chinese literature womanly virtue is not the monopoly of virtuous women. There are also romanticized prostitutes like Miss Li, whose story is told by Po Chü-i's brother, who concludes by exclaiming: 'It is strange that a woman of easy virtue should have such loyalty that women who have been held up as models of behaviour in the past would not be able to surpass her!'[51] This is the story of a young man who fell in love with a prostitute called Miss Li and went to live with her and her 'mother', but was deserted by them after about a year when he had gone through the whole of his fortune. Later he became a professional mourner and, while working in this capacity, he was found by his father, who thrashed him to the brink of death for disgracing the family. When he recovered he was reduced to beggary. One day he happened to beg outside the house where Miss Li was now living. She recognized his voice and took him in, blaming herself for his tragic decline. She gave him food and clothing and nursed him back to health, and then bought him books and encouraged him to resume his literary studies. Predictably he passed the examination at the first attempt. Miss Li now wished to fade out of his life so that he could make a more appropriate match. The young man reluctantly agreed, but his father, who had now become reconciled with his son, insisted that he marry Miss Li. She proved to be a devoted wife and bore four sons, all of whom attained high rank. This romantic view of the woman of easy virtue contrasts strongly with the figure of Golden Lotus, who is cunning and ruthless in her struggle for power and security within that squabbling household. Having won her place in it by the murder of her former husband, she tries to secure it by training the cat to kill a rival wife's baby.[52]

In Miss Li's time women had more freedom than later, when seclusion was their common lot. A frequent theme in poetry is the neglected wife or palace lady bemoaning her solitude and pining for her absent lover. Yet there were women of action in Chinese literature, female knights-errant who avenged the innocent victims of injustice and made their living by robbing corrupt officials. And the story of a warrior-maiden disguised as a man was told in the *Ballad of Mu-lan*, about a girl who joined the army in her father's place and fought in countless battles before returning triumphantly to her native village twelve years later, her true sex undiscovered by her unobservant comrades.[53]

But were there any whose militancy was in the cause of women's liberation? Wu Ching-tzu had a humane and enlightened attitude towards women, and in *The Scholars* he portrays a girl of good family who is taken as a concubine by a rich salt merchant against her will. She escapes and supports herself by writing poetry and doing embroidery; and when runners are sent to apprehend her, she also reveals her talent for the martial arts, felling them with powerful blows.[54] Much earlier, from a third-century poet called Fu Hsüan, comes an unusually understanding attitude to women's position in society:

> Bitter it is to have a woman's shape!
> It would be hard to name a thing more base.
> If it's a son born to the hearth and home
> He comes to earth as if he's heaven-sent,
> Heroic heart and will, like the Four Seas,
> To face ten thousand leagues of wind and dust!
> To breed a girl is something no one wants,
> She's not a treasure to her family.[55]

There are also books describing a separate country of women, which ultimately carry a strong feminist message. The earliest description of such a land appears in the *Classic of Mountains and Seas*. In this version there are no men at all, and women become pregnant by bathing in the Yellow Sea. Such a country is even mentioned in the official T'ang histories, and according to that account men are regarded as the inferior sex. Women of rank have male concubines, who wear their hair long and paint their faces green and are only employed on agriculture and warfare. The men are restricted to the same inferior occupations in the Country of Eastern Women described by the T'ang Dynasty pilgrim Hsüan-tsang, who also writes of a Country of Western Women where there are no men at all. The novel *Monkey*, whose hero the monk Tripitaka is based on Hsüan-tsang, also features a Women's Kingdom; but the culmination of this tradition is in the late eighteenth-century novel *Flowers in the Mirror*, which satirizes concubinage and foot-binding and other feminine misfortunes in a most telling manner, by putting the man in the woman's shoes – or rather foot-wrappings.

This book is set in the time of Empress Wu of the T'ang Dynasty. One day Little Hill, the daughter of the main character T'ang Ao (which means 'Wandering Chinese'), says in her childish innocence that there must be examinations for women, because there must be female ministers and advisers at court to serve a female ruler. Sure enough, later in the book Empress Wu does institute such examinations, successful candidates at the three stages being known as Damsels of Literature, Virtuous Ladies of Literature, and Talented Ladies of Literature, while those who pass the palace examination with highest honours are to be dignified with the title of Lady Scholars.

The early part of the book is mainly devoted to a sea journey to strange lands with weird customs, such as the Country of Gentlemen, in which others' desires matter more than one's own selfish interest; the Land of Ranging Vision, in which men have a single eye located on the hand; the Nation of Pedants, where the travellers discern a sourness in the air while still at sea and mistake the local wine for vinegar; the Country of the Swollen-headed, who feed on flattery and have hands as long as their bodies; and the Country of Surpassing Intelligence, where men are hoary-headed before they reach the age of thirty.

One of the strange lands is the Country of Women, where men wear skirts and tunics, call themselves women, and run the household; whereas the women wear boots and tall hats, call themselves men, and preside over public affairs. The high point of the satire is reached when Merchant Lin, who had hoped to make a good sale in cosmetics in this country of women, finds himself adopted as queen and surrounded by maids of honour:

They stripped him clean of every garment outer and inner. The serving maids were all mightily strong, and like a sparrow in the grip of a hawk there was no way that he could master them. As soon as they had stripped him clean, the serving maids, who had long before prepared hot scented water, gave him a bath. They took away his trousers and coat and put on him a skirt and blouse, and for the moment put silk stockings on his 'enormous golden lotuses'. They dressed his hair into a chignon, applying a great deal of hair oil, placed a phoenix headdress on his head, smeared his face with scented powder, and coloured his lips bright red. They slipped rings on his fingers and gold bracelets on his wrists.[56]

The climax of horrors is reached when a waiting woman approaches, saying: 'Madam, by your leave, we have orders to bind your feet.' Poor Lin has to submit to all the agony of foot-binding and the prolonged beauty treatment inflicted on young princesses. Eventually he is in such anguish that he asks that the king be informed that he would prefer instant death to having his feet bound. But still there is no escape for him. After all this beauty treatment Merchant Lin is inspected by the king, who finds that 'his face is like the blossom of the peach tree, his waist as the pliant willow, his eyes hold autumn waters, and his brows are like distant hills' – in other words, he looks like a conventional Chinese beauty. Poor Lin has to submit to the king's amorous attentions and eventually to the nuptials. He is smitten with anguish at the thought of his wife and daughter as the king cries: 'You and I have "plighted our eternal troth". After such a happy event, why do you still look so sad? Since you have met with such good fortune, it has been worth your while to be born a woman. Now you are the first lady of the realm, what other wish have you which is still unsatisfied?'

Let us now turn to descriptions of the more normal type of love and marriage in Chinese literature. The amount of love poetry in Chinese is sometimes underestimated, as if arranged matches ruled out romantic love. On the contrary, feelings of great affection often developed within the conventional marriage-bond. But indecorous and violent expressions of passion would be out of place in a literature dominated by Confucianism, so love poetry is generally in a low key, and is marked by yearning and sadness rather than passion and desire. Sometimes editors removed love poems from a poet's collected works, and very few frankly physical ones escaped the scissors of Neo-Confucian moralists. But despite these inhibitions Chinese love poetry does cover many aspects of the love affair. There is love at first sight, dating, treasuring a simple gift from a loved one, the agony of separation and the despair of loss, and even the suicide pact. It also ranges from the outdoor naturalness and simplicity of the *Book of Songs* to the boudoir artificiality, the powder and paint and heavily scented atmosphere of late T'ang love poetry, illustrated in these two contrasting examples:

> Poplar at the Eastern Gate,
>> Your leaves so glossy growing;
> Dusk was the time set for our date,
>> Now morning stars are showing!

> Poplar at the Eastern Gate,
>> Your leaves so thickly twining;
> Dusk was the time set for our date,
>> Now morning stars are shining![57]

The T'ang poet's style is much more ornate:

> In her chamber, jade-white in the moon, she is filled with longing;
> Willow-fronds toss gracefully, languid as the spring;
> Outside her gates new grass grows thick again;
> Coming to say goodbye she hears his horses neighing.
> On the painted curtains are golden kingfishers,
> The scented candle is melting into tears.
> Among the falling flowers a nightjar cries,
> Shattered at a gauze window, her dream dies.

The same poet, Wen T'ing-yün, also gives us this over-adorned beauty:

The golden gleams on the folds of the bed-screen fitfully come and go;
Her cloudlike hair is about to fall across fragrant cheeks of snow.
Lazily she rises to make up moth-arched brows,
Languidly combing and washing, her toilet slow.
In mirrors before and behind her flowers reflect,
And face and flowers gaze brightly to and fro.
Embroidered on the silk of her new jacket
Pair after pair of golden partridge glow.[58]

These verses from a widow's lament in the *Book of Songs*, as so often even in these ancient writings, compare Man and Nature:

The spreading creepers choke the thorns,
The ivy covers field and hill;
Since my lover went away
Who can I meet? Alone I dwell.

Through summer days,
Through winter nights,
After a hundred years have passed,
I'll come back to his home at last.

Through winter nights,
Through summer days,
After a hundred years have passed,
I'll come back to his house at last.[59]

A man's voice speaks in the practical domesticated grief of Yüan Chen:

We used to joke together of a love surviving death;
This morning what we said comes back to me.
Your clothes have all been bundled out of sight,
I still can't bear unwrapping your embroideries.
I am sorry for your favourite maids because they cared for you,
And moved by kindly dreams of you, reward them well.
I do know all men suffer this same sorrow,
But when a couple shared hard times, a hundred things cause grief.[60]

There are also many plays and stories in which love is the central theme. The ideal pair of Chinese lovers is a beautiful maiden and a talented student destined for examination success, and the ideal conclusion to a story – instead of 'they lived happily ever after' – is the birth of numerous sons who in turn achieve top places in the examinations and attain high office. One well-known love story with a very Chinese flavour

is *The Peony Pavilion* by T'ang Hsien-tsu of the Ming Dynasty, in which
the sheltered and secluded heroine's longing is expressed in a dream in
which she pictures her ideal lover.[61] Losing her heart to this dream-hero
she languishes and dies, and is buried in the garden where she dreamt
she saw him. He has also dreamt of the girl, whose name is Fair Bride;
and one day he finds himself in this very garden, which has now been
converted into the grounds of a temple. Fair Bride's spirit visits him,
and he induces the nun in charge of the temple to exhume her; and she
is granted a new lease of life by the judge of the underworld. The pair
are married and, although the hero is accused of violating the tomb, he
eventually achieves outstanding success in the examinations and he and
his bride are received in audience by the emperor.

Typically Chinese too is the T'ang tale *The Story of a Soul leaving its
Body*, of which there is also a stage version by the Yüan playwright
Cheng Te-hui.[62] Two young lovers, Wang Chou and Ch'ien-niang, are
expecting to be married, but are separated because a different match is
arranged for the boy. As Wang goes off by boat to the capital, he is
overtaken by Ch'ien-niang and they flee to Szechwan together. After
five years, by which time they have two children, they return home because Ch'ien-niang is homesick. When Wang begs her father's forgive-
ness, the old man is quite incapable of understanding what has happened,
for Ch'ien-niang is lying ill in her room. When the bed-ridden
Ch'ien-niang hears what has happened, she smilingly rises from her bed,
goes out to greet the other Ch'ien-niang, and merges with her. So in this
story the lovers' ordeal has been relieved by the separation of soul from
body. Another very different, but also very Chinese, solution to problems of the heart comes in the play *Female Phoenixes Courting the Male*, by
the seventeenth-century dramatist Li Yü. In this play three girls con-
tend for the hand of the same man, but they eventually patch up their
differences and are content to serve him harmoniously together.

Unless it is to be made fun of, the wedding itself occupies little space
in novels and short stories. The conventional happy union comes as a
brief curtain-call at the end of the story. But plenty of things can go
wrong to provide material for satire or coarse good humour. Unsuitable
marriages or illicit amours are plotted by evil go-betweens, brides protest
their abhorrence of matrimony, the wrong husband gets the bride, or
the bride even turns out to be a man in disguise: all these possibilities
provide the plot for a good story. Two of the most sinister matchmakers
in Chinese literature are the old woman Wang, who brings Hsi-men
Ch'ing and Golden Lotus together, and Dame Hsüeh in the Ming story

The Pearl-sewn Shirt. In *The Pearl-sewn Shirt* a travelling vendor named Chiang Hsing-ko marries a girl called Fortune, and they make 'a pair like figures of jade, carved and polished by fine craftsmanship'.[63] Soon Chiang goes off on a business trip. Encouraged by a fortune-teller to expect his early return, Fortune is constantly on the look-out for him, gazing out on the street from behind a curtain. One day as she keeps watch she is noticed by another travelling vendor, Ch'en Ta-lang, who falls in love with her at first sight. He decides to consult the old jewel-vendor Dame Hsüeh, who knows the locality well and is also 'skilled in the arts of persuasion'. Ch'en goes and tells her of the particular jewel he wishes to procure, and the old crone agrees to help. They stage a scene in front of Fortune's house, Ch'en refusing to give the right price for her jewels. Fortune is watching, and she asks her maid to invite Dame Hsüeh in so that she can look at her wares. Dame Hsüeh flatters the lonely woman and gradually builds up a close relationship with her. She talks disparagingly of merchants who take concubines when on their travels and never bother to come home. She becomes a regular caller, and Fortune invites her to stay. Sleeping in the same bedroom, she rouses Fortune with tales of her own youthful amours, and eventually contrives to get Ch'en into bed with her. The seeds of a very complicated plot have thus been sown.

When Hsi-men Ch'ing falls for Golden Lotus, he confides in the old woman Wang, a tea-seller who lives nearby. After several visits and much banter and double-entendre he gets round to the real business of his visit. The old woman then reveals a cunning ten-stage plan to get the two alone together and bring Hsi-men Ch'ing to the brink of success, the last and conclusive stage being when he knocks down a pair of chopsticks with his sleeve and touches Golden Lotus's foot when picking them up. If she is not angry at this, victory is certain.

Feng Meng-lung's short story *The Perfect Lady by Mistake* is a good example of the wrong person getting the bride.[64] An ugly young man seeks a match with the beautiful Autumn Fragrance, and persuades a talented cousin to impersonate him, both when making the preliminary arrangements and when going to fetch the bride. The bride's home is on an island in a large lake, and bad weather prevents the cousin returning with Autumn Fragrance for her wedding; so it is suggested that the happy event should take place on the island at the bride's home. The cousin has no alternative but to accept the suggestion; but after the ceremony, to the bride's disappointment, he goes to sleep fully clothed. But when the weather improves and they are able to return, the ugly young man refuses to believe that his talented cousin has not taken full advantage of the situation in which he found himself. He picks a quarrel, which develops into a general brawl. The local magistrate happens to be passing, so he has the disputants brought to court so that he can clear the matter up. As a result of his investigations he confirms the match and the ugly young man is left to bemoan his wifeless lot.

After marriage and childbirth the chapter on the social experience of the Chinese goes on to deal with death and ancestor worship. We need not dwell on death, for enough has been said earlier in this chapter to indicate that attitudes range from Chuang Tzu's ready acceptance of it as part of the natural order to the repugnance of those who bitterly regretted the passing of time and sought to postpone the end by producing an elixir of immortality. Attitudes to the deceased are naturally also varied. The vengeful take the heads of executed villains and offer them up in sacrifice to the spirits of their victims, and the bereaved tend in various ways the spirits of their loved ones. There is a detailed description of Hsi-men Ch'ing's mourning for his wife Lady of the Vase, which includes an account of what happens at mealtimes: when the food is brought to him, it is also offered by the maids to the spirit of his dead wife; and when he takes up his chopsticks, he turns to her spirit tablet and invites her to eat with him.[65] It was the duty of the living to keep the dead informed about family affairs, and news of bureaucratic careers must often have played an important part in these communiqués. Po Chü-i addressed his brother's soul with news of his latest appointments: 'Last year in the spring I became head of the Palace Library and received the order of the Purple Sash, and this spring was appointed Vice-President of the Board of Punishments. But I feel so utterly desolate without you and have also been in such bad health that I do not care much what becomes of me. In official life at any rate I have definitely lost all interest.'[66] Bereavement, like weddings, certainly provides an opportunity for the family to proclaim its status in the eyes of the world! But a much more moving example of bereavement is Miss Chao's distress as she tries to draw likenesses of her parents-in-law to take with her so that she can sacrifice to them on her journey. How was she to portray them, when their faces were so thin and haggard when they died?

So far we have been concerned only with family relationships, but friendships were also important in Chinese society, and the literature has striking examples of strong attachments between friends. In the Ming Dynasty story *The Journey of the Corpse* the two friends become devoted to each other even without meeting.[67] An army officer called Wu

Pao-an hears of the great reputation of Kuo Chung-hsiang, who comes from the same district as himself. He writes to him to ask for the chance of joining him to fight the barbarians, and Kuo secures him a position with the Military Governor. Before long Kuo is captured by the barbarians, who demand an enormous ransom for his return because he is the prime minister's nephew. He tries to get a message to his uncle via Wu Pao-an, but the prime minister dies before Wu Pao-an can succeed in his mission. Wu now feels bound to take upon himself the burden of raising the money to ransom his benefactor. Leaving his wife and child to their own devices, he goes off and works as a merchant, but after ten years of hard slog he has still only accumulated seven hundred of the thousand rolls of silk needed. At this time the hapless wife sets out with her child to search for her long-lost husband. On the way the sounds of her weeping reach the ears of the new Military Governor of the region who, out of admiration for her husband's loyalty to his friend, promises to find him and make up the rest of the ransom out of his own resources. Wu Pao-an is duly found, and is at last able to hand the ransom over and so meet his friend face to face for the first time ever. Kuo Chung-hsiang has had his feet nailed to boards after making repeated attempts to escape, but he quickly recovers his health and resumes his career. Having lost touch with Wu Pao-an, he hears much later that he and his wife have died in poverty. Full of remorse, he journeys to their crude grave and disinters their bones so that he may rebury them in their native place (marking them each with ink so that he makes sure that he reburies them in proper order). He sets out on foot, carrying the bones on his back. Wherever he stays the night, he sets wine and food before the basket containing the bones. Finally he submits a memorial, begging to retire and hand over his job to Wu's son. Eventually the local people erect a temple of Twin Loyalties, where sacrifices are offered to both Wu Pao-an and Kuo Chung-hsiang.

In *The Water Margin*, too, friendship is the most important of the ties between human beings. It is an extension of the brotherly relationship, as expressed in the Confucian saying, 'Within the four seas all men are brothers.' It binds the outlaws together, and its practical manifestation is seen in the tradition of knight-errantry. Knights-errant date back to antiquity in China, and there are classic examples in Ssu-ma Ch'ien's history, like Chu Chia:

The brave men whose lives he saved by taking them into hiding were numbered by the hundred, and he rescued an untold number of ordinary people. Yet he never bragged of his abilities or enjoyed the fruits of his virtue, and his only fear was that he might run into all the people whom he had once done a favour. In relieving those in want he started with the poorest and humblest. At home he had no money to spare, and his clothes were worn and shabby. He had little to eat, and when he went out he rode in a bullock-cart.[68]

Unlike their European counterparts, Chinese knights-errant were not motivated by romantic love or religious inspiration, and they were often persons of plebeian origin or occupation. Those who were aristocrats treated their social inferiors with respect if they were men after their own heart, as shown in the biography of Prince Wu-chi of Wei, who went out of his way to cultivate the acquaintance of the gate-keeper Hou Ying and the butcher Chu Hai, because he had heard of their fine qualities although they lived in obscurity.[69] They treated him in an off-hand fashion to assert their independence: thus, when Hou Ying was finally persuaded to accept an invitation from the prince, he went along in his shabby clothes to be guest of honour at a banquet attended by members of the royal family, but insisted on making a detour to call on his friend Chu Hai in the market-place, while the outriders cursed under their breaths and the prince waited deferentially, and in the palace the assembled throng of dignitaries were already in their places. But when Wu-chi was in need they rallied to his aid, and Hou Ying even committed suicide at the moment when he calculated that the prince was certain to meet his end in battle against the mighty Ch'in armies, so as to serve him in the next world.

Knight-errantry was a disruptive force in society, not only because it broke social barriers, but also because it meant taking the law into one's own hands. It meant 'robbing the rich to help the poor', in the manner of Robin Hood; and it meant wreaking justice and vengeance, as the Liangshanpo heroes did in a society in which officials were corrupt and the law perverted. There are many stories of knight errantry in Chinese literature, from Ssu-ma Ch'ien's biographies to T'ang period tales of chivalry, and there are many descriptions in poetry also. But it is in the stories of injustice set to rights by the outlaws of Liangshanpo in *The Water Margin* and in the numerous plays based on these stories that this aspect of the Chinese experience finds its most popular expression.

The bandit-hero plays of the Yüan Dynasty are an especially coura-geous voice of protest against the oppression of the times, and *The Water Margin* itself follows closely the pattern of popular uprisings, both in the stories of how individual heroes flee from injustice to form the rebellious band in their mountain lair and in the millenarian atmosphere which pervades the novel. It is a great work of protest against injustice and exploitation, which looks forward to a time when the world will be set to rights again. And if we are going to look for literary manifestations of the economic experience of the Chinese, which is the next main topic of this book, we must certainly expect to find eloquent expressions of protest against economic injustice and exploitation. And indeed descriptions of peasant life are sometimes idyllic and sometimes full of grievance. Already in the *Book of Songs* happy harvest scenes alternate with the theme that the luxury of the lords depends on the hard work of the peasants:

> Chop, chop, cut the sandalwood,
> Pile it by the river where
> The swift stream flows so clearly!
> If *we* did not sow and reap
> Would your yards hold so much corn?
> If *we* did not hunt and trap
> Would badger furs your courts adorn?
> What a noble lord this is
> That earns his bread so fairly![70]

The peasant idyll has its roots in Confucian and Taoist concepts of primitive simplicity, when people lived happy and undisturbed lives in their isolated villages. Po Chü-i has a long idyll of village life, which echoes the same attitude. It begins:

> In Hsüchou, in the District of Kufeng
> There lies a village whose name is Chüch'en –
> A hundred miles away from the county town,
> Amid fields of hemp and green of mulberry-trees.
> Click, click, the sound of the spinning-wheel;
> Donkeys and oxen pack the village streets.
> The girls go drawing the water from the brook;
> The men go gathering firewood on the hill.
> So far from the town Government affairs are few;
> So deep in the hills, men's ways are simple.
> Though they have wealth, they do not traffic with it;
> Though they reach the age, they do not enter the Army.
> Each family keeps to its village trade;
> Grey-headed they have never left the gates.
> Alive, they are the people of Ch'en Village;
> Dead, they become the dust of Ch'en Village.[71]

But in more realistic mood, as he watches the reapers toil

> Whose feet are burned by the hot earth they tread,
> Whose backs are scorched by the flames of the shining sky

he feels guilty about his own comfort and affluence, and asks:

> In virtue of what desert
> Have I never once tended field or tree?[72]

This theme of unease or protest aroused by the inequality between rich and poor echoes down the centuries. It comes in Mencius complaining to King Hui of Liang that he has fat horses in his stables, while people are dropping dead from starvation.[73] It comes in Tu Fu's vivid couplet:

> In crimson gates a stink of meat and wine;
> On roadsides lie the bones of frozen men.[74]

These privations and inequalities were, as Tu Fu felt, a certain prelude to war. This too is an object of revulsion in much of Chinese literature. Between the tales of ancient heroes and the valiant deeds of derring-do recorded in *The Water Margin*, the keynote is horror and protest. One recurrent theme is the heart-breaking separations caused by war. In the vast land of China long farewells had to be said in times of peace, but war conditions intensified this shattering of close-knit family groups. A man's dread of being drafted was heightened by the knowledge that he would no longer be able to make offerings before the tablets of his ancestors and that his own bones might lie untended on the battlefield and his spirit uncared for. Po Chü-i has a well-known poem about a very old man telling how, as a youth, he broke his arm to evade military service.[75] Tu Fu wrote of the harshness of the recruiting officer, of piled up corpses and rivers of blood, and of the desolation left behind when the menfolk have gone:

> Strong women in ten thousand villages
> Wield hoe or plough, but fields lie choked with weeds
> And east and west the dykes are broken down.[76]

Li Po also wrote of war with gruesome realism:

> Men die in the field, slashing sword to sword;
> The horses of the conquered neigh piteously to Heaven.
> Crows and hawks peck for human guts,
> Carry them in their beaks and hang them on the branches
>   of withered trees.

Captains and soldiers are smeared on the bushes and grass;
The general schemed in vain.
Know therefore that the sword is a cursed thing
Which the wise man uses only if he must.[77]

Service on the northern frontier was especially disagreeable. The late T'ang poet Li Ho thus describes the atmosphere:

Barbarian horns draw out the northern wind;
Paler than water lies the Thistle Pass;
Sky swallows up the road to Kokonor;
Moonlight, a thousand miles along the Wall.
Our sagging banners drizzle in the dew,
Cold brass cries out the watches of the night.
Tibetan mail is meshed like serpents' scales,
Their whinnying horses graze the Green Mound* bare.
In autumn stillness, see the Pleiades,
Remote in thorny deserts, feel the grief.
North of our tents, the sky must end somewhere.
Beyond the pale, the River murmurs on.[78]

The suffering of women in wartime receives classic treatment in *The Lament of the Lady of Ch'in*, which dates from 883, when Changan was sacked and occupied by the rebel Huang Ch'ao. Many people were slaughtered, but the 'lady of Ch'in' lived to tell how she was forced to become a rebel's mistress:

At night I slept enclosed a thousand-fold by swords and spears;
For breakfast always the same dish, minced human liver.
How could I come to happiness in such a marriage-bed?
Their plundered treasure was immense, but not what I desired.
Their heads were tousled, faces grimed and bushy eyebrows red.
However often I glanced that way, I could not look at them.
Their clothes were all dishevelled and they spoke in foreign
    tongues,
And on their faces, boasting of their deeds, signs were tattooed![79]

The topic of war concludes this survey of how the Chinese experience has been reflected in literature. War is often the end of a period of glorious civilization, as when the calamities which destroyed the T'ang swept away its brilliant capital so that the land reverted to the peasants.

---

*The tomb of Wang Ch'iang, the heroine of *Autumn in the Han Palace*. It was said that the grass always grew on it.

But sometimes war offers a chance of a new beginning, as when the civil war of a generation ago ushered in the People's Republic of China. About the twentieth-century experience of the Chinese, material fit for another whole volume, a few brief words must be said to bring this book to an end.

EPILOGUE

THE TWENTIETH-CENTURY EXPERIENCE

It was in the nineteenth century that the seeds of change were sown, when the Western powers forced China to accept a place in the family of nations instead of being the centre of the universe. Military pressures won men of God the freedom to traverse the country and bring Western learning as well as Christian religion to the Chinese people. The foreigners also brought along with them all the paraphernalia of the industrial revolution. By the end of the century the old regime was on the verge of collapse, internal weakness having been compounded by external pressures.

Although there had been some recovery from the Taiping Rebellion of 1850–64, which was one of the most devastating catastrophes in world history, the Chinese were slow to understand that they could not absorb technical know-how from the Europeans while preserving their own traditional culture intact. The railway engine and the steamship would attract curiosity about the ways of life and thought which made these wonders possible. But much of the hinterland was still little affected by Western influence, so the Chinese clung as long as possible to their belief that their country was a place of superior culture surrounded by barbarian savagery. But, after a shock defeat by the Japanese in 1894 and the humiliation of the court's flight from Peking in 1900 as foreign forces broke the Boxers' siege of the Legation Quarter, events moved rapidly towards the inglorious abdication of P'u-yi in 1912. At this time China seemed so weak and helpless that some Europeans thought that her carcase, like Africa's, would be shared out by the European powers.

After this there ensued the kind of chaos which was apt to follow the downfall of major dynasties, and until the foundation of the People's Republic in 1949 no strong regime or ideology established itself. Yüan Shih-k'ai made an abortive attempt to restore the empire in 1915, with himself occupying the dragon throne; and Sun Yat-sen, inspirer of the revolution which overthrew the Manchus, was confined to the south while warlordism prevailed in the north. After Sun's death in 1925 Chiang Kai-shek marched north to try to reunite the country, but the Communists soon became a thorn in his flesh, and in the 1930s the Japanese began their encroachments. In 1932 they made Manchuria into the puppet state of Manchukuo and in 1937 began hostilities inside China. Before the outbreak of the Second World War most of eastern China was in Japanese hands and Chungking had become the capital. The end of the War freed China from the Japanese menace, and left the Communists and Chiang Kai-shek's Kuomintang, who had been uneasy allies against the common enemy, to engage in the final struggle for supremacy which ended with the founding of the People's Republic in 1949.

If we look at the Chinese experience in the twentieth century under the four major headings which have provided the framework for this book and start with the political viewpoint, we see firstly how Chinese imperial institutions were swept away when the last emperor made his exit into the wings in 1912. He did not take the stage again until he became puppet ruler of Manchukuo, the third and final act of his career being as an ordinary citizen under the People's Republic. The imperial palace has become a museum where the curious can see what remains of imperial treasures after the depredations of P'u-yi and the removal to Taiwan of vast quantities of them by the retreating Kuomintang. When all-under-Heaven no longer made sense, how could there be a Son of Heaven?

The long-gowned mandarins too have long since departed, the death-blow to Confucian elitism being the abolition in 1905 of civil service examinations based on the Classics. During the early years of the Republic, when China was shopping around for new political solutions, the First World War was not a good advertisement for the virtues of Western European civilization; and what proved to be a more appropriate model of political organization came on the market with the success of the Russian revolution. The Chinese Communist Party was founded in 1921 in a girls' school in the French concession of Shanghai, but it took another generation of civil war and resistance against Japanese aggression – a period of terrible hardship and great fortitude, typified by the Long March – before the dedicated band of comrades could take their places at the Gate of Heavenly Peace, and receive the salutations of the masses at the very entrance to the stronghold of the Son of Heaven.

The Chinese revolution diverged greatly from its Russian model. It was based on the peasant rather than on the urban proletariat. As Mao

put it, 'We must unify appropriately the general truths of Marxism
with the concrete practice of the Chinese revolution.' Stalin viewed the
revolution coolly and did not believe in its success until success was
imminent, and the period of Sino-Soviet friendship can now be seen as
a short interlude in the mutual hostility felt by two large countries
sharing a long land frontier. The revolution used a foreign political language, but its heart and sinews were Chinese. It drew its strength and
will largely from shame at the humiliations of the nineteenth century
and the wasted years of the early twentieth century, and from disgust at
how the 'Imitation Foreign Devils' of the early republican era disparaged
Chinese culture and aped the West. It was inspired by a leader who was
deeply rooted in Chinese tradition and saw little of the outside world,
who based his military stratagems on the ancient writer Sun Tzu, who
treasured the example of the heroes of *The Water Margin*, who sprinkled
his conversation with earthy colloquialisms, and who wrote old-
fashioned Chinese poetry. The foreigner living in this vast country is
conscious that other lands still seem peripheral to the Chinese world,
that foreign influences are kept at bay and that internal affairs are the
people's sole concern. Foreign visitors are again closely controlled after
a century when freer access only spelt humiliation.

But even if the revolution is deeply rooted in Chinese soil, surely the
contemporary ideology cannot owe anything to the philosophies discussed in the second part of this book? Chiang Kai-shek attempted to
use Confucius for ideological purposes, and the sage's birthday was still
being celebrated in China on the eve of Liberation; but Confucianism,
as we have seen, could no longer stand up once it was forced to try to
survive as a national religion rather than a universal philosophy. Communist writers initially paid some respect to Confucius as a great teacher
of the Chinese people, but more recently the name of the ancient sage
has been coupled with that of the arch-traitor Lin Piao in a criticism
campaign. Taoism and Buddhism have also dwindled; for, although the
People's Republic gave its blessing to freedom of religion, the slogans
have constantly condemned superstition. Both religions had in any case
been in decline for centuries and now only a few aged priests remain,
although the Buddhist colouring has not entirely faded from the attitudes of the Chinese people. Christianity has also become anonymous in
China. In the nineteenth and early twentieth centuries Europe and the
United States invested enormous human and material resources in the
attempted conversion of the Chinese people. But after all her sufferings
from foreign interference it was natural that, after 1949, China should

want to put her own house in order. Foreign missionaries had to leave and the Chinese church had to adopt the policy of the 'three selfs', to be self-governed, self-supporting, and self-propagating.

But although the Confucian label on the package has been discarded, some of the essential ingredients remain, just as Christian assumptions still influence the lives of professed non-believers in our society. In presenting Communism to the Chinese people ideological writers of the 1930s and 1940s not only used the familiar language of proverbial phrases and classical quotations to give this alien philosophy a homely look, but also assimilated Communist ideas to familiar philosophical themes from the native tradition. Confucianism placed strong emphasis on self-cultivation and moulding of the personality as the basis of moral and political life, and this is fertile soil in which to sow Communist ideas of self-education and of the kind of remoulding necessary to acquire the appropriate proletarian class attitudes. Soon after Liberation it was decided that criticism and self-criticism should be spread among the people by the traditional device of presenting examples of proper conduct. Marx, like the early Confucians, had insisted that man was capable of basic change; and Marxist sages could be imitated, just as anyone might become a Yao or a Shun. In his essay *How to be a Good Communist* Liu Shao-ch'i even went so far as to argue that the problem of 'goodness' was so similar in Communism and Confucianism that concepts from the latter might be used to elucidate the former. Moreover, the traditional acceptance of a strict orthodoxy based on the Confucian Classics had its counterpart under the People's Republic when the sayings and writings of a great latter-day sage, Chairman Mao, were adopted as a standard of correctness. The old-style mandarins who knew the Classics by heart have their modern equivalent in the cadres who are expert in the current orthodoxy. Very traditional, too, is the emphasis on political correctness to the detriment of technical expertise. Just as Confucius himself disparaged specialization, so that the ethos of the imperial civil service favoured generalists schooled in the ethico-political orthodoxy, so under the People's Republic it has generally been more important to be 'red' than to be 'expert', since nothing can be achieved except on the basis of right thinking.

It may be argued, too, that the social and economic changes which have taken place are not so fundamental as might be expected. Of course the physical environment has been changed by the gadgetry of the modern world, and no family attains respectable social status without its bicycles, wrist-watches, sewing-machine, and transistor-radio.

But past patterns of social and economic life have certainly not become irrelevant to the present-day experience. It has been said that when factory workers began to live in small apartments suitable only for a couple and their children, this marked a sharp break with the tradition of the extended family; but it has to be remembered that in the old days neither urban hovel nor peasant shack provided accommodation in which large numbers of people could live together. Modern life may be thought to make people more mobile, and it is true that many have been directed to the countryside or moved to settle sparsely populated regions. But such movements also took place in the old society. Families scattered by famine or military incursions were resettled in new development areas, merchants travelled long distances and spent much time away from home, husbands were driven by poverty to seek a living away from their native region, families split because there were too many sons to eke a living from their small acreage of land, civil servants were moved about at the whim of government, and candidates travelled long distances to take their examinations. By contrast the commune system of today strongly militates against mobility. Although the communes are mainly concerned with agricultural production, they also have workshops for the repair of agricultural machinery and manufacture of spare parts, factories to supply some consumer goods, and stores to sell those which need to be brought in from outside, as well as hospitals and schools to cater for the health and education of the people. Spreading industry and services throughout the country and establishing a high degree of local self-sufficiency, communes tend in fact to reduce movement of population.

When they were introduced in 1958, the communes were supposed to lead to the rapid realization of a truly Communist society, but before long the most radical features of the system had to be modified because families did not wish to merge their identity so completely with the larger community. Communal feeding retreated before the preference for home cooking, and private plots had to be restored so that people could grow their own vegetables and keep their own pigs and chickens.

In fact, although it was anticipated that the communes might have a weakening effect on traditional family ties in China, this has not been the case. The family as an economic unit sustained a heavy blow when land was taken into communal ownership. But this loss has been compensated for by the extreme economic importance to the family of its labour resources, which are now its only guarantee of economic welfare and consequent social status. Since a family can no longer hire labour but can only acquire it by the short-term expedient of matrimony or the long-term measure of reproduction, the large family of male children has become even more desirable than it was in the old society, despite the government's propaganda in favour of late marriage. With economic stability, improved agricultural productivity, and the decline of infant mortality, more households now have the resources to attain the extended family ideal, which was achieved by few in the old society.

These economic factors have prevented women from fully enjoying the new freedoms and equalities they have ostensibly gained elsewhere, notably in educational and vocational opportunities. In the first half of the twentieth century foot-binding was gradually abandoned so that, although there were still many women with tiny feet in the early years of the People's Republic, they have now almost all died. Liberated young women in the cities had begun to choose their own husbands in the early republican period, and one of the first acts of the new Communist government was to introduce a marriage law which gave women equal rights in a marriage contract freely entered into. The act of marriage became a simple and unceremonious registration of a union arranged by the two partners, instead of the complicated family ritual practised in the old society. But in fact the deep-seated traditions of the Chinese people are not changed so easily. Comparatively few marriages take place strictly in accordance with the new ideal, although it is also true that few marriages of the old-fashioned type now take place. Generally what happens is a compromise between the two, with more conservative features prevailing in rural weddings, and the young couples having greater independence in the towns. In the countryside matches are still often arranged by the families, although the marriage partners do have the right of veto. It is common to have a party after the marriage has been registered, and family prestige still demands an expensive celebration. Bridal sedan-chairs are still sometimes used. Afterwards, however, the new daughter-in-law does not become a domestic skivvy under her mother-in-law's thumb. As an able-bodied person she is part of the family's work-force, able to contribute to its earnings, and it is the mother-in-law who tends to do the domestic chores and eventually moves on to the grandparental child-minding role. So in the new world of the commune the family remains close-knit and preserves strong traditional features, although in the cities the social pattern is different, with small nuclear families being the norm.

The last quarter of this book is devoted to the aesthetic experience of the Chinese, and here too the past is still with us. In the world of art old styles and themes have persisted. Although painters naturally sought inspiration abroad, and particularly from Paris after the First World War, when the long hair and floppy bow ties of the Latin Quarter were to be seen in the French Concession of Shanghai, the power of tradition remained strong. In contemporary China, side by side with the works of revolutionary romanticism, which portray workers, peasants, and soldiers with their chests thrust forward and eyes gazing idealistically into the future, there are many conventional landscapes which embody the traditional union of painting, poetry, and calligraphy. Although such paintings may proclaim a contemporary theme, the serenity of nature is but little disturbed by the minute red flags seen on the horizon, or by the tiny figures building a railway or conquering a mountain. These works illustrate the irreconcilability of the Taoist and Maoist visions of man, for how can one who is insignificant in the context of the infinite be portrayed as the conqueror of nature? Craftsmen also – in addition to modern subjects – continue to turn out traditional figures from ancient mythology, complaining bitterly that they were prevented from doing so under the Gang of Four; while the rich archaeological discoveries of the past decades have enabled the Chinese to praise the glorious artistic achievements of the labouring masses of past centuries. Pride in her ancient art has been an important element in the restored sense of past greatness which has had much to do with the present success of what is ostensibly a most untraditional regime.

In literature naturally more radical changes have taken place, since the old literature was so closely tied to the discredited imperial institutions. The old classical language was effectively pensioned off as a medium of literature in 1917; and this dramatic change not only brought new recognition to the masterpieces of Chinese vernacular literature, but also stimulated much new writing in the idiom of the day and in the manner of influential European writers. A theatre in the European style also emerged, and eventually a cinema. But at the same time the traditional Chinese theatre showed great vitality, and the Peking Opera continued to flourish until the Great Proletarian Cultural Revolution, when old plots were replaced by revolutionary operas based on episodes in the struggle for Communist victory, and when the gorgeous old costumes and make-up gave way to PLA uniforms and peasant dress. For now art was 'to serve the workers, peasants and soldiers', and little was to be bought in the bookshops apart from the works of Chairman Mao; but since the downfall of the Gang of Four artists and literary men have begun to emerge and express themselves again, and traditional theatre has been revived.

But under the present regime literature has been and will continue to be the literature of a closed society working out its own problems. Although these are the problems of a new society, the strongly didactic flavour of the literature, which is designed to present models of correct or desirable behaviour, is obviously in keeping with Chinese tradition. (The isolation of Chinese literature is underlined by the retention of the characters – albeit with many simplifications; for, although romanization is the avowed aim, it is bound to be a long time coming.) Indeed, although modern inventions and European political ideas have had an important impact, China has been remarkably successful in sealing itself off from the rest of the world and retaining its own culture. To visit China today is to be among people with whom one can feel completely at home because of the common human experiences which we share with them, but at the same time still conscious that they are the children of a tradition and heirs to a past experience very remote from our own, which this book has tried to illuminate.

Let us end where we began, in Peking, which has changed more in the past thirty years than in the previous three hundred. It is no longer the old two-dimensional city, the flat box set on the flat North China plain. It has spread on all sides, as if the huge old walls, now demolished, no longer keep it within bounds. It has become three-dimensional as factories and administrative buildings have shot up (a seventeen-storey hotel now dares to look down on the Forbidden City) and, below ground, a maze of air-raid shelters has been tunnelled. Until recently this new world was presided over by a figure of cosmic magnitude, even in frailty revered for his epoch-making achievement, even in his life celebrated with colossal statues, and finally after death immortalized by a huge mausoleum of imperial magnificence. On a Peking bus a Chinese mother was once heard to say as she pointed to the great red sun in the evening sky: 'Look, my son. That is just like Chairman Mao!' In China, as Mao insisted, the past does indeed serve the present.

NOTES

Translations are by the author except where otherwise indicated. Where the translation is previously unpublished, a reference (introduced by cf.) is given to a published translation, where one exists, so that the reader may see the passage within its context, if he or she wishes to do so. Space does not permit these notes to give much more information than the sources of quotations included in this book.

CHAPTER I

1 R.E. Latham, tr., *The Travels of Marco Polo* (Harmondsworth, 1958), p. 83.
2 Du Halde, quoted in A.H. Rowbotham, *Missionary and Mandarin: the Jesuits at the Court of China* (Berkeley, 1942), p. 223.
3 A. Waley, *The Way and its Power* (London, 1934), p. 134.
4 cf. W.T de Bary, ed., *Sources of Chinese Tradition* (New York, 1960), p. 175.
5 2b, 2.
6 7b, 14.
7 ch. 9. cf. B. Watson, tr., *Hsün Tzu: Basic Writings* (New York, 1963), p. 37.
8 ch. 27. *Hsün-tzu chien-shih* (Peking, 1956), p. 376.
9 *Analects*, XII, 7; *Mencius*, 2b, 1.
10 *Tso-chuan*, Duke Hsiang, year 14.
11 1a, 7.
12 quoted in C.O. Hucker, ed., *Chinese Government in Ming Times* (New York, 1969), p. 51.
13 B. Watson, tr., *Records of the Grand Historian of China* (New York, 1961), vol. 2, p. 16.
14 cf. B. Karlgren, *The Book of Odes* (Stockholm, 1950), 243.
15 quoted in P. Wheatley, *The Pivot of the Four Quarters* (Edinburgh, 1971), p. 175.
16 quoted by Ssu-ma Ch'ien. *See* Watson, *Records*, vol. 2, p. 16.

17 E.R. and K. Hughes, *Religion in China* (London, 1950), p. 92.
18 J. Legge, *The Religions of China* (London, 1880), p. 49.
19 2a, 8.
20 quoted in S.H.L. Wu, *Communication and Imperial Control in China* (Cambridge, Mass., 1970), p. 16.
21 cf. H.L. Kahn, *Monarchy in the Emperor's Eyes* (Cambridge, Mass., 1971), p. 173.
22 W.J.F. Jenner, tr., *From Emperor to Citizen* (Peking, 1964), pp. 58–9.
23 7b, 35.
24 ch. 16. cf. J. Legge, *Li Ki*, in *Sacred Books of the East*, vol. 28 (Oxford, 1885), p. 88.
25 quoted in H.G. Creel, *The Origins of Statecraft in China* (Chicago, 1970), p. 167.
26 quoted in de Bary, *op. cit.*, p. 171.
27 e.g. *Record of Rites*, *see* Legge, *Li Ki* (SBE, vol. 27, pp. 254–5; vol. 28, pp. 222, 231).
28 Watson, *Records*, vol. 2, p. 48.
29 1b, 4.
30 Legge, *Chinese Classics*, vol. 3, pt 1, pp. 35 ff.
31 quoted in Wu, *op. cit.*, p. 25.
32 cf. Karlgren, *op. cit.*, 205.
33 Jenner, *op. cit.*, p. 46.
34 quoted in D.C. Twitchett, *Financial Administration under the T'ang Dynasty* (Cambridge, 1963), p. 194.
35 Jenner, *op. cit.*, p. 39.
36 *ibid.*, p. 41.
37 5a, 4.
38 quoted in Kahn, *op. cit.*, p. 229.
39 quoted in J. Ch'en, *Yuan Shih-k'ai* (London, 1961), p. 129.
40 quoted in Kahn, *op. cit.*, p. 198.

CHAPTER 2

1 ch. 1. Watson, *Hsün Tzu*, p. 19.
2 I. Miyazaki, *China's Examination Hell* (New York, 1976), pp. 57–8.
3 *ibid.*, p. 57.
4 *ibid.*, pp. 77, 79.
5 Yang Hsien-yi and Gladys Yang, tr., *The Scholars* (Peking, 1957), p. 74.
6 A. Waley, *Yüan Mei* (London, 1956), p. 24.
7 *Analects*, II, 12.
8 quoted in T.T. Ch'ü, *Local Government in China under the Ch'ing* (Cambridge, Mass., 1962), p. 93.

9 ch. 21. cf. Watson, *Hsün Tzu*, p. 130.

10 *see* S.Y. Teng, 'Chinese Influence on the Western Examination System', in *Harvard Journal of Asiatic Studies*, vol. 7, pp. 267–312.

11 ch. 1. Watson, *Hsün Tzu*, p. 19.

12 6b, 2.

13 3a, 4.

14 P.T. Ho, *The Ladder of Success in Imperial China* (New York, 1962), pp. 274 ff.

15 *ibid.*, pp. 303 ff.

16 quoted in Chü, *Local Government*, p. 16.

17 e.g. Galeote Pereira, *see* C.R. Boxer, *South China in the Sixteenth Century* (London, 1953), p. 17.

18 *Analects*, XII, 13.

19 quoted in S. van der Sprenkel, *Legal Institutions in Manchu China* (London, 1962), p. 77.

20 *Tso chuan*, Duke Chao, year 6. cf. Legge, *Chinese Classics*, vol. 5, pt 2, p. 609.

21 quoted in J.R. Watt, *The District Magistrate in Late Imperial China* (New York, 1972), p. 229.

22 cf. Legge, *Chinese Classics*, vol. 3, pt 1, p. 50.

23 A. Waley, *Chinese Poems* (London, 1961), p. 169.

CHAPTER 3

1 quoted in Wheatley, *op. cit.*, p. 411.

2 cf. Karlgren, *op. cit.*, 305.

3 quoted in Wheatley, *op. cit.*, p. 430.

4 quoted in Wheatley, *op. cit.*, p. 428.

5 7a, 21.

6 *Tso chuan*, Duke Hsiang, year 9.

7 quoted in A.F. Wright, 'Symbolism and Function: Reflections on Changan and other Great Cities', in *Journal of Asian Studies*, vol. 24, p. 669.

8 D. Hawkes, *A Little Primer of Tu Fu* (Oxford, 1967), p. 27.

9 tr. A.M. Lonsdale. cf. L. Giles, tr., 'The Lament of the Lady of Ch'in,' in *T'oung Pao*, vol. 24.

10 quoted in L. Sickman and A. Soper, *The Art and Architecture of China* (Harmondsworth, 1956), p. 255.

11 Latham, *op. cit.*, p. 184.

12 quoted in J. Gernet, *Daily Life in China on the Eve of the Mongol Invasion* (London, 1962), p. 224.

13 Latham, *op. cit.*, p. 190.

CHAPTER 4

1 2a, 2.

2 3b, 9.

3 5a, 4.

4 ch. 9. cf. Watson, *Hsün Tzu*, p. 36.

5 cf. Legge, *Chinese Classics*, vol. 1, p. 221. On the concentric squares mentioned at the end of the previous paragraph *see* J. Needham, *Science and Civilization in China* vol. 3, (Cambridge, 1959), p. 500.

6 *Tso chuan*, Duke Chao, year 25. cf. Legge, *Chinese Classics*, vol. 5, pt 2, p. 708.

7 ch. 17. cf. Watson, *Hsün Tzu*, p. 80.

8 cf. Legge, *Chinese Classics*, vol. 1, p. 280.

9 *Han-shu* (Chung-hua shu-chü edn, 1962), p. 2523.

10 cf. Legge, *Chinese Classics*, vol. 1, p. 249.

11 W.T. de Bary, in J.K. Fairbank, ed., *Chinese Thought and Institutions* (Chicago, 1957), p. 197.

12 VIII, 13.

13 4a, 7.

14 2b, 1.

15 7b, 24.

16 ch. 14.

17 1b, 9.

18 ch. 21. cf. H.H. Dubs, *The Works of Hsüntze* (London, 1928), p. 265.

19 5a, 6.

20 7b, 15.

21 cf. Legge, *Chinese Classics*, vol. 1, p. 237.

22 cf. Karlgren, *op. cit.*, 241.

23 *Analects*, VII, 1.

24 cf. Legge, *Chinese Classics*, vol. 1, p. 238.

25 ch. 19. cf. Watson, *Hsün Tzu*, p. 108.

26 ch. 9. cf. *ibid.*, p. 41.

27 4a, 9.

28 4b, 19.

29 ch. 9. cf. Watson, *Hsün Tzu*, p. 45.

30 2a, 6.

31 ch. 23. cf. Watson, *Hsün Tzu*, p. 160.

32 ch. 23. cf. *ibid.*, p. 167.

33 6b, 2.

34 XVII, 2.

35 *Analects*, XII, 5.

36 *ibid.*, XV, 38.

37 ch. 1. cf. Watson, *Hsün Tzu*, p. 22.

38 ch. 1. cf. *ibid.*, p. 19.
39 ch. 1. cf. *ibid.*, pp. 20-1.
40 *Peking Review*, June 2, 1967, p. 13.
41 *Analects*, XIII, 19.
42 4a, 3.
43 *Analects*, XIII, 18.
44 ch. 9.
45 VIII, 20; VIII, 1.
46 1a, 7.
47 ch. 11.
48 III, 3; III, 26.
49 XII, 1.
50 ch. 17. cf. Watson, *Hsün Tzu*, p. 85.
51 ch. 15. cf. *ibid.*, p. 71.
52 *ibid.*, p. 94.

CHAPTER 5

1 ch. 18. cf. B. Watson, *The Complete Works of Chuang Tzu* (New York, 1968), p. 192.
2 chh. 25 and 1.
3 ch. 3. cf. Watson, *Chuang Tzu*, p. 50.
4 ch. 2. cf. *ibid.*, p. 43.
5 ch. 21. cf. *ibid.*, p. 224.
6 ch. 2. cf. A.C. Graham, *The Book of Lieh-tzu* (London, 1960), pp. 36-7.
7 ch. 5.
8 ch. 17. cf. Watson, *Chuang Tzu*, p. 179.
9 *ibid.*
10 chh. 18 and 19.
11 *Shih-chi*, ch. 63.
12 ch. 37.
13 ch. 60.
14 ch. 78.
15 ch. 1. cf. Watson, *Chuang Tzu*, p. 35.
16 ch. 4. cf. *ibid.*, p. 67.
17 ch. 80.
18 ch. 2. Watson, *Chuang Tzu*, p. 49.
19 ch. 6. *ibid.*, p. 85.
20 ch. 22. cf. *ibid.*, p. 238.
21 quoted in M. Kaltenmark, *Lao Tzu and Taoism* (Stanford, 1969), p. 109.
22 ch. 39. cf. B. Watson, *Mo Tzu: Basic Writings* (New York, 1963), p. 127.
23 ch. 39. cf. *ibid.*, pp. 132-3.

24 ch. 11. cf. *ibid.*, p. 35.
25 ch. 16. cf. *ibid.*, p. 40.
26 xv, 24.
27 ch. 16. cf. Watson, *Mo Tzu*, p. 49.
28 ch. 21. cf. Watson, *Hsün Tzu*, p. 125.
29 ch. 31. cf. Watson, *Mo Tzu*, p. 94.
30 ch. 35. *ibid.*, p. 117.
31 ch. 33. cf. Watson, *Chuang Tzu*, p. 366.
32 ch. 11. cf. Y.L. Fung, *A History of Chinese Philosophy* (London, 1952) vol. 1,
   p. 335.
33 ch. 7. cf. B. Watson, *Han Fei Tzu: Basic Writings* (New York, 1964), p. 33.
34 ch. 49. cf. *ibid.*, p. 102.
35 ch. 50. *ibid.*, p. 127.
36 cf. J.J.L. Duyvendak, tr., *The Book of Lord Shang* (London, 1928), p. 172.
37 ch. 49. cf. Watson, *Han Fei Tzu*, p. 97.
38 cf. Duyvendak, *op. cit.*, pp. 172–3.
39 ch. 49. cf. Watson, *Han Fei Tzu*, p. 110.
40 ch. 49.
41 ch. 6. cf. Watson, *Han Fei Tzu*, p. 28.
42 ch. 50. cf. *ibid.*, p. 125.
43 ch. 6. cf. Watson, *Han Fei Tzu*, p. 26.
44 ch. 8. cf. *ibid.*, p. 38.
45 ch. 5. cf. *ibid.*, p. 20.
46 cf. Duyvendak, *op. cit.*, p. 275.
47 *Shih-chi*, ch. 68 (Chung-hua shu-chü, 1959, p. 2230).
48 ch. 49. cf. Watson, *Han Fei Tzu*, p. 117.
49 A. Waley, *Three Ways of Thought in Ancient China* (London, 1939), p. 221.
50 cf. Duyvendak, *op. cit.*, p. 279.

CHAPTER 6

1 quoted in K.K.S. Ch'en, *The Chinese Transformation of Buddhism* (Princeton, 1973), p. 29.
2 E.O. Reischauer, tr., *Ennin's Diary* (New York, 1955), p. 342.
3 Ch'en, *op. cit.*, p. 107.
4 A. Waley, *Chinese Poems* (London, 1961 edn), p. 131.
5 Reischauer, *op. cit.*, p. 301.
6 Ch'en, *op. cit.*, pp. 264–5.
7 *ibid.*, p. 230.
8 quoted in E.O. Reischauer, *Ennin's Travels in T'ang China* (New York,
  1955), p. 223.
9 quoted *ibid.*, p. 226.

CHAPTER 7

1 e.g. *Shih-chi*, ch. 77, p. 2381.
2 1b, 5.
3 ch. 29. cf. Legge, *Li Ki* (SBE, vol. 28), p. 341.
4 ch. 41. cf. *ibid.*, p. 428.
5 e.g. *Tso chuan*, Duke Hsi, year 23. See Legge, *Chinese Classics*, vol. 5, pt 1, p. 187.
6 4a, 26.
7 ch. 1. cf. Legge, *Li Ki* (SBE, vol. 27), p. 78.
8 M. Freedman, *Family and Kinship in Chinese Society* (Stanford, 1970), p. 181.
9 D. Hawkes, tr., *The Story of the Stone* vol. 2, (Harmondsworth, 1977), p. 407.
10 tr. T. T. Sanders, cf. W. Bauer and H. Franke, *The Golden Casket: Chinese Novellas of Two Millennia* (London, 1965), p. 190.
11 e.g. *Tso chuan*, Duke Hsi, year 23. See Legge, *Chinese Classics*, vol. 5, pt 1, p. 187.
12 M.C. Yang, *A Chinese Village* (London, 1947), p. 145.
13 2b, 2.
14 Yang, *op. cit.*, p. 11.
15 quoted in C.K. Yang, *Religion in Chinese Society* (Berkeley, 1961), p. 48.
16 *ibid.*, p. 41.
17 quoted *ibid.*, p. 63.
18 M. Freedman, *Lineage Organization in Southeastern China* (London, 1958), p. 123.
19 T.T. Ch'ü, *Law and Society in Traditional China* (New York, 1961), p. 269.
20 *ibid.*, p. 76.
21 ch. 20. cf. Legge, *Li Ki* (SBE, vol. 28), pp. 207–8.

CHAPTER 8

1 3a, 3.
2 quoted in M. Elvin, *The Pattern of the Chinese Past* (London, 1973), p. 80.
3 quoted *ibid.*, p. 248.
4 1a, 7.
5 Y.L. Feng, in *International Journ. Ethics*, vol. 32, no. 3 (1922).
6 quoted in Y.S. Yü, *Trade and Expansion in Han China* (Berkeley, 1967), p. 217.
7 quoted in Ho, *Ladder of Success*, pp. 158–9.
8 W.E. Willmott, ed., *Economic Organization in Chinese Society* (Stanford, 1972), p. 44.
9 2b, 10.

10 quoted in Y. Shiba, *Commerce and Society in Sung China*, tr. M. Elvin (Michigan, 1970), p. 140.

10 quoted in Y. Shiba, *Commerce and Society in Sung China*, tr. M. Elvin (Michigan, 1970), p. 140.
11 *ibid.*, p. 141.
12 Elvin, *op. cit.*, p. 165.
13 *Mencius*, 1b, 14.
14 ch. 51 (Chung-hua shu-chü, 1962), p. 2328.
15 quoted in Elvin, *op. cit.*, p. 303.
16 *ibid.*, p. 136.
17 Latham, *op. cit.*, p. 180.
18 J.S. Burgess, *The Guilds of Peking* (New York, 1928), p. 80.
19 *ibid.*, pp. 92–3.

CHAPTER 9

1 W.R.B. Acker, tr., *Some T'ang and pre-T'ang Texts on Chinese Painting* (Leiden, 1954), p. xii.
2 J. Cahill, *Chinese Painting* (Cleveland, 1960), p. 47.
3 A.C. Soper, tr., *Kuo Jo-hsü's Experiences in Painting* (Washington, 1951), p. 11.
4 quoted in R. Whitfield, *In Pursuit of Antiquity* (Princeton, 1969), p. 43.
5 quoted in Cahill, *op. cit.*, p. 11.
6 cf. Acker, *op. cit.*, p. 59.
7 quoted in A. Waley, *An Introduction to the Study of Chinese Painting* (London, 1923), p. 162.
8 Soper, *op. cit.*, p. 10.
9 The Han Dynasty philosopher Wang Ch'ung, in *Lun-heng*, ch. 13.
10 Soper, *op. cit.*, p. 9.
11 Wen Fong, *Sung and Yüan Paintings* (New York, 1973), p. 34.
12 Cahill, *op. cit.*, p. 15.
13 quoted in Acker, *op. cit.*, p. 151.
14 H. Munsterberg, *The Arts of China* (Rutland, Vermont, 1962), p. 111.
15 *Analects*, VI, 21.
16 Lu Chi, *Wen fu*, tr. Shih-hsiang Chen, in C. Birch, ed., *Anthology of Chinese Literature* (Harmondsworth, 1967), p. 225.
17 G. Rowley, *Principles of Chinese Painting* (Princeton, 1947), p. 61.
18 Kuo Hsi, *An Essay on Landscape Painting*, tr. Shio Sakanishi (London, 1935), pp. 44–5.
19 *ibid.*, p. 37.
20 Karlgren, *op. cit.*, 55.
21 Cahill, *op. cit.*, p. 129.
22 quoted in S. Bush, *The Chinese Literati on Painting* (Cambridge, Mass., 1971), p. 20.

23 quoted in J. Cahill, 'Confucian Elements in the Theory of Painting', in A.F. Wright, ed., *The Confucian Persuasion* (Stanford, 1960), p. 135.

24 quoted in Bush, *op. cit.*, p. 41.

25 S. Sakanishi, tr., *The Spirit of the Brush* (London, 1939), p. 40.

26 Kuo, *op. cit.*, p. 35.

27 quoted in Cahill, 'Confucian Elements', p. 135.

28 *ibid.*, p. 130.

29 quoted in Cahill, *Chinese Painting*, p. 91.

30 Acker, *op. cit.*, pp. 124–5.

31 quoted in Elvin, *op. cit.*, p. 285.

32 Père d'Entrecolles. *See* S. Jenyns, *Later Chinese Porcelain* (London, 1951), pp. 6–14.

33 The second-century AD dictionary *Shuo-wen chieh-tzu*.

34 *Tso chuan*, Duke Wen, year 18, in Legge, *Chinese Classics*, vol. 5, pt 1, p. 283.

CHAPTER 10

1 XVII, 9.

2 quoted in A. Waley, *The Life and Times of Po Chü-i* (London, 1951), p. 108.

3 cf. Birch, *op. cit.*, p. 231.

4 cf. J.J.Y. Liu, *The Art of Chinese Poetry* (London, 1962), p. 66.

5 quoted in J.J.Y. Liu, *op. cit.*, p. 73.

6 Translations from *Song of Everlasting Sorrow* are by A.M. Lonsdale. cf. Birch, *op. cit.*, pp. 281 ff.

7 quoted in W.C. Liu, *An Introduction to Chinese Literature* (Bloomington, 1966), p. 177.

8 tr. J.E. Liu, in *Six Yüan Plays* (Harmondsworth, 1972), pp. 189–224.

9 tr. A.M. Lonsdale. cf. J.D. Frodsham, *An Anthology of Chinese Verse* (Oxford, 1967), p. 151.

10 tr. in Bauer and Franke, *op. cit.*, pp. 45–57.

11 Translations from *Shanglin fu* are by A.M. Lonsdale. cf. Birch, *op. cit.*, pp. 168 ff.

12 Both passages from *Golden Lotus* tr. T.T. Sanders. cf. C. Egerton, *The Golden Lotus* (London, 1972), vol. 3, p. 297 f.

13 cf. A. Waley, tr., *Monkey* (Harmondsworth, 1961), p. 126.

14 cf. Yang and Yang, *op. cit.*, p. 359–60.

15 tr. in C. Birch, *Stories from a Ming Collection* (London, 1958), pp. 15–36.

16 partially tr. in H.C. Chang, *Chinese Literature: Popular Fiction and Drama* (Edinburgh, 1973), pp. 79–121.

17 *ibid.*, pp. 273–4.

18 tr. E.B. Howell, *The Restitution of the Bride and Other Stories* (London, 1926).

19 tr. T.T. Sanders. cf. W. Dolby, tr., *The Perfect Lady by Mistake, and Other Stories by Feng Menglong* (London, 1976), p. 78.
20 tr. T.T. Sanders. cf. Waley, *Monkey*, p. 43.
21 tr. T.T. Sanders. cf. *ibid.*, p. 330.
22 cf. Yang and Yang, *op. cit.*, p. 461.
23 cf. *ibid.*, p. 456.
24 cf. Birch, *Anthology*, p. 175.
25 ch. 39. tr. Watson, *Mo Tzu*, p. 127.
26 ch. 29. cf. Watson, *Chuang Tzu*, pp. 324–5.
27 cf. Yang and Yang, *op. cit.*, p. 99.
28 cf. P. Buck, tr., *All Men are Brothers* (London, 1933), p. 247.
29 cf. Waley, *Monkey*, pp. 27, 64, and 66 (tr. by T.T. Sanders).
30 Waley, *Chinese Poems*, p. 173.
31 A. Waley, *The Poetry and Career of Li Po* (London, 1950), p. 44.
32 tr. A.M. Lonsdale. cf. Frodsham, *op. cit.*, p. 156.
33 Waley, *Chinese Poems*, p. 122.
34 Waley, *Li Po*, p. 46.
35 tr. A.M. Lonsdale. cf. A.R. Davis, *The Penguin Book of Chinese Verse* (Harmondsworth, 1961), p. 54.
36 Frodsham, *op. cit.*, p. 67.
37 Frodsham, *op. cit.*, p. 135.
38 tr. A.M. Lonsdale. cf. J.R. Hightower, *The Poetry of T'ao Ch'ien* (Oxford, 1970), p. 52.
39 Frodsham, *Anthology*, p. 189.
40 tr. A.M. Lonsdale.
41 tr. W.C. Liu, *op. cit.*, p. 133.
42 tr. T.T. Sanders. cf. Egerton, *op. cit.*, vol. 3, p. 45.
43 tr. T.T. Sanders. cf. *ibid.*, vol. 3, pp. 38–9.
44 cf. Buck, *op. cit.*, p. 71.
45 tr. T.T. Sanders. cf. Egerton, *op. cit.*, vol. 1, p. 119.
46 all passages in this para. tr. T.T. Sanders. cf. Waley, *Monkey*, pp. 315, 197, 349.
47 tr. A.M. Lonsdale. cf. Waley, *Chinese Poems*, p. 105.
48 Buck, *op. cit.*, pp. 736, 750, 752, 765.
49 tr. Chang, *op. cit.*, pp. 79–121.
50 tr. J.E. Liu, *op. cit.*, pp. 115–58.
51 tr. T.T. Sanders. cf. Birch, *Anthology*, p. 323.
52 Egerton, *op. cit.*, vol. 3, p. 80.
53 W.C. Liu, *op. cit.*, p. 68.
54 Yang and Yang, *op. cit.*, chh. 40, 41.
55 tr. A.M. Lonsdale. cf. Frodsham, *Anthology*, p. 51.
56 all passages from *Flowers in the Mirror*, tr. T.T. Sanders. cf. Chang, *op. cit.*, pp. 429, 430, 436, 446.

57 tr. A.M. Lonsdale. cf. Karlgren, *op. cit.* 140.
58 tr. A.M. Lonsdale. cf. Birch, *Anthology*, pp. 344–5.
59 tr. A.M. Lonsdale. cf. Karlgren, *op. cit.*, 124.
60 tr. A.M. Lonsdale. cf. Davis, *op. cit.*, p. 22.
61 tr. Chang, *op. cit.*, pp. 262–302.
62 tr. J.E. Liu, *op. cit.*, pp. 83–113.
63 cf. Birch, *Stories*, p. 49.
64 tr. Dolby, *op. cit.*, pp. 16–56.
65 Egerton, *op. cit.*, vol. 3, p. 185.
66 Waley, *Po Chü-i*, p. 174.
67 tr. Birch, *Stories*, pp. 117–49.
68 *Shih-chi*, ch. 124. cf. J.J.Y. Liu, *The Chinese Knight Errant* (London, 1967), p. 35.
69 *Shih-chi*, ch. 77.
70 tr. A.M. Lonsdale. cf. Karlgren, *op. cit.*, 112.
71 Waley, *Chinese Poems*, p. 125.
72 *ibid.*, p. 114.
73 1a, 4.
74 tr. A.M. Lonsdale. cf. W.C. Liu, *op. cit.*, p. 82.
75 Waley, *Chinese Poems*, pp. 119–20.
76 tr. A.M. Lonsdale. cf. Birch, *Anthology*, p. 258.
77 *ibid.*, p. 246.
78 tr. A.M. Lonsdale. cf. A.C. Graham, tr., *Poems of the Late T'ang* (Harmondsworth, 1965), p. 97.
79 tr. A.M. Lonsdale. cf. Giles, *op. cit.*

FURTHER READING

I have only been able to include a small proportion of the books used in writing this volume, so I have tried to pick out ones which are not too specialized for the general reader. More extensive bibliographies will be found in many of the works mentioned below.

HISTORICAL SURVEY

Recent authoritative surveys of Chinese history are *China's Imperial Past* by C.O. Hucker (London, 1975) and *East Asia: Tradition and Transformation* by J.K. Fairbank, E.O. Reischauer, and A.M. Craig (London, 1973), which also covers Japan, Korea, and South-east Asia. R. Dawson's *Imperial China* (London, 1972) is the middle volume of a trilogy on Chinese history, the final volume of which, by J. Ch'en, is to be published shortly. A multi-volume *Cambridge History of China* is also expected soon. *The Legacy of China*, edited by R. Dawson (Oxford, 1964), contains authoritative articles on various aspects of Chinese civilization, as does *Half the World* (London, 1973), a lavishly illustrated survey edited by A. Toynbee, devoted half to China and half to Japan. M. Loewe's *Imperial China: Background to the Modern Age* (London, 1966) is another useful introduction to traditional Chinese society.

PART ONE: THE POLITICAL EXPERIENCE

The best insight into the personality of an individual emperor is J.D. Spence's *Emperor of China: a Self-portrait of K'ang-hsi* (London, 1974), a montage of extracts from the emperor's own writings. The same author's *Ts'ao Yin and the K'ang-hsi Emperor: Bondservant and Master* (New Haven, 1966), which is about the relationship between the emperor and the grandfather of the author of *Dream of the Red Chamber*, also sheds much interesting light on the imperial role, as does H.L. Kahn's *Monarchy in the Emperor's Eyes: Image and Reality in the Ch'ien-lung Reign* (Cambridge, Mass., 1971). The last emperor's autobiography is *Aisin-gioro Pu Yi: From Emperor to Citizen*, tr. W.J.F. Jenner (Peking, 1964). The story of the only woman who reigned over China is told by C.P. Fitzgerald in *The Empress Wu* (Melbourne, 1955).

A recent account of the civil service examination system is *China's Examination Hell* by I. Miyazaki (New York, 1976). The sophisticated methods of recruitment and promotion developed a thousand years ago can be studied in E.A. Kracke's *Civil Service in Early Sung China* (Cambridge, Mass., 1953). C.O. Hucker's *The Traditional Chinese State in Ming Times* (Tucson, 1961) gives a general account of Ming governmental organization, and the same author's *The Censorial System of Ming China* (Stanford, 1966) describes the function of that unique institution. P.T. Ho's *Ladder of Success in Imperial China* (New York, 1962) deals with the examination system in the context of a general discussion of social mobility in the Ming and Ch'ing periods. Information about the role of the individual official can be found in J.R. Watt, *The District Magistrate in Late Imperial China* (New York, 1972). T.T. Ch'ü's *Local Government in China under the Ch'ing* (Cambridge, Mass., 1962) and T.A. Metzger's *The Internal Organization of Ch'ing Bureaucracy* (Cambridge, Mass., 1973) are also authoritative works.

The only book-length study of one of the old Chinese capitals is J. Gernet's description of Hangchow in *Daily Life in China on the Eve of the Mongol Invasion* (London, 1962).

PART TWO: THE PHILOSOPHICAL EXPERIENCE

The most useful translation of the *Analects* is still by A. Waley (London, 1938). His *Three Ways of Thought in Ancient China* (London, 1939) deals with Mencius, Chuang Tzu, and the Legalists. His version of the *Tao Te Ching* is called *The Way and its Power* (London, 1934), but the most accessible of the numerous translations of this work is D.C. Lau's *Lao Tzu: Tao Te Ching* (Harmondsworth, 1963). The same author's *Mencius* (Harmondsworth, 1970) is the best available rendering of that philosopher. A prolific translator of ancient Chinese literature is B. Watson who, in the philosophical field, has produced *The Complete Works of Chuang Tzu* (New York, 1968), *Hsün Tzu: Basic Writings, Mo Tzu: Basic Writings*, and *Han Fei Tzu: Basic Writings* (New York, 1963, 1963, and 1964). *The Book of Lieh-tzu* has been translated by A.C. Graham (London, 1960). The standard general account of Chinese philosophy is still Y.L. Fung's, *A History of Chinese Philosophy*, tr. D. Bodde, 2 vols (London, 1952–3); and *Sources of Chinese Tradition*, compiled by W.T. de Bary, W.T. Chan, and B. Watson, contains basic source-material for the history of Chinese thought.

A.F. Wright's *Buddhism in Chinese History* (Stanford, 1959) is a most useful introduction for the general reader, who could then go on to study K.K.S.

Ch'en's *Buddhism in China: a Historical Survey* (Princeton, 1964) or his *The Chinese Transformation of Buddhism* (Princeton, 1973).

PART THREE: THE SOCIAL AND ECONOMIC EXPERIENCE

An impression of traditional patterns of family life and changes in them during the first half of the twentieth century can be gained from M.J. Levy's *The Family Revolution in Modern China* (Cambridge, Mass., 1949). More recent developments were covered in C.K. Yang's *The Chinese Family in the Communist Revolution* (Cambridge, Mass., 1959). A decade later a collection of papers called *Family and Kinship in Chinese Society*, ed. M. Freedman (Stanford, 1970) was a valuable addition, although the authors' field research was necessarily confined to overseas Chinese communities. M.C. Yang's *A Chinese Village* (New York, 1945) includes interesting material on the traditional family based on his own youthful experiences, and there is much valuable information on clan organization in Hui-chen Wang Liu's *The Traditional Chinese Clan Rules* (New York, 1959). M. Wolf's *The House of Lim* (New York, 1968) is a very readable study of a Taiwanese farm family with which the authoress and her husband lived for two years. I. Pruitt's *A Daughter of Han* (New Haven, 1945) relates the autobiography of a Chinese serving woman. On the roles of law and religion in Chinese society the most important books are T.T. Ch'ü's *Law and Society in Traditional China* (New York, 1961) and C.K. Yang's *Religion in Chinese Society* (Berkeley, 1961).

No satisfactory comprehensive economic history of China is possible yet, but M. Elvin's *The Pattern of the Chinese Past* (London, 1973) deals with some major themes; and on the economic history of separate dynastic periods there is much to be learnt from the same author's translation of Y. Shiba's *Commerce and Society in Sung China* (Michigan, 1970), from D.C. Twitchett's *Financial Administration under the T'ang Dynasty* (2nd edition, Cambridge, 1971), from Y.S. Yü's *Trade and Expansion in Han China* (Berkeley, 1967), and from P.T. Ho's *Studies in the Population of China, 1368–1953* (Cambridge, Mass., 1959). On individual topics D.H. Perkins, *Agricultural Development in China, 1368–1968* (Chicago, 1969) and L.S. Yang, *Money and Credit in China: a Short History* (Cambridge, Mass., 1952) are specially recommended. On scientific and technological matters J. Needham's multi-volume *Science and Civilization in China* (Cambridge, 1954–   ) is supreme.

PART FOUR: THE AESTHETIC EXPERIENCE

L. Sickman and A. Soper, *The Art and Architecture of China* (Harmondsworth 1956) is an authoritative introductory work, but it covers only painting, architecture, and sculpture. The minor arts are included in M. Sullivan's introductory surveys, the most recent of which is his *Arts of China* (London, 1973). J. F. Cahill's *Chinese Painting* (Cleveland, 1960) is perhaps still the best general survey of that topic, and on calligraphy there is Chiang Yee's *Chinese Calligraphy: an Introduction to its Aesthetic and Technique* (Cambridge, Mass., 1973). A novel approach to the topic is adopted in W. Watson's *Style in the Arts of China* (Harmondsworth, 1974). Books on archaeology soon go out of date, but K.C. Chang's *The Archaeology of Ancient China* (revised edn, New Haven, 1968) is probably still the best.

On the modern Chinese language a useful introductory description is R. Newnham, *About Chinese* (Harmondsworth, 1971). R. Dawson's *An Introduction to Classical Chinese* (Oxford, 1968) is a teach-yourself description of the language of Mencius's time.

On literature the best survey is W.C. Liu's *An Introduction to Chinese Literature* (Bloomington, 1966). B. Watson's *Early Chinese Literature* (New York, 1962) describes ancient history, philosophy, and poetry. On the latter subject the best introduction is J.J.Y. Liu's *The Art of Chinese Poetry* (Chicago, 1962), and D. Hawkes's *A Little Primer of Tu Fu* (Oxford, 1967) gives the reader who does not know the language a good idea how Chinese poetry works. C.T. Hsia's *The Classic Chinese Novel* (New York, 1968) gives a useful account of all the major novels described in this book, and there is an up-to-date *History of Chinese Drama* by W. Dolby (London, 1976).

Two valuable anthologies are C. Birch, ed., *Anthology of Chinese Literature, from Earliest Times to the Fourteenth Century* (Harmondsworth, 1967) and *Anthology of Chinese Literature, From the Fourteenth Century to the Present Day* (New York, 1972). H.C. Chang's *Chinese Literature: Popular Fiction and Drama* (Edinburgh, 1973) has a representative selection of translations with useful introductions. There are many other translations of Chinese literature readily available. Of these I have most enjoyed (in alphabetical order) W. Dolby, tr. *The Perfect Lady by Mistake, and Other Stories by Feng Menglong* (London, 1976); C. Egerton, tr. *The Golden Lotus* (London, 1972); J.D. Frodsham, tr., *An Anthology of Chinese Verse* (Oxford, 1967); A.C. Graham, tr., *Poems of the Late T'ang* (Harmondsworth, 1965); D. Hawkes, tr. *The Story of the Stone* (vols 1, and 2, Harmondsworth, 1973 and 1977); J.E. Liu, tr., *Six Yüan Plays* (Harmondsworth, 1972); A Waley, tr., *Chinese Poems* (London, 1946); and, for a sample of historical writing, B. Watson, tr., *Records of the Grand Historian of China* (New York, 1961). A Waley's biographical works, *The Poetry and Career of Li Po*, *The Life and Times of Po Chü-i*, and *Yuan Mei, Eighteenth Century Chinese Poet* (London, 1949, 1951, and 1956) are interesting accounts of the lives of individual members of the cultured elite.

INDEX

landscape poetry, 264
language, 88, 117, 235–8, 241, 291
Lao Tzu, 63, 95–6, 98, 102–3, 166, 261–2
Laughing Buddha, 131
law, 21–2, 37–8, 44–8, 51, 109, 112–13, 140, 144–5, 151, 153, 158, 161–4
Legalism, xvii, xviii, 15, 38, 42, 51, 87, 95, 108–15, 140, 162, 183
Li Ho, 283
Li Po, 209, 239–40, 256–7, 262–3, 282
Li T'ang, 221
Li Yü, 276
Liang K'ai, 126, 209, 222
Lieh Tzu, 98, 103
Lin Piao, 287
Ling, emp. (168–189), 224
Ling Meng-chu, 245
liquor monopoly, 194
Literary Mind and the Carving of Dragons, The, 217
literature, general description of Chinese, 238–49
literature in modern China, 291–2
Liu Pang (Kao-tsu, 202–195), 10–11, 22, 24, 30, 43, 148, 188, 191
Liu Pei, 246
Liu Shao-ch'i, 288
Liu Tsung-yüan, 265
Liu Yin, 263
Lo Kuan-chung, 245
lock-gates, 182, 191
love in literature, 146, 274–8
loyalty, 43, 89–91, 139
Loyang, 56, 59, 61, 117, 127, 209
Lu Chi, 239
Lu Pan, 193
Lungmen, 209

Ma Yüan, 214, 221
Macartney, 13

Macartney Embassy, 4, 189
magic, Buddhist, 118, 267
magnetism, 6, 180
Mahayana, 119, 127–9, 131
Maitreya, 118, 122, 124, 131
Man vis-à-vis Heaven and Earth, 76, 84, 87, 104
Mao Tse-tung, 68, 80–1, 83–4, 88, 286–8, 292
market towns, 186
markets, 60, 63, 185–6, 192
markets, frontier, 189–90
marriage, 141–5, 148–9, 151, 154, 186, 232, 274, 276–8, 290
matchmakers, 142, 276–7
Mean, 72, 76–7, 84
memorials, 17–19, 42, 105
Mencius, 5, 7–9, 17, 23, 25, 27, 30, 39, 43, 56, 71–4, 78, 81–94, 106–7, 139, 141, 150, 172, 177, 185, 243, 260, 269, 282
merchants, 59–60, 62–3, 115, 117, 171, 175, 179, 183–95, 224
Mi Fu, 221, 223
Mi Yu-jen, 221
migration, 176
Ming, emp. (57–75), 214
Ming founder (Hung-wu emp., 1368–1398), 11, 20, 27
Ming Tombs, 28–9, 81
model emulation, 79–80, 238
modernization of China, 48, 84, 285
Mohism, 78, 87, 92, 95, 103–8, 112, 121, 260
money, xvi, 6, 130, 165, 178, 182, 195–6
monopolies, state, 194
motherhood, 141, 269
mourning, 30, 50, 54, 106, 131, 145, 151–3, 163, 229, 270, 278–9
music, 20, 61, 88, 106, 115
mutual responsibility, 51, 114, 140
mysticism, 97–8, 217

INDEX

Revenue, Board of, 41

Ricci, Matteo, xxi, 200

rice, 174, 176, 187

righteousness (i), 85, 92, 104, 110

Rites, Board of, 41, 167

ritual (li), 20, 73, 85, 88, 90–4, 109, 115, 152, 155, 161–3, 217

roads, xvii, 190–1

Robber Chih, 260

Romance of the Three Kingdoms, The, 245

Rowley, G., 212

runners, yamen, 39, 46, 49, 50

sacred (*sheng*), 10, 27

Sacred Edict, 52

sacrifice, 14, 57, 86, 93, 168, 230

sacrifice, human, 3, 57, 152

sagehood, 5–6, 76, 78–9, 86–7, 91, 111

sagehood, Taoist, 101

salaries, official, 54

salt, 182, 184, 194

Scholar and the Courtesan, The, 146–7

scholar-bureaucrat class, 39, 50, 156, 171, 211, 215, 229, 247

scholar-painters, 220, 223

Scholars, The, 37, 139, 148, 247, 254, 256, 259–61, 271

script, Chinese, xv, xvii, 201, 237, 292

sculpture, 209–11, 228

seal-carving, 180

secret societies, 160–1

servants, yamen, 45–6

Shanglin Park, 252–3, 260

Shen Chou, 222

Shen-nung, 6

shih (knights), 72, 91

shih (power, authority), 114

Shih Nai-an, 246

shipbuilding, 182, 191

shu (art of governing), 113

shu (reciprocity), 185

Shun, 6, 13, 17, 19, 23, 30, 39, 53, 56, 78, 86, 110, 230, 288

Shun-chih, emp. (1644–1661), 17

Sian, 62

silk, xv, 67, 173, 177–9, 189, 231

silk route, 59, 178, 190

silver, 196

six arts, 88, 202

six ministries, 19, 41–2, 49

six principles of painting, 218

social mobility, 40

soil, god of, 58, 90

Song of Everlasting Sorrow, 249–50

Soochow, 179

soul, 155

Speeches of the States, 242

spinsterhood, 148

sponsorship in the civil service, 39

Spring and Autumn Annals, 33, 79–80, 238, 242

Ssu-ma Ch'ien, 12, 71, 114, 243–4, 279–80

Ssu-ma Hsiang-ju, 252

stirrups, 181

story-tellers, 148, 244–5, 266

Story of a Soul Leaving its Body, The, 276

Su Tung-p'o, 217, 219–20

suicide, 144, 152, 158, 162, 280

sumptuary laws, 153, 163, 183

Sun Tzu, 287

Sun Yat-sen, 285–6

Sung founder (T'ai-tsu, 960–976), 9, 11, 62

sworn brotherhoods, 180

symbols on art objects, 232–3

ta-t'ung (great unity), 77

T'ai, King, 188

T'ai-po, 92, 259

T'ai-tsung (626–649), 60, 208

Taiping Rebellion, xxii, 148, 161, 285

316